contents

Caesarea. Relics from the Hippodrome. The second century Roman amphitheatre (below).

BAZAK GUIDE TO ISRAEL

PRODUCED BY
AVRAHAM and RUTH LEVI

Get the most out of your visit to Israel with BAZAK

HarperCollins, Publishers, New York
Grand Rapids, Philadelphia, St. Louis, San Francisco
London, Singapore, Sydney, Tokyo, Toronto

Text: Anthony S. Pitch, Alec Israel, Joel Rebibo, Carol Novis.
Restaurant guide written by Daniel Rogov.
Edited by Lindsey Taylor
Production: A. & R. Levi
Typeset by Keter Press, Jerusalem
Illustrations: Ronit Ida
Press: Hamakor Press
Photography: Studio Magnes Jerusalem
Red Sea photography: Howard Rosenstein, Fantasea Cruises, P.O.B. 234, Hofit, Israel 40295.
Other photographs: Yoachim Schwartz.

BAZAK
ISRAEL GUIDEBOOK PUBLISHERS LTD.
P.O.B. 4471
Jerusalem 91043

Distributed by HarperCollins Publishers Inc.

Introduction

It is impossible to be neutral and dispassionate about Israel, and a visitor's responses will more likely than not be determined by attitudes formed before arrival.

One of the many astonishing facts about the country is its relatively small size. Only 240 miles long and about 10 miles wide at its narowest point, it is bordered by a crescent of nations comprising Lebanon, Syria, Jordan and Egypt. But the dramatic events linked with this diminutive strip of real estate known as the Holy Land have turned it into a perennial source of attraction for pilgrims, immigrants and other seekers of inspiration and refuge.

For the vast majority of Jews, a visit to the Western Wall and other sites connected with their recorded history in the Bible evoke the deepest feelings. Here Abraham, Solomon and David walked and lived out their lives; here the Matriarchs nurtured a nation; here the zealots of Massada preferred suicide to captivity.

Along with Jerusalem, the hills and the Sea of Galilee and other areas have associations for Jews and Christians alike that far transcend the prosaic reality of existing sites. Nazareth and Bethlehem are linked in the minds of Christians everywhere with Jesus and his promise of salvation. For Islam, the Mosque of El Aksa on the Temple Mount is associated with Mohammed's night journey, and is an important pilgrimage site, after Mecca and Medina.

But the country is more than the clichéd cradle of the three monotheistic faiths. Above everything else, perhaps, it is the reconstructed national home of the Jewish people, who were deprived of a country of their own for 2,000 years and condemned to restless wandering and often extreme intolerance in the many countries of their disper-

Bet Shean: A 5,000-seat Roman amphitheatre (top); Tel Bet Shean (middle); volunteers at a Bet Shean dig help excavate relics from the Byzantine era.

Ashkelon National Park

sion. It is ironic that the ownership of this land should still be disputed, when it is arguably the only country whose title deeds — in the Bible — may be found in hundreds of millions of homes throughout the world.

Small as it is, Israel is surprisingly varied geographically and climatically. The great Rift Valley runs from Syria down to Africa through Israel, where it has scooped out the basin of the Dead Sea, the lowest point on earth. In addition to stretches of desert, lunar landscape, there are also fertile plains permeated with the smell of orange blossoms.

It is possible to swim in the tranquil Sea of Galilee in the morning and still experience the big-city atmosphere of Tel Aviv in the afternoon. From the glory of rock-hewn Jerusalem to the underwater coral treasures of Elat, from the ancient mosaics of 1,500-year-old synagogues to the still-used amphitheatre built by Herod at Caesarea, the visitor is exposed to adventure and excitement wherever he turns. And whatever his beliefs, he is likely to find Israel a unique and stimulating experience.

SECURITY

The question of security may be one that concerns visitors to Israel today. Is Israel really safe?

Although newspaper reports may give the impression that a terrorist lurks behind every bush, the vast majority of residents and tourists usually do not have to contend with the kind of activity that reaches the headlines.

This doesn't mean that people are careless. On the contrary, Israelis are very security-conscious. You may notice that suspicious parcels are immediately checked, and handbags are inspected at the entrance to most cinemas and large shops. But these are simply wise precautions.

Israel is still safer than many large cities in Europe and North America. It is perfectly safe to stroll down the main streets of, say, Tel Aviv at midnight, and thousands of people do. Naturally though, the wise tourist will avoid more problematic areas, such as Gaza, and will not hike alone in Judaea and Samaria. Hitchhiking, particularly for women, should also be avoided.

LOOKING UP PLACES OF INTEREST

The index at the end of the book lists the important locations, which are graded from one to three stars on a scale of general interest, with special-interest grading for Jews, Christians, Moslems, archaeology enthusiasts and nature lovers. If you are looking for a place you have heard of, or if you generally want to know what to see first, the index is the place to turn to.

We recommend that you carefully read through the book at the start of your trip and draw up a list of priorities, allowing enough time for rest and relaxation. But most of all, take the time to talk to the people you meet and allow yourself to form relationships that you will carry with you long after your journey has ended.

The key:

*** A must   ** Special interest   * Interesting

J Jews
C Christians
M Moslems
V View
A Archaeology

הילטון

Jerusalem at daybreak.

The Land

Israel forms part of the Fertile Crescent lying between the sea, the desert and the mountains. It is bordered by Lebanon in the north, by Syria in the northeast, by Jordan in the east, by Egypt in the south and by the Mediterranean in the west.

RELIEF

It takes a modern jet fighter less than a minute to cross parts of the width of Israel. Nevertheless, the geographic portrait is as varied as that of North America.

Five main areas stand out in relief: the Coastal Plain, the Hills, the Afro-Syrian Rift, the Negev and the Golan Heights.

The Coastal Plain

Bordered by the Mediterranean Sea on the west, it begins with broad sand dunes in the south, which taper off in the centre and culminate in steep, white limestone cliffs on the northwestern tip of the country.

The coast is almost a straight line, broken by the inward-curving crescent of Haifa Bay and then numerous coves and inlets to the north. The Sharon Valley, stretching for 54 km. in the centre of the Plain, pushes inland for some 16 km. and is the citrus-growing centre because of its mild, frost-free climate.

The Hills

These are found throughout most of the remainder of the country but differ from each other in formation and climate.

In the north is the Upper Galilee, whose mountainous heights frequently top 1,000 m. Geological faults and tilts create a succession of gorges, ridges, isolated peaks and basins. The rolling hills of the Lower Galilee, divided from the Upper Galilee by the Bet HaKerem Valley, do not exceed 600 m.

Separating the Lower Galilee from the central hill ridges are the Harod and Jezreel Valleys, branches of the Afro-Syrian Rift.

The Judaean Hills stretch down the centre of the country, with Jerusalem dominating them at 800 m. above sea level. To their west are the foothills, 65 km. long and 12 km. wide, and rising from 100 m. to more than 400 m. in the east. Within these foothills are the Ayalon, Soreq and Elah Valleys.

The hills take on a different complexion in the Judaean Desert. Their folds stiffen into rock walls near the Dead Sea, forming spectacular canyons gouged out by floodwaters.

The Afro-Syrian Rift

The Dead Sea is the lowest point on earth, lying 394 m. below sea level. It forms part of the Afro-Syrian Rift, one of the longest gashes in the earth's rock crust. Some 6,500 km. long, it cuts through Turkey, Syria and Israel, passing through the Gulf of Elat and Africa down to the Zambezi River.

The terrestrial section of the Rift forms Israel's south-eastern border, from the Arava in the south up to the Dead Sea, Jordan Valley, Sea of Galilee and Hula Basin in the north.

The Negev

The triangular Negev, with its base just above Beer Sheva and its apex at Elat, encompasses about 12,000 sq.km. The Elat Hills in the south enclose many gorges hemmed in by rock walls.

Above this is the Paran Plateau, largely flat with majes-

Nebi Mussah

Succot in Jerusalem. Purchasing the four species for the Succot (Tabernacles) celebration.

tic scarps and rock pillars on both sides of the largest "river" in the country, Nahal Paran. Dry for most of the year, it is 240 km. long and at times 3 km. wide.

The central Negev hills are divided by the Zin Canyon into higher and lower halves. Some hills top 1,000 m. The region includes the Ramon Crater in the south and large and small craters to the north.

One-third of the northern Negev, which includes the Beer Sheva region, comprises sand dunes. It rises from 50 m. above sea level in the west to 500 m. in the east.

The Golan Heights

A volcanic high plateau in the northern corner of Israel on the eastern side of the Jordan River. The Israeli part of the Golan is 11,200 sq. km. in area. Its western slopes tower some 900 m. over the Afro-Syrian Rift and Israel's villages and towns. Its central plain is surrounded by volcanic rocks that are twisted into dramatic hills and deep gullies, strewn with basalt stones.

FAUNA

Once there were lions and hyenas and the Seleucids used elephants in their battles against the Maccabees. Unrestricted hunting and neglect of the land put an end to their presence.

Since 1948 the land has undergone a metamorphosis, and the effects on animal life have been significant.

Water-fowl, for instance, were plentiful in the Hula Valley before it was drained.

The Nature Reserves and the National Parks Authorities have increased the areas where hunting and fishing are prohibited and wild life, including gazelles and ibex, are safe from human predators.

There are about 80 species of tortoises, lizards and snakes. Many of the snakes are harmless but the dangerous ones include a cobra and two kinds of viper. Geckoes are the most common of the lizard family.

Most terrifying among the invertebrates are the black widow spider and the two local species of scorpion.

There are about 350 species of birds. Some of them, the hawk, vulture and eagle owl, have retreated to remoter areas with the spread of human habitation.

Gulls are found on the Mediterranean coast. The Dead Sea sparrow may be seen in the barren parts. The wagtail arrives during September and leaves in March. What makes Israel interesting for the bird-lover is the fact that the country is on the migration route of birds from Europe to Africa and back again. The Hula Valley, Nahariyya and Elat in particular are good spots for bird-watching.

About 25 varieties of fish can be caught with a rod and line. The best seasons along the Mediterranean coast are spring and autumn when the sea is normally calm. Common along this stretch are bream, grouper, barracuda, bonito (skipjack), tuna, blue-fish, skate, hake, mullet and mackerel.

St. Peter's fish is the most widely known of those caught in the sweet water Sea of Galilee. Among the other varieties are grey mullet, barbel and silver carp.

Down at the Gulf of Elat there are barracuda, farida, red snappers, turkey-fish with poisonous back spikes, sharks, hammerfish, sawfish and multi-coloured coral fish.

FLORA

Israel's exotic plant life numbers some 2,250 species. Dozens of wild flowers start blooming in January, and splash the hills and fields with intoxicating colours during spring and summer. They are under the protection of the Nature Reserves Authority and include the rare dark-brown iris, the red turban buttercup, the mountain tulip and common anemone found in abundance in the Galilee and Judaean foothills, the delicate Persian cyclamen, the white Madonna lily and the spotted Nazareth iris.

Cacti are a common sight all over Israel, serving as hedges in most Arab villages.

The huge afforestation schemes are the work of the Keren Kayemet LeIsrael, which has transformed thousands of dunams of rocky hills by planting coniferous forests with Jerusalem pines, cypresses and poplars. Australian eucalyptus have drained the swamps and arrested erosion in the arid south.

The sycamore, which the Bible notes was "plentiful" in the lowlands during the days of King Solomon, is particularly common just south of Ashqelon.

Meron on Lag Be'Omer.

The Jordan Valley. The fish ponds of Kibbutz Hamadia.

Western Galilee teems with the thick, leathery leaves of the carob tree. Also to be found in large numbers here are the purplish-rose flowers of the Judas tree.

Most sections of the hills have evergreen Palestinian oaks, whose roots penetrate through dolomite.

Israel's desert areas promote entirely different species. Loess and poor calcareous soils in the Beer Sheva region account for the low brush or dwarf bushes. Similarly, the marl and basalt soils of the hot Bet Shean and lower Jordan Valleys are ideal for the deep-rooted lotus tree shrubs.

History

CHRONOLOGICAL TABLE

Prehistoric Periods:	
Palaeolithic (Early Stone Age)	50,000-15,000 BCE
Mesolithic (Middle Stone Age)	15,000-8000 BCE
Neolithic (Late Stone Age)	8000-4000 BCE
Chalcolithic	4000-3150 BCE
Historical Periods: Early Bronze Age	3150-2200 BCE
Middle Bronze Age (Patriarchs)	2200-1550 BCE
Late Bronze Age (Moses and Joshua)	1550-1200 BCE
Iron Age (Israelite)	1200-587 BCE
Destruction of First Temple	587 BCE
Babylonian and Persian Period	587-322 BCE
Hellenistic Period	322-167 BCE
Hasmonaean Period	167-63 BCE
Roman Period	63 BCE -324 CE
Destruction of Second Temple	70 CE
Byzantine Period (Christianity)	324-640 CE
Persian Conquest	614-628 CE
Arab-Moslem Period	640-1099 CE
Crusader Period	1099-1291 CE
Mameluke Period (Moslems)	1291-1516 CE
Ottoman Period (Turkish)	1516-1917 CE
First Jewish Colony	1878 CE
First Zionist Congress	1897 CE
British Mandate	1917-1948 CE
State of Israel	14 May 1948
Sinai Campaign	1956
Six Day War	June 1967
Yom Kippur War	1973
Israel - Egypt Peace Treaty	1979
Operation "Peace for Galilee"(Lebanon War)	1982
Gulf War, Scud attacks	Jan–Feb 1991
Middle East Peace Talks open in Madrid	Oct. 1991

BAT-YAM
Sea & Sun

The 3 km.-long Bat-Yam promenade merges with the municipal park, which extends over 60 dunams, comprising a leisure and entertainment center. There are hotels of various grades in Bat Yam, overlooking the Mediterranean and the lush gardens along the golden beaches.

The coastal strip, which extents for 3.5 km of golden sands and marvelous sea, offers vacationers a variety of swimming options for youngsters and families.

The unique Sela Beach is protected by a jetty and is ideal for swimming for both adults and children.

The Brichof: a new resort and sports center on the beach with fresh-water swimming pools for children and adults, as well as lawns and sports facilities.

The Resort and Sports Center: the center, which is the largest in the city, has swimming pools for adults and children, a sophisticated health club with a sauna, sports facilities and lounge rooms, as well as tennis courts and a cafeteria.

Ice Skating Rink: a new rink, built next to the Resort and Sports Center, which combines sport with great enjoyment possibilities for all ages.

EARLY BIBLICAL TIMES

Though abundant traces have been found of prehistoric man in this land, notably at the Carmel caves near Haifa, Israel emerges from the mists of history during the second millennium (about the nineteenth century BCE), when a West Semitic people called the Amorites began their nomadic movements in Mesopotamia, now Iraq. These were the ancestors of the people of Israel.

During the Patriarchal period, Abram left the city of Ur in modern Iraq, according to the Bible, and ultimately arrived in Canaan. Here he, his descendants and their increasing tribe of followers developed a monotheistic creed different from that of all other existing tribes. It was based on the idea of an ethical God as the one and only creator, who in a divine covenant with Abram (now renamed Abraham, or "the father of the multitudes") granted the Hebrew people the land as an inheritance.

As time passed, and others succeeded Abraham, the Hebrews moved to Egypt where they were eventually enslaved. This ended with the dramatic story of the Exodus, thought by some historians to have taken place during the reign of Rameses II (1290–1224 BCE).

The Bible describes the Exodus from Egypt as a divinely inspired escape from slavery, followed by forty years of wandering in the desert. During this period, Moses received the Torah (Bible) from God. This momentous event welded the Hebrews into a people united by the spiritual code encompassed in the Torah and a longing to return to the land of Israel.

Moses himself died outside the promised land, but under his successor Joshua, the Hebrews penetrated and conquered many parts of Canaan during the thirteenth and fourteenth centuries BCE.

The wandering nomads now became settled farmers, with different tribes settling in different parts of Canaan. Although the climate was difficult and water always short, the Israelites managed to eke out their livelihoods.

But the ruling system of local tribal leaders proved insufficient to unite the Hebrews, some of whom were beguiled by the ways of other inhabitants of the area and absorbed their ways of worship and customs. In these times of moral crisis and physical threat, a new type of leader arose. These were the Judges – whose numbers included warriors such as Samuel, Deborah, Samson and Gideon.

THE KINGS OF ISRAEL

Even the Judges proved insufficient as a leadership model. After the demoralizing success of a new enemy, the Philistines, in conquering many Israelite towns, the Israelites decided to institute a line of monarchs.

Saul became the first king around 1025 BCE, and was followed by David, who initiated a golden age of creativity and expansion during a reign which started about 1000 BCE.

A brilliant military commander, David extended his kingdom as far south as the Gulf of Aqaba on the Red Sea, defeated the Philistines on the Mediterranean and conquered large stretches of land to the east and north. Most significantly, he captured Jerusalem from the Jebusites and set up his capital there. Jerusalem now became the home of the revered Ark of the Covenant, dating from the days of Moses, which housed the tablets of the Ten Commandments. Now serving as a central religious and political central fulcrum, Jerusalem became a uniting focus for the Israelites. The city has retained that mystical role ever since.

THE KINGDOM SPLITS

David was succeeded by his son Solomon (c. 971–931 BCE), who built a magnificent Temple in Jerusalem, and under whose reign the Israelites prospered materially and culturally. His merchant fleet traded thoughout the known world. But as international trade and commerce with other nations flourished, so did assimilation and discontent. Taxes and forced labour caused unrest among the people. By the end of Solomon's reign, a popular uprising had split the Israelites. Ten of the original twelve tribes now became known as the kingdom of Israel, while the tribes of Judah and Benjamin formed the kingdom of Judah with Jerusalem as capital.

So began a period of dissent, factionalism and partial return to the practices of heathen cults, such as Baalism, among the northern tribes. Though Israel prospered materially under Omri (c. 886–874 BCE) and his son Ahab, the cult of Baalism also thrived, until it was stamped out by the prophet Elijah. He and such other prophets as Isaiah and Amos served as the spiritual spear-bearers of the nation at a time of moral laxness.

In 736 BCE, the conquering Assyrians reached the northern kingdom, which was unable to counter the threat. By 722, the last bastions had fallen. The northern kingdom of Israel was dispersed.

Meanwhile, the southern kingdom of Judah had chosen, for a time, a more peaceable path. Under the reign of Asa and Jehoshaphat, the people remained loyal to their one God, but later kings introduced Baalism. When the northern kingdom of Israel fell to the Assyrians, Judah escaped the fate of dispersion and slavery, but it became a subject territory.

In 609 BCE, the Assyrian empire came to an end and Babylon, under Nebuchadnezzar, superseded the Assyrians in Judah. Jerusalem was seized and burned in 586 and most of the people of Judah dispersed to Babylon. So ended the proud period of independence. From a people in exile came the poignant poem "By the waters of Babylon we sat down and wept, when we remembered Zion."

EXILE AND RETURN

Though military defeat meant a crushing end to Jewish national hopes for a time, it did not mean the end of Judaism. Ironically, throughout history scholarship and creativity have flourished in exile, as they did in Babylon.

Total exile, though, proved to be short. When the Babylonian empire was in turn defeated by the Persian king Cyrus in 538 BCE, Jews were allowed to return to Judah. Many did, and the Temple was rebuilt.

In 333 BCE, Persian rule ended and Alexander the Great took command of the region. He introduced a way of life which was to have a seductive influence on the world. This was Hellenism, a sophisticated, brilliant Mediterranean culture from Greece, the centre of the civilized world at that time.

THE MACCABEE REBELLION

Although Jews flourished under Alexander and under the Ptolemaic dynasty who succeeded him, the Greek Seleucids, who took control about 200 BCE, were intolerant of any culture other than their own. Once again the Jews of the area suffered. Antiochus IV attempted to hellenize the Jews by force. All Jewish observances were prohibited and the Temple converted to a place of worship for the Greek god Zeus. In a final outrage, a pig was sacrificed on the altar.

The result was consternation and, inevitably, revolution. In the small town of Modiin, a priest named Mattathias of the Hasmonaean family and his five sons led a guerilla rebellion against the Hellenist oppressors. One son, Judah, led an attack on Jerusalem in 164 BCE and recaptured the Temple. To this day, Jews celebrate the winter festival of Chanukah in memory of this feat.

Though Judah became independent in 142, its independence lasted less than a century of intensive political rivalry. By 63 BCE, Judaea was ruled by Rome.

ROMAN RULE

In some ways, the area prospered under the Romans. Herod, king from 37–4 BCE, was an imaginative and ambitious leader who rebuilt Jerusalem and founded magnificent fortresses at Caesarea, Massada and Herodion. Their remnants can still be visited today.

But by the time Herod died, the country was rife with factionalism and discontent. The Jews had become politically and religiously splintered; they now included Pharisees, the rabbinic community who adhered strictly to the tenets of the Torah regardless of political expediency; the Sadducees, or landed gentry who lived by the Torah but not the oral tradition and were more pragmatic in relations with their neighbours; the Essenes, an ascetic sect, and others.

It was in this turbulent atmosphere that a young Jewish preacher, Jesus of Nazareth, won a wide following. He was charged with sedition and crucified outside Jerusalem. After his death, his followers, who believed that Jesus was the long-awaited messiah and the son of God, took a separate path and began spreading the gospel of the Christian movement.

Meanwhile, the Jews rose in revolt against their Roman overlords in 66 CE. But their hopes of independence were fruitless against the power of the Roman empire. Within four years, the Romans had conquered the country, including Jerusalem, where the second Temple was plundered and destroyed. The Arch of Titus in Rome, which depicts Titus and his army triumphantly bearing off the great menorah of the Temple, is a bitter reminder of Israel's great defeat.

Massada, an isolated desert stronghold, alone remained to the Jews. Within three years, the Zealot men, women and children under siege at Massada had chosen to die by their own hands rather than face certain defeat by the Roman army. The contemporary historian Josephus tells us what the Jewish leader on Massada told his followers before their suicide: "I cannot esteem it but a favour that God hath granted us that it is still in our power to die bravely and in a state of freedom."

The Jews of Israel now entered on a period of spiritual rather than political growth. A leader of the time was Rabbi Yochanan ben Zakkai, who had moved from Jerusalem to Yavneh, which now became a centre for religious and legal study. Distinguished rabbis such as Akiva and Judah compiled the fundamental teachings of the traditional Oral Law in what became the Mishna and Gemara, which together form the religious, legal and moral precepts of the Talmud.

Still religious persecution continued, provoking Bar-Kochba and his followers to rise in revolt against the persecutions of Hadrian (117–138 CE) After a four year struggle he was defeated and conditions worsened for the Jews. Hadrian closed the centre at Yavneh, suppressed the ruling legal body, the Sanhedrin, prohibited the practice of Judaism, and even forbade Jews to enter Jerusalem except once a year, on the anniversary of the destruction of the Temple. Even the name Judaea was changed to attempt to destroy all remnants of the Jewish past. The area now became known as Palestine.

Meanwhile, the Roman empire was disintegrating. Christianity thrived, and in the fourth century, the Roman emperor Constantine converted to Christianity. Palestine, as the place where Jesus had walked and preached, became a holy centre for Christianity.

ARAB INVASION AND THE CRUSADES

About 640 CE, the armies of Islam swept over Palestine, as they were to conquer lands as far distant as northern India, and Spain. To the Moslems too, Jerusalem was holy because they believed that Mohammed had visited the city on his ascension to heaven. The Dome of the Rock is a sacred Moslem site in Jerusalem dating from this period.

What of the Jews during Arab rule? Many prospered in

such occupations as fishing and weaving, though they were always considered less than first-class citizens. But worse was to come.

Christians reacted with passion to the usurpation of their Holy Land, and the Crusades, a series of papal-inspired campaigns to wrest Palestine from Moslem rule, began. Fanatical bands swept through Europe, killing and plundering, and the Jews, once more, were caught in the middle. At the conquest of Jerusalem in 1099 great numbers of Jews were slaughtered or exiled. But by 1291, after two centuries of local oppression, the Crusaders had been driven out by the Egyptian Mamluks.

A SLOW DECLINE

For the next seven hundred years, the Holy Land slowly deteriorated economically, culturally and intellectually. Natural disasters such as plagues, locust infestations and earthquakes in the fifteenth century further taxed the population. Palestine became an impoverished backwater, languishing in squalor. When the Ottomans conquered the land in 1516, bringing to an end Arab rule, which had lasted some 700 years, things improved for a time, but as the Ottoman empire declined, the land sank back into a morass of poverty and inefficiency. Local pashas warred; Bedouin robber bands roamed the country. Still, the Jewish presence continued, estimated at some 5,000 residents at the beginning of the Ottoman conquest.

Jews may have been impoverished and many existed on charity, but they stubbornly held on to their life in Israel. For a time Zefat flowered as an intellectual and spiritual centre. And slowly, their numbers and their ambitions grew.

In the mid-1800s, Sir Moses Montefiore of England and the Rothschilds of France undertook projects to improve the life of the Jews in the Holy Land – hospitals, schools, agricultural teaching institutes were established. Thus were laid the first tentative foundations for a renewed, flourishing Jewish life in Israel.

Although Israel was no longer important politically during the Ottoman period, it was still strategically important on the world stage. From time to time, the greater world intruded. Napoleon made a quixotic attempt to capture the Holy Land in 1799, and later, one of the reasons for the start of the Crimean War in 1853 was the disagreement between France and Russia about who had the right to guard the holy places. Palestine may have been a backwater, but it never entirely lost the interest of the outside world.

A JEWISH STATE RISES

The yearning for Zion has been a central tenet of the Jewish religion since the Babylonian exile. An observant Jew is never allowed to forget this; every day he prays "Gather us together from the four corners of the earth."

But the transformation of Israel from the decrepit backwater home of a few thousand religious Jews mainly existing on charity, to a vital, reborn homeland for vigorous idealists was a process that took more than a hundred years.

Several historical developments kindled the Zionist spark. The continued persecution of Jews in the diasporas of central and eastern Europe evoked a yearning for a national homeland where Jews would no longer be oppressed. In addition, the movement towards political emancipation coupled with the Haskalah, or enlightenment movement, with its emphasis on national and personal freedom, made the very idea of achieving a renewed Jewish state seem within the realm of possibility.

In Europe, Theodor Herzl, a young Austrian journalist traumatized by the unfair trial of Dreyfuss, a French army officer of Jewish faith, wrote his seminal call for a homeland in his book "Der Judenstaat". Others also felt the need. The first Zionist Congress was held in Basel in 1897. Meanwhile, pogroms and persecutions in Russia increased in strength and number.

In this charged atmosphere, some 25,000 young, idealistic Jews entered Palestine between 1882 and 1903, in a movement called the First Aliyah. They could hardly have been prepared for the hardships they were to find. The Jews who already lived there had little sympathy for these newcomers, and work was scarce. When they did find work, they were forced to wrestle with disease, swamplands, poverty, and weather that was difficult to bear. Many left or died.

From 1904 until 1914, a second wave of idealistic pioneers – the Second Aliyah – poured into the country. They were fervent secular socialists, devoted to reclaiming the land, who suffered the difficult conditions with the zeal of fanatics. Among them was David Ben-Gurion who was to become the first prime minister of Israel. Land was purchased and both communal settlements and towns were founded. Local Arabs became alarmed and hostile at the encroachment.

After the First World War, the Holy Land became a mandate of the British, who in the Balfour declaration of 1917 agreed to support a Jewish homeland. Jewish joy was soon tempered. Britain showed more sympathy for Arabs than for Jews in handling Arab riots in 1920 and 1922, and continued to show little enthusiasm for the idea of a Jewish homeland. Still Jews came. In the early 1920s, the Third Aliyah of some 37,000 pioneers swept into the country, establishing labour institutions such as the Histadrut federation, and building up the unique agricultural settlements of kibbutz and moshav that still flourish today.

After a fourth wave of immigration in the late 1920s, Arab riots increased. In 1929, mobs killed over 133 Jews and the British responded with a White Paper that proposed limiting the number of Jews who could enter Palestine.

Now Jews faced a new threat as the rise of National Socialism caused a massive exodus of Jews from Germany, many of whom entered Palestine. In turn, the local Arab population became frightened and inflamed. New Jewish underground defence organizations were formed to counter further rioting.

As Jews in Palestine became aware of the dangerous plight of their brothers in Nazi-dominated Germany, they attempted rescue missions by boat. The British refused to allow boats to enter, and in 1939, on the eve of war, issued a White Paper limiting Jewish immigration. Thus the doors were shut on a possible escape route for the doomed Jews of Europe.

Six million Jews were to die over the next six years, and a determination was born that Israel should become an independent homeland for world Jewry. Even before the end of the war, Jewish underground groups began a campaign of terror to attempt to expel the British from Palestine. The determination of the Jews of Palestine was heightened by the fact that when the war ended, battered refugees of the Holocaust were still not allowed to enter freely. Boats were turned back and refugees thrown into internment camps in Cyprus. Meanwhile the Irgun underground organization blew up the British headquarters at the King David Hotel in Jerusalem, killing 91, and the Hagana, the semi-official underground army, blew up bridges. Britain, faced with problems elsewhere in the world and a general desire to extricate itself from its colonies, referred the problem to the United Nations.

In 1947, the UN produced a partition plan dividing the country between a Jewish and an Arab state, a plan which was accepted by the General Assembly. If the Arabs had accepted it, the subsequent history of the area would have been different, but instead the Arab armies massed for battle.

In spite of ominous threats of war, Jews rejoiced in their new state, when the British left on 14 May 1948. After 2000 years, Israel had been reborn. As Golda Meir was to recall "The long exile was over... now we were a nation like other nations, masters for the first time in 20 centuries of our own destinies."

STATEHOOD

Though the first four decades after Israel's independence brought hostility and recurring war, they also brought an economic and creative flowering. Statehood provided the opportunity for a great ingathering of Jews from threatened communities and from countries where Jews were free.

Israel and its Arab neighbours have yet to come to terms, as the many battles since 1948 attest. In 1967, the Six Day War reunited Jerusalem and gave Israel control over territory in the Golan, Sinai, and Judaea and Samaria. The Arab countries made an effort to regain this land in a surprise attack on Yom Kippur in 1973, which was repelled. In November 1977, President Anwar Sadat of Egypt electrified the world by travelling to Jerusalem to promote peace in exchange for the return of the Sinai. In 1982, a war was launched in Lebanon to secure Israel's northern settlements against the PLO threat.

More than a decade later, the threat from Lebanon persists, albeit more perhaps from the Islamic fundamentalist Hizbullah organization than from the Palestinian terror groups based there.

And more than 15 years after Sadat visited Jerusalem, the Palestinians, along with Lebanon, Syria and Jordan have still not made peace with Israel, although negotiations under the sponsorship of the United States and Russia have been going on since October 1991.

Yet despite the unremitting hostility of its neighbours, Israel survives and thrives, melding the legacies of its rich historical past with the vigorous, democratic institutions of a thoroughly modern State.

The State

Since its foundation in 1948, Israel has been a parliamentary democracy founded on principles of freedom, justice, equality before the law and responsible government.

Who Runs the State?

The state is headed by a president (currently President Ezer Weizman) who is elected every five years by Parliament. His duties are largely ceremonial. The actual decision-making process, though, is undertaken by the Prime Minister and his cabinet and by a unicameral legislature called the Knesset ("Assembly"), which has 120 members.

How Elections Work

Members of the Knesset are elected by universal suffrage under a proportional representation system. This system has a tendency to lead to the proliferation of small parties, and visitors may be surprised at the large number of political parties which vie for Knesset representation. There is some support for proposals to modify the system to one based partly on regional constituencies and partly on proportional representation.

Israel's proportional representation system was designed to reflect the ethnic, cultural and ideological diversity of Israeli society. That something-for-everybody approach may well make Israel the most democratic society in the world.

For each election, the various parties prepare lists of candidates which are appointed by the party's central committee or elected by the party rank and file, and then listed according to importance within the party. Electors then choose between lists of candidates, and seats are allocated in proportion to the votes obtained.

Every citizen over 18, irrespective of sex, race or religion, can vote, and any citizen over 21 can stand for election. Perhaps because of the lively expression of so many views, Israelis take a huge interest in their elections.

Coalition Governments

Since no single party has ever succeeded in gaining an overall majority in Israel, all governments have been formed from coalitions between leading parties. From 1948, such coalitions were dominated by the Labour Party, but in 1977, the Likud Party, led by Menahem Begin, took power. Labor ended 15 years of Likus rule when it won the 1992 elections; its current coalition partners are Shas and Meretz.

THE LEGAL SYSTEM

The law of Israel consists of five different systems: relics of Ottoman law, Orders-in-Council and Ordinances enacted by the British Mandatory Administration, the substance of English Common Law, Religious Law, and Israeli legislation.

There is no written constitution in Israel. In its absence, several Basic Laws have been enacted, and citizens' rights, on universal lines, are safeguarded by them and by the general law of the State. There is absolute equality before the law with no discrimination on grounds of creed, race or sex. Freedom of movement, freedom of speech, freedom of the press, freedom of worship and freedom of association are taken for granted.

THE COURTS

The law guarantees the complete independence of the courts. Civil judges are appointed by the President on the recommendation of a special nomination committee. **Civil Courts** are divided into three categories: Magistrates' Courts, District Courts, and the Supreme Court. The last is the highest court in the land, consisting of ten members, only three or five of whom hear any one case. It hears appeals against District Court judgments, and also sits as the High Court of Justice. In this capacity it deals with complaints proffered by any citizen against governmental bodies.

Religious Courts deal with all matters of personal status – marriage, divorce, wills, adoption, etc. They rule according to religious law – be it Jewish (Rabbinical), Moslem (Shari'a), Druze, or one of the Christian Codes – insofar as that law does not contradict the law of the land. Supervised by the Ministry of Religious Affairs, their judgments are carried out by the process of the Civil Courts.

LABOUR ORGANIZATION

The largest of the four central labour organizations is the **Histadrut,** or General Federation of Labour. It is open to all workers, including members of cooperatives and of the liberal professions.

Almost all parties are represented at the Histadrut Convention, which is elected on a countrywide basis. Trade union work is done through elected works committees, local labour councils and national unions. Collective agreements with employers protect the workers' rights and conditions of work. Once an embodiment of socialist-communist economic theory, the Histadrut is now undergoing adaptation.

Women in Israel

"I think women often get not so much an unfair deal as an illogical one. Once in the Cabinet we had to deal with the fact that there had been an outbreak of assaults on women at night. One minister (a member of an extreme religious party) suggested a curfew. Women should stay at home after dark. I said: 'But it's the men who are attacking the women. If there's to be a curfew, let the men stay home, not the women.'"

– Golda Meir

Since its inception in 1948, the State of Israel has guaranteed the civil rights of all its female citizens through a body of highly liberal, non-discriminatory legislation.

The reality of the Israeli woman's life, however, is shaped by the constant need for national defence, and by the pervasive struggle for economic independence. It is tempered in the compromise between religious and secular elements in public life and, like the State itself, is a unique mixture of paradox and progress.

The advances in women's rights during the last five decades have had the greatest effect on female immigrants from Asian and African countries. In a single generation, many of them have leaped from a condition of feudal subjugation to one of active involvement in a modern society.

The younger the Israeli woman, the better are her chances of a university education. The proportion of women enrolled in institutions of higher learning has nearly tripled since the mid-'60s.

The average woman in Israel has served up to two years in the Israel Defence Forces; hers is the only country in the free world where compulsory military conscription applies to women as well as men. Although Orthodox Jewish women are not required to serve, many fulfil their defence obligations within special Nahal units which combine military duty with agricultural work in border settlements. Others elect to do voluntary service as teachers' aides, or as outpost nurses, and so on.

The position of Arab women is more difficult to generalize, depending strongly as it does on the family's economic standing and social tradition, and on the degree to which women's freedom has been circumscribed by religious dictates and community attitudes. By law, Arab women have full legal rights concerning education, ownership of property, and personal status, equal to all other women in the State of Israel. But, in practice, the decisions which determine whether an Arab woman will be free to pursue an education, plan and embark on a career, own property, or even drive a car, have frequently been shaped by forces at work for decades before her birth.

The likelihood that the "average" Israeli woman will enter the work force, and stay in it, has increased steadily. The professional woman will encounter virtually no prejudice in advancing through the lower and middle ranks. But she may face problems reaching the very top.

Although concerned with equality, the Israeli woman has not adopted extreme measures to pursue that end. The more radical programmes of Women's Lib have not been seriously entertained by more than a small number here. However, the ultimate egalitarian aims of Women's Lib have for decades been a central part of the programmes of several powerful women's organizations, which number among their members virtually every educational, social, and economic group in Israel.

Women who travel alone in Israel (and there are very many who do), should know a few things:

The only places where a woman will feel uncomfortable alone are some of the shadier night clubs in the large cities.

This is a Mediterranean country. The low whistle and muttered or even shouted comments are not uncommon, mainly from teenagers.

In the Arab neighbourhoods (the Old City in Jerusalem, Acre, Nazareth, Hebron, etc.) Moslem customs are severely chaste. The very way a Western woman dresses seems indecent to people who were used to women covering their faces in public. Scanty outfits may cause tragic misunderstandings.

It is not advisable to hitch-hike anywhere.

Communities of Israel

What is an Israeli? An Israeli can come from Yemen, from Ethiopia, from Russia or from America. An Israeli can be a Christian, a Moslem, a Jew or of the Bahai faith. His home might be a kibbutz (collective settlement), a Christian monastery, a tent in the desert or a modern skyscraper. An Israeli, in short, is a member of one of the most diverse communities in the world.

JEWS

About 4,247,000 of Israel's population of over 5 million are Jews. Israel's Jews are like Joseph's coat of many colours. They come from more than 100 countries, speak many languages, have different customs and outlooks and are white-skinned, brown and black. They reflect the dispersion of the Jewish people and the great "ingathering of the exiles."

Broadly speaking, the Jews are divided between **Ashkenazim** and **Sephardim,** with the latter constituting the majority, though intermarriage is changing the picture.

SEPHARDIM

Though Israel's founding generation were Ashkenazim who came mainly from Eastern European countries and from Russia, today Israel has a majority of Jews who are labelled Sephardim.

The word "Sephardim" is in fact a misnomer. It is derived from the word "Sefarad", which means Spain, and originally referred to Jews of Spanish descent whose common tongue (besides Hebrew) was Ladino. Some of them live in Israel today, but more commonly the term Sephardim is a blanket one applied to Jews from North African countries such as Morocco and Tunisia or from Middle Eastern countries, including Yemen and Syria. Today, a more commonly applied term is "Edot Hamizrach", "Communities of the East".

The Sephardi community in 19th century Palestine formed the elite of the Jewish population. Later, however, the situation changed. Because most of the Sephardim came to Israel later than the Ashkenazi pioneers, they were often faced with an Ashkenazi-dominated society and culture that appeared strange and alien, and a population that seemed unsympathetic to their cultural traditions. It has taken several generations for Eastern Jews to take their place among the country's political, academic, artistic, army and business leaders. A high intermarriage rate between Jews of Ashkenazi and Sephardi background has hastened the process of acculturation.

Though Sephardim have become part of the mainstream in Israel, they have not lost touch with their rich heritage. In the religious sphere, an ultra-orthodox religious party, Shas (Sephardi Torah guardians), has achieved electoral popularity in recent years, and in the secular sphere, Sephardi-influenced pop music, businesses and local leadership attest to their strong influence on Israeli life today.

ASHKENAZIM

The term Ashkenazi derives from the name given in the Middle Ages to the Jews of northern France and western Germany. Later it came to mean all Jews whose culture originated in Europe, and whose everyday language was Yiddish. Until the great waves of immigration in the 1950s, the Ashkenazim were the elite, who devised and developed such institutions as the Histadrut labour cooperative, the kibbutz and moshav collective settlement movements. They include Jews from Russia, Romania, Poland, the "Yekkes" (a nickname given to the orderly, formal German community), and the "Anglo-Saxim", or

Jews from the prosperous communities of North America, Britain, South Africa, Australia and New Zealand.

While most of the Ashkenazi pioneers were secular socialists, many of today's Ashenazim (as indeed, many Sephardim) are religious: some indeed are ultra-Orthodox. Hasidic and "Haredi" or ultra-Orthodox men can be frequently seen on the streets, particularly in Jerusalem or B'nei Brak, sporting the black caftans or frock coats, the fur hats and the white or black stockings of nineteenth-century eastern Europe. Some Israeli Jews, of course, are neither secular nor ultra-Orthodox, and practise Conservative or Reform Judaism.

Other Jewish groups

Not all Jews fit neatly into the broad categories "Ashkenazi" and "Sephardi". Others include **Indian** Jews, from Cochin, India, who have settled mainly in Kfar Yuval and Mesillat Zion, or the Bene Israel, mostly from Bombay, India, and now settled in large numbers in Beer Sheva, Dimona, Lod and Elat. They claim to have arrived in India before the Hasmonaean revolt.

Also adding to the Israeli mosaic are the **Kurdistani** Jews from Iraq, the **Bukharan** Jews from central Asia, and among more recent arrivals, the **Ethiopian** Jews (or Beta Israel), about 23,000 of whom now live in Israel. They come mainly from the north-western region of Ethiopia where they were persecuted throughout the centuries for their beliefs. They consider themselves descendants of King Solomon and the Queen of Sheba. In 1973 they were recognized as descendants of the tribe of Dan by the Sephardi Chief Rabbi of Israel. Some 8,000 arrived in Israel in 1984 during a dramatic rescue operation named "Operation Moses", and another 14,000 arrived in 1991 in "Operation Solomon".

Another group is the **Karaites**, who are a community of Jews who follow the precepts of the Bible, but not the Oral Law or Talmud. Their sect broke away from mainstream Judaism in the eighth century. The few hundred living in Israel are to be found mainly in the Ramla district, and in Ashdod and Beer Sheva.

A type of community unique to Israel is the **kibbutz** (collective settlement). Although only 4 percent of Israelis live on the 230 or so kibbutzim scattered around the country, they wield a lot of influence in Israeli society. From primitive beginnings (the first kibbutz was founded at Deganya in 1909), the kibbutzim have evolved into beautiful, well-tended settlements, often with luxurious standards of living which would have astounded – and probably shocked – their founders. Many have added industrial enterprises to their traditional agricultural pursuits. While the kibbutzim are structurally the same, they differ radically in their political and religious beliefs. Each is affiliated to one of the Kibbutz Federations, drawn along political lines from the far left to the centre. For information about volunteering to work on a kibbutz, see the section on Youth Travel, under "Miscellaneous Information".

ARABS

There are about 900,000 Arabs living in Israel, and a further 1.6 million in Judaea, Samaria and Gaza. Most are **Sunni** Moslems, though a few communities of **Shi'ite** Moslems exist.

Though some Arabs still live in rural areas, particularly in the Galilee, today many more reside in towns and villages. Some Israeli cities, such as Jaffa, Akko, Ramla, Jerusalem and Haifa, have mixed populations of Jews and Arabs.

About 80% of these Arabs are **Moslem**, while most of the others are **Christian**, usually Greek Catholic, Greek Orthodox, Roman Catholic or Maronite. Some 10% are Bedouin or Druze.

Although the Arabs of Israel live in a somewhat ambivalent position as Moslems or Christians within a Jewish state, their freedoms are guaranteed by law. Arabs have the same civil rights, including representation in the Knesset, as Jews or any other citizens have, with the exception of compulsory military service.

As the standard of living in Israel has improved over the years, so has that of Israeli Arabs. Modernization has led to a decline in the birthrate, a decrease in infant mortality, an improvement in health and a much higher level of general education. This is true also in Judaea and Samaria, where several universities were established in the years after 1967.

DRUZE

A loyal minority group which elected to send its sons

for compulsory service in the Israel Defence Forces, the Druze number 84,800 in 18 Galilean villages, notably at Dalyat el-Carmel and Isifiya.

They speak Arabic and dress much like Arabs,but the community split from Islam in the 11th century.

Although known for their warm hospitality, the Druze are not forthcoming when probed about the secrets of their religion. They are known, however, to believe in one God and seven prophets - Adam, Noah, Abraham, Moses, Jesus, Mohammed and Mohammed Ibn Ismail. They revere Jethro, father-in-law of Moses, and make an annual pilgrimage to his tomb at the Horns of Hittin (see Route No. 11).

SAMARITANS

From hundreds of thousands in biblical times, the Samaritans number only a few hundred today. Centred in Nablus and Holon, they claim to be direct descendants of Ephraim and Manasseh. Popular belief claims they are descended from the offspring of Assyrian colonizers of the 8th century BCE.

They believe that the Five Books of Moses are the only scriptural guide and that Moses was the sole prophet.

The Samaritans worship in synagogues, after first removing their shoes. They also circumcise their children and hold the equivalent of a Bar Mitzvah celebration. Pilgrimages to the summit of Mt. Gerizim near Nablus are held on Passover - for the ritual slaughtering of sheep - and on Shavuot and Succot.

BEDOUIN

A picturesque example of life in ancient days, the Bedouin are nomads or semi-nomads who live today in much the same way as the Patriarchs did thousands of years ago - with a slight difference: it is no rare sight to see them driving jeeps instead of riding a camel, and transistor radios accompany the tribe on its wanderings.

The Bedouin are Semitic in origin, hailing from Saudi Arabia from where they spread northwards in order to find new grazing grounds and sources of livelihood. Throughout history we see the Bedouin periodically coming forth from the desert in times of drought and attempting to penetrate the settled areas. These attempts were always marked by warfare between the Bedouin and the city dweller.

The semi-nomad and the settled Bedouin have a stronger link with urban civilization than the wandering Bedouin, who only reaches settled areas once or twice a year for a short period. The former supply the towns with produce from their herds, and buy all their needs from there. On Thursday mornings, the Bedouin market in Beer Sheva is a colourful event attracting many visitors.

Bedouin hospitality is famous for its ritual sumptuousness and it is a grave insult to refuse it without good reason.

Religion

Enshrined in the Declaration of Independence is a passage declaring that "the State of Israel will guarantee freedom of religion and conscience and safeguard the holy places of all religions."

This was put to the test after the Six Day War when Jerusalem was reunited and Samaria and Judaea came within the administrative rule of Israel. Since then every religious community has had access to its shrines, in marked contrast to the situation during the 19 previous years when Jordan occupied East Jerusalem and barred Jews from praying at the Western Wall and Arabs living in Israel from worshipping at the Dome of the Rock and the El-Aksa Mosque.

These inalienable rights are now guaranteed by law and every denomination is free to worship in its own way, to maintain its religious and charitable institutions and to administer its internal affairs.

The Ministry of Religious Affairs is the arm of government charged with liaising with leaders of religious denominations. It also works in conjunction with the Israel Antiquities Authority in restoring and renovating places of worship and sacred sites, and in keeping them accessible.

Following is some background to the three great monotheistic faiths – Judaism, Christianity and Islam – which coexist in the land sacred to all.

JUDAISM

Judaism is the oldest of the three faiths and for the first time since the fall of the Second Temple in 70 CE and their expulsion to the far corners of the world, the Jews are free to apply their religion to daily life without restriction.

The Jew in Israel does not normally have to ask for the day off work on Saturday (the Sabbath) or on the festivals. They are national holidays and all offices and most factories close, regardless of whether the employees go to synagogue or on a picnic.

The fact that there are 4.2 million Jews in Israel (pop. 5 million) makes it the only country in the world where the Jew is the majority population group. For this reason, yarmulkas (skull caps) and peyot (side curls), far from being freakish, are part of the everyday scene, like the Hebrew script and Star of David pendants.

Israel is a secular state, but political reality has put the religious parties in an advantageous position as coalition partners without whom neither Labour nor the Likud can form a government. So although they are a minority (app. 15%), the religious groups have been able to ensure that there is no public transportation on the Sabbath and Jewish holidays (except in Haifa, a city that has always been noted for its secularity).

It is for this reason that Jewish dietary laws (kashrut) are observed in the Israel Defence Forces, and in all government and public institutions. Bible studies and the Talmud form part of the curriculum of all Jewish schools.

Supreme religious authority is vested in the Chief Rabbinate, comprising an Ashkenazi and a Sephardi Chief Rabbi and the Supreme Rabbinical Council. It decides on the interpretation of the Jewish law in matters beyond the jurisdiction of the eight regional rabbinical courts and the Rabbinical Court of Appeal.

Religious Jews live with the aim of sanctifying every detail of their lives by observing 613 commandments, derived from the Torah (the first five books of the Bible). These regulate every aspect of existence, from dress and food to ethical behaviour and the celebration of festivals.

To be present during one of the many religious or national holidays in Israel is an exciting and moving experience, and one that should be considered when planning the time of a trip. One way to get to know Israel is to be with Israelis when they celebrate or mourn during days of solemn remembrance. Judaism observes a lunar calendar month, so that religious holidays occur at slightly different times each year.

Sabbath – Friday evening after the setting of the sun,

until after sunset on Saturday. Shops, public transportation and most places of entertainment close down. Traditionally, Sabbath is a time of rest and spiritual regeneration.

Rosh Hashana – usually falls in September-October. The beginning of the Jewish year, when many Jews attend synagogue services and get together for family festive meals. Traditionally, honey and apples are eaten to symbolize the entry of a sweet year.

Yom Kippur – September-October, ten days after Rosh Hashana. The Day of Atonement, when Jews search their souls, fast and pray for forgiveness, is the most solemn day in the Jewish calendar. The atmosphere in the country is hushed and respectful. It is a day without television, radio, or public transportation (with the exception of ambulances).

Succot – September-October. Festively decorated succot (booths) are built in the open air, in which people eat and sometimes sleep. The booths symbolize the life of the ancient Israelites in the wilderness after the Exodus from Egypt. Also part of the festival is the ritual waving of the four species – palm, citron, myrtle and willow – over which a blessing is said.

Simchat Torah – September-October, on the eighth day of Succot. The annual reading of the Torah in synagogues begins its cycle on this day, which is marked by singing, dancing and festivity. Children wave special decorated flags.

Chanukah – December. Chanukah celebrates the Maccabaean victory over the Hellenistic Seleucid empire. For eight days, candles on a "chanukiah" or candelabrum are lit, adding one each night. Children are traditionally given gifts or money, special games are played with a top, and fried jelly-filled doughnuts and potato pancakes are eaten.

Tu B'Shvat – January-February. The new year for trees, when saplings are planted all over Israel.

Purim – February-March. To commemorate the victory of Queen Esther and her uncle Mordechai over the evil machinations of Haman in ancient Persia, children dress up in costumes and everyone parties. In synagogues, the book of Esther is read. Holiday food includes triangular filled pastries called "Oznei Haman" or "Haman's ears".

Passover (Pesach) – March-April. A "Seder" or family

gathering and feast is held at which the traditional "Haggadah" text is read and sung, telling the story of the exodus from Egypt. Since unleavened products are not eaten for the 8-day holiday period, bread is generally not available. Instead, unleavened bread (matza) is eaten.

Shavuot – May-June. The festival commemorates both the giving of the Torah and the harvest of the first fruits. On kibbutzim particularly, the harvest parade is a favourite tradition. Dairy foods are traditionally eaten.

Tisha B'Av – August. A day of mourning and fasting for the destruction of the First and Second Temples.

Other significant days include **Holocaust Day**, in April-May during which television and radio feature only solemn programmes and the country marks its memory of the greatest disaster to befall its people; **Remembrance Day**, in April-May, in memory of fallen soldiers, and **Independence Day**, on the day following Remembrance Day, during which most cities and towns hold festive street parties with entertainment and fireworks.

CHRISTIANITY

Unlike Judaism, Christianity owes its presence and most of its shrines in Israel to the existence of one man alone. For this reason pilgrims find themselves following a well-charted course first trodden by their saviour, Jesus of Nazareth.

Bethlehem is the inevitable starting point for those who prefer to follow the chronological sequence of events in the life of Jesus. Then to Nazareth, where he grew up to be rejected as a false prophet. Kafr Cana, the site of his first miracle at the wedding feast, is close by, as are Capernaum and the Mt. of Beatitudes on the shores of the Sea of Galilee, where fishermen became apostles and where multitudes thronged to witness miracles and hear immortal words.

The final acts in his brief life were played out in Jerusalem, where he was arrested, summarily tried and crucified. Here, too, is the Via Dolorosa, along which he stumbled while carrying his cross to Calvary, and a veritable plethora of shrines.

The visitor to the Holy Land will see at a glance how Christianity, alone among the major monotheistic religions, spawned centuries of reclusive monks, spending their lives in meditation and prayer in the wilderness. The

Judaean desert is dotted with caves and precariously perched monasteries to which hermits have withdrawn, from the beginnings of Christianity. As Christians also revere Mt. Sinai, tourists will find the ruins of many Byzantinc churches and chapels within ancient Negev settlements guarding the pilgrims' route south.

The Christian population of Israel is small compared with the number of sites holy to them. The community numbers about 128,000, of which the vast majority are Christian Arabs. Of the 30 denominations, the principal ones (in terms of numbers) are Greek Catholic, Greek Orthodox, Latin and Maronite. There are also about 3,000 Protestants (Anglicans, Presbyterians, Baptists and Lutherans) and more than 3,500 members of Eastern Monophysite Churches (including Armenian Orthodox, Coptic, Ethiopian and Syrian Orthodox). About 14,000 Christians live in Jerusalem; there are several Christian villages in the Galilee.

Most of the Roman Catholic shrines are supervised by the brown-garbed Franciscan friars who remained custodians of many Christian sites in the Holy Land in the face of intermittent harassment and persecution at the hands of the Moslems.

It may come as something of a surprise for you to learn of the delicate relationship between many of the Christian denominations. They stem from early squabbles that led on occasion to physical blows among the prelates for the rights and privileges connected with major holy sites. Order is maintained through rigid adherence to the status quo. If you visit the Church of the Nativity in Bethlehem, or the Church of the Holy Sepulchre in Jerusalem, you will witness the daily ritual of Greek Orthodox, Armenian Orthodox and Latin churchmen walking along well-defined routes to specified altars for tightly controlled schedules of services.

The Christian pilgrim would do well to time a visit to Israel for Easter or Christmas. The colourful Palm Sunday procession down the Mt. of Olives recreates the triumphal return of Jesus to Jerusalem. Christmas Eve in Bethlehem's Manger Square, amid carollers of all denominations, is undeniably the peak of any Christian pilgrimage to the Holy Land. The Ministry of Tourism has a special pilgrims' department for Christians.

Different Christian denominations in Israel observe some of their holy days on different dates. For further information, contact the Christian Information Centre in Jerusalem, tel. (02)272692.

On Christmas Eve and Christmas Day, Catholic services are held at the Church of St. Catherine and in the Grotto of the Nativity in Bethlehem. Protestant services are held in St. George's Cathedral. Greek Orthodox and Armenian services in Bethlehem are held later in January, according to the Julian calendar.

ISLAM

The religion that broke like a tidal wave over the Middle East and half the world in the 7th century owes its origin to Mohammed (570-632 CE). Moslems regard him as the last and the greatest of a line of prophets including Abraham and Christ. His legendary ascent to heaven from the Temple Mount in Jerusalem makes this city the third holiest in the world to Moslems, after Mecca and Medina.

Mohammed claimed to have had visions of the Archangel Gabriel and to have received revelations from Allah, the true and only God. His sayings, recorded in the Koran (reading), are recited daily in Moslem schools and at regular services in hundreds of mosques in Israel. The Koran contains many episodes from the Old Testament and the New. It offers daily guidance for every Moslem ("one who submits to the will of God"), portrays paradisiacal rewards in the after-life for those who follow its teachings, and holds out the promise of a burning hell for transgressors.

Like Judaism, Islam prohibits the eating of pork or carrion. Believers are forbidden to drink alcohol or to gamble. The Koran upholds honour and justice in all dealings and directs the faithful to honour their parents, assist the poor and protect orphans. Daily readings from the Koran, as well as prayers and sermons, are broadcast by the Arabic station of the Israel Broadcasting Authority.

The overwhelming majority of Israel's Arabic population of about 900,000 are Moslems. Their highest dignitaries are the Qadis, of the Shaari'a courts, who have exclusive jurisdiction in matters of personal status, including marriage, divorce and inheritance.

Wherever a Moslem lives, in Akko or in Karachi, he is expected to observe the Five Pillars of Islam, prescribed by Mohammed. The first of these is faith in Allah, defined thus: "Allah is mighty; there is no God but Allah; Mohammed is his messenger."

The second is prayer, to which Moslems are called five times daily by the cry of the muezzin from the minaret. Moslems need not be in a mosque to pray, but they must face the holy city of Mecca, Mohammed's birth-place. Before entering the carpeted mosques, they wash their hands and feet to purify themselves and then place their shoes outside before prostrating themselves before Allah. Women pray in separate rooms or in balconies set aside for them. Fridays and the festivals of Islam are recognised in Israel as official holidays for Moslems.

Almsgiving is also a pillar of the faith and every Moslem is expected to give a part of his income for the support of the mosque and the poor.

The fourth pillar is the month-long Fast of Ramadan, commemorating Mohammed's first revelations, when Moslems abstain from eating and drinking during the daylight hours. At the end of the month gifts are exchanged between friends during the festival of goodwill known as Little Bairam.

The fifth pillar of Islam is the haj (pilgrimage) to Mecca, which every believer is expected to make once during his lifetime. Tourists get a glimpse of departing busloads of pilgrims from Judaea and Samaria during the two months following Ramadan. Moslem citizens of Israel, alone among the millions of Moslems around the world, were until recently forbidden to make the haj by the Arab governments concerned.

Islam follows a lunar calendar and dates of holy days vary from year to year. Some of the most important are Id el-Adha – the sacrificial festival; Mohammed's birthday; New year; Fast of Ramadan – for one month, devout Moslems do not eat or drink during the hours of daylight. Id el-Fitr marks the conclusion of Ramadan.

BAHAIS

Haifa is the spiritual and admininstrative centre of the world Bahai faith, whose principal shrines are in Akko and Haifa. There are more than 100,000 centres of the faith in 315 different countries and dependencies.

The golden-topped shrine on the slopes of Mt. Carmel holds the remains of the "Bab," who was the martyr-herald of the Bahai faith. In 1850 he was executed in

Tabriz, Persia, because of his religious teachings. His remains were brought to the Holy Land and entombed in 1909.

The Bahai faith teaches that religious truth is progressive, not final: God educates the human race through a series of prophets who have appeared throughout history and will always appear to guide the destiny of Man: Moses, Zoroaster, Buddha, Jesus and Mohammed are all examples of these "Divine Educators." The last of the prophets was Baha'ullah, the founder of the Bahai faith. He is buried at Akko, where he died in 1892.

Archaeology

When in the summer of 1947 a young Bedouin shepherd, Muhammad Adh Dhib, lost a goat in the wilderness between Bethlehem and the Dead Sea, he couldn't have imagined that he would end up making one of the greatest discoveries in biblical archaeology this century. In a cave in the vicinity of Khirbet Qumran, he stumbled upon seven ancient scrolls, among them manuscripts of the Book of Isaiah about a thousand years older than any previously known Old Testament text.

Predictably, the Dead Sea Scrolls fired the imagination of the world. They constituted a part of the library of an ascetic Jewish sect, the Essenes, who, although never mentioned in the New Testament, were active in this area around the time of Jesus – a crucial period in man's history, and one of the most poorly documented.

Archaeologists subsequently examined the area carefully and found 40 other caves in which there were more scrolls and tens of thousands of fragments. Many questions about the origins of the Christian faith could now be answered.

As the cradle of Western civilization, Israel is a veritable treasure house of relics of the past. And accidental finds are common.

Typical is the freak discovery of "Jason's Tomb," a 1st century BCE rock-cut extravagance in the heart of a plush Jerusalem suburb. After builders had exposed part of it a neighbour rushed to alert professional archaeologists who crawled through the debris and found Maccabean coins, pottery, bronze mirrors and bottles.

Even the skilled archaeologists trust in Lady Luck. Israel's best-known excavator, the late **Yigael Yadin,** was exploring the caves at Nahal Hever, which had been combed by many before him, when his team electrified the country by announcing the discovery of the letters of the 2nd century Jewish leader, Bar Kochba, masses of legal documents, household utensils and tatters of clothing from the same period.

It should be pointed out that although written evidence is often discovered during an archaeological investigation, it does not – strictly speaking – constitute the subject matter of archaeology proper, which concerns itself with the material remains of the past in order to fill in details that are missing from recorded history.

Frequently an archaeologist unearths a cache of historical objects after acting purely on a hunch. Dr. **Benno Rothenberg** was working near the Timna copper mines when it occurred to him that the brooding pillars of Solomon, carved by nature out of pinkish Nubian sandstone, might have been a place of cult worship. He dug a trench and, over the same spot where tourists had walked for decades, unearthed an Egyptian temple, only a metre below the sand.

Finds such as these have turned thousands of Israelis into passionate students of the past. More often than not the rewards lie on the surface of the sand or gravel. Caesarea, the Roman capital of Palestine, has yielded many ancient coins to hawk-eyed amateurs carefully scanning the sandy beaches around the colossal ruins.

Sherds of pottery literally lie scattered over the land and are the tell-tale signs of previous civilizations.

So great has been the impact of Israel's fund of archaeological treasure that outsiders periodically swarm in to join the digs. Many of them write in advance to the **Israel Antiquities Authority, P.O.B. 586, Jerusalem,** for information on forthcoming digs. **Note**: it is forbidden to excavate, dig, etc., without permission from the authority. All archaeological finds are the property of the State of Israel.

When Prof. Yadin prepared to unravel the secrets of Massada, he was flooded with thousands of applications from volunteers in 28 countries, even though they knew in advance that they would have to pay their round-trip fares and sleep 10 to a tent in the blistering heat of the Dead Sea rift.

The Israel Defence Forces have added a flamboyant touch to archaeological digs in the Holy Land. Soldiers helped to construct the paths down the cliff face to the caves at Nahal Hever and they brought in mine-sweepers to detect coins. Air Force helicopters have been used for aerial surveys and for ferrying finds from these remote areas to the safety of the cities.

The rubble has been cleared from the great Nabataean cities of 2,000 years ago and we can see how their advanced system of water conservation supported vast settlements in the arid Negev. We can follow the art of warfare and the subtle minds behind the tacticians and strategists of yesteryear. Solomon's gates were built in such a way that enemy forces could smash their way through the first enclosure, only to find themselves trapped within it.

Ahab, the Israelite king, and Hezekiah, king of Judah, were formidable engineers. Ahab's stupendous water tunnels at Hazor and Megiddo show that however much he led his people astray from the laws of Moses, he nevertheless proved that they were masterly builders. Hezekiah's tunnel, cut through solid rock, is almost 600 metres long and runs below the City of David; it remains one of the wonders on view to the 20th century tourist.

The burrowing archaeologist has also focused on the religious practices of buried civilizations. Man either believed in an after-life or practised ancestor worship as long as 11,000 years ago in Jericho. Some human skulls unearthed there are pasted over with plaster and the hollows of the eyes are set with sea shells. The great stone temples of the Canaanites uncovered at Gezer, and elsewhere, were contemporaneous with cultic figurines, including goddesses of fertility.

The archaeologist's spade and the builder's bulldozer have thrown much light on the burial customs of the previous inhabitants of Israel. A Nabataean cemetery at Mampsis (Kurnub) revealed that the bodies lay face up with the legs pointing east. Wealthy Hellenized Jews were often buried in family tombs. Those at Bet Guvrin were handsomely painted within. On the other hand terracotta ossuaries uncovered at Givatayim point to a 2,000–year–old practice of a second burial after the flesh had decayed.

A dig conducted by Prof. **Benjamin Mazar** near the Western Wall in Jerusalem after the Six Day War of 1967 unearthed ruins and relics that go back almost 3,000 years.

Stones toppled by the Romans from the walls of the Second Temple enclosure in 70 CE were found lying on

Herodian streets below, presenting vivid testimony of the destruction of the colossal Temple.

Mazar's team uncovered part of the huge supporting walls of the Herodian Temple Mount, public works of the Herodian period – paved streets, stairways leading to the gates of the Mount, complex water systems and various types of building.

It is true to say that excavations conducted in this key area since 1968 have revealed more about the city's past than had all the previous excavations conducted during the last century.

In addition to the Second Temple period, the other main periods in Jerusalem's history are the Byzantine (4th-7th centuries CE) and the Early Islamic (7th-8th centuries CE). Excavations south of the Mount, at the Ophel – initiated by Mazar and continued by Meir Ben Dov – produced important finds from these periods, especially the latter. One massive and beautiful construction behind the El-Aksa Mosque, for instance, was an Umayyad palace; flanked by other large buildings, it suggests a centre for Caliphs in Jerusalem. A papyrus discovered in Egypt 80 years ago mentions two carpenters being sent to build a palace in Jerusalem. No one made much of this knowledge until this first Early Islamic palace was discovered.

Less than half a kilometre away from the Temple Mount, in the Jewish Quarter of the Old City, Prof. **Nahman Avigad** and other experts have sorted out and assembled crate-loads of jars and vases from successive epochs in Jerusalem's history.

A large-scale investigation of the Ophel and the City of David began in 1978. The site of the original Jerusalem, the area was within the city boundaries of every king of Judah and was inhabited by Jebusites even before the Israelites invaded Canaan under Joshua.

The dig was headed by the late Dr. **Yigal Shiloh.** Within two months of starting to work at the site archaeologists uncovered a water tunnel from the Siloam spring going back to 900 BCE, which predates by 200 years the famous tunnel cut by order of King Hezekiah. They also found remains from the earliest settlement period known in Jerusalem, Early Bronze I (c. 3000 BCE).

In August 1981 the scientists and students at the dig were harassed by religious zealots who claimed to have found human bones at the site and persuaded the country's chief rabbis to declare the area a Jewish cemetery and out of bounds to archaeologists. The High Court of Justice, however, ruled that the dig could continue.

The main goal of the excavation was to explore what remained of the city from the First Temple period and before. "Since 1967, everything we knew about Jerusalem changed," said Shiloh. "This is the last part of the puzzle for this generation."

EXCAVATION SITES FOR VOLUNTEERS

A number of archaeological excavation sites are open to volunteers from abroad.

Volunteers must be over 17 years of age and physically fit. They are expected to pay their own fares to and from Israel and to take care of all their accommodation and other arrangements not connected with their work on the dig.

For a detailed list of digs, dates and general information contact: **Israel Antiquities Authority,** P.O.Box 586, Jerusalem, tel. (02) 292627.

PRACTICAL INFORMATION

Entry Regulations

VISAS

The visa or transit visa (valid for five days), can be obtained at any Israeli Diplomatic or Consular Mission abroad and may be applied for by post or in person. It is valid for a stay of three months from the date of arrival.

Citizens of the following countries do not require a transit or visitor's visa for entry into Israel:

Austria, Bahamas, Barbados, Belgium, Bolivia, Colombia, Costa Rica, Denmark, Dominican Republic, Dutch Antilles, Ecuador, El Salvador, Fiji, Finland, France, Greece, Guatemala, Haiti, Holland, Hong Kong, Iceland, Jamaica, Japan, Liechtenstein, Luxembourg, Maldive Islands, Mauritius, Mexico, Norway, Paraguay, Surinam, Swaziland, Sweden, Switzerland, Trinidad-Tobago, and the United Kingdom (including Northern Ireland, the Channel Islands and the Isle of Man).

Citizens of the following countries receive the visa free of charge at the port of entry:

Argentina, Australia, Brazil, Canada, Central African Republic, Chile, West Germany (those born after 1 Jan., 1928), Italy, New Zealand, San Marino, South Africa, Spain, Uruguay and the U.S.A.

Citizens of the Republic of Ireland (Eire) also receive the visa at the port of entry but are required to pay the requisite fee.

Citizens of the following countries receive the visa free of charge **but must apply for it, before departure, at any Israeli Diplomatic or Consular Mission:**
Cyprus, West Germany (those born before 1 Jan., 1928).

Citizens of the countries not mentioned above must submit their visa application to the nearest Israeli Diplomatic or Consular Mission and pay the prescribed fee.

Landing for the day card: Tourists arriving by boat or airplane who wish to stay a short period and leave by the same boat or airplane may be issued a landing for the day card by frontier control authorities. It may be extended at their discretion for the time the boat or airplane remains in the country.

Collective visas: Collective visas are issued to organized groups of from 5 to 50 persons who arrive and leave together.

Transit Visa: A transit visa, valid for five days, is also available from any Israeli Diplomatic or Consular Mission. It can be extended, following arrival, for a further 10 days by applying to any district office of the Interior Ministry in Israel.

Note: all of the foregoing applies only to people wishing to enter Israel for travel or touring purposes. Anyone wishing to enter the country for the purposes of work, study, or settling must apply, while still abroad, to an Israeli Diplomatic or Consular Mission for the appropriate visa.

FORM AL.17

All visitors to Israel, including diplomats, are required to fill in an entry form, AL.17, on arrival.

Visitors who intend to continue to Arab countries (except Egypt) after their visit to Israel may ask the frontier control officer to put the entry stamps on this form and not on their passports.

EXTENSION OF STAY

Tourists who wish to stay in the country longer than three months must obtain an extension of stay. This applies also to citizens of those countries which are exempt from entry visas. The extension may be obtained through any district office of the Ministry of Interior.

The addresses of the main offices are:

Jerusalem: Generali Building,
Rehov Shlomzion Hamalka, tel. (02)290222
Tel Aviv: Shalom Mayer Tower,
9, Rehov Ahad Ha'am, tel. (03)5193333
Haifa: Government Building (opposite
Municipality), 11, Hassan Shukri, tel. (04)616222
Beer Sheva: Derekh Hanesseim, tel. (057)231789
Nazareth: Government Offices, tel. (06)570510
Ramla: 74, Rehov Herzl, tel. (08)270170

HEALTH

There are no vaccination requirements for tourists entering Israel.

Tourists in Israel can obtain vaccination against yellow fever at any district office of the Ministry of Health. Further information from any of the 15 public health offices of the Ministry of Health located in all major cities. Ministry of Health headquarters: (02)705705.

CUSTOMS REGULATIONS FOR TOURISTS

Dual Channel Customs Arrangements at Ben-Gurion Airport

A person entering Israel via a port where the dual channel "Red-Green" system operates may pass through the "Green Channel" if he has only those items which are listed below as non-dutiable. If he carries other items, even if brought temporarily and he is entitled to exemption on them, the "Red Channel" should be used.

Personal effects (Green Channel)

The following items are exempt only if brought with the person on the same plane or ship on which he arrived:

Alcoholic drinks - Spirits up to 1 litre and wine up to 2 litres, for each person aged at least 17 years.

Alcoholic perfumes (such as eau-de-cologne) – up to 14 litre per person.

Tobacco products - up to 250 gr. tobacco or 250 cigarettes, for each person aged at least 17 years.

Gifts - various articles imported as gifts or for personal use, provided that they do not include alcoholic drinks, alcoholic perfumes, tobacco products or a TV set and that their total value – as determined by the official at the port of importation, according to price lists in his possession and after adding expenses for freight, insurance and port costs in Israel (c.i.f.) – does not exceed $125 (non-cumulative). This category may also include foodstuffs of various kinds up to a total weight of 3 kg., provided that foodstuffs of each kind do not exceed 1 kg. in weight. This exemption (including foodstuffs) is granted to each person who arrives on his own, and, in the case of a family, to each member who is at least 17 years old, non-cumulative, as noted above, even if several persons enter together.

Travellers' hand luggage — clothing, footwear and toilet articles of types and in quantities customarily carried as part of a traveller's hand luggage.

Other used, portable effects with which Green Channel may be passed and which must be taken out on departure:
Baby carriage.
Bicycle – one, without auxiliary motor.
Binoculars – one pair only.
Camera – one ordinary; also up to 10 rolls or 10 plates of suitable, unexposed photographic film may be included.
Camera-movie – one less than 16mm.; also up to 10 reels of suitable, unexposed photographic film.
Camping equipment – and sports requisites.
Gramophone – one (portable).
One sound recorder and reproducer.
Musical instruments.
Personal jewellery – in reasonable quantity.
Radio receiver and tape recorder – not suitable for installation in a motor vehicle; 2 cassettes.
Typewriter – one (portable).

Appliances to be declared (Red Channel)

Appliances detailed in the following list are subject to cash deposit of taxes and must be brought with the person entering:
Caravan trailer and boats.
Diving equipment – portable and used.
Hand-operated tools – of a type that during their use or operation are held in the hand and of a total value not exceeding $1,650 including cost, insurance and freight.
TV set – one, portable and used.
Videotape – videotape and cameras.

All of the items listed above must be re-exported on

your departure from Israel, unless the customs official fixes another date.

Customs Deposits

The Customs authorities are entitled to demand deposits or guarantees on any article brought in by the tourist or sent separately by him. Thus, tourists who bring in temporarily or send separately effects such as video equipment or any of the other items included in the "appliances to be declared' list, are required by the Customs authorities to deposit with them appropriate guarantees.

You can use your Visa credit card, instead of cash, for the deposit. The sales slip will be held by the Customs Authority at the airport until you leave the country. When you show the officials that you still have the item in question, i.e. video camera, they will return the sales slip.

The guarantee or deposit is returned to the tourist when he leaves the country and takes the article(s) out with him. Since the formalities take some time, it is advisable to make all arrangements a day or two before departure and preferably at the port of entry of the goods so that the return of the guarantee can be carried out more conveniently.

Further information from: The Department of Customs and Excise, 32 Rehov Agron, P.O.B. 320, Jerusalem 91 002, tel. (02)703333.

Export of Antiquities

It is forbidden to export antiquities from Israel unless a written export permit has been obtained from the Department of Antiquities and Museums of the Ministry of Education and Culture, Jerusalem. This applies also to antiquities which accompany tourists who are leaving the country. Antiquities proven to have been imported after 1900 will be exempted.

Antiquities are defined as objects fashioned by man before the year 1700.

A 10 percent export fee is payable upon the purchase price of every item approved for export.

The article(s) must be despatched by post, with an accompanying cheque for the appropriate amount, or taken in person to: The Israel Antiquities Authority,

Museums, Rockefeller Museum, near Herod's Gate, P.O.B. 586, Jerusalem. For personal visits, it is advisable to phone (02)292627 for an appointment.

The Antiquities Authority accepts no responsibility for the authenticity of antiquities, even if they have been approved for export. Visitors should, therefore, make sure that the antiquities they buy are authentic.

Some shops selling antiquities are listed by the Ministry of Tourism.

CURRENCY

A tourist is permitted to bring into Israel any amount of foreign currency, without any declaration at all. Upon leaving the country, all the money remaining can be taken out.

Hold on to all receipts when buying shekels. During their stay, tourists are entitled to reconvert to foreign currency money exchanged through licensed money changers since the last entry to Israel, that is by showing the original bank receipts for the exchange. The amount is limited to $5,000 per visit. At the end of the visit, after passing through border control at the point of exit, a tourist can exchange shekels to dollars up to a value of $100 without showing any documentation.

PETS

Dogs and cats must be accompanied by a veterinarian's health certificate from country of origin. Dogs should be vaccinated against rabies. Dogs and cats from Asia, East Europe, Africa, Central and South America will be quarantined for at least 30 days, while the quarantine period for animals from other countries will be decided by the health authorities.

Value Added Tax

Value Added Tax (VAT) of 17 per cent is imposed on all purchases except in Elat, which is a free-trade zone.

Tourists in all other centres are exempted from VAT only on the following if paid in foreign currency: accommodation, regular tours, car hire, Arkia flights and tours, meals provided by tour operators on regular tours, and meals taken by hotel guests in hotel restaurants which are included in the hotel bill.

Refund of VAT and Discount on Foreign Currency Purchases

Tourists are given refunds on goods purchased with foreign currency at shops listed by the Ministry of Tourism. They also get a discount of at least 5% exclusive of VAT. The total value of purchases must add up to a minimum of $50 on each invoice and the goods must be taken out of the country in the tourist's hand luggage.

What You Should Request From The Store

1. A discount of at least 5% from the listed price.
2. The original receipt, with the VAT, which you paid, marked in the proper place, both in Israeli shekels and U.S. dollars.
3. That the product you have bought be packed in a plastic bag with at least one transparent side.
4. That a copy of the receipt be placed inside the bag in such a manner that the entries on it can be read without opening the bag.
5. That the bag be heat-sealed or glued. The bag should remain sealed during your entire stay in Israel.

Do not lose the original receipt you obtained from the store.

When you come to the departure hall at either Ben-Gurion or Elat Airport, or to the departure hall of Haifa Port, please apply to the official of Bank Leumi in the departure lounge, and present the sealed bag and the original receipt to him. He will stamp the original receipt and refund, in U.S. dollars, the amount of VAT which you paid (in round figures).

Airport & Harbour Taxes

On leaving Israel every passenger must pay the airport tax (about $15) or harbour tax, unless they leave from Elat.

Miscellaneous Information

BEACHES, BATHING AND WATER SPORTS

With a long coastal strip along the Mediterranean Sea, two inland seas (Sea of Galilee and the Dead Sea) as well as the tip of the Red Sea at Elat, Israel has a great number of pleasant beaches. Most of them offer many facilities, either free or for a small entrance fee. Do not swim in areas where there are no lifeguards or where signs forbid you to swim. Although the Mediterranean appears calm, it can be deceptive. In addition, most large hotels have swimming pools, open to guests and sometimes to visitors for a fee, and the large cities have municipal pools.

Water sports include waterskiing, snorkelling, skin diving and scuba diving, particularly along the Red Sea coast near Elat, where spectacular coral reefs make underwater sport an unforgettable experience. The water temperature near Elat is warm all year round. Courses and equipment rental are available.

Contact the **Federation for Underwater Activities in Israel**, P.O. Box 6110, Tel Aviv, tel (03)457432.

BUSINESS HOURS

Shopping hours

Sunday to Thursday: 8.30 a.m. – 1 p.m.
4.00 p.m. – 7 p.m.
Friday and days preceding Jewish holidays:
8.30 a.m. – 1 p.m.

Some shops in the larger cities stay open all day. Some small grocery shops stay open until 3 p.m. or even an hour or two later on the half-days. In addition, many shops are closed on Tuesday afternoons. Most hairdressers close on Monday afternoons and travel agents don't work on Wednesday afternoons. The Sabbath (Shabbat) begins on Friday evening and ends on Saturday night. Christian Arab shops are closed on Sundays. Moslem shops and institutions are closed on Fridays.

Banks

Sunday, Tuesday, Thursday: 8.30 a.m. – 12.30 p.m., 4 – 5.30 p.m. Monday, Wednesday: 8.30 a.m. – 12.30 p.m., Friday: 8.30 a.m. – 12 noon. Some banks keep longer and different hours in the afternoons. Branches in leading hotels offer convenient additional hours.

Government offices are generally open to the public Sunday to Thursday: 8.30 a.m. – 12.30 p.m.

Banks, Government institutions, and Jewish shops, offices and places of entertainment are closed on Saturdays and on Jewish religious and national holidays.

CLIMATE

Israel has hot summers with no rain, and a rainy season in winter. Spring and autumn are generally mild and pleasant, though there may be some days of "sharav" or hot, dry wind. In winter, the Dead Sea and Elat are pleasantly warm and dry. Weather forecasts are available in newspapers and on radio and television.

The weather forecast after the 9 p.m. news on television is generally reliable. You do not have to understand any Hebrew to get a clear picture of what is expected in the next 24 hours.

Average Temperatures:

	Jan.	Aug.
Jerusalem	F43-53 C6-11	F66-83 C19-28
Tel Aviv	F48-63 C9-17	F72-85 C22-29
Haifa Carmel	F48-59 C9-15	F71-82 C22-28
Elat	F49-69 C9-21	F78-102 C25-39

Average Annual Rainfall:

Jerusalem	486 mm (19.13 in).
Tel Aviv	539 mm (21.22 in).
Haifa	601 mm (23.66 in.)
Elat	N25 mm (0.98 in).

CULTURE AND ENTERTAINMENT

MUSIC

Israel is justly proud of the quality of music it produces – both popular and classical. Its symphony and chamber orchestras, particularly the Israel Philharmonic, are internationally renowned, as are popular singers such as Ofra Haza, Dudu Fisher, Yehoram Gaon and Arik Einstein. In the short years of its existence, Israel has also developed a distinctive style of folk music and a high level of choral singing.

Concerts of all types of music are performed all over the country, but particularly in the large cities. See the Friday edition of the Jerusalem Post (or, if you read Hebrew, any of the other newspapers) for a full listing of what is currently on. As a bonus, great musicians such as Isaac Stern and Zubin Mehta appear frequently in Israel and may provide the music lover with a chance to enjoy a famous soloist or conductor. Booking in advance is almost always necessary, either at the box office or through ticket agencies.

Among the many international music festivities held in Israel are an international harp competition every three years, the Arthur Rubinstein piano competition, the Zimriya choir festival, and annual festivals in Jerusalem and Kibbutz Ein Gev, among others.

DANCE

Israel has several respected dance companies, including the Batsheva, Bat Dor and the Israel Ballet companies.

The Kibbutz Dance company performs widely, as does the Inbal troupe which specializes in ethnic dance. See the newspapers for performance schedules.

Israeli folk dance is immensely popular at the grass-roots level, and almost every city and village has folk-dancing instruction groups at which everyone is welcome. Ask at the sports department of local municipalities for information.

THEATRE

Theatre is remarkably lively and original in Israel, but of course almost always performed in Hebrew. Some of the main theatrical companies are Habimah, Cameri, and the Haifa Municipal Theatre. Popular contemporary playwrites include Hanoch Levin and Yehoshua Sobol. Theatrical productions in English and Yiddish can be seen from time to time.

ART

The best places to see both modern and seminal works of Israeli art are the Tel Aviv Museum and the Israel Museum. In Tel Aviv, galleries are concentrated in the Gordon Street area, and also in the old city of Jaffa. Worth seeing in Tel Aviv is the house of Reuven Rubin, who painted life in the early days of settlement on the sands of Tel Aviv among other themes. Haifa and Jerusalem also have many galleries. Ein Hod and Zefat have picturesque artists' quarters.

CINEMA

Israel has its own film industry and local films can be seen from time to time in the country's theatres. Serious films can be seen at the Jerusalem, Tel Aviv and Haifa cinematheques.

See newspapers for daily film listings. Usually, performances are scheduled for about 4 p.m., 7 p.m. and 9:30 p.m.

NIGHTCLUBS AND PUBS

Tel Aviv is the main night-life centre of Israel, with folk, pop, rock and sometimes jazz on offer till the early hours.

Jerusalem too has a modest night-life. See the newspapers for listings.

CURRENCY

Israel's main currency note is the shekel (also called the new Israeli shekel = NIS), which is divided into 100 agorot. Coins come in denominations of 5, 10 and 50 agorot (brass-coloured) and one shekel and five shekels (silver-coloured). Larger denominations are in paper bills. The exchange rate is regulated and is the same at every bank. Current rates of exchange can be found in newspapers and displayed outside some banks. Banks usually offer a better rate than shops or hotels.

Many international credit cards, such as Visa, Diners, American Express and Eurocard are widely accepted, as are travellers' cheques.

ELECTRICITY

Power supply is 220 volt AC – 50 cycles. Therefore, if you have an electric razor or other appliances, see that they are suitable or equipped with adapters. Israeli sockets take three-pronged plugs.

FIRST AID & MEDICAL SERVICES

The standard of medicine in Israel is extremely high and should a medical emergency arise, you may be confident of receiving capable care. Most doctors can speak adequate English.

It is a wise precaution to obtain medical insurance before leaving home. If you don't have insurance and need hospital treatment, bring your passport and money to cover the bill, which is likely to be less than equivalent services in the United States. Ask for a receipt in English for your insurance company.

Many hospitals including Hadassah in Jerusalem honour Blue Cross–Blue Shield coverage. In addition, Israel now has a number of private multi-doctor clinics, such as the Herzliyya Medical Centre, which can provide access to specialists.

EMERGENCY MEDICAL NUMBERS:

Magen David Adom (equivalent of Red Cross, which provides emergency service): 101 in most parts of the country.

Poison control counselling service – (04)529205.

Rape crisis centre – Tel Aviv – (03)5234819, Jerusalem (02)514455, 514466, Haifa (04)660111.

Kupat Holim Information Centre – (03)433300, Sun. –Thurs. 8 a.m.–8 p.m., Fri. 8 a.m.–3 p.m.

Eran – Emotional First Aid by telephone. Usually only available in Hebrew. Jerusalem (02)610303, Tel Aviv (03)5461111, Haifa (04)672222.

Off-hour duty hospitals are listed daily in the Jerusalem Post newspaper, as are the location and telephone numbers of emergency off-hours pharmacies. In the event of an emergency, any hospital will offer treatment. Bring your passport, insurance papers and money to cover payment. Keep receipts to obtain refunds from insurance companies.

For less serious cases – e.g. strep throat – inquire at MDA, or if you are staying at a hotel, you can ask at the desk for the doctor who is associated with the hotel.

Another option is a new service called Terem, a private, full-service urgent care centre that is staffed by board certified physicians from the U.S. They are open Sun.–Thurs. 7 a.m. till 11 p.m., Fri. 7 a.m. – 4 p.m. and Sat. 7 a.m.–midnight, and can handle anything from a sore throat to a serious illness or injury. Ask for a receipt for your insurance company back home. Rehov Kehilat Saloniki 9, Tel Aviv (facing Derech Herzliya), tel. (03) 499978; Rehov HaMem-Gimel 7, Jerusalem (02) 521748.

HEBREW PHRASE GUIDE

Hebrew is the first official language of Israel (Arabic is the second), and is written from right to left. For many centuries, Hebrew was only used as the language of study and prayer among Jews, but with the beginning of the Zionist movement, an attempt was made to make it the language of daily life. Today, Hebrew is a flourishing, living language.

Note: "kh" is the gutteral "khet" or "khaf" sound, sometimes written as "h" or "ch", and pronounced like the "ch" in the Scottish "loch".

DAYS OF THE WEEK

Sunday – yom ri-shón
Monday - yom shey-ní
Tuesday – yom shli-shí
Wednesday – yom re-vi-í
Thursday – yom kha-mi-shí
Friday – yom shi-shí
Saturday – sha-bát

NUMBERS

one – a-khát
two – shtá-yim
three – sha-lósh
four – ár-ba
five – kha-mésh
six – shesh
seven – shé-va
eight – shmó-ne
nine – té-sha
ten – é-ser
eleven – a-khát es-rey
twelve – shtém es-rey

TIME

What time is it? – ma ha-sha-á?
It is one o'clock – ha-sha-á a-khát
It is 2:15 – ha-sha-á shtá-yim va-ré-va
It is 3:30 – ha-sha-á sha-lósh ve-khétzi
It is a quarter to four – ha-sh-á ár-ba pa-khót réva
At six o'clock – be-shésh
morning – bó-ker
afternoon – a-kha-ráy ha-tzo-ho-rá-yim
day – yom
evening – é-rev
night – lái-la
today – ha-yóm
yesterday – et-mól
tomorrow – ma-khár
week – sha-vú-a
month – khó-desh
year – sha-ná

GENERAL

hello – shá-lom
goodbye – shá-lom le-hit-ra-ót
How are you? – ma shlom-khá (m) shlo-mékh (f)?
I'm fine – be-sé-der
see you later – le-hit -ra-ót
good morning – bó-ker tov
good evening – é-rev tov
good night – lái-la tov
excuse me – sli-khá
please – be-va-ka-shá
thank you – to-dá
yes – ken
no – lo

DIRECTIONS

Can you help me? – tu-khál la-a-zór li?
Where is the central bus station? – éfo ha-ta-kha-ná ha-mer-ka-zít?
How do I get to the museum? – ekh a-ní ma-g-ía la-mu-zé-on?
How many kilometres to Haifa? – ká-ma ki-lo-mét-rim le-khéy-fa?
Tell me when to get off – ta-gíd li ma-táy la-ré-det
Take me to the theatre – kakh o-tí la-te-a-trón
Where is bus no. 5? – é-fo kav mis-pár kha-mésh?

straight on – ya-shár, ya-shár
to the right – ye-mí-na
to the left – smó-la
traffic light – ram-zór
taxi – tá-ksi (mo-nít)
up – le-má-la
down – le-má-ta
bus – ó-to-bus

SHOPPING

How much is this? – ká-ma ze o-léh?
store – kha-nút
clothing – b'ga-dím
gift – ma-ta-ná
jewellery – takh-shi-tím
market – shuk
newspaper – i-tón
books – se-fa-rím
bookstore – kha-nút se-fa-rím
shoes – na-a-lá-yim
money – ké-sef
expensive – ya-kár
cheap – zol

POST OFFICE

post office – dó-ar
postcard – glu-yá
aerogramme – i-gé-ret a-vír
stamps – bu-lím
air mail – dó-ar a-vír
registered – ra-shúm
How much is a postcard to the U.S./Europe? – ká-ma o-láh glu-yá le'artzót ha-brít/Eyrópa?
Give me three stamps for an air mail letter – ten li shlo-shá bu-lím le-mikh-táv dó-ar a-vír
Send this registered – shlakh et ze dó-ar ra-shúm

CHEMIST

chemist (drugstore) – bet mir-ká-khat
soap – sa-bón
toothpaste –mish-khát shi-ná-yim
toothbrush – mi-vré-shet shi-ná-yim
comb– mas-rék
shaving cream – mish-khát gi-lú-akh
razor blades – sa-ki-néy gi-lú-akh

EMERGENCY

doctor – ro-féh
dentist – ro-féh shi-ná-yim
hospital – bet kho-lím
accident – te-u-náh
police – mish-ta-ráh
fire – esh
first aid –ezrá rishoná

AT THE RESTAURANT

restaurant – mi-sa-dá
dining room – khá-dar ó-khel
salad – sa-lát
fish – dag
chicken – off

menu – taf-rít
waiter – mel-tzár
breakfast – a-ru-chát bó-ker
turkey – tar-ne-gól hó-du
orange juice – mitz ta-pu-zím
bread – lé-khem
white cheese – gvi-ná le-va-ná
salt – mé-lakh
yellow cheese –gvi-ná tze-hu-bá
water – má-yim
egg – be-tzá
omelette – kha-vi-tá
coffee – ka-fé
black coffee – ka-fé sha-khór (or) túrki
thank you – to-dá
coffee with milk – ka-fé im kha-láv
milk – kha-láv
lunch – a-ruk-khát tzo-ho-rá-yim
supper – a-ru-khát é-rev
first course – ma-ná ri-sho-ná
soup – ma-rák
main course – ma-ná i-ka-rít

meat – ba-sár
veal – é-gel
lamb – ké-vess
vegetables – ye-ra-kót
dessert – ki-nú-ach
fruits – pei-rót
pepper – píl-pel
cold drink – ma-shké kar
ice – ké-rakh
ice cream – gli-dá
please – be-va-ka-shá
glass – kos
plate – tza-lá-khat
knife – sa-kín
fork – maz-lég
teaspoon – ka-pít
spoon – kaf
serviette – ma-pít
white wine – yá-yin la-ván
red wine – yá-yin a-dóm

THE MENU

For those who are mystified by the names of local dishes on the menus, we offer a short list of definitions.

Baklawa: Oriental sweetmeat made of thin dough, honey, pistachio nuts and ground nuts.

Blintzes: thin pancakes usually filled with cheese and served with cream or apple puree.

Burekas: a leafy pastry pie filled with either salty cheese, spinach, or mashed spiced potatoes.

Calamari: squid.

Cholent: one variation includes pearl-barley, potatoes, kishke, beans, fat, cooked slowly all night.

Felafel: ground chick pea paste fried in small patties which are then put into a pita with salad and tehina; if you like hot food ask for "harif" – a chili-type red sauce which also goes into the pita.

Houmus: a spicy paste made with ground chick peas as

the base, and sharp spices added. Often eaten with tehina sauce.

Kebab: grilled minced meat on a skewer.

Kishe: beef derma stuffed with flour and shortening.

Kreplach: a sort of ravioli with minced meat or cheese stuffing.

Kubeh: wheat and flour sculptured by hand and filled with lamb or other meat, onions and pine seeds, and then fried.

Mamitze: Rumanian dish; the fat back part of a cow's tongue.

Moussaka: baked eggplant, minced meat, onion and parsley.

Mousakhan: baked chicken.

Pita: round white bread.

Shakshuka: eggs cooked in tomato sauce with onion.

Shishlik: pieces of meat grilled on a skewer.

Shwarma: lamb on a spit.

Snia: flat hamburger of beef or mutton, baked in the oven with tehina and pine seeds or tomatoes.

Tehina: a sauce made with ground sesame seeds as the base. May be eaten by itself, or with houmus or felafel.

MEDIA

RADIO

The Israel Broadcasting Authority runs the First Station (Reshet Alef), which has mainly classical music and discussion programmes on 576 kHz, 1440 kHz (Jerusalem) and 1458 kHz (south); the Second Station (Reshet Bet), with lighter music, plus advertisements, at 657 kHz, 1206 kHz (Jerusalem), 1206 kHz (Haifa), 846–882 kHz (north) and 927 kHz and 90–103 FM, and the Third Station (Reshet Gimel) with pop music at 88 kHz FM, 530 kHz AM. There is also Kol Hamusica, with classical music, betwen 88–100 FM, as well as the immigrants' station, Reka, 954 kHz, which broadcasts the 8 p.m. English news.

The military station, Galei Tsahal, broadcasts lighter programmes 24 hours a day and is popular among all Israelis.

You can hear English-language news at 7 a.m., at 1 p.m., at 5 p.m. and at 8 p.m. The most extensive broadcast is at 1 p.m., with 15 minutes of news followed by a 15 minute magazine programme.

The Voice of America and the BBC World Service also have good reception. VOA broadcasts at 1269 kHz and BBC usually at 1323 kHz.

TELEVISION

There are two channels, as well as the cable channels. Broadcasts are mainly in Hebrew, though there are also Arabic broadcasts in the afternoon. Educational Television runs excellent children's programmes in the morning and afternoon. Daily television listings appear in the Jerusalem Post; the week's listings appear on Fridays.

NEWSPAPERS

The only national English language newspaper is the Jerusalem Post. Also available in English from newsstands are magazines such as the Jerusalem Report and the Israel Economist.

NATURE

Israel, despite its small size, is dotted with nature reserves and forests and is a wonderful place for hiking, spelunking, and even canoeing. There are 160 nature reserves, serving as sanctuaries for a plethora of wildlife and plants. For information, contact the **Nature Reserve Authority**, 78 Yirmiyahu St., Jerusalem, (02)536271.

The **Nature Parks Authority** supervises 40 national parks all over the country. For information contact 4 Aluf M. Makleff St., Hakirya, Tel Aviv, tel. (03)6952281.

The **Jewish National Fund** is in charge of land development in Israel. It carries out soil conservation programmes, land preparation for new immigrant housing and prepares land for agriculture. The JNF also implements drainage projects and helps solve regional water problems by preparing dams and reservoirs. Among its tasks are all aspects of afforestation and the opening of forests to the public for recreation. You can plant a tree with your own hands at special planting centres all over the country. For details, contact JNF Head Office, Jerusalem (02) 707402 or 707411.

Probably the best way to explore the outdoors in Israel is though the facilities of the **Society for the Protection of Nature in Israel.** They organize walking tours to little-known areas of beauty, sometimes combined with car rides, swims and even camel and donkey tours. All tours are in English. Guides are particularly informative. The SPNI has field centres all over the country, many of them hostels open to the public. For details, contact SPNI, 4 Hashfela St., Tel Aviv (03)5374425; 13 Helene Hamalka St., Jerusalem (02) 252357, 244605.

A firm running off-the-beaten track tours, including desert safaris, is Neot Hakikar Jabaliya, 36 Keren Hayesod St., Jerusalem, (02)699385.

If archaeological excavations interest you, the Israel Antiquities Authority, Ministry of Education and Culture, POB 586 Jerusalem, tel. (02)292627, can offer information on current excavations and how to volunteer to work on a dig.

Finally, if you prefer your nature tamed, try one of Israel's zoos or speciality farms. The largest is the Safari Park in Ramat Gan (03)776181. Others are the Jerusalem Biblical Zoo, (02) 430111, the Haifa Zoo (04)377018 and the Hai Bar Reserve, north of Elat (07)331518.

Speciality farms include the ostrich farm at Kibbutz Ha'on on the Sea of Galilee (06)757555 and the alligator farm at Hamat Gader (06)751039.

POLICE

You will probably never need them, but if something goes wrong during your vacation, you'll be happy we told you about the Tourist Police.

This 20-man unit was established in Jerusalem in 1986 to help tourists with problems ranging from snatched purses to lost relatives. These police officers speak English, French, German and have access to volunteers who understand other languages.

The unit is based at the Kishle police station just inside Jaffa Gate in the Old City of Jerusalem. If you're in the city centre when trouble arises, you can get help at the police headquarters at the Russian Compound, near the Central Post Office. (Unfortunately, so far the Tourist Police only operate in Jerusalem.)

They can be reached by dialing the police emergency number, 100, or by phoning them directly at 273222. They are open from 6:30 a.m. to 10:30 p.m., but in the event of an emergency involving a tourist, they will be summoned round the clock.

The head of the unit told us that in addition to criminal complaints, his men handle any kind of emergency involving tourists.

He has the following tips for tourists:
- Don't leave luggage in cars.
- Don't carry large sums of money on you.
- Conceal your money on your body, in a money belt, instead of in your pockets.
- Separate your valuable documents. Don't keep everything in one place.
- When walking with a bag slung over your shoulder hold it in front of you.
- Don't leave anything of value in your hotel room.
- Above all don't be naive. Crime does take place even in the holiest city in the world.

POSTAL INFORMATION

The Postal Authority

Most post office branches are open from 8 a.m. until 12.30 p.m. and from 4.00 p.m. until 6 p.m. daily, except Wednesday, when they are open from 8 a.m. until 1.30 p.m., and Friday when they are open from 8 a.m until noon. They sell phone tokens (asimonim) as well as stamps. Fax and telex services are also available.

The main post office in each of the major cities (see below for addresses) is open from 7 a.m. until 10 p.m., but facsimile and telex service is available 24 hours a day. The post office at Ben-Gurion Airport is open 24 hours a day.

You can send telegrams of up to 50 words, by calling 171. The service is available 24 hours a day.

You can have packages picked up and delivered. To send a package, call the "Rapid Services." Express Mail Service gets letters or packages weighing up to 20 kilos (4 pounds) to 120 countries – including Egypt – within 48 to 72 hours. Express mail can be delivered the same day to 58 places within Israel.

The Postal Authority also offers two other services that may be of interest to tourists. Travel insurance can be bought at all Tel Aviv post office branches and at the airport branch. And the Philatelic Service puts out a year book of all the new stamps issued that year.

The main branches: Jerusalem, Jaffa Road 23, tel. (02)

241954; Tel Aviv, Rehov Mikve Yisrael, tel. (03) 5643679; in Haifa, Rehov Hanevi'im, tel. (04) 669500.

For further information, call the Authority's toll-free number: 177-022-2121.

ROAD DISTANCES (IN KM.)

	Jerusalem	Tel Aviv	Haifa	Lod	Tiberias	Nazareth	Beer Sheva
Jerusalem	-	61	161	46	188	169	122
Tel Aviv	61	-	97	22	134	105	107
Haifa	161	97	-	105	70	39	201
Acre	180	117	25	125	57	49	223
Bethlehem	9	70	170	31	197	178	120
Elat	310	348	439	337	404	403	240
Gaza	92	78	175	70	215	185	45
Hebron	32	92	190	78	216	200	45
Jenin	113	100	50	104	70	30	225
Jericho	35	97	198	80	200	175	120
Metula	222	196	120	206	65	96	303
Nablus	55	70	98	85	120	86	187
Netanya	95	34	67	48	103	74	141
Rehovot	55	22	120	16	156	127	85
Safed	223	164	75	168	35	56	264
Sodom	124	196	288	183	326	294	87

SHABBAT (Saturday)

If you have your own car, remember to keep away from the very religious areas like B'nei Brak, or Mea She'arim in Jerusalem from Friday afternoon until Saturday night.

Public transportation, except in East Jerusalem, Haifa, Nazareth and environs, doesn't operate on Shabbat, but there is private transportation – sherut taxis, taxis and tourist buses.

If you're looking for a meal on Saturday in Tel Aviv you'll find restaurants open on Rehov Dizengoff, on Rehov Allenby near the sea - and on Rehov Kedem (Rehov "Shishim") in Jaffa. In Jerusalem, restaurants and cafes in the Old City and in East Jerusalem, as well as a few places in the "German Colony" and Ein Karem are open on Saturday. In Haifa several Oriental restaurants in the port area and several cafes and restaurants in Hadar HaCarmel and central Carmel are open on Shabbat.

Of course, in Bethlehem, Hebron, Nablus, Nazareth, Gaza and other Arab centres, shops, restaurants and cafes remain open on Saturday.

SHOPPING IN ISRAEL

Israel combines the best of modern design in textiles, fashion and crafts, with the best of the past. The boutiques of internationally famous designers such as Gidon Oberson feature creations as avant-garde – and as expensive – as their equivalents elsewhere in the world. On the other hand, Israel also abounds in old world markets where haggling can result in a real bargain.

What to look for:

Judaica

Israel, and particularly Jerusalem, has become a world centre for Jewish ritual art, ancient and modern. Look for menorot (Hanukah lamps), candlesticks, wine goblets, mezuzot and spice boxes. The work of silversmiths, calligraphers, ketubah makers and papercutters combine the sensibilities of past and present, East and West.

Many modern craftsmen maintain studios. Replicas of famous historical artefacts are on sale in the gift shops of the Israel Museum, the Diaspora Museum and the Eretz Israel Museum in Ramat Gan. Places to look for modern creations include, in Jerusalem, the Jewish Quarter, Khutzot HaYotzer – Arts and Crafts Lane, the House of Quality and many shops in the Mea Shearim quarter. At Kuzari, 10 David St in the Bukharan Quarter, look for traditional Near Eastern style embroidery designs. In the Tel Aviv area, try Old Jaffa and the central shopping areas. The Wizo shops also carry a fine supply of ritual objects as do the Maskit stores. Ancient maps and prints, in many of which Israel figures prominently, are also good buys.

Shopping Malls and Department Stores

Israel has no extremely large department stores, although the Kol Bo Shalom in Tel Aviv, Herzl Street, and the Hamashbir chain come the closest. In recent years, shopping malls have sprung up all over the country, which are very similar to their North American equivalents. Perhaps the best known are Dizengoff Centre in Tel Aviv and the Canion in Ramat Gan, and the Canion in Jerusalem's Manahat neighbourhood, not to mention the Ben Yehuda pedestrian mall.

Leather and Furs

Perhaps surprisingly, given the mild winter weather, furs and leather are well-designed and widely available in Israel. When buying a fur, look for the symbol of the Association of Furriers in Israel. Israeli furs are tax-free and exempt from customs in the USA and EEC.

Diamonds and Jewellery

Did you know that diamond transactions throughout the world are sealed with the Hebrew words "Mazal u Bracha" (luck and blessings)? Israel is the world's largest exporter of polished diamonds, so it comes as no surprise that diamonds (emeralds too) are a good buy. The Israel Diamond Exchange Centre is located in Ramat Gan. Other diamond polishing centres are Netanya and Tel Aviv. Jewellery is also individual and appealing. Many jewellery makers combine ancient coins or glass with silver and gold to produce truly distinctive items.

Fashion

The swim-wear of Gottex, Gidon Oberson and others is justly renowned. Take a stroll along Dizengoff or Ben Yehuda in Tel Aviv to discover other fashion finds. At the other end of the shopping scale, try the Carmel Market or Bezalel Market off Allenby Street, for low, low-cost fashion bargains.

In Jerusalem, the new Canion in Malha has already acquired a reputation for the latest fashions; the Canion in Talpiot also has interesting boutiques. And of course the Ben-Yehuda mall and the downtown area are full of elegant clothing shops.

Markets

As well as the Carmel and Bezalel markets in Tel Aviv, try the Flea Market in Jaffa for inexpensive jewellery, brass, and copper. In the Old City of Jerusalem and markets in Bethlehem, Akko, Nazareth and the Druze villages, look for olive wood, bamboo, hand-blown glass and ceramic items.

SPORTS IN ISRAEL

If you believe that Israel is associated only with the past, you will be surprised to find that sporting activities abound. As well as the usual sports, visitors can have fun camel-riding, orienteering, and even playing cricket or American-style baseball. You can even find roller-skating, arm-wrestling and tug-of-war!

The mild winter climate makes sporting activities such as scuba diving and tennis possible all year round, while winter sports can be found on the slopes of Mt. Hermon.

Perhaps the best-known sporting spectacle is the Maccabiah, in which Jewish athletes from all over the world take part. The Maccabiah is held every four years in the year following the Olympic games and has been held 13 times so far. Other events include the Hapoel Games and the annual Sea of Galilee marathon. But even not-so-fit enthusiasts are welcome to take part in the annual spring march to Jerusalem, usually held in April.

Sports for the handicapped are also well developed. For detailed information on local sports, contact sports associations in Israel:

Israel Sport-For-All Association 5 Warburger St., P.O.B. 56200, Tel Aviv 61560, tel.(03)5281968. Issues annual programme of scheduled non-competitive sporting activities.

Sports Federation of Israel 4 Marmorek St., Tel Aviv (03)5616262. Established in 1931, it organizes sports events in 20 sports.

Elitzur Religious Jewish Sports Association 14 Raoul Wallenberg St., Tel Aviv 69719. Tel. (03) 498458. Numbers 12,000 athletes in 11 sports, operating in 111 clubs.

Maccabi Sports Association Kfar Maccabiah, Ramat Gan 52105, tel. (03) 715715. Established in 1912, it numbers 40,000 athletes in 130 clubs.

Betar Sports Association 24 Kalisher St., Tel Aviv

(03)660637. Established in 1924, it numbers 2,400 athletes in 48 clubs.

The Israel Olympic Committee 6 Ha'arba St., Tel Aviv (03)561089.

Some of the more popular sports in Israel are:

GOLF

Israel has only one 18-hole golf course, located on a spectacular site near the ancient port of Caesarea, between Tel Aviv and Haifa. Contact the Caesarea Golf Club, POB 1010, tel. (06)361174

TENNIS

This sport has made immense strides in recent years, and can be played on excellent courts around the country all year round. The Israeli Tennis Centre in Ramat Hasharon, with its 16 courts and stadium, is well worth a visit. Tel. (03)481803. For further information, contact the Israel Tennis Association, 79 Maze St., Tel Aviv, tel. (03)613911.

RIDING

Although racing does not exist as a sport in Israel, trail-riding and show-riding and breeding are popular. Stables can be found thoughout the country. For further information: Equestrian Sports Committee, 8 Ha'arba St., Tel Aviv, tel. (03)5613322.

SQUASH

The three centres for squash around the country are the Herzliyya Squash Centre, tel. (09)539160; the Haifa Squash Centre, tel. (04)539160 and the Kfar Hamakabiya, tel. (03)715737.

WATER SPORTS

(See also 'Miscellaneous Information')

To dive in the Red Sea among the coral reefs and spectacular fish is a truly unforgettable experience that can be enjoyed year-around. The Mediterranean and the Sea of Galiliee are also good places for diving, mainly in autumn and spring. Divers must have a 2 star licence or take a course. Snorkelling is also popular in Elat, at the Nature Reserve on Coral Beach. Equipment can be rented. Yachting is well developed, particularly from the Tel Aviv Marina, tel. (03)282972.

For information on all underwater sports contact the **Federation For Underwater Activities in Israel**, Tel Aviv port, POB 6110, Tel Aviv, tel. (03)5236436.

WINTER SPORTS

Considering Israel's Mediterranean climate, skiing is an astonishing sport to find, yet it exists in the Hermon area in northern Israel during the winter. For information, contact the Hermon Ski Site, tel. (06)740121 or the Israel Snow Ski Centre, 43 Montefiore St., Tel Aviv, tel. (03)290645.

Ice-skating is also popular on several indoor rinks: Hechal Hakerach in Bat Yam, Hakomemiut Blvd., tel. (03)5517063 and Hechal Hakerach in Kiryat Motzkin, near Haifa, tel. (04)750977.

TELEPHONES

The most expensive way to make long-distance phone calls is to dial from your hotel room. Therefore, we recommend that you take advantage of the Public Telephone Centres – located in all major cities – to dial directly (see list below). These centres are staffed by Bezek telephone personnel who can tell you the cheapest time of day to call. You can bill long-distance calls to the U.S. on your ATT credit card.

Reversed charge (collect) phone calls can be made from any public telephone with one token, or "asimon," which is returned to you at the end of the conversation. Dial "188" for the international operator. (The only two countries that do not accept collect calls from Israel are Germany and Austria.) Asimonim can be bought from a post office or your hotel.

Local calls at public boxes are made with asimonim – one for telephoning within the area of the call, and more the further away you dial. Be well equipped with asimonim, since when they run out, your call is cut off without warning.

A new service introduced by the telephone authority (Bezek) is a series of cards to be sold in units of 10, 20, 50, 120 and 240. These can be used for telephone calls, including international calls.

Public Telephone Centres:

Jerusalem	**3 Koresh St. (behind Central Post Office)** **236 Jaffa St.** **Sun.–Thurs. 8 a.m.–9 p.m.; Fri. 8 a.m.–2 p.m.**
Tel Aviv	**13 Frishman St.** **Sun.–Thurs. 9 a.m.–11 p.m.; Fri. 9 a.m.–2:30 p.m.**
Elat	**Bezek offices, Old Commercial Centre, Hatmarim Blvd.** **Sun.–Thurs. 7 a.m.–1 p.m.**
Netanya	**14 Ha'azmaut Sq.** **Sun.–Thurs. 8 a.m.–10 p.m.; Fri 8 a.m.–2:30 p.m.**
Tiberias	**Bezek offices – Midrehov promenade** **Sun.–Thurs. 9 a.m.–11 p.m.; Fri. 8 a.m.–2:30 p.m.**

Emergency Numbers
(in Jerusalem, Tel Aviv, Haifa)
First Aid (Magen David Adom) 101
Police 100
Fire Brigade 102
Telephone Services
Information 144
International Telephone Calls 188
Time 155
Telegrams by Phone 171
Automatic Alarm Service 174 (then your number, then the hour required)

TIME

Israeli Standard Time is two hours ahead of G.M.T. (Greenwich Mean Time), one hour ahead of mid-European time, and seven hours ahead of Eastern Standard Time, U.S.A. In summer the clock is moved forward an hour; "summer time" is usually in effect from April to September.

TIPPING

The custom is for bills to include a service charge. By and large, Israelis do not tip, except at the barber's and hairdresser's, and in restaurants.

Your fellow tourists, however, have made tipping quite popular, and it is the expected thing in some restaurants and other places which cater primarily to the tourist trade. Tipping is mandatory where "service not included" appears on the bill, when 10-15% is expected.

TOURIST INFORMATION OFFICES

Beer Sheva	
6 Ben Zvi St.	(057)236001/2/3
(opp. central bus station)	
Ben-Gurion Airport	(03)9711485/6/7
Information Desk	
Bethlehem	(02)741581
Manger Square	
Elat	
Khan Centre	(07)334353
Rechter Centre	(07)374233
Haifa	
18 Herzl St.	(04)666521/2
	(04)643616, 645692
Jerusalem	
24 King George St.	(02)754888
Jaffa Gate	(02)282295/6
17 Jaffa St.	(02)228844
Nazareth	(06)573003
Casanova St.	(06)570555
Tel Aviv	
5 Shalom Aleichem St.	(03)5101451, 660257
Tiberias	(06)720992
23, Habanim St.	(06)722089
Zefat	
2 Jerusalem St.	(06)930633

TRANSPORTATION

AIR

Inland air services are provided by Arkia Israel Airlines Ltd and by several charter companies. Arkia flies from Jerusalem to Tel Aviv, Haifa, Rosh Pinna and Elat, from Tel Aviv to Jerusalem, Rosh Pinna and Elat, from Haifa to Jerusalem, Tel Aviv and Elat and from Elat to Jerusalem, Tel Aviv, Haifa. Contact Arkia at Sde Dov Airport tel. (03)6902222.

BUSES

Buses are frequent and relatively inexpensive, both within cities and on inter-city routes. Buses generally do not run on the Sabbath. Monthly tickets are available.

Central bus stations – Egged: Jerusalem (02)304704
Tel Aviv – 142 Derekh Petah Tikvah (03)5375555
Haifa – (04)549131
Beer Sheva – (057)274341
Elat – (07)375161

Dan bus line – 36 Shaul Hamelech Blvd; Tel Aviv (03)7543333

CARS

Most major international rental firms plus local firms maintain offices in Israel for car rental. An international driving licence or national licence issued by a country which has reciprocity with Israel in this matter is necessary. The licence must be printed in English or French or else confirmed in Hebrew.

HITCH-HIKING

Hitch-hiking is not recommended.

TRAINS

Trains run fairly infrequently on several routes, principally Haifa–Tel Aviv–Jerusalem. Trains are slower than buses, but offer an interesting and worthwhile ride. For information call Central Station, Arlozoroff St, Tel Aviv, (03)5421515.

TAXIS AND SHERUTS

Taxis are frequent and can be hailed on the major streets of large cities. They can also be ordered by telephone. Make sure the driver uses the compulsory meter. Tipping is not compulsory, though of course welcomed.

In case of complaints against taxis, contact the Transport Ministry (02)319411, with details of the complaint, the cab number from the sign on the vehicle roof, the personal licence number posted inside the taxi. Ask for a receipt if you think the fare is too high.

Sherut taxis are vehicles which carry up to seven passengers at a time and follow a fixed route, such as along Ben Yehuda Street in Tel Aviv and between cities. They are much cheaper than taxis and cost slightly more than buses.

VOLUNTARY TOURIST SERVICE (VTS)

Israel's Voluntary Tourist Service offers a helping hand to tourists and welcomes visitors to this country with friendship and warmth. It has desks in the major hotels in the major cities in the evenings. It has a non-commercial approach to aiding tourists - people-to-people contact, bridging gaps between races and religions. Over the years it has fulfilled several hundred thousand visitors' requests, ranging from assistance in finding lost suitcases to locating distant relatives and arranging visits with Israeli families in their homes. Address enquiries to: 7 Mendele St., tel. (03)222459, P.O. Box 3381, Tel Aviv 63431. Jerusalem: P.O.B. 810, tel. (02)633819. Haifa: 106 Hanassi Blvd., tel. (04)374010. Elat: 14 Zofit St., tel.(07)372344. Nahariyya: 18 Sokolov St., tel.(04)920135. Tiberias: 20 Ahuzat Kineret St., tel. (06)795072.

No matter where you come from, there are people from your country who are living in Israel. If you would like to meet them you can be pretty sure that there's an association of immigrants from your country and that they'll be pleased to see you. The head offices are in Tel Aviv:

Association of Americans and Canadians (AACI) 22 Mazeh St. (03)299799.

South African Zionist Federation (Telfed) Beit Clal, 5 Druyanov St. (03)290131

British Olim Society, 76 Ibn Gvirol St. (03)265244
Irgun Olei Holland, 7 Tarsat St. (03)290901

WATER

The water in Israel is safe to drink, though bottled water is also available, if preferred.

WHAT TO BRING AND WHAT TO WEAR

Two basic rules apply: dress for comfort, and dress informally. Israeli men rarely wear a tie and suit, except to the most formal dinner occasions. Even at weddings and synagogue services, a neat open-neck shirt is usually acceptable, with a sports jacket in winter.

Since touring involves walking, often over uncomfortable surfaces, bring comfortable walking shoes.

Laundromats are available, but not as common as they are in North America or Europe, so drip-dry clothing is useful. Of course major hotels have laundry service.

Summers are long and dry, with fairly constant daily temperatures and bright sun. Therefore women should equip themselves with light dresses or trousers and shirts for day. Avoid all-polyester fabric which can be uncomfortably hot. A cotton or linen mix is best. A sun hat and sunglasses are obligatory and a water canteen can be useful. Stockings are unnecessary, even for evening. Be sure and bring a bathing suit.

For men, open-necked shirts and light trousers in a cotton blend are advisable. A sweater can be useful in mountain areas or the desert for evenings, though not in the Tel Aviv area.

Winter is rainy and chilly, though not excessively cold. A light-weight winter coat, leather coat or jacket is sufficient. Overseas visitors may find that Israeli homes are chillier than they are used to, since in many areas small heaters rather than central heating are used. A heavy sweater for indoor use is useful. (Hotels, of course, are well heated). If planning to visit a resort such as Tiberias Hot Springs or Elat, don't forget a bathing suit.

In the evening, women tend to wear elegant dresses or cocktail dresses when attending nightclubs or big functions in the major cities, but dress much less formally when visiting homes. Israeli fashion, by the way, is elegant and attractive and if any item has been forgotten in packing, it can easily be purchased in Israel.

Religious customs dictate a few dress habits. In the very religious Jewish quarters such as Mea She'arim in

Jerusalem, men are expected to wear long pants and women to keep their arms and shoulders covered. This also applies in synagogues. Women should dress modestly in churches and mosques.

Clothing Sizes

Shirts:	American	14½	15	15½	16	16½	17
	Local	37	38	39	41	42	43
Trousers and Jackets:	American	36	38	40	42		
	Local	46	48	50	52		
Dresses:	American	10	12	14	16	18	20
	Local	36	38	40	42	44	46
Sweaters and Blouses:	American	34	36	38	40	42	44
	Local	40	42	44	46	48	50

Shoe Sizes

Local sizes differ from both American and English sizes, so it is advisable to have your feet measured by the shoe shop staff.

YOUTH TRAVEL AND PROGRAMMES

The **Israel Student Tourist Association (ISSTA)** has offices in the three main cities:

Tel Aviv: 109, Ben Yehuda St., tel. (03)5440111, Dizengoff Centre, tel. (03)5250037, 5250039.

Jerusalem: Hebrew University, Mt. Scopus, tel. (02)826118; 5 Eliashar Street, tel. (02)257257.

Haifa: 29 Nordau St., tel. (04)669139/660411.

ISSTA arranges cheap flights to and from Israel and offers a variety of tours, safaris, work camps and other services for young visitors, such as the issuing and renewing of International Student Identity Cards.

The **Jewish Agency** has a **Youth Department** which deals with such things as placing volunteers who wish to work in their professions. The office is at 19, Keren Hayesod St., Jerusalem, tel. (02)208511.

The **Youth Section Promotion Department** of the **Ministry of Tourism** provides maps and other printed information and helps youngsters to join archaeological digs (see "Archaeology" section). Address: 23, Hillel St., Jerusalem, tel. (02)237311. Details of digs may also be obtained from the **Israel Antiquities Authority**, P.O. Box 586, Jerusalem, tel. (02)278602, 278603.

Many youngsters like to spend time observing the lifestyle and working on a kibbutz, or co-operative settlement. Generally, volunteers must be between 18 and 32. Some kibbutzim offer Hebrew language instruction as well. Information from the various kibbutz associations:

Hakibbutz Ha'artzi – 13 Leonardo da Vinci St., Tel Aviv (03)435222
Hakibbutz Hadati (religious) – 7 Dubnov St., Tel Aviv (03)6957231.
Ikhud ve Hameyukhad – 10 Dubnov St., Tel Aviv (03)250231
Kibbutz Programme Centre, Volunteer Department, TAKAM-ARTZI, 124 Hayarkon St., P.O.B. 3167, Tel Aviv 63573. Tel. (03)221325, 5246156.

For the student who wishes to combine learning about Israel with formal education, many universities and colleges offer excellent courses in English, both during the summer and winter.

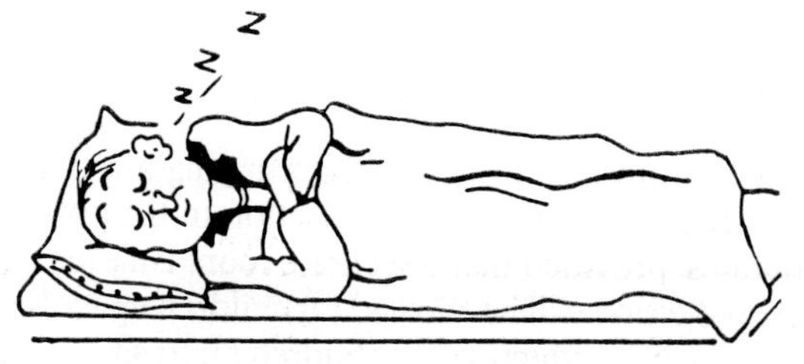

Accommodation

HOTELS

The Israel Hotel Association office is in Tel Aviv, at 29 Hamered St., tel. (03)5170131. Hotels, holiday villages and aparthotels are recommended for tourists.

Some hotels in resort areas accept bookings only for full board during their peak season, but most offer a choice of full board, half board or bed and breakfast.

Tariffs

Tourists paying in foreign currency are exempt from Value Added Tax and other local taxes in the hotel in which they are residing.

Special rates for groups are quoted by hotels on request.

Grades

The Tourism Ministry bases its grading system on service as well as the quality of the facilities and includes a new top grade, "five star-deluxe", in addition to the standard "five star" to "one star."

Extra Charges

Small extra charges are made for room service, and for the supply of TV sets on request.

Telephone calls made through the hotel exchange are subject to a hotel surcharge.

Children

Children up to the age of 12 occupying a room with their parents are entitled to a reduction in the published room rates, provided that a separate room isn't required. A 50% reduction will be allowed for children up to the age of 6, and a 30% reduction for children up to age 12.

YOUTH HOSTELS

Youth hostels, located throughout the country, are generally of a fairly high standard and provide basic facilities. Many of them have family accommodation in addition to the usual dormitories.

If you are not a youth hostel member and wish to use youth hostel facilities, information about becoming a member is available from the **Israel Youth Hostels Association**, P.O.B. 1075 Jerusalem, tel. (02)250685.

During the summer, on holidays and weekends some hostels are full: **to book, contact each hostel directly.**

The **National Parks Authority** has reduced entrance rates for hostellers.

Following is a selection of some of Israel's youth hostels; a full list may be obtained from the Israel Youth Hostels Association.

Akko – (04)911982; Beer Sheva – (057)277444; Elat – (07)370088; Haifa (04)531944; Jerusalem, Louise Waterman-Wise Hostel – (02)423366; Jerusalem, Bet Bernstein Hostel – (02)258286; Jerusalem, Old City – (02)288611; Jerusalem, Bet Shmuel – (02)203466; Karei Deshe (Sea of Galilee) – (06)720601; Massada – (057)584349; Rosh Pinna (between Tiberias and Zefat) – (06)937086; Tel Aviv – (03)5441748; Tel Hai (Upper Galilee) – (06)940043.

YOUTH TRAVEL BUREAU

The Youth Travel Bureau is the travel agency of the Israel Youth Hostels Association. They specialize in low budget tours for young people but also study programmes, adventure tours, pilgrim tours and any other group travel plans requested. They can organize any kind of progamme requested for a group of no fewer than 10 persons.

The Youth Travel Bureau also offers attractive tour packages for the individual traveller looking for economical travel plans. For further information contact: Youth Travel Bureau, P.O.B. 1075, Jerusalem 91009.

CHRISTIAN HOSPICES

There are Christian hospices near most of the places in the Holy Land revered by Christians the world over. Many of them have either facilities for full board or only lodgings. Arrangements for staying in them should be made in advance. Rates are usually very reasonable. (See "Accommodation" in Jerusalem, Haifa, Tiberias, Mt. of Beatitudes, Nazareth and Mt. Tabor.) For a full list, including facilities and prices, ask for the brochure "Christian Hospices in Israel" from the Ministry of Tourism, Pilgrimage Promotion Dept., P.O. Box 1018, Jerusalem, tel. (02)240553.

CAMPING

The **Israel Camping Organization** has established standards for its member camps. These include a fenced-in area, electricity, running water, central toilet facilities, watchman service, garbage collection, shaded picnic areas and barbecue pits. Contact the ICO at P.O. Box 53, Nahariyya, tel. (04)925392, for lists of sites, rates and facilities.

Health Resorts

In addition to Israel's long beaches on four seas - the Mediterranean, the Red Sea, the Sea of Galilee and the Dead Sea - there are well-known health resorts in the north and in the centre of the country.

TIBERIAS HOT SPRINGS (Map: Northern Sheet, N-6)

Both in recent and in ancient times the waters of the Tiberias hot springs have been put to good use. There is evidence that in all periods of antiquity these springs were a source of health to the ailing who visited them.

In 1929, Tiberias Hot Springs Co. acquired the rights to run the baths, and exploitation of this natural boon has since restored to Tiberias its importance as a holiday and health resort. Seven physiotherapists who immigrated from Russia are on the staff. Tel. (06)791967.

GENERAL INDICATIONS

Rheumatic ailments, diseases of the joints and of the spine, muscles, etc.

THERAPEUTIC FACTORS

Two hundred metres below sea level, the temperature at Tiberias seldom falls below 14°C (57°F), and the average winter temperature is a pleasant 18°C (62°F). The Juvenile springs have a heat of 60°C (140°C), and contain twelve different salts. Piloma (therapeutic mud) is used for mudpack treatment.

FACILITIES FOR TREATMENT

Aerated-mineral pools, mineral baths and pools, Piloma mudpacks, sauna, gymnastics, physiotherapy, underwater hydrotherapy and massage, inhalation.

The premises include a modern clinic with a staff of doctors, nurses and physiotherapists. In the reception hall, which is air conditioned, there is a cafe. Visitors relax in the large park and on the beaches.

The baths are open every day from 7 a.m. to 4 p.m. Tiberias Hot Springs tel. (06)791967.

SPA CENTRE

The spa and recreation centre opened on the lake in 1978 is comparable with the famous European spas in terms of equipment, design, facilities and comfort.

There is an indoor mineral pool at 32°C, an outdoor mineral pool at 34°C; a wing for hydrothermal treatments, physiotherapy and electrotherapy; and a gymnasium.

A heated (seasonal) pool was recently added to the centre.

The new building, which is across the road from the older buildings, is air-conditioned throughout.

Enquiries: Tiberias Hot Springs Co., Tiberias., tel (06)791967.

ZEFAT AND THE GALILEE (Map: Northern Sheet)

The cool mountain climate and the pleasant surroundings of the Galilee have always attracted vacationers in the hot summer months. Zefat, Metula and a number of kibbutzim in the region have a regular clientele and facilities to serve them. (Route No. 20)

Mitzpe Hayamim Natural Clinic: On Rosh Pinna – Zefat Road. Tel. (06)937013. Provides nature cure treatments and vegetarian cuisine all year round.

HAMAT GADER (EL HAMA) HOT SPRINGS

Hamat Gader is located in the Yarmuk Valley on the eastern shore of the Sea of Galilee, about 20 kilometres from Tiberias. It is an area rich in vegetation and springs (one of sweet water and four of mineral water).

Visitors can bathe in a natural open-air mineral pool. This is oval-shaped, about 60 metres x 30 metres in size; the maximum depth is 1.5 metres, but most of it is considerably shallower and therefore ideal for sitting or lying in. There is also a covered pool for bathing during winter.

The year-round water temperature is 42°C. Air temperatures range from 20°C-25°C in winter to 30°C-40°C in summer. Among the many minerals which the water contains are sulphur, chloride, calcium and magnesium. A short dip is therapeutically beneficial and very relaxing.

Facilities at the site include: changing rooms, showers and toilets; children's playing and swimming area; landscaped pool and grounds; picnic tables and barbecues in shaded areas (visitors may bring their own tents and other equipment); benches; fresh-water taps; a lookout onto the Yarmuk River and over into Jordan; an archaeological site with reconstructed Roman baths, which are regarded as the most impressive in the world; an amphitheatre and a 5th century synagogue. There is also a crocodile farm (the only one in the Middle East); a buffet for refreshments next to the pool; a first-aid station; parking facilities and a self-service restaurant.

Access to Hamat Gader is via the Tiberias – Zemach road, 11 kilometres from the Zemach Junction. The road is clearly signposted, but is very narrow and requires all your attention. There is bus transportation on weekdays from Tiberias to Hamat Gader.

The park is open from 8.00 a.m. - 3.30 p.m. Entrance fee. Tel. (06)751039. (Route Nos. 17 and 19)

ARAD AND THE DEAD SEA REGION (Map: Southern Sheet, J,K,L-23,24,25)

The Dead Sea has been known for generations for the richness of its mineral deposits; but its therapeutic properties have been exploited only in the last few years. The stretch of coast between Neve Zohar and En Boqeq constitutes a spa of international standard. Visitors can avail themselves of the healing properties of the Dead Sea and of the hot springs. For further information contact the Dead Sea Regional Tourist Organization, Dead Sea Post, 86910, tel. (057)84181. (Route No. 22)

THERAPEUTIC FACTORS

The **climate** of the Dead Sea region is warmer and drier than that of the rest of Israel (with the exception of the Arava and Elat). It is characterized by low rainfall, comfortable temperatures, high atmospheric pressure, low humidity and weak ultraviolet rays.

The air of the Dead Sea region, 400 metres below sea level, is the richest in the world in oxygen - with 10 per cent more than at sea level. And the absence of polluting factors (industry, heavy traffic, etc.) and of intensive vegetation makes for some of the cleanest air in the world.

The town of **Arad,** at 620 m. above sea level, overlooks the Dead Sea 1,000 m. below it. Its climate is dry and relatively mild, with temperatures rarely going above 34°C (92°F) in summer. There are two types of ultraviolet rays: UVA, which treat disorders of the skin and give it a pleasant tan; and UVB, which produce sunburn and other side-effects. Because the Dead Sea is 400 metres below sea level, few of the UVB can penetrate while the long wave ultraviolet rays, UVA, have no trouble reaching ground level. This means that people can expose themselves to the sun almost without restriction.

Dead Sea Water: hypertonic, containing a concentration of salts that is ten times higher than in ocean or sea water. There is a fundamental difference in the quality of the main ions. It is the saltiest and most mineral-laden body of water in the world.

Zohar Hot Springs and Mazor (Ein Gedi) Hot Springs: hyperthermal and hypertonic, classified as radioactive thermal sulphur springs. The water can be heated for special baths, up to 38°C. The high magnesium content is a special property of this water, though some are wary of the radioactivity. (Route No. 22)

GENERAL INDICATIONS

HAMEI ZOHAR and HAMEI MAZOR (Ein Gedi Hot Springs):
Recovery after surgery, neurological metabolic disorders, traumatic ailments, allergies, bronchial asthma.

Medicinal Mud: rheumatic illnesses, post myelitic and post-paralytic illnesses.

EN BOQEQ:
Skin diseases, especially psoriasis; atopic dermatitis.

ARAD:
Its desert location, altitude, dry air and lack of vegetation form a unique combination which is of benefit to sufferers from asthma, allergies and breathing complaints.

FACILITIES FOR TREATMENT

In **Hamei Zohar** there are private and public baths and pools, massage facilities, a dispensary, change rooms and showers, restrooms, and a buffet. Open daily from 7.30 a.m. to 5.00 p.m. Tel. (057)902612.

In **En Boqeq** guests are offered a solarium, change rooms and showers, a buffet, physiotherapy facilities and cosmetic advice. There is also a dermatological clinic. Open daily from 6.00 a.m. to 7.00 p.m.

At **Mazor Hot Springs**, near Kibbutz Ein Gedi, there are three covered pools, therapeutic mud treatment and rest rooms.

ACCOMMODATION

There are several luxury hotels in Arad, Hamei Zohar and En Boqeq, in addition to comfortable guest-houses along the Dead Sea coast, youth hostels and a camping site. There is a regular bus service from Arad, Tel Aviv, Beer Sheva and Jerusalem to the baths. (See the end of Route No. 22.)

Israeli Cuisine

And the house of Israel called the bread Manna; and it was like coriander seed, white; and the taste of it was like wafers made with honey.

–Exodus 16:31

INTRODUCTION

For forty years, as they wandered in the Sinai Desert, the children of Israel dined almost exclusively on quail and manna. Even though this may have been a nutritionally satisfying diet, one can reasonably assume that after not too many years it tended to become rather monotonous. Of two things, however, we may be certain: the recipe for manna has been irretrievably lost and that was the last time in history that all of the children of Israel shared a single culinary style.

Some 4,500 years later, the descendants of those wanderers, now settled in the Promised Land, are enjoying a far more diversified cuisine, one that is set with the dishes of people who have come from eighty different nations and a host of distinct culinary back-grounds. While there is a rapidly increasing awareness of the sophisticated culinary styles of France, Italy and the Far East, especially in the better restaurants throughout the nation, many of the dishes served in homes of ordinary and in simpler although often charming restaurants have their roots in the traditions of the countries of the people who brought their favourite dishes with them when they immigrated.

INFLUENCES

The most pervasive culinary influences in Israel are the cooking styles of the Middle East, North Africa, the Mediterranean basin, and Central and Eastern Europe.

Of all these cookery styles, the best known and most popular remains that of the Middle East. Because most of the inhabitants of the Middle Eastern nations are Moslems who, like Jews, are forbidden to eat pork, Israelis have been readily able to adapt this culinary style to their own tables. In addition to the indigenous cookery of Israeli Arabs, Jews from Iran, Iraq, Kurdistan, Syria, Egypt, Libya and Yemen have each made unique contributions to the national table.

Middle East, North Africa, the Mediterranean

From Iran comes the tradition of cooking meat together with fruits, lentils or split peas. From Lebanon comes an appreciation of fish flavoured with cayenne pepper, paprika, cinnamon and other spices. Jordanian kebabs, whether of plain or marinated lamb or a mixture of lamb and beef have also become indispensable to local cookery. Syrian or Kurdish **kubbeh** – lamb and cracked wheat paste served in fried patties stuffed with meat, onion and pine nuts – is a well-beloved dish wherever one travels within Israel, as are **sfeeha**, small pastry shells filled with spiced ground lamb, pine nuts and yoghurt, which originated in Egypt.

No culinary style is more unique than that of Yemen, whose cookery has earned a special place on the Israeli palate. This style is not especially sophisticated, and its highly flavoured cookery relies on special spice mixtures. The cereal and burghul dishes of Yemen, along with a range of specially tasty breads, have also received wide acceptance throughout Israel.

Another major culinary influence comes from the peoples of the Maghreb, the North African nations of Morocco, Algeria and Tunisia. Among the most renowned dished of these countries are **couscous** and **chakchouka**. Originally devised by wandering Berber tribesmen some 4,000 years ago, couscous is a stew based on hard wheat semolina, topped with simple-to-prepare meats and a variety of vegetables and accompanied by side dishes. Algerian couscous invariably includes tomatoes; Moroccan versions rely on saffron; and Tunisian couscous is highly spiced. The side dishes also vary widely, depending on the whims of individual cooks. **Chakchouka** is another beloved dish of the Maghreb. In this dish, to be found everywhere in Israel, eggs are poached to near hardness over peeled tomatoes that have been sautéed together with onion, garlic and a generous variety of herbs.

From Greece and Turkey have come such popular dishes as **moussaka** (a baked aubergine, cheese and meat pie), **dolmas** (stuffed grape leaves), and the incredibly light, honey-soaked **baklava** pastries. Israelis are particularly fond of the Greco-Turkish style of frying or grilling fish after seasoning it with fresh herbs and lemon.

Because it reflects a blending of European and Middle Eastern influences, and because of substantial numbers of immigrants from these countries, the cookery of the Balkan states – Yugoslavia, Romania and Bulgaria – is particularly well known in Israel. **Mititei**, the thumb-shaped minced meat patties of Romania and the mixed meat grill **kebabsha** of Bulgaria are both grilled on skewers and are not dissimilar to Middle-Eastern shishkebabs. Other well-known dishes include Romanian **tarator**, a cold yoghurt and cucumber soup sprinkled with chopped walnuts and dill; Bulgarian **ghivetch**, a medley of stewed vegetables similar to ratatouille, sometimes served with yoghurt; and Yugoslavian **sarma**, a variety of meat mixtures stuffed into cabbage leaves that have been pickled in brine. Especially popular are **ciorba**, the somewhat sour and hearty Balkan meat or fish and vegetable soup, and **mamaliga**, a sweetened solidified cornmeal Romanian dish similar to the Italian polenta.

Central and Eastern Europe

The style of Central and Eastern Europe that has made itself most evident is that of the Yiddish kitchen. Diverse but rarely subtle, having evolved primarily in the shtetls (the small towns and villages inhabited primarily by Jews until the Holocaust), these are the foods that most Americans and Europeans consider to be typically "Jewish." Much in evidence are dishes like **gefilte fish** (fish balls made of finely minced carp, pike or a mixture of both, generally served in their own jelly and often accompanied by horseradish); **cholent** (a slowly simmered beef stew traditionally prepared for the Sabbath meal); **kishke** (a peppery blend of breadcrumbs, chicken fat and onions stuffed into beef casings like sausages);

and **knaidlach**, egg and matzo meal based dumplings. Other popular offerings from this variegated cuisine are **kreplach**, dumplings filled with ground meat or cheese and boiled or fried; **latkes**, fried potato pancakes; and a large assortment of salt, pickled and matjas herring dishes.

It should be understood that there is nothing lean, light or subtle about the foods of the Yiddish kitchen. These are dishes that assault the nostrils, make their way to the stomach with a thump and then sit heavily in the intestines for seveal hours. Loaded with overcooked vegetables and incredible amounts of fat and cholesterol, such cookery ignores all the rules of what we have come to think of as refined cuisine. Despite these seeming faults, well-prepared old world Jewish cookery is a delight. The owner of one restaurant that specializes in these dishes claims that people come to his place and weep for joy. This is probably not much of an exaggeration, for whatever else one says about it, the Yiddish kitchen is *par excellence* the heartland of nostalgia. One should, however, bear in mind that, as popular as such foods are, they are far from being the most popular culinary style in the land.

Russia, Poland and Hungary have also contributed dishes from their countries of origin. From Hungary, whose cookery is marked by the liberal use of dozens of types of paprika, have come goulash soup and stew, a variety of carp dishes, dumplings and **tarhonya** (dried pedllets of flour and egg). Polish cooking has given the nation dishes that feature the heavy use of sour cream and dill as main cooking ingredients. Dishes from Poland include duck soup, cold fruit soups, **krupnik** (barley, potato and sour cream soup), a variety of stuffed cabbage rolls, and plain and filled noodle and dumpling dishes.

From the former Soviet Union have come a variety of dishes. From Russia has come **borscht**, the famous beetroot-based soup that can be red or clear, cold or hot, and may contain meats, vegetables and sour cream; **golubtsy**, stuffed cabbage rolls often served in a tangy tomato sauce; **kulebiaka**, a salmon mousse baked with a flaky pastry dough; and several quasi-French dishes including chicken Kiev, beef Strogonoff and chicken Pojarsky. Another well-known Russian dish popular in Israel is **pirozhki**, miniature turnovers stuffed with chopped meat, vegetables or fruit. From the Ukraine come **kasha** (buckwheat) dishes and **vareniki**, dumplings stuffed with a savoury or sweet filling such as cheese, potatoes, meat or fruit and from Georgia have come a variety of meat dishes served with plum sauce.

India, Ethiopia

Other styles that make themselves felt, albeit on a lesser scale, are those of India and Ethiopia. Traditional Indian delicacies such as eggs with lamb, chicken with chestnuts, chicken tandoori, split pea fritters and stuffed potatoes are to be found in the homes of Indian immigrants as well as in several fine restaurants. Ethiopian dishes such as **wat**, a highly spiced stew of chicken and dried legumes, and **kitfo**, an offering of raw chopped beef seasoned with a blend of hot chili peppers, garlic, ginger, fenugreek, cardamom, cloves, allspice, turmeric and nutmeg may be found in several small restaurants, are patronized primarily by Ethiopians.

CHANGING TRENDS

Awareness of international trends in cookery, especially in restaurants, has increased enormously over the last two decades. Several Hebrew language magazines are devoted exclusively to the culinary arts and nearly every newspaper in the country has regular food sections that, in addition to recipes and restaurant reviews, also contain articles about food and wine history and culture.

A little more than a decade ago, when most Israelis dined out it was at Middle Eastern, north African, Balkan or Yiddish restaurants. What this meant was that people were eating the same things in restaurants as at home. That picture has changed dramatically, and even though such establishments still thrive, many of the best and most popular restaurants now specialize in French, Italian and Far Eastern cookery. Even more important, from the point of view of both the gastronome and the food historian, the "new wave" of Israeli chefs has been making itself felt. Neither the heaviness of traditional French cuisine, the frivolity of California dining nor the sometimes moribund traditions of the Middle East could satisfy these rebellious chefs. What they were seeking, and what many have found, was a way of combining the best of traditional French or Italian cookery, the best of nouvelle cuisine, and the best of the Mediterranean.

Most concur, however, that despite these advances and an abundance of readily available and excellent foods, the nation has not developed its own unique cuisine. Alas, not even the street foods so popular throughout the nation are truly Israeli. **Felafel** – deep-fried balls of minced chickpeas, parsley, coriander, onions and garlic – has been mistakenly identified as indigenous to Israel, but ground chickpeas have been found in the tombs of several of the Pharaohs, and Egyptians, Moroccans, Algerians and Lebanese have been happily feasting on felafel for at least 200 years. The equally popular **shawarma** – marinated lamb slices roasting slowly on a rotating vertical skewer, which can be found everywhere in the land – is Turkish in origin, as are **bourekas**, which are delicious cheese or potato filled filo-dough pastry shells. Most important, however, is the fact that as a meeting point of European, Middle Eastern and North African cultures, the national table is a rich one, offering many pleasant surprises to those who sit at it.

A FEW WORDS ABOUT KASHRUT

Within Israel, the religiously based dietary laws of kashrut have played a role in determining cooking and dining habits. For those who follow these rules, pork and various other types of meat are forbidden, as are shellfish, fish without scales and fins and the flesh of any kind of scavenger. Nor will Orthodox or traditional Jews, following the proscription in the Book of Leviticus, cook or serve meat and dairy products at the same meal. The rules of dining for Moslems, as detailed in the Koran, are not dissimilar to those followed by Jews.

The restaurants that have succeeded best in presenting high quality cookery while maintaining a kosher kitchen have been those serving foods from nations where Jews made these adaptations over many centuries. Although there is a demand for kosher French, Italian and Chinese food, most of the restaurants serving the kosher versions of these dishes have not succeeded in attaining a high standard. This is partially because there are inherent contradictions between the cuisines of these nations and the demands of kashrut. Fine French cookery, for example, is absolutely dependent on being able to sauté meat in butter; Italian dishes often combine meat and cheese; and Chinese cuisine is heavily dependent upon the use of pork and shellfish. Eliminating one vital ingredient or another, substituting vegetable-based margarine for butter, or serving industrially processed North Sea pollack instead of shrimp is simply not conducive to fine dining. Without exception, the hotel dining rooms throughout the country are kosher, and some talented chefs have done well within these limitations. Few private restaurants have done as well; and with few exceptions, the best restaurants in the country are not kosher.

A HISTORY OF WINE

After they left Egypt and approached Canaan, Moses and the children of Israel sent twelve spies across the river to explore the Promised Land. When they returned to their encampment to advise Moses, only Joshua and Caleb were in favour of entering the new land. The other spies were not particularly impressed by what they had found, and because of their lack of enthusiasm, the Israelites began their forty-year trek through Sinai. Fortunately, however, two of the spies had returned with a cluster of grapes and, according to folklore, those grapes yielded enough wine to last the people for their forty years in the wilderness. Nobody today is sure just how that wine tasted. There is a good chance, however, that it was terrible.

Wine has been made in Israel since pre-Biblical times; but, if the truth be known, until recently there was no reason to be proud of these wines. The wines shipped to ancient Egypt were so bad that they had to be seasoned with honey, pepper and juniper berries to make them palatable, and those sent to Rome and England during the height of ancient Roman civilization were so thick and sweet that no modern connoisseur could possibly approve of them. So bad were most of these wines that it was probably a good thing that the Moslem conquest in AD 636 imposed a 1,200-year halt to the local wine industry.

Even in 1870, when wine production started again, thanks to the aid of Baron Edmond de Rothschild, not all went smoothly, and most of the wine that was produced was red, sweet, unsophisticated and unappealing. In 1875, for example, British Prime Minister Benjamin Disraeli was given a bottle of kosher red wine from Palestine. After taking a few sips, Disraeli observed that it tasted "not so much like wine but more like what I expect to receive from my doctor as a remedy for a bad winter cough." Well into the 1960s, Israel justifiably suffered from a reputation of producing wines too sweet and too coarse to appeal to knowledgeable drinkers.

Sophisticated wine lovers know that the local wineries have risen out of the morass of cheap, cloyingly sweet wines that burn the throat and bring tears to the eyes. Many local dry reds and white wines are now as good as some of the fine wines of California. Some are so good that they are compared favorably to the wines of the respected chateaus of France. Sometimes fruity and on other occasions crisply dry, often with excellent balance, body and bouquet, Israeli wines are now perceived as an integral and important part of dining out.

Not all of the local wineries have made this quantum leap in quality. The following list may, therefore provide a useful reference when deciding what wines to order with your meals or to purchase to take home for your own future consumption or as gifts. (It's worth bearing in mind that both the Ramat HaGolan Wineries and Carmel-Mizrachi offer tours of their wineries.)

The Ramat HaGolan Wineries: This excellent winery, largely responsible for the wine revolution within Israel, releases wines in three series, "Yarden," "Gamla," and "Golan," with the wines in the Yarden series considered the most prestigious. Regardless of the series, this winery produces some excellent reds and whites. The most serious and more full bodied of the reds are the Cabernet Sauvignon and the Merlots. The reds known as Har Hermon Adom and Golan Village are fruitier and meant to be consumed younger. The most notable whites from here are the Chardonnay and the Sauvignon Blanc, both of which are crisply dry and make for excellent drinking, and the Emerald Riesling which is semi-dry. Also worthy of note are two sparkling wines, "Bland de Blanc" and "Brut," both which are made in accordance with the traditional method of making champagne, and two dessert wines, the "Late Harvest

Sauvignon Blanc" and the "Port Blanc," neither of which need make any apology for its smooth, rich sweetness.

Carmel-Mizrachi: By far the largest wine producer in the country, now in its 110th year, Carmel produces three series that will be of interest to sophisticated drinkers. The most prestigious and often excellent wines are those in the "Rothschild" series. Included among these are some high quality Cabernet Sauvignons, Sauvignon Blancs, Chardonnay and Emerald Rieslings. The less expensive "Selected" series offers wines of the same varieties as well as a red Shiraz and whites such as Chenin Blanc and French Colombard. In the "Vineyard" series one finds Dry Muscat, an especially pleasing, crisply dry, but remarkably fruity white. The sparkling Chardonnay of this winery, made according to the traditional champagne method, is worthy of note, as is the White Muscat, a rich, sweet dessert wine in the Rothschild series. Also from Carmel is "Hilulim," a very young, fun and fruity red that is always the first wine to appear after the onset of the grape harvest.

Ashkelon Wineries: This small but progressive and highly respected winery, now in the sixth generation of the Segal family, produces wines in two major series – "Ben-Ami" and "The Wine of Segal." With the exception of a Cabernet Sauvignon and a dry Riesling, most of the wines from here are blends, some of which attain surprising levels of depth and sophistication.

Barkan Wineries: This still young winery is increasing its output and its sophistication every year and its mid-range whites, especially the Emerald Riesling, Sauvignon Blanc and Chardonnay, are all worth sampling.

Baron Wineries: Even though this winery is small and young it offers some fine, primarily white, wines. There are two series – Maestro and Baron – and in both one will find Sauvignon Blanc, Chardonnay and Emerald Riesling, all of which are delightful.

RESTAURANTS

The Rating System

Even though the quality of the cooking was the most important factor in evaluating the restaurants in this guide, decor, atmosphere and the quality of the welcome and service were also considered. The ratings are relative only in that one should not have the same expectations from a restaurant specializing in cookery from the Yiddish kitchen as from one that specializes in fine French cuisine. Restaurants that did not attain a high enough rating are not listed. The overall evaluations fall into four categories – Good, Very Good, Excellent and Exceptional – and these are indicated before the name of the restaurant, using the following symbols:

Category	Symbol
Good	•
Very Good	*
Excellent	**
Exceptional	***

Keep in mind that in Israel as elsewhere, many chefs have the bad habit of frequently changing restaurants, and thus a good restaurant can turn mediocre or even bad in just a few days. Restaurants whose chefs are also the owners are, in theory, more stable, but even they are liable to deteriorate if success turns the owner's head.

Although advance reservations are rarely needed for lunch, they are sometimes *de rigueur* in the evening. In such cases, an appropriate note is made alongside the name of the restaurant.

Prices

Prices are indicated as reasonable, moderate or expensive. Price evaluations that are followed by a star (*) indicate especially good value for money regardless of the rating of the restaurant.

Many restaurants offer a special fixed-price menu for lunch. In some cases, alas, these are merely inferior meals at lower prices, but in others they represent an excellent opportunity to sample the best of a chef's offerings at considerable savings. In those cases where the fixed-price lunches are exceptionally worthwhile, a note will be found in the description of the restaurant.

TEL AVIV - JAFFA

*** ALHAMBRA: 30, Sderot Yerushalayim, Jaffa. Open for lunch 12.30 – 3 p.m. and for dinner from 7 p.m. – midnight. Closed all day Friday and on Saturday afternoons. Reservations recommended. Tel. (03) 834453.**

When Christian Zaradez opened this restaurant, more than 35 years ago, it was the first French restaurant in the country. The mood here is formal: the mezzanine level is a comfortable cocktail lounge; the dining room is divided into several intimate areas; and the charcoal grey carpeting, antique copper hangings and several attractive paintings all add to a sense of serenity.

Christian's foie gras is superb, but for a lighter first course try the squash halves filled with sautéed liver and asparagus. As a main course consider the fillet steak with either mustard or pepper sauce, the young salmon in a piquant tomato-based sauce, or the mullard breast, which comes in a sauce based in part on quinces and red wine. The potatoes Anna, the green pasta and the barely cooked baby vegetables that are offered as side dishes are all excellent. My own favourite desserts here are the superbly rich sublime au chocolate, the creme brulée and the smooth, rich and satisfying quince parfait. Expensive.

*** BAIUCA: 103, Yehuda HaYamit St., Jaffa. Open Mon. – Sat. from 7 – 11:30 p.m. Closed Sundays. Tel. (03) 827289.**

Brazilian cuisine has never inspired delicate emotions or great passions. The fact is, however, that Brazilian food is easy to enjoy and the dishes served up by owner Arie Zack are as genuine as you will find in Rio de Janeiro or Porto Allegro. There is nothing fancy about the ambience here, but the traditional Brazilian music and the dozens of folkloric items on the walls catch the senses in positive ways.

It is well worth starting off with the spiced beef and vegetables that come in a tasty pastry shell. The culinary brave of heart will dip these into the accompanying chili pepper sauce, hot enough to bring beads of perspiration to the forehead but tasty enough to make a bit of suffering worthwhile. From here go on to soup. Shrimps are the most popular seafood in Brazil, and the cream of shrimp soup here is thick, has an abundance of fresh shrimp and is based on a well-seasoned fish stock. The heart of palm soup, another Brazilian favourite, is also excellent. The main meat courses come in gigantic portions and, as the waitress will inform new customers, a single portion is more than adequate for two. My own favourite is churasca, grilled lamb and fillet steak served on long heavy skewers all cooked over hot coals until they are lightly charred on the outside but still pink inside. Under no circumstnces should you pass by the side dishes that accompany the meats. The farofa, made from ground toasted cassava root, which Brazilians sprinkle over nearly everything they eat, has a good crisp texture and a nice, light touch of sweetness, and the traditional onion salad and heart of palm salad are both excellent. One can also make a meal here of the superb feijoada, the national dish of Brazil: a thick dark stew made from black beans, with beef, pork, sausage and other bits of meat added. Prices vary from moderate to expensive. (*)

• **BATIA: 197, Dizengoff St. Open daily from noon – midnight. Tel. (03) 221335.**

Even though it has been recently renovated, this Tel Aviv landmark, which has been serving food from the Yiddish kitchen in the same location for nearly 60 years, still maintains an ambience that falls somewhere between that of a Greek taverna and a bombed-out railroad terminal. Nevertheless, Batia maintains a distinct Jewish charm. This is a restaurant that seems to encourage disagreement. There are those who adore the food, and those who say it is terrible. Oddly enough, even those who seem to hate it keep coming back for more.

Whenever I come here, I start off with small orders of gefilte fish and chopped liver and go on to the cholent, which I always take with the kishke – marvellous because it has plenty of onion, pepper and chicken fat.

Because overeating seems to be *de rigueur* in Yiddish restaurants, I also take a small sampling of the simple but delicious baked beef. Reasonable prices.

• BEYBELE, 177, Ben Yehuda St. Open daily from noon – 1 a.m. or later. Tel. (03)5467486.

A relative newcomer to the Tel Aviv Yiddish food scene, the very "in" Beybele has already established itself as one of the most reliable and best eateries of its type. With an ultimately simple décor based primarily on tables with thick, graceless, painted wooden legs and two overhead fans to keep the flies confused, it is difficult to decide whether Beybele is trying to emulate the mood of Warsaw in the 1920s or Tel Aviv in the post-modern '90s.

Happiness here for a couple is sharing orders of gefilte fish, chopped liver, what may be the best kishke in town, a glass of borscht and some of the house pickles and then going on to the beef baked in red wine, lemon juice, oil, garlic and onions. The side dishes are equally marvellous; you must insist on tasting the tzimmes, based on thinly sliced carrots, pitted prunes, honey and perfect measures of nutmeg, cinnamon and ground cloves. If you have room for dessert, the strudel here is exquisite. Reasonable prices.

• CAPRICCIOZA: 56, Shenkin St. Open Sun. – Thurs. from noon – 3:30 p.m. and from 6:30 p.m. – midnight. Fri. open until 4 p.m. Closed Sat. Tel. (03) 614964.

The simple, unpretentious décor of this popular Italian restaurant is as appealing as the cuisine. The mixed antipasto platter, with prosciutto, fried eggplant and ham and vegetable quiche are good ways to start off, as is the seafood antipasto of shrimps and calamari coked in red wine and herbs. The gnocchi are especially good and come in a cream sauce that contains bacon and mushrooms; and the scallopini al limone, based on veal slices in a sauce based on brown stock, Marsala wine, lemon and herbs is excellent. Reasonable to moderate prices.

*** CASBAH: 32, Yirmiahu St. Open from 1 p.m. – 4 p.m. and from 7 p.m. – midnight. Closed Sat. night. Reservations recommended. Tel. (03) 6043617.**

This well-established French restaurant, one of the first to open in Israel, has been presided over by owner Emile Gatlin for more than thirty years. With an atmosphere that is a pleasing blend of old world formality and Middle-Eastern ease, this is French cuisine with not even a hint of the nouvelle. It is said that some people have been eating here so long that they have actually become addicted to Gatlin's classic duck in orange sauce.

As an hors d'oeuvre try the coquille Saint-Jacques with mushrooms and Mornay sauce, or the crêpes that have been filled with a meat and cream based bolognese sauce. Main courses specially worthy of note are the grilled shrimps that are served on breaded, deep fried forest mushrooms; the pink trout in caper sauce; or any of the fillet steaks. Expensive.

• DAKOTA: 11, Yehuda HaLevi St. Open daily from 11 a.m. – midnight. Tel. (03) 5100635.

Even though his fish and seafood restaurant is located inland – that is to say, in the heart of the banking and insurance sector of the city – chef Eliezer Loya does a good job in capturing the traditional flavours of the Mediterranean. That the restaurant is "typically Tel Avivian" is demonstrated in part by the fact that there are no tablecloths on the tables and the waiters dress with a kind of practiced informality that is almost unknown elsewhere. Although the brief, well-thought-out menu has some interesting offerings, one should make sure to check the specials of the day that are written on a blackboard hung near the entrance to the kitchen.

If crabs are among your passions, those served here are marvellous. Boiled in a court bouillon seasoned with thyme, bay leaves and salt, and then treated to a sauce that contains an abundance of garlic and herbs and a hint of Pernod, this is a first course worth remembering. Other good starters are the coquilles Saint-Jacques, prepared with mushrooms in a cream sauce and finished under the grill to melt the cheese topping, and the

Spanish-style seviche of thin slices of raw fish in a mixture of lemon juice, olive oil, chili pepper, onion, tomato, salt and oregano; the texture and taste of this offering is a treat. As main courses consider especially the smoked trout served with a good horseradish sauce, the calamari in a ginger-flavoured sauce, and any of the shrimp dishes. Reasonable to moderate prices. (*)

• **ESTHER'S DELI: 7, Ibn Gvirol St. Open Sun. – Thurs. from 7 a.m. – 9 p.m., on Fri. until 4 p.m. and on Sat. from 10 a.m. – 2:30 p.m. Tel. (03) 5617096.**

Esther, who comes originally from the Ukraine, has been serving Yiddish-style food here for 27 years. Her comfortable, homelike eatery is charming; and even though her kitchen is not much bigger than a closet, she manages to turn out enough food to keep her devoted clients happy. Everything here is good, but Esther's herring dishes are special. Matjas herring comes chopped and smothered in shmaltz (rendered chicken fat); with olive oil, sliced onions and whole peppercorns; with finely chopped apples; in a mayonnaise and vinegar sauce; or fried, sprinkled with dill and served with boiled potatoes. All are marvellous. Also try the excellent cholent, the delicious knishes, and whatever else you have room for, and then, if you can, close with the strudel, served with fresh cooked figs and a tantalizing sweet sauce. Reasonable prices. (*)

• **FISHERMAN'S RESTAURANT: In Jaffa Port. Open daily from noon – midnight. Tel. (03) 813870.**

Set on the water's edge, overlooking the comings and goings of hundreds of fishing boats that call Jaffa port home, this is simple Mediterranean dining at its best. Meals here open with a variety of Middle-Eastern salads and then go on to whatever fish and seafood the boats have brought in that day. Consider sharing a platter of deep-fried shrimps, calamari and finger-sized red mullets and then going on to the fried or grilled fish your waiter suggests. Don't hesitate to eat with your fingers here – it makes the fish taste even better. Moderate prices.

**** GARGANTUA: 3, Pinhas St., Jaffa. Open daily from 8 p.m. – midnight. Reservations recommended. Tel. (03)827938.**

The idea of creating a single menu with offerings from the cuisines of Japan, France, China and the Mediterranean is a bold one, and if it had not been put together wisely, it could have been catastrophic. Happily, owner-chefs Chenny Farber and Leon Alkalai have pulled it off with great charm and theirs is one of the most enjoyable restaurants in town. The first thing to make its way to your table, depending on the season, will be a kir aperitif or a glass of hot wine punch, and these will be accompanied by small plates of nicely spiced sliced zucchini, a few pickles and delicious hot fresh rolls. Only then do your problems begin, for there are so many tempting offerings that making one's selection is not always easy.

The dim sum and the shrimps with mango are both excellent, but then again, so are the salmon sushi, the marinated salmon with chives and coriander and the cold chicken livers that have been seasoned with soya sauce, green onion, anise and ginger. Nor will it be any easier deciding on a main course. The beef sirloin with a marchand de vin sauce, the duck in a sauce based on lemon and prunes, the veal fillet in basil-enriched red wine sauce, and the grilled fish seasoned with taragon and rosemary are all worthy of attention. Do not skip dessert. The creme Catalan, a Spanish-style custard flavoured with cinnamon, orange peel and nutmeg, is marvellous. Moderate prices. (*)

***** GOLDEN APPLE: 1, Karl Netter St. (on the corner of Montefiore St.). Open from noon – 3 p.m. and from 7 – midnight (last orders accepted at 10:30 p.m.). Closed Fri. afternoons. Reservations required. Tel. (03)5660932.**

For at least five years Israel Aharoni talked about his desire to open a fine French restaurant, and from time to time rumours would circulate that this opening was imminent. Many of Aharoni's fans agreed that his two existing restaurants, "Ying Yang" and "Tai Chi," were the best Chinese restaurants in the country, but because Aharoni's name had become so firmly linked with the cuisine of the Far East, many wondered whether he would succeed if he ventured into the world of French cuisine. Although Golden Apple as been open for less than a year at this writing, it has already established itself as a world-class French restaurant. Aharoni has definitely earned his stars.

This elegant restaurant, is decorated tastefully, the service is formal but not stiff, the greeting one receives on arrival is genuinely warm, and the atmosphere is dignified but not stuffy. The menu pleases because its tone of intelligent originality reflects a comfortable blend of modernism and tradition, of the classic and the playful. Best of all, Aharoni's dishes show a passion for lightness, balance and perfect cooking times.

Every dish here is special and worth your consideration. Among my favourite starters are the classic terrine de foie gras, which is as good as I have eaten anywhere, and the calamari salad in which thinly sliced calamari rings are heaped onto barely cooked green beans and treated to a perfect balsamic vinaigrette sauce. The herbed saddle of lamb is superb, with meat cooked precisely as it should be and so full of flavour that it brings tears of joy to the eyes; and the shrimps on soya-ginger sauce, which come with a garnish of black mushrooms in a pastry nest and a tiny braised lettuce, are a sheer pleasure. Prices are high but those who love fine food will not consider them expensive. Also definitely worthy of note is the very reasonable fixed-price menu offered at lunch. (*)

• HIPPOPOTAME: 12, Yirmiyahu St. Open daily from noon – 12:30 a.m. Tel. (03) 5466348.

With lots of well-worked dark wood and simple tables covered with tablecloths, on which sit sheets of glass to keep the linen clean, Shabi Bahar's hippopotame is one of Tel Aviv's most popular French eateries. Although this is not the kind of place at which you should expect to find the meal of the century, it is a comfortable and pleasant restaurant that leads you to anticipate a really good French meal. The regulars here are so at home that many of them never even look at the menu, preferring to simply ask for whatever happens to be the special of the day or to request whatever dish comes to mind.

The shrimps in calamari in a herbed bechamel-based wine sauce make excellent hors d'oeuvres, as do the large sautéed mushrooms that are filled with sea food, transferred to a personal-sized casserole, sprinkled over with breadcrumbs and then browned under a hot grill. I have two favorite main courses here. The first is the sirloin steak, served with an excellent sauce made by blending a brown and a white sauce together with wine and then adding mustard and parsley. The second is the escalope of goose liver, which is served with a bechamel-based sauce, artichoke hearts and almonds. For dessert try any of the parfaits (the pistachio, chocolate and lemon are special) or the "floating island," that beloved French dessert in which whipped egg whites are floated in a rich vanilla custard. Moderate prices. (*)

***** KEREN: 12, Eilat St. Open Sun. – Fri. from noon – 3 p.m. and from 7 p.m. – midnight (last orders taken at about 11:00 p.m.). Reservations required. Tel. (03) 816565.**

The old house on the corner of Eilat St. and Orbach St. had fallen into total decrepitude. Built in 1866 by the grandfather of Peter Ustinov and later used as a residence by the Knights Templar, the building lay abandoned for many years. Today, after it has been renovated from top to bottom, this house is the jewel that houses Keren, possibly the most beautiful restaurant in Israel and certainly one of the best.

The dark wood floors, oversized windows, and exposed beams on the first floor reception area call to mind early American architecture; and the outdoor terraces, trimmed with wooden railings and balustrades, are pure New Orleans. But the kitchen and the food are unquestionably French.

In the well-designed dining room on the second floor, one will sit in great comfort disturbed only by having to make the most agonizing choices about which of the tempting items on the menu to order. Chaim Cohen, who is the chef here, can hold his head high. After studying in France with chefs Roger Verger, Guy Savoir and Phillipe Grault, Cohen has evolved a personal style that is both rustic and modern, and his dishes are prepared with the precision that is the unmistakable sign of a serious chef. His dishes often touch on the exquisite.

The first courses are all excellent, but my own choice is often Cohen's squid salad. As a soup, it would be hard to beat the mushroom cappuccino, and as an intermediate course the calf's brain in caper sauce is unbeatable. Among my own favourite main courses are the double offering of carapaccio and a steak of baby lamb that comes in a superb brown sauce, or the shrimps in crab sauce. The desserts are also splendid. Try, for example, the extra ordinarily light creme brulée with its perfectly caramelized crust, or the superb apple tart. Expensive but well worth the investment. (*)

*** LA ITALIANA DI MONTEFIORI: 17, Montefiore St. Open for lunch daily except Sat. from 12:30 – 3:30 p.m. and for dinner daily except Fri. from 8 – 11:30 p.m. Reservations recommended. Tel. (03) 5608732.**

White tables, white walls, white ceilings, white tablecloths and white napkins, paisley upholstery on the chairs and paintings on the walls make this a lovely place for the eye. Best of all, this is genuine Italian cooking without tricks. For starters consider the mushrooms in cream sauce, the beef carapaccio which comes with a marvellous pesto sauce or the house paté. The pasta dishes are all good, but my favourites are the tortellini in a rich cream sauce, the salmon raviolis and the gnocchi. If you want another course, opt for the veal alle Marsella, the osso buco or the chicken with tarragon, all of which are excellent. Moderate prices. (*)

*** LE RELAIS JAFFA: 13, HaDolphin St., Jaffa. Open daily from noon – 2:30 p.m. and from 7 – 11:30 p.m. Reservations recommended. Tel. (03) 810637.**

The beautiful house in which this charming restaurant is set features impossibly high ceilings, intricate wrought-iron chandeliers, and arched windows that call to mind Alexandria as Lawrence Durrell described it. Here is an interior so beautiful that the contrast between Arabesque architecture and Mediterranean simplicity provides a visual feast for those who thrive on refined decor. With its intimate entrance hall, outdoor terraces, separate salons for aperitifs and after-dinner brandy or coffee, and a large but comfortable main dining room, Le Relais provides an ideal setting for voluptuous meals.

As starters, in addition to two excellent country-style patés, there is also a paté de foie gras that has a tantalizing hint of sage and thyme. Another first course to be considered is the egg with duxelles, a superb mixture of mushrooms and shallots enriched with bechamel sauce. My favourite main courses here are the entrecôte steak in a superb bordelaise sauce and the navarin tapenade, a ragout of lamb, olives, anchovy fillets and capers. In the winter months be sure to try the classic choucroute garni or the cassoulet, both of which represent French bistro cuisine at its best. For dessert try the profiteroles, puff pastry balls filled with vanilla ice cream and then topped with a rich chocolate sauce; they are exceptional. Prices moderate to high.

• **MAGANDA: 26, Rabbi Me'ir St. (in the Yemenite quarter). Open Sun. – Thurs. from noon – midnight and on Sat. night until midnight. Tel. (03) 661895. Kosher.**

Those who like noisy, friendly Middle-Eastern restaurants where the owners and waiters are helpful and the food is always reliable but never extraordinary, may find that this is a place much to their taste. In addition to a meze (the Middle-Eastern equivalent of an Italian antipasto assortment) that will include as many as twelve different salads, first courses also include Moroccan style beef-filled pastries, felafel and several stuffed vegetables, all of which are quite good. As main courses the calf's liver, steaks, shishliks and kebabs are all worth considering. Moderate prices.

• **MAMAIA: 192 Ben Yehuda St., Tel Aviv. Open daily from noon – midnight. Tel. (03) 5237784.**

A neighbourhood restaurant, but one that attracts knowledgeable diners from all over, Mamaia is a Romanian restaurant that combines the best of old-world European decor and politeness with the simple joys of genuine Romanian cuisine. The ciorba, a thick and hearty meat and vegetable soup with lots of lemon juice, is excellent; the mixed grill is marvellous; the mititei, thumb-shaped garlicky minced meat patties, are full of flavour; and the steaks, livers and kebabs here are all cooked precisely as they should be – charred on the outside and tender, rare and juicy inside. Definitely worth trying. Moderate prices.

• NELU: 11, Eilat St. Open daily from noon – 3 a.m. Tel. (03) 5101919.

Devoted carnivores among the Tel Aviv population learned long ago that one of the best ways to satisfy their lust for meat is to undertake a periodic pilgrimage to Chaim Nelu. Tucked away in the midst of the bleak industrial and wasteland that divides Tel Aviv and Jaffa, there is nothing fancy at this Romanian grill. A single picture adorns the walls of the main dining areas and that, frankly, is strongly reminiscent of the kind of junk one would find at a five-and-ten-cent store. The tables are simple, the tablecloths simpler; the service is a bit brusque, and the noise level sometimes just a bit too high. But nobody cares because nobody comes here to be "fancy." Whether at 1 pm. or 2 a.m., the only reason one comes here is to feast on meat.

In keeping with the country-style cookery of the Balkans, the meats here are unadorned by fancy sauces or garnishes. Chops, steaks and other standard cuts are all brushed with butter or oil before being treated to generous sprinklings of paprika, pepper, rosemary and oregano. Enough fat is left intact on each cut to ensure that the meat, which is then grilled over well-tempered charcoals, will remain as flavourful as possible. The mixed grill is a house speciality. Unlike the English version of this dish (bacon, steak, sausages, and perhaps liver), what is served here is precisely what one would expect to find in Bucharest or Cluj and reflects the Romanian love of variety meats. Cooked calves' brains, sweetbreads and spinal cord are brushed generously with melted butter, and dredged in paprika and pepper seasoned breadcrumbs before grilling. Sliced veal kidneys are broiled until nearly done on one side, basted with butter and then grilled until they are ready to be seasoned with lemon juice, salt and paprika. The plate also comes with grilled beef liver, pork medallion and a small entrecote steak. Those with truly Gargantuan appetites will open their meal with a traditional ciorba, a slightly sour, marvellously hearty vegetable soup with lots of tasty boiled beef. Prices are reasonable to moderate. (*)

• OSTERIA DA FIORELLA: 44 Ben Yehuda St., corner of Bograshov. Open from noon to midnight. Closed Fri. nights and Sat. afternoons. Tel. (03) 5288717.

Opened several years before the new-wave Italian restaurants saw the light of day, the food served at this simple, comfortable establishment is remarkably faithful to that found in many small, unpretentious restaurants throughout Italy. The minestrone soup and pasta e fagioli (bean soup with pasta) are excellent examples of the country-style cookery of Italy; the gnocchi is much to be recommended, and the fusilli puttanesca is an equally good pasta dish, served in a delicious sauce of tomatoes, black and green olives, mushrooms, capers, garlic and olive oil. As main courses, both the scallopine alla Marsala and the spezzatino prove excellent choices. In the first dish, veal scallops are dredged in herbed flour and then sautéed in butter and Marsala wine. The second dish, a Ligurian veal ragout, is rich with tomatoes, oil, butter and fresh herbs. For dessert do not miss the biscuitta da fiorella, based on crushed biscuits, chocolate mouse and cherry brandy. Moderate prices.

*** PICASSO: 88, Rehov Hayarkon St. Open daily from 8 a.m. – 6 p.m. Tel. (03) 5102765.**

There may be no place more typically Tel Avivian than Assi Aviv's ultra-popular restaurant, where the attractive waitresses, the view of the sea, and the sheer "in-ness" of being there keeps people coming back and smiling every time. Paris-born David Prozniak is in charge of the kitchen here, and in addition to the quiches, salads and light meals that are offered throughout the day, his menu also features the kinds of innovative and delicious dishes that have made the yuppies of the city indebted to him. Among my own favourite dishes are the spiral of young tuna and salmon, the poached salmon in a delicate remoulade sauce, and the rabbit stew. Also a good place to come for a coffee and a rich dessert. Moderate prices. (*)

**** THE PINK LADLE: 15, Balfour St. Open Sun. – Fri. from noon – 3 p.m. and from 7 – 11 p.m. Tel. (03) 202302. Reservations recommended.**

Ten years ago, when Tzahi Bukshester opened this restaurant, he was one of a small group of young chefs to represent a "new wave" in local dining. Though The Pink Ladle is the only restaurant of that new wave to have survived the decade, the influence of these chefs is now felt in the country's more serious restaurants.

Neither the restaurant nor the cooking here shows any signs of growing tired, and the cuisine is as light, innovative and appealing as ever. If any of the lamb specialities are on the menu when you visit, be sure to try them. If not, other house specialities include the veal with olives and tomatoes, and the chicken breast in peach sauce, as appetizers, and the steamed salmon in green horseradish sauce and goose livers that have been first fried and then treated to a demi-glacé sauce enriched with liqueur. Also worthy of note are the special luncheon menus which are in the hands of the young but talented Ayala Epstein, who worked as Bukshester's sous-chef for two years. Her style has an interesting combination of grace, lightness and boldness. Best of all, the lunch menu changes daily, depending entirely on what appeals to the chef when she visits the market early the same day. Dinner prices are moderate to expensive. The fixed-price lunch menu is surprisingly reasonable. (*)

*** PREGO: 9, Rothschild St. Open for lunch daily from 12:30 – 4 p.m. and on Sat from 1 – 5:30 p.m. Dinner served daily from 7:30 p.m. until after midnight. Closed Fri. evenings. Reservations recommended. Tel. (03) 659545.**

This was the restaurant that, about five years ago, brought the Italian version of nouvelle cuisine to Israel, and its genuinely charming atmosphere has made it one of Tel Aviv's most "in" places. The carapaccio of paper-thin slices of marinated beef, and the shrimp salad with red and green lettuce are both good, and the minestrone soup is excellent. My favourite main course here is the saltimbocca, veal scallops sprinkled with sage, salt and pepper and then rolled around thin slices of prosciutto (ham) before being sautéed in butter. For dessert, try the pinata, a marvellous concoction based on butter, egg whites, sweet cream, pine nuts, bittersweet chocolate and coffee. Prices range from moderate to high.

*** PRONTO: 26, Nachmani St.. Open daily from 12:30 – 3.30 p.m. and from 7 p.m. – midnight. Reservations recommended. Tel. (03) 299915.**

Owner Raphi Adar lived in Italy for some time and was wise enough to call his simply but charmingly designed and uncluttered place a "trattoria," thus acknowledging a happy lack of pretentiousness. Among the more delightful antipastos are large stuffed mushrooms, nicely coated with seasoned bread crumbs and then quickly deep-fried and served with pesto sauce, and the salad of mozzarella cheese and tomatoes in a light vinaigrette sauce. The chef here knows how to handle pasta. Be sure to try either the fettuccine with either salmon or peas and mushrooms, both of which come in a good cream sauce. The main courses are all tempting, but my own favourite is the veal scallopine that comes in an excellent Marsala sauce. For dessert consider the tiramisu, perhaps the best sample of this dish you will find outside of Milan. Moderate prices.

• CHEZ RAYMONDE: In the Cinema Club, 288, Hayarkon St. Open from noon – 4 p.m. and 7:30 – midnight. Closed Sat. lunch. Reservations recommended. Tel. (03) 5466784.

Raymonde, who has spent nearly twenty years in Paris, takes the culinary arts seriously and knows that attention to ambience and the serving of food can be just as important as the food itself. Hers is an intimate restaurant, seating only about thirty people. The intentionally unpolished wooden floors, a handsome wooden bar, salmon-coloured drapes, a selection of attractive prints on the walls and the handsomely set tables combine to create an atmosphere that is dignified but relaxed, formal but not pretentious.

As starting courses consider the foie gras or the simpler but no less charming paté de campagne, a rustic paté of ground pork and pork liver flavoured with cognac and fresh herbs, and then go on to the fish bisque, one of the best you will taste anywhere. As main courses give special consideration to the salmon scalopes done in the style of Escoffier, poached and served with a finely puréed mixture of vegetables, and the carré d'agneau, in which small medallions of lamb are first sautéd in butter and then finished under the grill. Do not pass by the excellent desserts, of which the iced soufflé may be the very best. Expensive.

• THE RED CHINESE: 326, Dizengoff St. Open from Mon. – Thurs. from noon – midnight and on Fri. and Sat. until 1 a.m. Tel. (03) 5466347.

This attractive and comfortable Chinese restaurant has been popular for many years and, even though many of the dishes have been adapted to the Western palate, the food is always of high quality. My own favorite dish here is Peking Duck (which should be ordered by telephone a day in advance). I also find that the standards, wonton soup, corn soup, sweet and sour soup, spare ribs, lemon chicken, sesame shrimp and Szechuan style shrimp or fish, are extremely rewarding here. Moderate prices.

• RETEVIM: 39, Bogroshov St. Open daily from noon – midnight. Tel. (03) 5280344.

Another "fun" restaurant, Retevim (which means "sauces" in Hebrew") specializes in one dish – chicken escalopes, which can be ordered with 49 different sauces. This might sound somewhat tedious, but because this spacious, comfortable and uncluttered restaurant refuses to take itself too seriously and insists on serving sauces that are well made, the whole thing is rather a delight. As first courses consider the excellent country-style salmon mousse or an order of sweet peppers that are lightly fried, marinated and served with shredded goats' cheese. Among the sauces I have sampled I recommend those based on bacon and mushrooms; basil with oranges; mushrooms, garlic and sweet cream; butter, lemon and white wine; and shrimps, red wine and brandy. My favourite, however, was the sauce based on pomegranate butter – grenadine syrup blended with a well-made white butter sauce to which grenadine syrup and fried onions had been added. For dessert try the pana-cotta, a custard-like dessert based on sweet cream, vanilla, lemon, rum and sugar, or the apple cake, both of which are excellent. Reasonable to moderate prices. (*)

• RITZ: 82, Hayarkon St. Open from noon – 3 p.m. and from 7 p.m. – midnight. Closed Fri. nights and open again after Shabbat until midnight. Tel. (03) 655160. Kosher.

Unlike the restaurants in the Ritz hotels throughout Europe, this establishment offers strictly kosher food. The decor in this spacious, well-decorated restaurant is pleasantly formal, quiet and dignified. The waiters are friendly but avoid familiarity, and, despite the limitations imposed by the laws of kashrut, the food is French in style. The best opening course here is the sautéed goose liver, and as main courses the fillet steak in demi-glacé sauce and whole peppercorns and the veal ribs are quite good. Moderate to high prices.

*** ROTHSCHILD RESTAURANT: 47, Rothschild Blvd. Open from noon – 3:30 p.m. and from 7 – 11 p.m. Closed Fri, afternoons. Reservations recommended. Tel. (03) 662467.**

Although this sophisticated and attractive French restaurant had its ups and downs (partially due to changing owners and chefs), it has always maintained an overall high standard. As starters, the terrine of chicken livers, seasoned with juniper and pepper, the beef carapaccio and the cream of carrot soup are all excellent. As main courses the mullard breast in blackberry sauce is especially good, the beef liver in mustard sauce is worth trying, and the steak offerings are all excellent. For dessert try the rich, dense chocolate terrine flavoured with Grand Marnier liqueur. As for the ostrich steaks and the crocodile tail meat that is sometimes found on the menu, I suggest simply ignoring these, treating them merely as jokes in dubious taste. Prices moderate to high.

*** RUSSALKA: 86, Herbert Samuel St. Open daily from 12:30 – 4 p.m. and from 7:30 p.m. – midnight. Reservations suggested. Tel. (03) 5173530.**

The marriage between the cuisines of France and

Russia was made in the 19th century, when it became de rigueur for wealthy Russian families to employ French chefs. The marriage was a good one – so good in fact that it eventually gave birth to now famous dishes such as chicken Kiev, beef Stroganoff and veal cutlets Pojarsky.

Since this exceptionally pleasant restaurant opened twenty years ago in Tel Aviv, it has served just such dishes. With an abundance of dark wood, attractive paintings and prints on the walls, and quiet piano music, this is a comfortable establishment. Other classic offerings are the Ukrainian-style borscht that has lots of cooked shredded cabbage, the cream of pepper soup, and the Caucasian shishlik (in which marinated cubes of lamb are placed on skewers and alternated with pieces of tomato, green pepper and onion). Expensive, but with a reasonably priced lunch menu.

• SHANGRILA: 105, Hayarkon St. (in the Astor Hotel). Open daily from 1 – 3:30 p.m. and from 7 p.m. – midnight. Tel. (03) 5238913.

A few traditional Thai arches, simply painted walls, comfortable tables and chairs and the marvellous view of the sea contribute nicely to the purposely understated decor of this restaurant, where nearly all of the dishes are genuinely Thai. One can order Western style (that is to say, a single course at a time) or in keeping with Thai tradition, by having the entire meal placed on the table at the same time. The tam yum soup, seasoned with lemon grass and garnished with fried mushrooms, onions, garlic and several whole shrimps, has much to recommend it, as do the chicken with green curry (which has a pleasant hint of coconut milk), the stir-fried shrimps seasoned with tamarind, and the Phad Thai, a traditional dish of rice noodles fried with eggs and chili peppers and then garnished with ground nuts and bean sprouts. Be sure to tell your waiter whether you want your food mild, hot or extremely hot. Even the desserts offered are genuinely Thai, and the pudding with water chestnuts and rice is a special delight. Depending on your selections, prices can range from moderate to expensive.

• SHMULIK COHEN: 146, Herzl St. Open Sun. – Thurs. 10 a.m. – 10 p.m. Tel. (03) 810222. Kosher.

When Gad and Rivka Cohen arrived in Palestine in 1920 they built a small house at what is now 146, Herzl Street. In 1936, the Cohens opened a Polish-Jewish restaurant on the ground floor. The restaurant has been there ever since. Although Yiddish is no longer the lingua franca, the air is charged with old-world Jewishness, and anyone who has expectations of what such an eatery should be like will not be disappointed with the ambience.

Even though the prices are high and some of the dishes are disappointing (the roast goose is almost always overcooked), this is one of the most popular and respected restaurants in its category and the many regulars who frequent this establishment defend it fiercely. My own favourites here are chicken soup, gefilte fish, cholent (be sure to take it with the marvellous kishke) and the baked beef. Also be sure to try the sweet cabbage and the sweet cooked carrots. Moderate to high prices.

• SPAGHETTIM: 18, Yavne St. Open Sun. – Thurs. from noon to 4:30 p.m. and from 7 p.m. – 1 a.m. Open all day Sat. Closed Fri. afternoons. Tel. (03) 294467.

The menu of this simple but charming restaurant lists one soup, two salads and 58 different kinds of spaghetti, including several sweet spaghetti dishes for dessert. All of this might sound a bit outrageous, but in fact this is one of the most "fun places" to dine in Tel Aviv. Most of the spaghetti offerings can be divided into three broad categories – those with tomato-based sauces, those with olive-oil-based sauces, and those with cream sauces. Some, such as the napolitana, with its herbs, and the carbonara, with bacon, ham, white wine, nutmeg, black pepper and cream, are well known. Others, like the arvieta, with tomatoes, sweet red and green peppers, hot peppers and garlic, or the one that comes with walnuts, ricotta cheese, parmesan cheese and cream, are a bit more adventurous. The first good thing about all of this choice is that absolutely everyone, no matter how normal or jaded his or her tastes, will find a pleasing dish here. The second thing is that each of the dishes is quite good. There is nothing fancy about the dishes offered here, but there is an undeniable element of fun in them. Young chef Gil Chaim is to be commended not only for his imagination but also for his tasty sauces and for the fact that he respects his spaghetti enough not to overcook it. The service is friendly and good, the food comes in generous portions, and the prices are very reasonable. (*)

• STAMBOUL: 16, Uriel Acosta St. Open daily from noon – midnight. Tel. (03) 812588.

Bondi Abursi, the owner of this small and delightful establishment, originally came from Istanbul, and his all-Turkish cooking staff make this a place definitely worth visiting. The food offered here is genuinely Turkish – simple, tempting, rewarding and great fun. At the same time as the waiter brings the menus to the table you will be served a plate of black olives. Lightly crushed and then marinated in oil that has been enriched with lots of garlic, these are as good as I have sampled anywhere in the Mediterranean basin. As a first course, be sure to try the fine tarama, a delightful light pink mixture of lightly smoked fish roe that has been pounded into a paste with garlic, breadcrumbs, lemon juice and olive oil. Also as a first course consider the vine leaves filled with pine nuts and rice. As main courses it will be difficult to beat the kebabs, the deep fried chicken croquettes or the shishlik, all of which are seasoned marvellously before being grilled or fried. Reasonable prices. (*)

**** TABOON: In Jaffa Port. Open daily from 12:30 – 01:00. Reservations recommended. Tel. (03) 811176.**

Those who are convinced that the only way to cook a fish is to grill it or fry it neither understand nor appreciate why I continually put Taboon at the top of the list among local fish and seafood restaurants. The simple truth is that the dishes at this Jaffa establishment have always shown touches of imagination, lightness, and sometimes even daring, which are missing from all other similar restaurants. Chef Ruby Portnoy is wise and talented enough to balance his menu so that everyone will find dishes to their taste.

The first courses here are extraordinarily good. It would be difficult, for example, to find a dish more elegant than the veal brain and shrimps with apple and lemon cream, or the Basque-style stuffed squid. Other equally well-made first courses include the salmon carapaccio, which comes in a sauce based on sweet red peppers, the gravad lax, the calamari rings in a gentle ginger and butter sauce, and the goats' cheese mixed with pumpkin seeds. Also worthy of note are the red mullet fillets that come in a creamy sauce of lemon, olive oil and herbs. Nor will one be let down by the main-course offerings. The Mediterranean-style shrimps, herbed just right and served with rings of fried sweet red pepper, are superb; the seafood ragout – a highly seasoned stew of shrimp, calamari, scallops, and clams – is special, and the salmon-filled raviolis are marvellous. If it is a more simple fish one wants, the grouper, sea bass, trout, fresh salmon and red mullet here are all herbed gently, cooked to perfection and served to your choice with or without a variety of simple but well-made sauces. Moderate to high prices. (*)

• **TARRAGON: 13, Montefiore St. (on the corner of Yavneh St.). Open daily from 12:00 – 24:00. Tel. (03) 200297.**

Even though it carries the name of a herb, this large but attractive and comfortable restaurant is a paradise for carnivores, and the small but intelligent menu features dishes ranging in sophistication and complexity from hamburgers to Tournedos Rossini. Among the best first courses are slices of goose liver that are fried and then treated to a well-made sauce nicely seasoned with Calvados, and the veal brain with capers in lemon butter sauce. The beefburgers come in a variety of styles, but my own favorite has chopped fresh herbs and comes in a simple but good pepper sauce. The steaks here are all excellent; I highly recommend the Tournedos Rossini and the fillet steak with either pepper or mustard sauce. The home-made butter pecan ice cream and the chocolate parfait make for fine desserts. Prices are reasonable and the fixed-price business lunch is an especially good deal. (*)

*** TAI CHI: 71, Ibn Gvirol St. (in the Gan Ha-Ir shopping centre). Open daily from 12:30 a.m. – 11:30 p.m. Tel. (03) 5449212.**

With its white, cream and black decor and extruded steel and glass structural components, this spacious, modern Chinese restaurant is one of Israel Aharoni's enterprises. Aharoni, one of the nation's best-known culinary figures, guarantees that the food served here is truly representative of the culinary styles of Canton and Szechuan. The menu is similar to that at Yin Yang (described below), and at both places the food and service are always excellent. Prices moderate to high. (*)

• TAJ MAHAL: 12, Kedumim Square, Old Jaffa. Open daily from 12:00 a.m. – 3:00 p.m. and from 7 p.m. – midnight. Reservations recommended. Tel. (03) 821002.

Set in a charming building and with beautiful decorations, this comfortable restaurant provides a festive setting for dining in the Indian style. Start off with an order of mixed traditional Indian hors d'oeuvres, breads and relishes and then go on to the tandoori chicken, the beef or lamb curries or the lamb biryani, a festive casserole dish in which rice, meat and saffron come together in delightful ways. For dessert give special consideration to the four different kinds of home-made kulfi, Indian ice cream based on mango, pistachio, orange or cream. Moderate prices.

*** TANDOORI: 2, Zamenhoff St. (adjoining Dizengoff Circle). Open daily from 12:30 – 3:30 p.m. for lunch and from 7 p.m. – 1 a.m. for dinner. Reservations recommended. Tel. (03) 296185.**

Reena and Vinod Pushkarna, who own this Indian restaurant, are not so much restaurateurs as masters at combining food, sight, scent, atmosphere and all the little things that prepare you for the pleasures of the table. A genuinely warm greeting, impeccable service, and cookery without any signs of uncertainty or amateurism come together to make this Indian food at its finest.

I enjoy so many of the dishes here that it is impossible to list them all. If I had to list favourites, I would include the mulligatawny soup, the lamb chops in green masala sauce, the tandoori chicken and the shrimp and lamb curries. For dessert do not miss the kulfi, a wondrously rich ice cream based on frozen milk, pistachio nuts and dried fruits, or the gulab jamun, balls of milk powder and white cheese soaked in syrup. All dishes can be ordered to the level of hotness one likes best, and those new to Indian food will find their hostess will be more than glad to advise concerning what dishes to order. Those who enjoy cocktails should know that the owners are masters of this art, and Tandoori's cocktails are marvels to behold. Moderate prices. (*)

• TSION: 28, HaP'dueem St., in the Yemenite quarter. Open Sun. – Thurs. from 11 a.m. – midnight, Fri. from 11 a.m. – 4 p.m. and Sat. night until midnight. Tel. (03) 5178714. Kosher.

This Middle Eastern cum Yemenite resturant has two distinct dining areas. The ground floor boasts simple but attractive rooms where the "real" people eat; the second floor is where, for the privilege of sitting in a fancier but not quite real imitation of Middle Eastern atmosphere, the tourists go. Before you select your table, however, be aware that the food is identical wherever you sit but the prices are about thirty percent higher upstairs. Despite this touristy aspect, the food here is genuinely Middle Eastern and genuinely good. The humous, tehina, kubbeh, meat-filled "cigars," variety of eggplant and tomato salads, hot sauces, and hot pita breads are always good as starters. For your soup course be sure to try the Yemenite meat soup and then go on to whatever meat or fish dish most suits your needs of the moment. My own favorites here are the standards – the excellent kebabs, the well-seasoned shishliks, and the grilled fish dishes. Moderate prices.

• TULIPAN: 7, Pasteur St., Jaffa. Open daily from noon – 3:30 p.m. and from 7 p.m. – midnight. Closed Sat. night. Tel. (03) 817979. Kosher.

The motif of stylized red, white and green flowers stenciled on the white walls and replicated on the linen tablecloths and napkins gives this establishment much of the flavour of what one hopes for in a refined Hungarian restaurant. The service is formal but pleasant, the quartet of musicians who make their way from table to table in the evenings are moving enough to break your heart, and even though the kitchen goes through its ups and downs, the cuisine is genuine and sufficiently good to make it interesting. For first courses try the mushroom-stuffed crêpes that come with a well-made remoulade sauce, or the cold goose liver that comes sprinkled with oil and paprika. For a main course consider the mixed grill of slices of goose liver, beef steak (be sure to tell them not to overcook it), veal cutlets and chicken breast, or the fillet steak Budapest which is garnished with crisp potato puffs, gnocchi and excellent ratatouille. The desserts are particularly good here. Try especially the gundel blintzes, filled with a tasty blend of white cheeses and served in a rich chocolate sauce, and the perfect apple strudel. Expensive.

• THE WHITE GALLERY: Kikar Habima 4. Open daily 10 a.m. – midnight. Tel. (03) 5614730.

This fashionable cafe-restaurant, with quiet piano music, and pale paisley banquettes, is particularly popular with theatre people and journalists, especially for light meals. The hot goose liver on lettuce leaves, the quiche lorraine and the pasta dishes are all worth trying, and all have a special Mediterranean touch. My own favourite is the fettuccine in cream sauce with salmon and dill. Be sure also to try the chocolate-based desserts. Moderate prices.

**** YIN YANG: 64 Rothschild Blvd. Open daily from 12:30 – 2:30 p.m. and from 7:30 – 11:30 p.m. Reservations suggested. Tel. (03) 621833.**

Few knowledgeable diners doubt that the best and only genuine Chinese cuisine in Israel is that served here by owner Israel Aharoni. The restaurant is situated in a small house on an attractive boulevard and the interior is divided into small dining rooms, each of which has its own attentive waiters. This is a comfortable place at which to dine and, best of all, because so many of the dishes are special here, there is no need to confine oneself to the old standbys of egg rolls and sweet and sour beef. For starters consider the chicken salad with lychees, the cold sliced pork with spicy garlic sauce, and the spicy cucumber salad. My own favourites among the main-course offerings include the deep-fried shrimps in bacon, Szechuan-style calamari, crabs in black bean sauce, beef with eggplant, chicken in hoy-sin sauce or with mushrooms, pork with black chinese mushrooms, and beef in anise sauce. As to the duck dishes, all are excellent. Prices moderate to high. (*)

• **YOSHI YEN: 56, Herbert Samuel St. Open daily from 12:30 – 11:15 p.m. Tel. (03) 5177559.**

With its view of the sea, this handsomely designed Chinese restaurant offers a warm welcome, excellent service, generous portions and food that, although it makes bows to Western tastes, retains a clear touch of the Far East. The shrimp soup, based on a rich brown stock and mushrooms, has lots of perfectly cooked shrimp in it; and the hot and sour soup, which is garnished with peas, julienned chicken and carrots, is equally good. For main courses consider the spicy calamari, the chicken in ginger, the beef in hot and sour sauce or the seafish served Szechuan style. Prices moderate.

JERUSALEM

• **ALLA GONDOLA: 21, King George St. Open daily from noon – 3 p.m. and from 6 – 11 p.m. closed Fri. nights. Reservations recommended. Tel. (02) 255944.**

With its attractive, muted decor and excellent service, this, the first Italian restaurant to open in Jerusalem (circa 1957), has always had a reputation for being expensive. Fortunately, it has also had a justified reputation for serving high quality Northern Italian cookery. The menu, which lists dishes that nearly all originated in Milan or in the area of Tuscany, avoids novella cuccina and stays with the classics. The stuffed canellonnis come in an excellent cheese-based sauce, and the tasty lasagna has several layers of well-seasoned chopped meat and a good cheese topping. The best main courses here are the veal with mushrooms, the osso buco, the veal steak in mushroom cream sauce, and the tournedo steaks which come with a marvellous sauce based on tomatoes and sweet red and green peppers. Expensive.

• EL MARRAKESH: 4, King David St. Open Sun. – Thurs. from noon – 4 p.m. and from 6 p.m. –midnight. Closed Fri. and reopens on Sat. night. Tel. (02) 257577. Kosher.

Showy and just a bit glitzy, this traditional Moroccan restaurant maintains a decor and atmosphere that closely approximate what one would find in its counterpart in Casablanca. The luxurious couches and chairs, the traditional large embossed copper table tops, the musicians, the belly dancers and the singers add to this ambience of comfort, and the food and service are exactly what one expects to find in such a place. Meals start when waiters deposit anywhere from eight to fifteen small bowls of Middle Eastern dishes on the table. The humous, tehina, six types of eggplant dishes, spiced and garlic seasoned black and green olives, cabbage salad, and spicy carrots are all good. Main course specialities worth sampling are the stewed veal with prunes and almonds; baked lamb with a delicate sweet sauce; stuffed spleen; and small chickens that have been stuffed with pine nuts, raisins and rice. For dessert be sure to try the flambéed crêpes and the various pastries. Expensive.

*** FINK: 2, Hahistradrut St. Open Sun. – Thurs. from noon – 3 p.m. and from 5:30 p.m. – midnight, and on Sat. night until midnight. Tel. (02) 234523.**

One of the best-known and in fact best bars in the world, Fink is to Jerusalem what Harry's New York Bar is to Paris. So renowned is this bar that it has been said that any diplomat, politician or public figure who has never been to Fink's is simply not worth knowing. No one has ever accused Fink of serving great food or original dishes, but they do serve delightful meals, the components of which may be French, Yiddish, Russian or Mediterranean in origin. Side by side, one may find one person eating fried shrimps in butter and garlic sauce and another munching contentedly on chopped liver, while a few yards away a trio at another table may be having beef Stroganoff, fillet mignon wth pineapple and bacon and tafelspitz (an Austrian dish of tender boiled beef from close to the tail) with horseradish sauce. An absolute joy to visit. Moderate prices. (*)

• FONTE BELLA 8, Rabbi Akiva St. Open from noon – midnight. Closed Fri. evenings and open again on Sat. night. Kosher.

With lots of wood, a nearly antique espresso machine and a charming garden area, this is the kind of simple but charming Italian restaurant you would expect to find comfortably tucked away in the hills of Tuscany. Best of all, the food is authentically Italian. Among my favorites are the gnocchi served with pesto sauce, the thick, rich minestrone soup, the chicken with rosemary, and the traditional osso buco, veal knuckles that are braised in white wine and tomato sauce together with garlic and onion. For dessert try the sublime lemon pie. Moderate prices.

• HATZRIF PIE HOUSE: 5, Horkenos St. (adjoining the Russian Compound). Open daily from noon – 1 a.m. Tel. (02) 242478.

One of Jerusalem's most popular eateries, this appealing and happily unpretentious restaurant features a menu that is an interesting blend between the cookery of France and that of Morocco. The beef and the paté de foie gras are uniquely French while the salad of dried tomatoes and the piquant meat soup are definitely Moroccan. The pink trout baked in salt and the steak au poivre are French, while the pie of beef and prunes could only be Moroccan. All in all, this is a good marriage made even more pleasing for guests by the pleasant ambience and good service. Moderate prices. (*)

*** KOHINOR: In the Jerusalem Hilton Hotel. Open for lunch Sun, – Fri. from noon – 4 p.m. and for dinner on Sun. – Thurs. from 6 p.m. – midnight. Reservations recommended. Tel. (02) 536667. Kosher.**

A sad but true fact of the local culinary scene is that when most Israeli restaurateurs decide to open chains, the quality of their food deteriorates and the service declines in direct proportion to the number of branches.

Reena and Vinod Pushkarna, who are respectively the mother and father of the Tandoori chain of Indian restaurants, are notable exceptions to this rule, and Kohinor, which is a kosher branch of their chain, maintains the same high level of cuisine, service and ambience found in all their other restaurants.

The restaurant is named after the fabulous 60-carat Kohinor diamond, a stone found in India and now part of the crown jewels of England. With intricate arches, delicate filigree woodwork, beige walls, and classic Indian prints and copper etchings on the walls, the restaurant is best described as exquisite. Best of all, even though the restaurant is kosher, the dishes offered suffer no loss in flavour or authenticity whatever. For a description of many of the dishes offered, refer to the listing of Tandoori in Tel Aviv. Those who are new to this style of cuisine can comfortably rely on the knowledgeable staff to suggest dishes that will come together to make up a thoroughly enjoyable meal. Moderate prices. (*)

**** MISHKENOT SHA'ANANIM: in the Yemin Moshe quarter. Open daily from noon – midnight. Reservations recommended. Tel. (02) 254424.**

Moise Peer, who holds court here, has two passions – traditional French cuisine and fine wine. And, in addition to its exquisite panoramic view of the Old City of Jerusalem, this elegant bastion of fine cookery also boasts what is probably the finest wine cellar in Israel. The restaurant itself, with its large windows, elegant table settings and service that is as close to perfect as one can imagine, is considered by many the *de rigueur* spot for entertaining important visitors.

The most traditional hors d'oeuvre here is probably the paté de foie gras, seasoned perfectly with juniper berries, cognac and red wine and then cooked to perfection. Equally worthy as starters are those dishes that feature smoked goose breast, the goose liver with strawberries, and the smoked salmon with hearts of palms. My own favourite main course is the Tournedos à la Rossini, in which thick cuts of fillet steaks are placed on artichoke hearts and then covered with truffles and served with an exquisite dark brown Madeira-based sauce. Equally memorable are the roast duckling served with figs, and the dishes based on fresh salmon. Expensive.

**** OCEANUS: 7 Rivlin St. Open daily from 1 – 3 p.m. and from 7 p.m. Last orders taken at about 10:30 p.m. Reservations recommended. Tel. (02) 247501.**

With its low arched ceiling, ceramic tile floor and seven tables (each set for four) set off only by the tall green stalks of the white lilies that stand in niches alongside the tables, this is a charming place at which to dine. A few years ago this was by far the best fish and seafood restaurant in the country. The quality has dropped somewhat, but even now Oceanus remains a truly fine restaurant, well worth visiting.

Eyal Sani has been the talented driving force in the kitchen at Oceanus since it opened. Despite occasional lapses, his is an intelligent cuisine based on the incomparable freshness of the sea bass, drumfish, sea bream, shrimps and crabs that make their way here from the sea in several daily deliveries. Opening courses include a delightful carapaccio of paper-thin slices of fish that have been marinated in a gentle mixture of olive oil, vinegar and fresh herbs. With this comes an excellent bread, prepared by spreading a dough of rye and whole wheat in the form of a pizza, sprinkling it with herbs and baking it quickly in a hot oven.

As an intermediate course seriously consider the salad of mixed red and green lettuces that are tossed together with basil, parsley and chicory before being treated to a tangy vinaigrette sauce. All of the fish dishes here are good, but the locus steaks served with butter sauce are special, and the mixed platter of crabs and shrimps, prepared in the Greek manner, are out of this world. Expensive.

*** PEER: Ben Shetah St., near the corner of Hasoreq St. Open daily from noon – 4 p.m. and from 7 p.m. until after midnight. Tel. (02) 231793.**

This sophisticated bistro features, among other things, good, simple Italian dishes. One can easily build a meal of the various antipasti offered (good sausages, several kinds of herring, cold hors d'oeuvres and a generous variety of cheeses), but many prefer to sample these and then go on to either a pasta or some other main course. The green raviolis, made with spinach, and with a filling of sweetbreads that have been sprinkled with sherry, are excellent; and the cheese-filled cannelloni, in a similar sauce and sprinkled with Parmesan cheese, are equally good. The lasagna and various fettuccine dishes are also worth trying. Main course specialities here include excellent fillet steaks that are offered plain or with one of the house sauces. Moderate prices. (*)

• **SIMA: 82, Agrippas St. Open 10 a.m. – 1 a.m. Closed Fri. night and Sat. until the end of Shabbat. Kosher.**

Despite its ultimately simple atmosphere, this Jerusalem landmark is nearly always packed, and most come here to feast on "Jerusalem grill" – a mixture of chicken hearts and livers with bits of lamb, all of which have been seasoned marvellously before being fried with generous amounts of onion and garlic. Also worth trying are good cole slaw, pickles, olives, and Turkish salad. Extremely reasonable prices. Mostly for lunch. (*)

• **SINGHA: 3, Rivlin St. Open daily from noon to midnight. Tel. (02) 231455.**

Once away from Bangkok, Thai cooks are a little like magicians. They show up as if out of nowhere and then, after enchanting us for a short while, they disappear in a puff of smoke. Hopefully, this is not about to happen at Singha, because one of the owners of this delightful restaurant is Thai. The food is also genuinely Thai, and although what is served makes a few concessions to the Western palate, the dishes are defintely not a compromise. Moderate prices.

HERZLIYA AND THE SHARON AREA

* **ART BISTRO: 7, Rothschild St., Rishon LeZion. Open daily from noon – 4 p.m. and 7 – 11 p.m. Tel. (03) 9671831.**

Located in a picturesque 100-year-old house that highlights the discreet charm of provincial life, one enters the restaurant by passing through an art gallery, climbing a narrow flight of wooden stairs and stepping into a dining room where more than half of the tables sit on a balcony that overlooks the gallery below. The recorded flute music, the attractively set tables and the pleasant formality of the dining area announce proudly that it is French cuisine that is served here.

Mickey Nir is the chef in this family-owned establishment, and his is a small but intelligent menu. If it is traditional cuisine you want, consider the sautéed goose liver with whole green peppercorns, the onion soup with puff pastry, the fillet of beef with bernaise sauce, the salmon in white wine sauce or the mullard breast in red wine sauce. If you are in a more daring mood, try the terrine of foie gras with kumquat, the mountain mushrooms with Sabra liqueur, or the poached trout stuffed with shrimp. The desserts are all good, but the mousse of white and dark chocolate and the fruit-flavoured parfaits are extraordinary. Prices moderate – expensive. (∗)

**** CLAUDINE: At the Paz Gas Station, Tsomet Savyon-Or Yehuda. Open daily except Fri. from 12:00 – 10:30 p.m. Reservations recommended. Tel. (03) 5336807.**

Tucked away in a gas station, not even the vaguest hint informs casual passersby that this little place is a well-beloved haven for those who admire fine French food. Claudine, who has studied with several fine chefs in France, has a wonderful flair for combining the traditional and the experimental. After many visits I have never regretted any of the good things I have said about her little restaurant. As first courses it would be hard to beat the asparagus flan or the goose liver paté. For main courses try the veal Provençal, the shrimps Diabalo or the entrecote steaks (perhaps the best in the country). Do not miss the superbly rich but remarkably light desserts here. Moderate prices. (∗)

• DONA FLOR: 22, HaGalim Blvd., in the Herzliya industrial area. open for lunch from Sun. – Thurs. from noon – 5 p.m., and for dinner every night except Fri. from 7 p.m. – 1 a.m. Tel. (09) 509669. Kosher.

Klarina Rosenberg comes from Rio de Janeiro and Vivien Bar-Tsin from Sao Paolo, and even though this is not a Brazilian restaurant per se, the food has a distinctly Brazilian soul. The plain white walls, dark rust-colored tablecloths, attractive glazed tile serving dishes and a decor that relies heavily on wood and terra cotta tiles gives the umistakable hint that the food here is going to be simultaneously earthy and sophisticated. The fact that the kitchen is open to view from the dining room, and that the first things you see in the kitchen are two huge cast-iron skillets, each more than a metre in diameter, pleasantly stimulate curiosity as to just what is going on here.

Among the excellent first courses are the smoked mackerel, served with fried quail eggs and an excellent horseradish sauce, and the mushrooms that are sautéed with garlic and chives. My favourite soup here is based on potatoes and carrots that have been seasoned with just the right amount of cinnamon and paprika. From here, go on to one of the smoked meat specialities. I confess to a passion for the smoked and fried lamb chops and the Wiener schnitzel, both of which are simple but because done so well are real culinary treats. Prices moderate.

• MEDITERRANO: 14, HaMelacha St. In the new industrial area of Or Yehuda. Open Mon. – Sat. from 8 p.m. Last orders taken at about 11:30 p.m. Tel. (03) 5331134. Reservations suggested.

Even though it is situated in an industrial area, this restaurant is extremely attractive; once you are inside, you quickly forget the outside ugliness. Opaque glass windows, high ceilings, a marvellously designed chandelier, beige-colored walls that are trimmed with natural wood, beautiful glazed clay serving dishes, and an abundance of marble all come together splendidly to make an attractive and comfortable dining area which is divided into two levels. Owner-chef Harel Duvdevani thinks very highly of his cuisine. Unfortunately, it is not always as good as he would have us believe.

This is a restaurant that draws heavily on the products and cooking styles of the Mediterranean, so one will do best to stay with regional starters such as calamari, spiced shrimp and leeks in vinaigrette. Of the main courses, according to my experience, the very best dish here is the roast quail. In this dish, boned quail meat is placed on a bed of thinly sliced and perfectly seasoned vegetables and the mixture is then enclosed in a case of flaky pastry and baked just to the point where the meat is perfectly succulent, retaining all of its flavour. Some of the other dishes I have tried here were not as successful. Expensive.

• HAMESILA: On the road from Rehovot to Nes Tziona, in the old Rehovot Railway station, Rehovot. Open daily from noon – 3:30 p.m. and from 7 p.m. – 1 a.m. or later. Tel. (08) 475129.

Not too many people remember the days when the British-Palestine Railroad had a daily passenger train that started in Syria and then wound its way through Lebanon before making its way to Rosh Haniqra, Atlit and Tel Aviv until it reached its final destination in Rehovot. Trains no longer ply this route but, situated in what was once the stationmaster's house, this unpretentious restaurant offers food and service where nothing is fancy but everything is tasty. The food is Middle Eastern in style. Rich, smooth tehina with plenty of fresh parsley; eggplant salad with sliced carrots and pickled cucumbers and lots of garlic; fried mushrooms in a sauce of cumin and curry make good starters; and the nicely seasoned kebabs, shishliks and steaks make good main courses. Although a special trip may not be in order from Rosh Haniqra or Alexandria to visit this charming place, one should be sure to stop by if in the neighbourhood. Reasonable prices.

**** PAPILON; 33, Bialik St, Ramat HaSharon. Open noon – 4 p.m. and 7 p.m. – midnight. Closed Sun. Reservations recommended. Tel. (03) 5401347.**

Now in its sixth year, Shimon Reiser's Provençal-style French restaurant has never wavered in the overall quality of its cuisine. The trees lining the pathway leading to this charming restaurant grow a bit more dense every year. Even the grass in the garden seems a bit greener between visits. All in all, the half-papered walls, coarse green tablecloths and overall ambience come together to give the happy illusion that one has been magically transformed to a Provençal paradise. Best of all, chef-owner Reiser continues to demonstrate that he is a talented cook who really cares about what he is doing.

There are several patés and terrines offered as first courses. All, frankly, are delightful, but my favourite is the terrine of pork liver and rabbit which is garnished with an exquisite confiture of baby onions. Equally noteworthy is the dish listed as a "Bell of Seafood," in which shrimps and crabmeat are cooked lightly with eggs, finished under the grill and served with a rosé-coloured sauce based on tomatoes, vermouth and crême fraiche. The soups are also excellent here but the seafood bisque and the purée of sweet yellow peppers are both worthy of special note. The main courses to which I am especially attached are the rabbit cooked in rum and the medallions of pork served with shrimp and a pleasant ginger-flavoured sauce. Moderate prices. (*)

**** REVIVA AND CELIA: 1, Hamayasdim St., Ramat HaSharon. Open daily from 9 a.m. – midnight. Tel. (03) 5400179.**

If perfection in a light meal or in cakes is what you are seeking, this is the place to try. Set among comfortable villas on a pleasant residential street, the atmosphere at this cafe-restaurant, where quality is obviously taken seriously, is one of refinement and quiet sophistication. The quiche lorraine here is the best you will find in the country, and the salads, omelettes and other light dishes are all prepared perfectly. The cakes, too, are truly special. The lemon meringue pie, the fruit pies and tarts, the chocolate cakes and the meringues are all of the quality one would expect at afternoon tea at the Ritz in London or at New York's Plaza Hotel. Prices are reasonable to moderate. (*)

****TAKAMARU: In Beit Hamerkazim, the Herzliya industrial center. Open daily from noon – 3:30 p.m. and from 7 – midnight. Reservations recommended. Tel. (09) 556782.**

With its neat, uncluttered design and open sushi bar, this restaurant could be nothing but Japanese. In fact, it is the only restaurant in Israel with an entirely Japanese menu. Owner Ari Grossman is experienced and wise enough to offer a cuisine that is excellent and sufficiently authentic to please the fussiest of purists, and intelligent enough not to shock those new to this style of dining.

Consider starting off with a platter that will include a sampling of excellent sushi and then go on to the miso shiro, a consommé made with red bean paste. Continue with a plate of the perfectly fresh and admirably sliced mixed sashimi which, depending on the season, may consist of such diverse fish as tuna, salmon, sole, mackerel and shrimp. From that go on to a sampling of gently fried tempura style fish and vegetables. Of the main courses it will be difficult to decide between the sukiyaki, grilled trout in yakitori sauce and the teriyaki. Personally, I have no such problem, for my favourite dish here is the shabu-shabu, paper-thin slices of beef, rice noodles, vegetables and bean curd, all brought uncooked to the table and then simmered in hot broth until they are just cooked. The ideal beverages to accompany such meals are warm sake or cold beer, but there is also a good selection of wines available. Expensive. (*)

HAIFA AND THE NORTH

• BAT YA'AR (CHAVAT BAT YA'AR) Mitzpe Amuka. Open daily from 9 a.m. – 2 or 3 a.m. For information tel. (06) 921788 or write to Mitzpe Amuka, D.N. Marom Hagalil 13905.

This charming ranch, exquisitely situated in the hills overlooking Mitzpe Amuka, features horseback riding and jeep trips. For the pleasure of gastronomes, the ranch also has an excellent steak house. The rustic, almost all-wood building that houses the restaurant fits in perfectly with its mountain environment. The wooden tables and benches, an antique pot-bellied stove, large windows with a view that takes in the entire Galilee and the Golan Heights, and a host of brass and copper lamps and bric-a-brac all give the nice feeling that there will be nothing pretentious in the cooking here. Even the paper napkins seem in place.

There are light offerings on the menu, but it becomes immediately clear that this is primarily a place for men and women who admire good steaks. The steaks are American cut: that is to say, there are T-bones, sirloins and rib steaks, and these can be ordered in sizes from anywhere from 225 grams to 750 grams. Excellent beef, charred on the outside and cooked just to the degree desired, and served with large baked potatoes, can be an ideal meal for a day in the country. Moderate prices.

• DOLPHIN: 13, Bat-Galim Blvd., Haifa. Open daily from noon – 4 p.m. and from 7 p.m. – midnight. Tel. (04) 523837.

A pleasant greeting upon entering, a dark but comfortable atmosphere, attrctive table settings and overall good service make this a pleasant place for a relaxed lunch or dinner. Best of all, the fish and other seafood that are served are fresh, the cook has a healthy respect for cooking times, and his sauces, which are simple, have the charm of adding to and not hiding the natural taste of fish. The fried calamari, the cold shrimp cocktail and the rich fish soup, based on an amply herbed tomato-flavoured stock, make for fine first courses. To select your main course, simply ask the waiter what fish or seafood are fresh that day. If oysters are in season, be sure to try these. Prices are moderate to expensive.

• BEN EZRA YAAKOV FISH RESTAURANT: HaZeytr 71a, Atlit. Open noon – 12:30 a.m. closed Fri. night and Sat. lunch and open again on Sat. night. Tel. (04) 842273. Kosher.

About twenty-five years ago, with one frying pan, fisherman Ben Ezra Yaakov and his wife decided that it might be pleasant and profitable to open a restaurant in which he could serve the fish he caught. Ten children, a larger dining room and quite a few frying pans later, Ben Ezra continues to go to sea nearly every day, and his restaurant continues to thrive. His is the kind of restaurant that might be found in any port of call throughout the Mediterranean. The ambience is ultimately simple and consists primarily of paper tablecloths, a collection of photos of Ben Ezra on the walls, a fisherman's net, and several not at all expertly stuffed sharks and barracudas and other fish hanging from the ceiling.

There is no written menu here, but diners in the know invariably start off with a few salads before going on to their fish. Begin your meal with green and red sweet peppers that are first roasted and then fried, the salad of lightly pickled white cabbage, and excellent green olives that are lightly crushed before being marinated in oil, fresh herbs and garlic. Then, whether you are having Spanish bream, sea bass, young barracuda, white bream or whatever other fish are offered and whether they have been grilled or fried, you will not be disappointed. Reasonable to moderate prices.

• DAHLIA'S RESTAURANT. Moshav Amirim: D.N. Bikat Beit Kerem 20115. Open daily from 8 a.m. – 8 p.m. Tel. (06) 989203.

Since it was established in 1958, the members of Moshav Amirim have devoted themselves to a natural-vegetarian way of life. Those with negative experiences in dining on such food will be delighted when they sample the food here, for these people have learned their culinary lessons well. In addition to being good for you, the food that is served up here is truly delicious.

The restaurant is situated in a simple but charming country-style building with wood-burning fireplaces, watercolours on the wall, converted gas lamps, and an exquisite view of the surrounding hills. The menu changes on a daily basis and, even though one can order à la carte, it would be hard to do better than ordering the fixed-price menu. A typical meal will open with lemonade sweetened with grape sugar, and this may be followed by multiple courses that include moussaka, squash filled with rice and pine nuts, crêpes filled with cheese and cinnamon, and a variety of salads. If the weather permits, take your dessert on the terrace adjoining the dining room and sample the apple and yoghurt dessert while sipping exquisitely scented herbal teas.

Another plus at Amirim is that whether one comes to visit for an hour or two or for a two-week vacation, breakfasts are available at the homes of those moshav members who accept guests. I have breakfasted here several times and always find such delights as sugar-free but marvellously rich jams, avocado salad with chives, cabbage and carrot salad, almonds and raisins, and a wonderful jam-like concoction made from olives and garlic. Definitely worth trying. Breakfast and restaurant prices are both reasonable.

• DAN EDEN TROUT RESTAURANT: In the national park at Tel Dan. Open daily from 8 a.m. – about 6 p.m. Tel. (06) 953826.

The place that gave simplicity its meaning, this may be one of the noisiest, most unsophisticated and most aesthetically unattractive restaurants anywhere. Despite this, it is a must place to dine in when visiting the Upper Galilee because the trout, pink trout and salmon, all of which are raised on the kibbutz that owns the restaurant, are superb.

Grilled, with nothing more than a dash of fresh lemon, or smoked and served hot or cold, they are exquisite; they are also available "au bleu," sprinkled with vinegar and then rapidly boiled in a highly seasoned concentrated soup stock and served with melted butter or Hollandaise sauce. I have discovered a way to avoid the restaurant itself – all one need do is have their fish served on a tray, wander outdoors and find the nearest quiet spot under the trees or on the bank of the river, there to have the picnic par excellence. Reasonable prices.

*** THE FARMYARD RESTAURANT: On the Dubrovin Farm, Yesod HaMa'ala. Open from noon – 5 p.m. and from 7:30 p.m. – midnight. Sat. open all day. Closed on Mon. night. Tel. (06) 934495.**

Set on a farm originally built in 1884, the restaurant's heavy wood beams, stone walls and large fireplace mark it as one of the most charming country-style establishments in the country. A warm greeting, an abundance of plants and freshly cut flowers, the well-polished heavy wood tables and a variety of wine racks give the first clues that here one has wandered upon the most sophisticated culinary aspects of country living.

Leah and Gadi Barkus are the proprietors and hosts here, and it immediately becomes evident that they have a broad knowledge of what they are doing. Start off with the goose liver prepared in the Hungarian style or the vine leaves filled with a mixture of lamb, onions, rice and pine nuts. Then, because they smoke their own meats here, go on to either the smoked goose breast, trout, or sausages that are served with country-style Dijon mustard with excellent sauerkraut made in the

German style with juniper berries and caraway. Those who arrive for lunch will have to pay an admission fee to the farm, but this will be refunded by the restaurant. Prices are moderate to high. (To find the farm drive north from Rosh Pina and make a right turn to Yesod HaMa'ala.) (*)

***THE HOUSE (HABAYIT): G'dud Barak St., Tiberias. Open for lunch and dinner on Fri. and for lunch on Sat. Reservations recommended. Tel. (06) 792353.**

Unlike most places featuring Chinese and Thai food, this attractive, airy place is uncluttered, has no imitation rice paper prints and not even a single electrified lantern to disturb one's sense of aesthetics. In fact, the only visual clue that this is a Far Eastern eatery is in the attractive bamboo-framed windows. The service is friendly but not familiar, the table settings and view are attractive, and the food, while not quite "world class," is definitely worth sampling. The appetizers I most enjoy here are the shrimp and chicken dim sum, the fried calamari, and the various shrimp dishes. As main courses I find the chicken in coconut sauce, the beef sate and the fish fillets in ginger all rewarding. Depending on individual orders, dishes will be served not at all hot, mildly hot, extremely hot or unbelievably hot. Moderate prices.

*** THE PINE CLUB: on Beit-Oren Road, Mount Carmel, Haifa. Open for dinner from 7 p.m. – midnight and for lunch on Sat. from noon – 3 p.m. Closed Mon. Reservations strongly recommended. Tel. (04) 323568.**

Set in an attractive villa on Mount Carmel, with a large wood-burning fireplace, a lovely view, and a pleasant interior design, this French restaurant is a culinary oasis. The welcome is not always as warm as it might be, but the formal service is excellent and the food, despite occasional ups and downs, maintains a quality high enough to make a visit worthwhile. Owner-chef Fadi Karaman's cookery has pleasant touches of both the classic and the nouvelle cuisines. In addition to some of the very traditional dishes (paté de foie gras, onion soup and steak au poivre), all of which are good, some of the dishes most worth trying are the goose liver sautéed and served in a delicate raisin sauce; the terrine of vegetables and roquefort cheese; the lamb in mint sauce; and the crêpes filled with a marvellously herbed minced beef. Expensive.

• **VERED HAGALIL: in Korazim on the road from Rosh Pina to Zefat. For road directions or reservations tel. (06) 935785.**

In addition to offering horseback riding, cross-country hikes and a magnificent view, this beautiful ranch set in the lush hills of Galilee also has a restaurant that is worthy of note, especially for lunch. With lots of wood and glass and a remarkable collection of bric-a-brac scattered on the walls, the atmosphere falls somewhere in style between camp and kitsch. Despite, or possibly because of this, there is a feeling of charm here; and because owner Yehuda Avni comes from Chicago, the luncheon salads have a distinctly American flavour.

The chicken salad, with plenty of finely chopped chicken and green pepper, is good, as is the tuna salad. The chopped liver, with lots of chicken fat and chopped onion, and the coleslaw are also worth trying. For lunch continue with a hamburger, but for dinner consider the smoked trout, the cold salmon with tartar sauce, the smoked beef served in barbecue sauce, or the fresh young salmon. Whether you are having breakfast, lunch or dinner, do not under any circumstances pass up the opportunity to taste the delicious apple or berry pies that are always on the menu. Reasonable to moderate prices.

EILAT

• **AU BISTRO: Eilot St., in the City Centre. Open daily from 5 p.m. – midnight. Reservations recommended. Tel. (07) 374333.**

The dark blue velvet on the walls, the linen tablecloths and the attractive table settings make this intimate French restaurant attractive to the eye; and although the dishes offered here are rarely daring, they are always appealing. The fact that owner-chef Michel Tordiman is Belgian also adds an interesting culinary twist to many of the dishes. The goose liver with a sauce based on Cassis liqueur, the grilled shrimps and the seafood bisque, which is generously laden with shrimps, calamari and fresh fish, are always reliable. The main courses show a light, modern touch, and two of my favourites here are the veal in red wine sauce and the beef fillet Romayer. A la carte prices are expensive, but a more reasonable fixed-price menu is also offered.

• **LA BOHEME: on the Coral Beach. Open daily from 6:30 p.m. – 1 a.m. Reservations recommended. Tel. (07) 374222.**

Its small size, muted gold and red decor, and several attractive prints on the walls make this a warm and appealing restaurant. Many of the dishes listed are traditionally French and among the best first courses are the artichoke and asparagus served au gratin, and the foie gras au cassis. My personal choice for a main course here is the Chateaubriand steak, a thick cut from the center of the fillet (always served for two) that is garnished, as it should be, with chateau potatoes, vegetables that have been cooked in butter, and an excellent bernaise sauce. Other main courses worthy of note are the Tournedos à la Rossini, the shrimps in butter and garlic, and any of the fried fresh fish that appear on the menu on the day of your visit. Expensive.

THE LAST REFUGE, on the Coral Beach. Open daily from 1 p.m. – midnight. Tel. (07) 372437.

Situated on a quiet inlet to the Coral Beach, the view of the water and the fishing and diving boats one sees from wherever one takes a table make this a pleasant place to sit. The weathered wood, fishing nets, lanterns and anchor chains that comprise the decor may be a bit kitschy, but they add nicely to the admosphere and increase one's appetite for the fish and seafood that are the speciality here.

As first courses consider the coquille of seafood in which shrimps, calamari and forest mushrooms are served in a large seashell with a pleasant cream sauce, or the mussels in garlic, both of which are simple but delightful. The fish soup is also good and makes a fine starter. The major treats here are the fish which are so fresh that owner Adi Aharon is wise to serve them simply, either grilled or fried and with no garnish other than lemon. If the fish known locally as "denise" is available, be sure to order it, because this firm-fleshed, not at all fatty fish is one of the reasons the Red Sea has such a good name among gastronomes. Moderate prices.

• **MAI THAI: in the Old Tourist Centre. Open daily from 1 – 3 p.m. and from 6:30 – 11:30 p.m. Tel. (07) 375217.**

Uncluttered walls, plenty of windows, attractive table settings and the intentionally underplayed decor make this Thai restaurant more appealing to the eye and more sophisticated than many of its competitors. The greeting one receives on entering and the attentive service throughout the meal add to one's comfort; and even though the food has some distinctly Western touches, it is definitely a cut above the average. Among the most authentic and best Thai dishes on the extensive menu are the beef won san, the tom yum soup, the coconut soup, the crisp batter-fried duck, the fish in hot chili sauce, and the noodles with meat, shrimp and pork. Moderate to high prices.

• **MANDY'S: on the Coral Beach. Open daily from noon – 3 p.m. and from 6:30 p.m. – midnight. Tel. (07) 372238.**

An abundance of heavy bamboo partitions, woven straw parasols and odd post-surrealistic paintings on the walls give this Chinese restaurant the clear atmosphere of kitsch; but the warm greeting, the excellent service and the generally high quality of the food make it worth a visit. One will do well to ignore the standard offerings, the kind one finds in Chinese restaurants all over the world (except in China), and consider some of the house specialties. The dim sum, the mixed seafood platter and the spare ribs make for excellent openers. The rich shark's fin soup and the sour shrimp soup are both quite good; for main courses consider the shrimp with butter and garlic sauce, the chicken with water chestnuts, or the five spices beef. Moderate to high prices.

• PAGO-PAGO, on the northern bank of the Lagoon. Open daily from 1 p.m. – 2 a.m. or later. Dinner reservations recommended. Tel. (07) 376660.

Situated on a large barge docked in the lagoon, this fish and seafood restaurant has been part of the Eilat scene since 1986 and is as important to the city's social life as to gastronomy. The spicy Thai-style shrimp soup makes a good starter, as does the calamari portion that is done in the Greek way by coating it with a light batter and then deep frying it. Also worth considering are the shrimp which are split down the middle, seasoned generously with garlic, and sprinkled over with olive oil before being grilled. The various fish available are done simply but well. To satisfy your need for a sweet, be sure to try the chocolate marquise for desert. Moderate prices.

*** TANDOORI: On the King's Wharf, behind the Laguna Hotel. Open daily from noon – 3 p.m. and from 6:30 – after midnight. Reservations recommended. Tel. (07) 333879.**

The Madras fabrics, flowers and handsomely set tables make this Indian restaurant – the Eilat branch of the Tandoori chain – extremely pleasing to the eye. Some say that this is the best restaurant in the chain. Be that as it may, the service and the quality of the food are all one could want. For a description of some of the dishes offered see the listing of the restaurant in Tel Aviv. Moderate prices. (*)

STREET FOODS, MOVEABLE FEASTS

If any group of people have raised stand-up dining to an art form, it is the Israelis. It is not so much that people are in too much of a rush to sit down as that wherever one wanders a feast of Middle Eastern treats is being hawked from streetside stands, moveable carts and eateries so simple that fancy is something left entirely to the imagination. The two most popular foods for stand-up dining are felafel and shawarma. Felafel, deep-fried balls of chickpeas and seasonings, may be of dubious nutritional value, but when well made they are delicious and fun to eat. Shawarma, which is made from small, thin pieces of lamb, beef or turkey meat that are built up on a skewer in cylindrical form to a height of about two feet and then cooked on vertically rotating grills, is no less a pleasure.

The felafel balls or shawarma slices are then placed in a pita bread (nearly everything considered edible here eventually makes its way into a pita) and seasoned with tehina, humous, a variety of salads and seasonings. One of the "tricks" to master is managing to put as much as possible into the pita and then avoid having the contents of your sandwich drip on your clothing. This sounds easy enough until one realizes that the condiments available include such diverse treats as sauerkraut, red cabbage, marinated sweet and hot peppers, an assortment of olives, pickles made out of cucumbers, onions, tomatoes and carrots, and at least five different preparations of eggplant. Some purists will put only tehina and one salad on their felafel or shawarma. Others have mastered the feat of loading their sandwiches with ten or more salads.

Even though fine samples of both of these treats can be found in almost every neighbourhood, some of the very best felafel and shawarma in the country is to be bought in and around Jerusalem's Mahane Yehuda market, and in Tel Aviv's Betzalel market and Yemenite Quarter (which adjoins the Carmel market). Especially good felafel is also available along Derech Ha'atzmaut and Rehov Herzl in Haifa and near the Central Bus Stations of Beer Sheva, Tiberias and Acre.

Felafel and shawarma are only the beginning of the story. Boiled, seasoned chick peas, hot grilled corn, and a variety of Middle Eastern breads are also available at streetside stands. Some say the best of these treats are to be found in Jaffa, but all agree that the offerings in Nazareth, Jerusalem and Beer Sheva are not far behind. One bakery in Jaffa, for example, makes twenty-five different kinds of bread, eleven kinds of rolls, and nine kinds of pitas, many of which are destined to be consumed either standing at the counter or while strolling. Be sure to try your pita bread sprinkled over with olive oil and za'atar – the Biblical hyssop – which is an exquisite herb.

A bit higher up on the fast-food ladder are "shipudim" – skewers of meat cooked over small charcoal braziers. It surprises very few to find bits of beef, chicken, turkey and lamb meat and liver on skewers, but it astonishes many when they learn that only in Israel do we also grill goose liver – the famous foie gras and then sell it at remarkably reasonable prices. Most of the places that serve such snacks arc so simplc that they have tables but rarely tablecloths. Knives and forks are always available at such places, but there is a good chance that the waiter will have to be reminded to bring them to the table. None of these factors should be taken as drawbacks, for these meat-laden skewers are culinary delights that would be the envy of many fine European and American chefs. The very best places in the country to seek out these delights is in the area known as the Hatikva Quarter of Tel Aviv. On Etzel Street alone there are at least twenty such places, any one of which serves marvellous foods. Personally, I always seek out the simplest of these places because the food there is invariably best and the prices lowest.

Because Israel is a Mediterranean country, fish has also become an integral part of informal dining. In addition to fine and sophisticated fish and seafood restaurants, many eateries in the port area of Jaffa, as well as in Caesarea, Atlit and Akko, specialize in what might be thought of as "just plain fish." Fried or grilled and garnished with lemon halves, there may be no better way to enjoy the sea. Despite the simplicity of such places, however, fish are not inexpensive. They are, however, well worth the investment.

TOURIST ROUTES

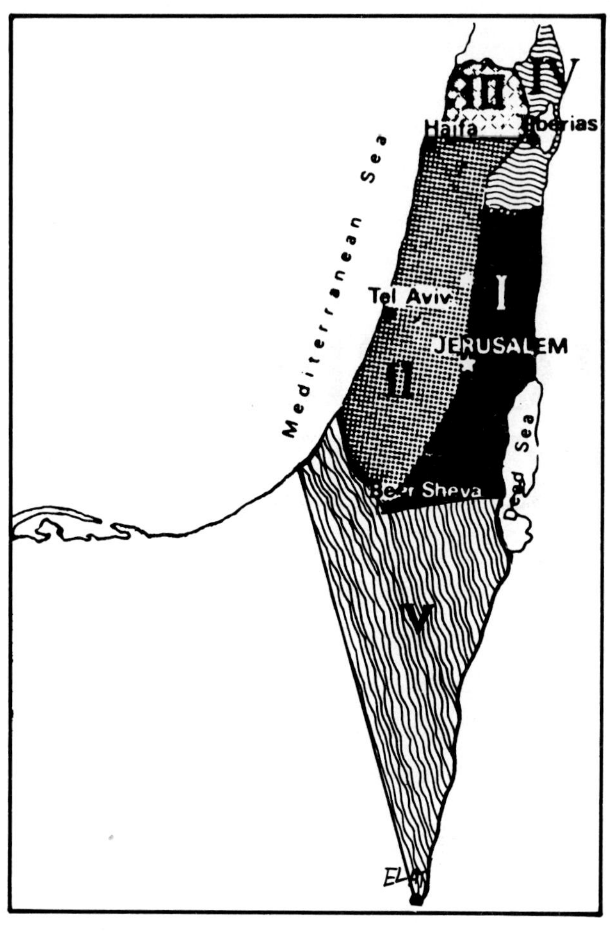

Explanation of Map of Tourist Routes

Area I includes Routes Nos. 1, 2, 3, 4

Area II includes Route Nos. 3, 5, 6, 7, 8, 9, 10, 11, 12

Area III includes Route Nos. 13, 14, 15, 16

Area IV includes Route Nos. 17, 18, 19, 20, 21

Area V includes Route Nos. 22, 23, 24

TOURIST ROUTES

Our driving routes radiate from five major cities – Jerusalem, Tel Aviv, Haifa, Tiberias and Beer Sheva.

Each of these centres is the point of departure for another major city. In some cases alternative destinations are suggested where a route reaches a principal tourist attraction near more than one major city.

Our map shows at a glance all the regions covered by the routes; we have listed accommodation available along the way. The selection caters to every taste, and includes hotels, Christian hospices, camp sites, holiday villages and youth hostels.

The highways and roads are numbered at the beginning of each route. (Road signs are in Hebrew, Arabic and English.)

Judaea and Samaria

(Map: Northern Sheet)

The Holy Land is quintessentially Judaea and Samaria. The Patriarchs were the first to endow Judaea (Yehuda) and Samaria (Shomron) with a mystical presence. Then the land became the assembly point for the conquering tribes of Israel. Forever after it became the centripetal force of Judaism following King David's proclamation of Jerusalem as the capital and King Solomon's construction of the Temple.

Much of Judaea is blanketed with pines and other species of trees under the Keren Kayemet's afforestation projects. They are the evidence of how much effort has gone into transforming this hallowed sector of Israel.

Samaria remains truer to its biblical past because time and technology have passed it by. Many are the villages sheltered by olive groves. The Arab farmers may be slow in substituting mechanized farming methods for the ox-drawn plough, but they retain a pristine ease of life and a clarity of values.

History stamped Judaea and Samaria with its stony imprint. The ancient ruins of houses, tombs, synagogues, churches and mosques are but stepping stones to the next historic site.

There is only one way to make the most of your visit. Take your Bible with you. It is an indispensable companion in Judaea and Samaria. The verses that you recite relate to the soil on which you stand. The experience is anything but melodramatic or sentimental. It is nothing short of personal witness at the cradle of monotheism and total involvement with elements that shaped the Western mind.

This area has been appearing a good deal on TV screens lately, but many places there are worth a visit. For information on specific routes and sites, apply to the Ministry of Tourism or to the Society for the Protection of Nature in Israel.

Jerusalem (Yerushalayim)

(Map: Northern Sheet J–K17–18. See also the coloured city maps, on Southern Sheet.)

INTRODUCTION

To visit Jerusalem is to visit one of the world's great cities. Jerusalem is not only glowing golden in colour (for all Jerusalem buildings must be faced in pale fawn-coloured stone from local quarries), but a golden repository of 3,000 years of history, sacred to three religions. With its ancient lanes and markets and its modern areas, Jerusalem is an exhilarating mixture of sights, sounds and cultures. There is no other city like it.

Jerusalem stands on the crest of rolling hills 835 metres above sea level. People talk of going "up" to Jerusalem from every other part of the country, in both a spiritual and physical sense. This is a city where crenellated 16th century walls enclose 200 acres of tightly packed history and archaeology. Here a colourful population of Moslems, Jews, and Christians tread the same paths that King David, Jesus and the Crusaders once walked.

Yet Jerusalem is far from being simply a memorial to the past. Outside the walls of the old town lies a modern, vital new city, where industry, luxury hotels, a thriving academic and medical community, the arts, parks and up-to-date residential sections – even discos – provide an everyday reality for more than 557,000 people.

And what a variety of people! Exotic sights lie around every corner. On Fridays, Franciscan friars in mediaeval robes lead pilgrims along the Via Dolorosa, the Way of the Cross, as they have been doing for 600 years. Narrow streets house churches and shrines of Armenian, Coptic, Syrian and Ethiopian Christians, to name but a few.

At the magnificent grey-domed El-Aksa Mosque on the Temple Mount, Moslem worshippers touch their heads to the ground in devotion, after the wailing voice of the muezzin has called them to prayer. In contrast, Orthodox Jews, in the black garb worn by eighteenth-century Polish noblemen, and women modestly dressed in stockings and long sleeves even on the hottest days, hurry along the streets in areas that resemble the intimate European ghettos of their ancestors.

And in the new city, well-dressed sophisticates survey the passing parade from cosmopolitan outdoor cafes on Ben Yehuda Street, and dance at night in up-to-the-minute discos. Definitely a city with something for everyone!

HISTORY

Has any other place in history been so turbulently and so hotly contested? For three thousand years, the city has waxed and waned in its fortunes, has been conquered and reconquered by a parade of Canaanites, Assyrians, Babylonians, Greeks, Romans, Jews, Moslems and Crusaders. Its extraordinary character remains. After every conquest, the city has risen again, leaving yet another layer of archaeological history under its stones.

We know that Jerusalem existed four thousand years ago because the place was mentioned in Egyptian hieroglyphic texts. Even in palaeolithic times, man lived here. In the Canaanite era, around the time of Abraham, the town contained a shrine to local gods.

Jerusalem first became a significant centre when David, as the Bible tells us, purchased the threshing floor on Mount Moriah and built an altar there (2 Samuel 24: 18–25), around the year 1000 BCE. Jerusalem became the political and spiritual capital of the twelve tribes of Israel.

Under the rule of David's son, King Solomon, Jerusalem became the centre of the nation. The splendid

First Temple, described in great detail in the Book of Kings, was perhaps Solomon's most important achievement.

When the kingdom split in two after Solomon's death in 925 BCE, Jerusalem remained capital of the southern kingdom, Judah. It continued to expand during the rule of King Hezekiah some two hundred years later. Under threat of attack from the Assyrian king Sennacherib, Hezekiah built a giant rampart connecting the sections of Jerusalem to the west, and an ingenious tunnel to bring water to the city from the Gihon spring. The attack was averted, and the tunnel survives today.

But in 586 BCE, the city fell to the Babylonian forces of Nebuchadnezzar and the First Temple was destroyed. The Jews were exiled, though many soon returned to rebuild the Temple when Cyrus of the Persians succeeded the Babylonians.

Two hundred years later, a new people took over control of Jerusalem. The Greeks under the Ptolemies and later the Seleucids introduced a seductive and oppressive Hellenistic culture to Jerusalem, which triggered a successful revolt by the Jewish Hasmonaeans (Maccabees). Once again for a short time Jerusalem was in Jewish hands.

Within three generations, though, a new ruling force came to the city – the Romans, under whose rule (particularly under King Herod in 37–4 BCE) the city grew and developed. Herod rebuilt and refurbished the Temple after enlarging the Temple Mount. He constructed palaces, theatres and sophisticated water systems – all the impressive appurtances of a successful Roman city. Its population has been estimated as a sizeable 150,000. It was shortly after this period that Jesus was crucified by the Roman procurator Pontius Pilate outside the city.

Once again the Jews revolted against Roman oppression in 66 CE, an uprising which was cruelly crushed by Titus. The Temple was destroyed, and its menorah and other treasures triumphantly borne off as booty.

In 132 CE, after Emperor Hadrian attempted to rid the city, which he renamed Aelia Capitolina, of its Jews, Bar Kochba led an unsuccessful revolt.

The following centuries introduced a parade of new rulers and faiths – the Christian emperor Constantine in the fourth century; the Moslems in the seventh century; the Crusaders in the eleventh century and the Ottomans in the sixteenth. Under the Ottoman emperor Suleiman, the city prospered and the walls were rebuilt in 1547, but from then on, it declined.

Nevertheless, the Jewish presence grew. In 1800, Jerusalem had about 1,800 Jewish inhabitants out of 9,000, a number which grew to 45,000 out of about 70,000 in 1914. As the population grew, so did expansion outside the old walls. Jews built residential neighbourhoods such as Mishkenot Sha'ananim, with its well-known windmill, and Mea She'arim; Christians built impressive churches, hostels and schools which still lend a European character to parts of the city today.

After the First World War, Jerusalem became the capital of Palestine under the British Mandate. This was a period of municipal expansion, with the construction of many Jerusalem landmarks, such as the YMCA building and the Rockfeller museum. At the same time, it was a period of Arab-Jewish disturbances and turmoil in the city. Jews in the Old City tended to retreat to the Jewish quarter, while Jewish resistance to what was seen as British anti-Zionist bias culminated in the blowing-up of British army offices in the King David hotel.

When the UN General Assembly voted to partition Palestine into Jewish and Arab sectors in 1947, Jerusalem was assigned the status of an international city. The War of Independence which followed prevented that; the Old City of Jerusalem was beseiged by the Jordanians.

In May 1948, the Jewish quarter in the old city surrendered to the Jordanian forces. The city was now partitioned into two halves, a situation which remained in force until the Six Day War in June 1967.

The war lasted only three days in Jerusalem. Israeli paratroopers surrounded and quickly occupied the whole of the Old City, in a move that electrified and moved the world. The barbed wire and ugly walls were torn down. Once again, the city was one, and the Western Wall lay in Jewish hands.

Jerusalem today – A mosaic of communities

Jerusalem has been legally united since 1967, but peace lies uneasy on these ancient stones. Though the two sides co-exist reasonably well, due in large part to the efforts of Jerusalem's innovative and tolerant mayor, Teddy Kollek, Jerusalem still remains a city of ethnically distinct and separate neighbourhoods. There are, for example, two separate downtown areas, two bus systems and even two electricity grids.

The city is divided between its many religious inhabitants and its secular population, and even between subgroups of religious communities.

When the Israeli government formally annexed East Jerusalem in 1967 the city had a population of about 65,000 Arabs and 200,000 Jews. Today about 401,000 Jews, more than 130,000 Moslems, and about 14,000 Christians live in this thriving city. Almost 1 million tourists add to the din and cosmopolitan atmosphere every year.

Once a dingy backwater, Jerusalem has undergone a frenzy of building since 1967, much of it exceptionally well planned by an international advisory committee of top world architects. Teddy Kollek has remarked that each of these architects has two cities: his own and Jerusalem. This careful and loving planning has led to architectural marvels such as the rebuilt Jewish quarter of the Old City, with its painstakingly restored Hurvah, Ramban and Four Sephardi synagogues, the new Tower of David museum and the impressive Jerusalem Theatre.

Today, because of the strains of the intifada, many tourists feel uncomfortable in parts of the Old City, such as the Arab market, where once they circulated freely. Still, Jerusalem continues to grow and to fascinate.

In spite of differences of opinion on many issues, Israelis of every political persuasion are convinced of one thing. The walls which once divided this extraordinary city must never rise again. Jerusalem must remain a free, undivided city where all faiths have unlimited access and rights to their own holy places.

ORIENTATION

Getting around in Jerusalem

Jerusalem is not an immensely large city, and it is not difficult to get from one place to another. The ideal way to get around is on foot (see section on Walks in Jerusalem) which gives the visitor a chance to know the city's streets, atmosphere and people. Public transport is also adequate, and taxis are readily available in main areas.

Buses are frequent and convenient, though they may

be crowded. The Central Bus Station, which serves most parts of the city, is on Jaffa St. at the western end of the city and has an information booth. Inter-city buses also run from here. Remember that bus service stops about an hour before Sabbath on Friday evening through Saturday evening. For information call (02)304704.

Bus Tour of the Main Sites

One of the best ways to tour the city is by Bus 99, the Jerusalem Circular line, which tours the main centres of interest. It departs from Jaffa Gate every two hours, Sun.–Thur. 9 a.m. to 5 p.m. and on Fridays 9 a.m. to 2 p.m.

Group tours are arranged by many private firms, including Egged. Details are usually available at hotels.

Shopping

Although ancient crafts and coins, copper, jewellery and Judaica are good buys in Jerusalem, the city also has a good selection of up-to-date stores and boutiques. Main shopping areas in the new city are Jaffa St., King George St. and the Ben Yehuda pedestrian mall, and the Mea She' arim quarter for Judaica. The Old City market (shuk) is colourful and fun, as is the fruit and vegetable market of Mahane Yehuda, on Jaffa Road. Other shopping places of interest are the Cardo in the Jewish Quarter and Khutzot Hayotzer (Artists' Lane) opposite Jaffa Gate.

Culture and Entertainment

The world-famous Jerusalem Symphony Orchestra performs at the Henry Crown Symphony Hall, in the Jerusalem Theatre complex. Concerts are also held at the YMCA Auditorium, Binyanei Ha'uma, the Lutheran Church in the Old City and at the Dormition Abbey on Mount Zion. From time to time in summer, outdoor concerts are presented at the Merrill Hassenfeld Amphitheatre at the Sultan's Pool, outside the Old City near Jaffa Gate.

Theatrical performances are regularly held at the Jerusalem Theatre and the Khan Theatre, among others.

There are many cinemas in Jerusalem, showing popular films in their original language, subtitled in Hebrew. At the Cinematheque on Hebron Rd and Maison Alliance Française (for French films) on Agron St., serious films are screened.

Bars and discotheques are popular, particularly in the area of the Nahlat Shiva quarter and Zion Square.

For listings of entertainment in Jerusalem in English, see the Friday edition of the Jerusalem Post.

ACCOMMODATION

HOTELS

K = kosher.

King David. Tel.(02)251111. 23 King David St. K.
Hyatt Regency Jerusalem. Tel.(02)331234. 32 Lehi St. K.
Seven Arches. Tel.(02)894455. Mt. of Olives.
Jerusalem Hilton. Tel.(02)581414. Givat Ram. K.
Sheraton Jerusalem Plaza. Tel.(02)259111. 47 King George St. K.
King Solomon Tel.(02)241433. 32 King David St. K.
Laromme Tel.(02)756666. 3 Jabotinsky Street. K.
Moriah Jerusalem. Tel.(02)232232. 39, Keren Hayesod St. K.
Jerusalem Renaissance. Tel.(02)528111. 6 Wolfson St. K.
St. George Jerusalem. Tel. (02)282571. Salah Eddin St.
American Colony. Tel.(02)285171. Nablus Rd.
Ariel. Tel.(02)719222. 31 Hebron Rd. K.
Caesar. Tel.(02)382156. 208 Jaffa St. K.
Central. Tel. (02)384111. 6 Pines St. K.
Holyland West. Tel.(02)437777. Bayit Vegan. K.
Jerusalem Panorama. Tel.(02)272277. Hill of Gethsemane.
Kings. Tel. (02)247133. 60 King George St. K.
Knesset Tower. Tel. (02)511111. 4 Wolfson St. K.
Mount Zion. Tel.(02)724222. 17 Hebron Rd. K.
Mount Scopus. Tel. (02)828891. 10 Sheikh Jarrah.
National Palace. Tel.(02)273273. 4 Az-Zahra St.
Shalom. Tel.(02)752211. Bayit Vegan. K.
Sonesta Jerusalem. Tel.(02)528221. 2 Wolfson St. K.
Windmill. Tel.(02)663111, 3 Mendele St. K.
Zohar. Tel.(02)717557. 47 Leib Jaffa St. K.
Alcazar. Tel.(02)281111. 6 Almutabi St.
Gloria. Tel.(02)282431. Jaffa Gate.
Holyland East. Tel.(02)272888. 6 Rashid St.
Jerusalem Meridian. Tel.(02)285212. 5 Ali Ibn Ali Taleb.
Jerusalem Tower. Tel.(02)252161. 23 Hillel St. K.
Palace. Tel.(02)271126. Mount of Olives.

Pilgrims Palace. Tel.(02)272416. Sultan Suleiman St.
Reich. Tel.(02)523121. 1 Hagai St., Beit Hakerem. K.
Tirat Bat Sheva. Tel. (02)232121. 42 King George St. K.
YMCA. Tel.(02)257111. 26 King David St.
Lawrence. Tel.(02)894208. 18 Salah Eddin St.
Metropole. Tel.(02)282507. 6 Salah Eddin St.
Mount of Olives. Tel.(02)284877. Mt. of Olives Rd.
New Regent. Tel.(02)284540. 20 Az-Zahra St.
Palatin. Tel.(02)231141. 4 Agrippas St. K.
Pilgrims Inn. Tel.(02)284883. Rashidia St.
Rivoli. Tel.(02)284871. 3 Salah Eddin St.
Ron. Tel.(02)253471. 44 Jaffa St. K.
Victoria. Tel.(02)274466. 8 Masudie St.
Christmas. Tel.(02)2825888. Salah Eddin St.
Jerusalem Gate. Tel. (02)383101. 43 Yirmiyahu St. K.
Ritz. Tel.(02)273233. 8 Ibn Khaldoun St.
Azzahra. Tel.(02)282447. 13 Az-Zahra St.
YMCA. Tel.(02)282375. 29 Nablus Rd.
YWCA. Tel. (02) 282593. Wadi Jose.
Holiday Village Recreation Centre, Jerusalem Forest. Tel. (02) 416060. P.O. Box 3353. K.

KIBBUTZ GUEST HOUSES

Shoresh. Tel.(02)341171. Judaean Hills. K.
Neve Ilan. Tel.(02)341241. Judean Hills. K.
Qiryat Anavim. Tel.(02)348999. Judaean Hills. K.
Ma'ale Hahamisha. Tel.(02)342591. Judaean Hills. K.
Mitzpeh Rachel. Tel.(02)702555. M.P., North Judaea 90900. K.

CHRISTIAN HOSPICES FOR PILGRIMS AND STUDENTS

Armenian Catholic Church Tel. (02) 284262
41, Via Dolorosa, 3rd Station. P. O. B. 19546.
Austrian House, Jerusalem Tel. (02) 286545
Catholic. 37 Via Dolorosa. P.O.B. 19600.
Casa Nova Tel. (02) 282791
Franciscan. Casa Nova Rd. Old City. P. O. B. 1321.
Centre Bethesda Tel. (02) 285587
(ladies only). Roman Catholic, French. 22 St. Mark St.
Centre Notre Dame Tel. (02) 289723
Opposite New Gate. Roman Catholic, ecumenical. P.O.B. 20531.

Christ Church Hospice Tel. (02) 289234
Anglican. Jaffa Gate. P. O. B. 14307.
Dom Polski Tel. (02) 285916
Catholic (Polish). 8 Hahoma Hashlishit St., West Jerusalem. P. O. B. 277.
Dom Polski Tel. (02) 282017
Catholic (Polish). Near Damascus Gate, Old City. P.O.B. 20256.
Ecce Homo Convent Tel. (02) 282445
(Sisters of Zion. Guest House. Youth Hostel for girls only). Catholic. Via Dolorosa. P. O. B. 19056.
Filles de la Charite Tel. (02) 284726
Catholic (French). Bethany Shiya. P. O. B. 19080.
Foyer St. Joseph Tel. (02) 383674
Catholic. 66, Rehov Hanevi'im. P. O. B. 771.
Franciscans of Mary Tel. (02) 282633
(White Sisters. For girls). 9, Nablus Rd. P. O. B. 19049.
Greek Catholic Patriarchate Tel. (02) 282023
Jaffa Gate, Old City. P. O. B. 14130.
Lutheran Hostel Tel. (02) 282120
St. Marks St. P. O. B. 14051.
Lutheran Hostel Tel. (02)282543
(for girls). Church of the Redeemer, Muristan Rd., Old City. P. O. B. 194076.
Maison d'Abraham Tel. (02) 284591
(for poor pilgrims, by special application to director.) Mount of Offence. P. O. B. 19680.
Pie Madri of Nigrizia Tel. (02) 284724
Catholic (Italian). Bethany Shiya. P. O. B. 19504.
Sisters of the Rosary Tel. (02) 228529
Catholic (French). 14, Rehov Agron, P. O. B. 54.
Sisters of Zion Tel. (02) 415738
Haoren St., Ein Karem. P. O. B. 3705
St. Andrew's Hospice Tel. (02) 732401
Church of Scotland. Near Railway Station. P. O. B. 14216.
St. Charles Borromaeus Hospice Tel. (02) 637737
Catholic (German). German Colony. P. O. B. 8020
St. George's Hostel Tel. (02) 283302
Anglican. 20 Nablus Rd. & Saladin St. P. O. B. 19018.
St. John's Convent Tel. (02)413639
Franciscan. Groups only. Ein Karem. P.O.B. 1704.

The Old City of Jerusalem. Arab women at market.

YOUTH HOSTELS

Louise Waterman Wise
8 Rehov Hapisgah Tel. (02)423366
Bayit Vegan 420990
Beit Bernstein
1 Keren Hayesod St. Tel. (02)258286
Registration on Friday, before sunset.
Jewish Quarter Youth Hostel Tel. (02)288611
Old City. 2 Ararat St.
Kfar Etzion, Gush Etzion Tel (02)935133
Near Hebron. Closed Friday afternoon to Saturday night & holidays.
En Karem Tel. (02)4162822
3 kms. from Mt. Herzl.
Beit Shmuel 13 King David St. Tel. (02)203466
Jerusalem Forest Tel. (02)416060
Kiryat Anavim Tel. (02)342770

USEFUL ADDRESSES AND NUMBERS

Government Tourist Information Offices: 24 King George St., tel. (02)241281. Open: Sun. – Thurs. 8.30 a.m. – 5 p.m. Fri. 8.30 a.m.– 2 p.m.; Jaffa Gate, Old City, tel. (02)282295/6. Hours as above.

Municipal Tourist Information Office: 17 Rehov Yafo, tel. (02)228844. Open Sun. – Thurs. 8 a.m. – 6 p.m. Fri. to 1.30 p.m.

Christian Information Centre: Jaffa Gate, tel. (02)272692. P.O.B. 14308.

Postal Services: the main post office at 23, Rehov Yafo, is open daily between 7 a.m. and 7 p.m.; Fridays, until noon; closed on Saturdays. There is a 24-hour telegram service. (see Postal Information).

Magen David Adom (first aid): tel. 101. (In addition to running the ambulance service, they arrange emergency home calls from 8 p.m. to 7 a.m. by doctors at fixed rates.)

Police: tel. 100.

Fire Brigade: tel. 102.

WORSHIP

SYNAGOGUES

Baba Tama Synagogue – Bukharan Quarter.

Centre for Conservative Judaism – Agron St.

Emeth Ve'emuna – 1 Rehov Hanarkis (Conservative).

Habad Synagogue – Rehov Habad, Jewish Quarter, Old City.

Har-El Synagogue – 16, Rehov Shmuel Hanagid (Reform Progressive).

Hebrew Union College Synagogue – 13, Rehov David Hamelekh (Reform).

Hechal Shlomo Great Synagogue – 58 Rehov Hamelekh George.

Issa Bracha – 31, Rehov Jabotinsky, Talbieh (Sephardi and Ashkenazi).

Italian Synagogue – 24, Rehov Hillel.

Midrash Porat Yosef Synagogue – Rehov Geula.

Mt. Zion Synagogue – Mt. Zion (Ashkenazi and Sephardi).

Rehavia – 22, Rehov Ussishkin (Ashkenazi).

Western Wall – Services are held whenever a minyan is formed, which is quite often. Always open. Many go to the Wall for Shabbat prayers.

Yeshurun Central Synagogue – 44, Rehov Hamelekh George (Ashkenazi).

CHURCHES

Roman Catholic:

Note: There is a daily procession at the Holy Sepulchre at 4 p.m. and from the First Station along Via Dolorosa on Friday at 3 p.m. Gethsemane Holy Hour is marked the first Thursday of each month at 4 p.m. in winter. During daylight saving time, services are one hour later.

Church of the Holy Sepulchre – Old City.

Chapel of Flagellation – Via Dolorosa, Old City.

Church of St. Stephen – Nablus Rd.

Church of St. Anne – Lions' Gate.

Church of the Visitation – (Franciscan) Ein Karem.

Church of St. John the Baptist – (Franciscan) Ein Karem.

Dormition Abbey – (Benedictine) Mt. Zion.

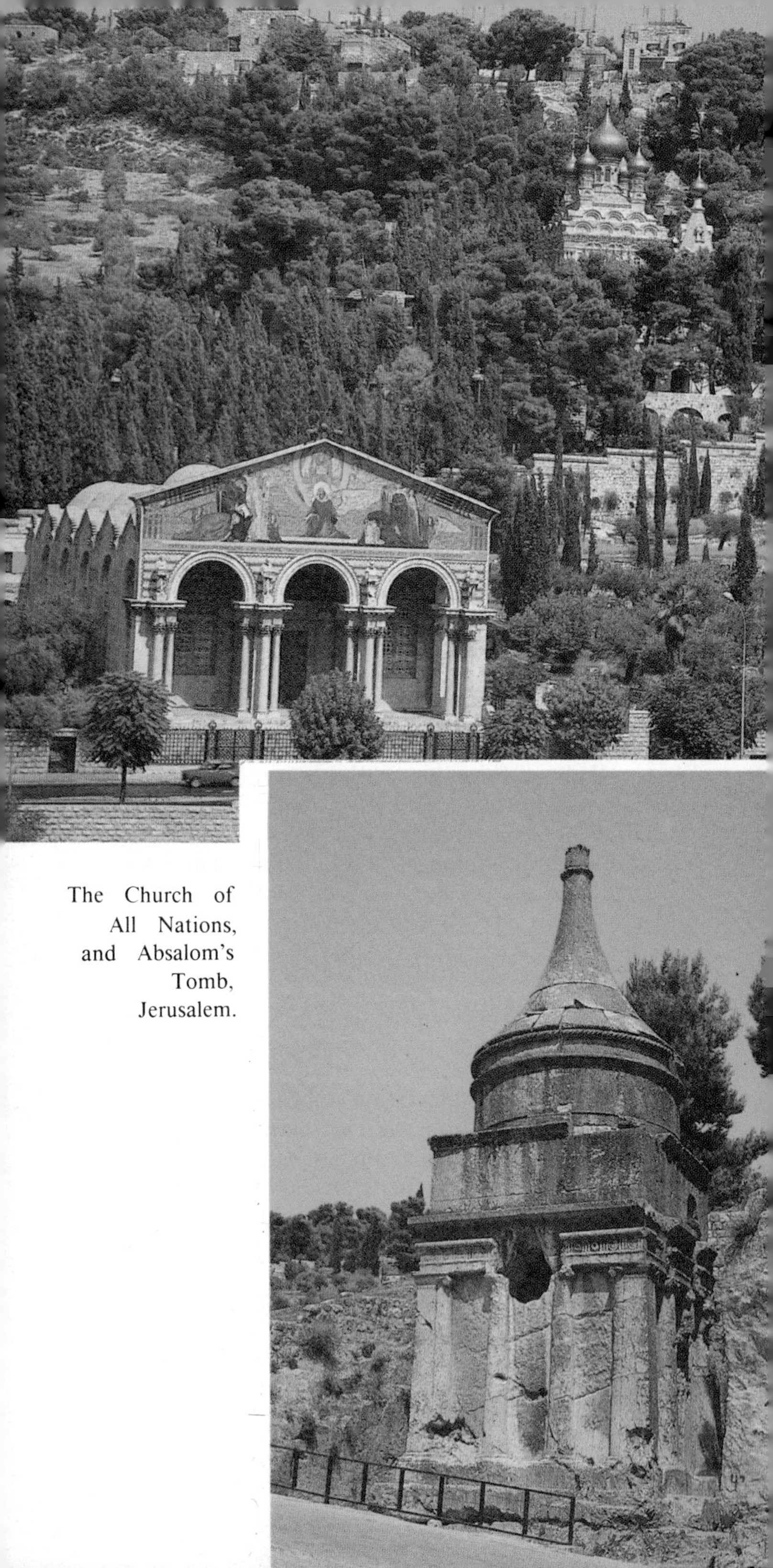

The Church of All Nations, and Absalom's Tomb, Jerusalem.

Dome of the Rock (above), and the Jordanian mountains seen from the Mt. of Olives.

Dominus Flevit – (Franciscan) Mt. of Olives.
Latin Patriarchate – Jaffa Gate or New Gate.
Lithostrotos (Sisters of Zion) – Via Dolorosa, Old City.
Notre Dame de France – (Assumptionists) 18 Rehov Shivtei Yisrael.
St. Saviour's Parish Church – St. Francis St., New Gate.
Terra Sancta College – Rehov Hamelekh George.

Greek Catholic:

Greek Catholic Patriarchate – Jaffa Gate.

Armenian Orthodox:

Cathedral of St. James – Armenian Orthodox Patriarch Road.

Coptic:

Coptic Orthodox Patriarchate – Souq Khan e-Zeit.

Protestant:

Church of the Nazarene – 33, Nablus Rd.
Anglican Church – St. Paul's Church, Rehov Shivtei Yisrael.
Baptist Chapel – Rehov Hanarkis.
Baptist Southern Worship – Al-Rashid Street.
First Baptist Bible Church – (Independent) Saladin St.
Church of Scotland – St. Andrew's Church, Rehov Harakevet.
Seventh Day Adventists – Advent House.
Y.M.C.A. – Rehov David Hamelekh.
St. George's Cathedral (Anglican) – Nablus Rd.
Christ Church – (Anglican Charismatic) opposite Citadel, Old City.
Church of the Redeemer – (Lutheran) Muristan, Old City.

Eastern Orthodox:

Ethiopian Orthodox Church – Rehov Ethiopia.

Greek Orthodox Church – St. Simeon, Katamon.

Russian Orthodox Cathedral of St. Trinity – Russian Compound.

Russian Orthodox Church of St. Maria Magdalena – Mt. of Olives.

OBSERVATION POINTS

Walter and Elise Haas Promenade: Perhaps the most impressive view of Jerusalem is that from the ridge leading from Hebron Road to the former British Government House (today the UN Headquarters) and to the new suburb of East Talpiot. A promenade 600 yards long and six wide has been built here out of golden Jerusalem stone. Special lighting has been installed. From the promenade, you look down across the valley to the walls of the Old City, Mt. Zion and the Arab village of Silwan. In the distance, the Mount of Olives and Mount Scopus can be seen. Leading onwards from the Haas Promenade and sweeping down and around to the Abu Tor neighbourhood is an even newer walkway – the **Gabriel Sherover Promenade**. Opened recently, this promenade descends through beautifully landscaped and carefully tended gardens, with equally magnificent views over the Old City and the surrounding areas.

(Bus Nos. 8, 48)

Mount of Olives: Spectacular views of the Temple Mount, Kidron Valley and beyond.

(Bus No. 99)

Mount Scopus: Looks towards the Temple Mount and Old City; the new suburb of Ma'ale Adumim can also be seen, as well as the 2,000-year-old fortress of Herodion, and the Dead Sea.

(Bus Nos. 4, 9, 26, 28)

Nebi Samuel: The traditional tomb of the Prophet Samuel, near the Ramot neighbourhood. Looks towards western Jerusalem, the Mount of Olives, Mount Scopus and Ramallah.

(Bus No. 36)

Bethlehem.

Church of the Holy Sepulchre

City Tower: King George St. Marvellous views of the entire city, old and new, from the restaurant at the top.

(Bus Nos. 4, 9, 14, 32)

Ramparts Walk: (see entry in section "Places to Visit").

A Selection of Interesting Places Arranged by Area

The Old City: Walk along ramparts, see Jewish sites – Western Wall, Temple Mount excavations, Ramban Synagogue, ruins of Hurva synagogue, Sephardi synagogues, Cardo, Burnt House, Old Yishuv Court Museum. Christian sites – Via Dolorosa, St. Anne's Church, Church of the Holy Sepulchre, Greek Orthodox Patriarchate Museum, Armenian Church of St James, Armenian Museum. Moslem sites – Temple Mount, El-Aksa Mosque, Dome of the Rock.

Mount Scopus: Hebrew University, Hadassah Hospital.

Mount of Olives: (viewpoint), Chapel of the Ascension, Jewish cemetery, Dominus Flevit, Church of St. Mary Magdalene, Basilica of the Agony.

Outside the walls: From Mt. Zion – King David's Tomb, Cenaculum (Hall of Last Supper), Church of the Dormition, Yemin Moshe area and Montefiore's windmill.

Mea She'arim: Ultra-Orthodox Jewish area.

Knesset Area: Knesset, Wohl Rose Park, Israel Museum, Monastery of the Cross.

To the West: Yad Vashem, Mount Herzl, Second Temple Jerusalem model at Holyland Hotel. Ein Karem, Church of St. John the Baptist, Hadassah Hospital (Chagall windows), Kennedy memorial.

PLACES TO VISIT

Any meaning to be derived from the sites of Jerusalem must be based on some knowledge of its history. But more than the raw material of facts one needs an imagination alive enough to grasp the texture of vanished societies from gutted ruins or restored shrines that hardly resemble their former shapes.

The story of Jerusalem is still unfolding; as archaeologists excavate new sites, new – often contradictory – light is thrown on old "facts." Some of the sites around which tourists are shown aren't always what some claim and other believe them to be. Nonetheless, the very stones form a genuine link with antiquity and serve to remind visitors of events which in most cases undoubtedly occurred, albeit perhaps in locations other than those pointed out.

An asterisk indicates that the site is within the **Old City**. See coloured maps on Southern Sheet. We have also indicated the numbers of the walks and the bus routes that lead to the site or pass near it.

Absalom's Pillar: Kidron Valley, off Hashiloah Road, opposite Gihon Spring. A large conical monument above one of the several tombs to be found in the valley. Absalom was David's son and tradition incorrectly ascribes this Second Temple pillar-like construction to him – (2 Samuel, 18:18). Also known as Pharaoh's Tiara because of its Egyptian appearance.

(Bus Nos. 42,43)

Abu Tor: east of Railway Station. Panoramic view of Old City and Kidron and Hinnom Valleys. Arabic name "Abu Tor" means "Father of the Ox."

(Bus Nos. 5, 6, 7, 21)

***African Quarter:** Ala 'Uddin (Aladdin) Street, Moslem Quarter. Inhabitants may be descendants of 16th century pilgrims or labourers from Sudan, Chad and Somalia. Housed in 13th century Mameluke school and hospice, former of which Ottomans converted into prison cells for condemned men.

(Walk No. 2)

Agnon House: 16, Klausner St. Talpiot. The house of

Barmitzva celebration at the Western Wall.

author S.Y. Agnon, winner of the Nobel Prize for literature, has been renovated and opened to the public. The house contains Agnon's study and library of 10,000 books with its original furnishings, including the desk at which he wrote. Visting hours: Sun.–Thurs. 9 a.m. to noon. Tel. (02)716498.

(Bus No. 7)

Agricultural Museum: 13 Rehov Heleni Hamalka, off Rehov Yafo, was inaugurated in 1961 by the then Minister of Agriculture, Moshe Dayan. Israelis justifiably take pride in their advanced agricultural technology; exhibits here range back to farming methods used 2,000 years ago (presses, pipes, wells, etc) Open: daily, 7.30 a.m. – 3 p.m. Friday until 2 p.m. Admission free.

(Bus Nos. 4, 18, 21)

American Colony: northeast of city. Quarter founded by American Christians in the 19th century. Contains U.S. Consulate, St. George's Cathedral, the YMCA in East Jerusalem and the American Colony Hotel.

(Bus Nos. 25, 27)

Ammunition Hill (Givat Hatahmoshet): flanked by Sderot Eshkol and Nablus Road, near foot of Mt. Scopus. It was a strategic military area in Jordanian hands from 1948 to 1967 when, after heavy fighting, the Israelis took it and went on to take East Jerusalem. Jordanian bunkers left as memorial to dead who fell in bitter fighting. The memorial and museum are dedicated to the reunification of Jerusalem after the Six Day War. Open: Sun.–Thurs. 9 a.m.–4 p.m., Fri. 9 a.m.–1 p.m. Admission free. Tel. (02)828422.

(Bus Nos. 4, 9, 25, 26, 28, 48)

***Antonia Fortress:** remains of Herodian palace-fortress guarding north side of the Temple. Pontius Pilate resided in it when Jesus was brought before him. Remnants at start of Via Dolorosa.

(Walk No. 3)

Arab Legion Camp: constructed with Jewish tombstones pulled from Mt. of Olives cemetery during Jordanian occupation 1948–67. East of Bethany, on the old road to Jericho.

(Route No. 1)

Archaeological Excavations: Many landmarks give a revealing insight into Jerusalem's exciting history. Some of the most fascinating are the **Citadel, the City of David** and **Warren's Shaft** and the **Ophel Archaeological Garden** (see separate entries.)

Armenian Bird Mosaic: in St. Polyeuctus' Chapel, on Rehov Haneviim one block away from Damascus Gate – a 5th century CE pavement dedicated to an "unknown soldier," and all the Armenians who fell in battle and whose names are known only to God. Possibly the earliest memorial of its kind, the mosaic depicts various birds around a vine.

(Bus Nos. 1, 27)

***Armenian Orthodox Monastery:** extending over the summit of Mt. Zion, the monastery adjoins the Armenian Patriarchate, the Cathedral of St. James, a library (established by oilman/philanthropist Calouste Gulbenkian in 1929), and a seminary. Of special interest is the collection of Armenian manuscripts in the Church of St. Theodoros.

The **Patriarchate,** built in 1853, has an impressive salon.

The **Cathedral of St. James:** beautiful ornate interior. Named after two saints – the Apostle James and James, son of Zebedee, cousin of Jesus. The latter's remains were discovered in the Kidron Valley below more than 300 years after his martyrdom (by stoning) and reinterred on Mt. Zion under what is now the main altar of this 11–12th-century Crusader building. (There was a Byzantine monastery on the site in the 7th century and a Georgian church in the 11th century.) The head of James the Greater (the Apostle), which was severed from his body in 44 CE, is entombed in the chapel to the left as you walk in. There are three altars: one to St. James the Less, one to the Virgin, and one to John the Baptist. The carvings and the painted tiles are remarkable. Admittance only if modestly dressed and during services. Open: daily 7–8 a.m., 3–3.30 p.m.

The **Chapel of Etchmiazine** was formed in the 17th cen-

Damascus Gate

The Citadel

tury when the arcades of a vestibule leading to the monastery were sealed off.

Before leaving, ask to be shown the **Mardigian Museum of Armenian Art and History** and the **Gulbenkian Library** (which houses over 50,000 volumes). There is a separate entrance to the library and the museum. Open: Mon.–Sat. 10 a.m.–3 p.m. Entrance fee IS 2.

(Walk No. 1, Buses to Jaffa Gate Nos. 3, 13, 19, 20, 30))

***Armenian Quarter:** southwestern section of Old City and Mt. Zion; the boundaries are the city's Walls to the west and the south, St. James' St. to the north and Ararat St. to the east. The Quarter comprises churches, the patriarchate and the House of Caiaphas. Armenians officially converted to Christianity in the 4th century and established religious and secular communities in Jerusalem, where they enjoyed relative tranquillity. Today's community numbers between three and four thousand.

(Walk No. 1)

Artists' House: 12, Rehov Shmuel Hanagid. Exhibition Hall of Jerusalem's painters and sculptors. Meeting place for artists and art-lovers. Includes a gallery of Jerusalem and Israeli artists' works, art-supply shop and restaurant. Open Sun. –Thurs. 10 a.m. – 1 p.m., 4–7 p.m. Fri. 10 a.m. – 1 p.m. Sat. 11 a.m. – 2 p.m. Admission free. Tel. (02)252636.

(Bus Nos. 4, 7, 8, 9, 31, 32, 48)

Artur Rubinstein Panorama: near the Kennedy Memorial; an observation point in the shape of a piano, with marble keys.

Augusta Victoria Hospital: on ridge between Mt. Scopus and Mt. of Olives. Built 1910 by Germans as sanatorium, following visit of Kaiser Wilhelm II to Jerusalem. British Government House 1920–27. Scene of fierce fighting in Six Day War. Now hospital maintained by Lutheran World Federation.

(Bus Nos. 4, 9, 26, 28)

Basilica of the Agony (Church of All Nations): on Jericho Road, facing the Golden Gate. It was designed by the renowned Barluzzi around the **Rock of the Agony** on which Jesus went down on his knees to pray prior to his arrest. Its 12 cupolas give the church a strikingly unusual roof; the mosaic over the entrance is extraordinary, and the mosaics inside are also worth noting. Theodosius I built a basilica here (4th century); destroyed in 614, it was rebuilt by the Crusaders, then destroyed again by Saladin. Franciscans consecrated the present church in 1924; the small enclosed garden is beautifully kept and forms part of the larger area of Gethsemane. Open from 8 a.m. to 12 p.m. and from 2.30 p.m. to sunset. Easiest access from the Old City is down through Lions' Gate. One can also walk down from Dung Gate, but the road is a narrow one and not at all suitable for pedestrians.

(Walk No. 4. Bus Nos. 1 and 42 or 43 from Damascus Gate)

Bernard M. Bloomfield Science Museum: Opened in 1992, the first exhibition here explores the world of motion, with plenty of hands-on exhibits to try out. Open: Mon., Wed., Thurs. 10.00 a.m.–6 p.m., Tues. 10.00 a.m.–10.00 p.m., Fri. 10.00 a.m.–1 p.m., Sat. 10.00 a.m.–3 p.m., Sun. closed. Entrance fee: Adults and children over 5, NIS 10. Tel. (02)618128.

(Bus Nos. 9, 24, 28)

Bethany: a small settlement on the Jericho Road at the outskirts of Jerusalem. The new Franciscan Church of St. Lazarus is dedicated to the man raised from the dead by Jesus. Crusader remains, Lazarus's tomb and the 400-or-so-year-old mosque near it should also be seen.

(Route No.1)

Bethpage: on the eastern side of the Mount of Olives, the Monastery was built by Franciscans in the late 19th century and is today the starting point for the Palm Sunday (Easter) procession. Jesus' last ride to Jerusalem started here and the rock from which he mounted the donkey is thought to be the one shown with scenes from his life painted on it.

Israel Museum (above); military cemetery (right); Herzl's tomb (belov

Sidewalk cafes on the Ben Yehuda Mall Jerusalem

Bezalel Academy of Arts and Design: Mt. Scopus, within the university campus. Israel's only art and design college, Bezalel was founded in 1906, and its graduates have had a profound influence on Israeli art. Subjects taught include fine art, industrial design, ceramics, gold and silversmithing, environmental design and graphic design as well as photography, animation and video. Tours by arrangement. Tel (02)893333.

(Bus Nos. 4a, 9, 23, 26, 28)

Bible Lands Museum Jerusalem: Opened in 1992, this museum houses one of the world's most important collections of objects representing the cultures and civilizations of the ancient lands of the Bible. On view in the striking building are seals, bronzes, ivories, mosaics, sarcophagi, stelae and other artefacts. Open: Sun., Mon., Tues., Thurs. 9.00 a.m.–5.30 p.m., Wed. 9.30 a.m.–9.30 p.m., Fri. 9.30 a.m–2.00 p.m., Sat. 11.00 a.m.–3.00 p.m. Entrance fee.

(Bus. Nos. 9,17,24)

Biblical Zoo (Jerusalem Biblical and Zoological Gardens): Manahat. Recently moved to more spacious grounds. Houses many species of animals and birds common in the Land of Israel during biblical times. Open every day – except Rosh Hashana, Yom Kippur and Memorial Day – from 9 a.m. to 4 p.m., Entrance fee. (Tickets for Saturday can be bought ahead of time at the ticket agencies "Klaim" and "Bimot" in the centre of town.) Tel. (02)430111.

(Bus Nos. 6, 18, 19, 24, 31)

Binyenei Ha'ooma (Convention and Concert Hall): opposite Central Bus Station. Seats more than 3,000 people. Venue for World Zionist Congress, Eurovision Song Contest, Israel Song Festival and other major events.

(Bus Nos. 1, 5, 6, 7, 8, 9, 11, 13, 14, 15, 17, 18, 20, 21, 23, 25, 26, 27, 28, 29, 31, 32, 33, 35, 36, 37, 39, 40, 50)

Boys Town: 20, Rav Frank St., Bayit Vegan. Campus and educational community of 1,300 boys in a Tora and technology environment. Free tours by appointment only.

Sun. – Thurs. 10 a.m. – 12 noon, 2–4 p.m. Special tours tel. (02) 441204, 441205.

(Bus Nos. 16, 39, 40)

British Military Cemetery: northern base of Mt. Scopus, next to Hadassah Hospital. Final resting place of those who fell in Palestine campaign, World War I.

(Bus Nos. 4, 9, 26, 28)

Bukharan Quarter: established towards the end of the 19th century by wealthy Jewish immigrants determined to preserve the distinct customs of their native Bukhara (subsequently incorporated in the U.S.S.R.). See the **Baba Tama Synagogue** (on Rehov Habukharim near the Turkish baths).

(Bus Nos. 3, 4, 9, 27, 35, 36, 37, 39, 40)

Burnt House: Tiferet St., Jewish Quarter. Archaeological museum in the ruins of house that was burnt a month after the Second Temple was destroyed in 70 CE. Multi-slide show – English: 9.30, 11.30, 1.30, 3.30. Hebrew: 10.30, 12.30, 2.30, 4 p.m. French and Spanish by arrangment. Open Sun.–Thurs. 9 a.m. – 5 p.m., Fri. 9 a.m. – 1 p.m. Entrance fee – adults IS 2. Tel (02)288141.

(Walk No. 1)

Caiaphas' House: site within grounds of Couvent Armenien St. Sauveur, Mt. Zion. Where Caiaphas imprisoned Jesus. There are Byzantine and Crusader remains and Armenian graves near the church.

(Walk No. 1, Bus Nos. 1, 13, 20)

***Calvary:** where Jesus was crucified. See Church of Holy Sepulchre (Stations X to XIII).

(Walk No. 1)

Canion Yerushalayim: The largest shopping mall in the Middle East opened in March 1993. It houses eight cinemas and 180 shops, including such well-known boutiques as Laura Ashley, Benetton and Levis, and 20 restaurants. Special events include fashion shows, dance and other entertainment. The 100,000 sq m complex situated in

Mahane Yehuda Market, Jerusalem

Malha, near the Zoo, cost $85,000,000 to build and also provides a baby-sitting service and a car wash. Open: Sun. –Thurs. 9. a.m.–9 p.m., Fri. 9. a.m.–one hour before Shabbat, Sat. after Shabbat. Information: (02)791333.

(Bus. Nos. 6, 18, 19, 24, 31)

***Cardo:** Rehov Hayehudim, Jewish Quarter. Remains of Roman road laid down in the 5th century CE, once the main thoroughfare of the city. Includes remains of Israelite walls and tower, and Byzantine and Crusader structures. Restored and opened to the public. Includes an information centre and a shopping area with some exclusive boutiques. Toward the end of the Cardo there is a duplicate of the Madaba mosaic map and a slide show (free). The site is illuminated and open also at night.

(Walk No. 1)

***Cathedral of St. James:** see Armenian Orthodox Monastery, Armenian Quarter.

Cellar (or Chamber) of the Holocaust: Mt. Zion, near David's Tomb. There's a synagogue and a small museum to remind one of the Nazi death camps. Open 9 a.m. to 5 p.m.

(Walk No. 1. Bus Nos. 1, 38)

Cenacle: (Cenaculum, Room of the Last Supper): Mt. Zion. Accepted by Christians except the Syrian Orthodox as the place where Jesus and his disciples met for the Last (Passover) Supper and where the Holy Ghost later appeared to the Apostles. It served as a centre for the first Christians and was attached to the 4th century Hagia Zion Basilica subsequently destroyed by the Persians and rebuilt by the Crusaders in 1100. The Crusader church was destroyed in 1219 by Moslems who by 1551 had evicted the last Franciscans from the mount and turned it into a strictly Moslem preserve. The room of the Last Supper is situated one floor above King David's Tomb.

(Walk No. 1. Bus No. 1, 13, 20)

Chapel of the Ascension: off the Mount of Olives Road, near the Tomb of Hulda the Prophetess. The dome was added by Moslems above a Christian shrine around the rock from which Jesus ascended to the heavens and upon which his footprint may be seen. Apparently, the Dome of the Ascension provided the visual inspiration for the Dome of the Rock; it is not to be confused with the Dome of Ascension on the Temple Mount or the Tower of Ascension.

(Walk No. 4, Bus Nos. 42 and 43 from Damascus Gate)

***Chapel of the Flagellation:** within Franciscan Monastery of the Flagellation, which includes Station II of the Cross, Via Dolorosa. The traditional spot where Jesus was scourged; nearby is the Chapel of the Condemnation and the Franciscan Faculty of Biblical and Archaeological Studies, which includes a library and a museum.

(Walk No. 3)

***Christian Quarter:** northwestern section of Old City. With few exceptions, all the residents here are Christians. First established in the 4th century CE when the Church of the Holy Sepulchre was erected, the area is bounded by the city-wall in the north and the west and by David St. – Bazaar St. and Souq Khan-ez-Zeit to the south and the east, respectively. Patriarchates, monasteries, churches, hospices and charitable and educational establishments abound here.

(Walk No. 3)

Church of the Dormition: Mt. Zion. Consecrated in 1910, the basilica commemorates the death of Virgin Mary. Crypt has a life-sized effigy of her. Note the golden mosaic on the inside of the dome above the main altar, and the signs of the Zodiac underfoot. The church was damaged during the wars of 1948 and 1967. It is a well-known venue for organ recitals. Open daily (including Sunday) until sundown; closed 12–2 p.m.

(Walk No. 1. Bus Nos. 1, 13, 20)

***Church of the Holy Sepulchre (Stations X to XIV):** in the Christian Quarter; the easiest approach – if you aren't following the Stations of the Cross – is through Jaffa Gate, down David Street (which leads into the bazaar) and left at Christian Quarter Road or Muristan Street further down.

First built in the 4th century CE by Constantine's mother Helena over the site of a Roman pagan temple to Venus, this Christian holy of holies (which today bears no resemblance to the original construction) encloses the area formed by the last five Stations of the Cross. Helena was the world's first and most successful archaeologist – wherever she dug she found exactly what she was determined to find. Showing little respect for Jesus' burial place, the Persians early in the 7th century destroyed the basilica, which was rebuilt by the Crusaders in the 12th century. By the beginning of the 19th century travellers reported that Moslem so-called guards lounged about the place in an offensively relaxed fashion. In 1927, the basilica was hit by an earthquake. Destroyed and rebuilt many times, the church is shared by six Christian communities.

The main entrance is on the south side where the building and decoration around the portals dates to the Crusaders.

Immediately as you walk in, upstairs, to your right, are **Stations X, XI, XII** and **XIII** which are commemorated by the two **Chapels of Golgotha.** This is where Jesus was stripped, nailed, killed and removed from the cross. The Greeks own the chapel on the left, where the cross was fixed; the Franciscans own the one on the right where Jesus was impaled. Directly below this area (Calvary), downstairs, is the Chapel of Adam around the rock of Golgotha, which was said to have cracked during the earthquake that marked the crucifixion. At a spot facing the entrance is a red slab of stone where Jesus was anointed before burial. The circular slab to the left (enclosed by rails) marks the point from which the three women watched the crucifixion (this belongs to the Armenians, as does the chapel up the stairs from here). Next is the Rotunda – enormous pillars, a hideous cupola at the centre of which is the **Holy Sepulchre;** two enclosures here: the **Chapel of the Angel,** showing part of the stone used to seal the tomb, and **Station XIV,** the tomb itself (with room for not more than four or five people; a benevolent-looking, white-bearded priest offers to light candles). Behind the edicule is the tomb of Joseph of Arimathea and the **Chapel of the Syrian-Jacobites;** the Copts, too, have a chapel here. Opposite the entrance (to the Sepulchre) is a Greek chapel with a stone at the centre indicating the centre of the earth. To the right, beyond the Sepulchre, is the **Chapel of Mary Magdalene** where the resurrected Jesus is said to have first revealed himself. This leads to the Franciscan chapel and a fragment of the Column of Flagellation. Following the extended gallery (Arches of the Virgin), you come to the **Prison of Christ,** a Greek chapel, as is the next one, the **Chapel of Longinus** (the Centurion who pierced Jesus' side). An Armenian chapel comes next, where Roman troops divided Jesus' raiment amongst themselves. Downstairs, the eerie **Chapel of St. Helena** and the cave where the cross was found in the 4th century. Back on ground level, walking towards the main entrance, is the (Greek) **Chapel of the Mocking** where Jesus sat and was insulted by Roman troops, and an entrance leading to the living quarters of the Greek monks who are the current custodians of the basilica. A group of Ethiopian monks live on the roof of the church, and possess two chapels in an adjoining building. The basilica is open from 4.30 a.m.–7 p.m. Greek Orthodox mass is celebrated at 1 p.m. daily; Armenian mass at 2.30 p.m.; Roman Catholic mass between 4 and 7 p.m. There is a daily Franciscan procession in the basilica at 4 p.m.

(Walk No. 3)

Church of Pater Noster: Jesus gave the world the Lord's Prayer somewhere near the site of this 19th century Carmelite church on the Mount of Olives. In the 4th century, Queen Helena (the super-archaeologist who, it will be recalled, commissioned the first Church of the Holy Sepulchre) built an Olive Tree ("Eleona") Church here to remind residents and visitors of Jesus' prophecy concerning the destruction of Jerusalem. In today's Pater Noster Cloister, the interesting feature is the Lord's Prayer painted on coloured tiles in 44 languages.

(Walk No. 4)

***Church of St. Anne:** just before the start of the Via Dolorosa, in the Moslem Quarter. To the right as you come in from Lions' Gate. The portals lead to a pleasant courtyard and to the church, which was built by the Crusaders and is an imposingly bare rock construction vaulting upwards with enormous columns – ascetic simplicity – no pictures or painted walls, etc. – windows of plain glass, perfectly plain. Downstairs, a small chapel marks

Mary's birthplace. The history of the site is a familiar one: the first basilica to honour Mary was probably built by the Empress Eudoxia in the 5th century, destroyed by the Persians in 614, rebuilt by the Crusaders, converted to a Moslem religious centre by Saladin, etc. After the Crimean war, Napoleon III was presented with the site in gratitude for the help he'd given the Turks; the church was restored and in 1878 placed under the care of the White Fathers. **The Pools of Bethesda,** around which archaeologists excavated a Byzantine basilica and Hasmonaean bath, is where Jesus healed a cripple on the Sabbath. Open: 8 a.m. – 12 noon and 2 – 5 p.m. Closed Sundays.

(Walk No. 3)

***Church of St. John the Baptist:** small, domed, situated just off Christian Quarter Road and David Street. The present structure dates to the 11th century and was apparently built over 5th century Byzantine ruins. Greek Orthodox priests guard a largish splinter of the True Cross.

Church of St. Mary Magdalene: on the slope above the Basilica of the Agony, a typically Russian-looking church (onion-shaped domes, 16th century Muscovite style), which could be transplanted to the heart of the Kremlin without any danger of physical rejection. It was built in the late 19th century by Czar Alexander III who wanted to do something for his late mother. Grand Duchess Elizabeth (killed by the Bolsheviks) and other Russian royals are buried here. The icons and other paintings inside repay close scrutiny. Open Tues., Thurs. 10 a.m. – 12 noon.

(Walk No. 4)

Church of St. Peter in Gallicantu (Cock Crow): Malchei Zedek St. Consecrated in 1931. The Apostle Peter heard a cock crow and wept with remorse for having thrice denied Jesus (Luke 22:16–62). A passage of ancient steps leads from here to the Kidron Valley and could have been used by Jesus after the Last Supper on the eastern slope of Mt. Zion.

(Bus No. 1)

***Citadel (see also Tower of David, Museum of the History of Jerusalem):** to the right as you walk into the Old City from Jaffa Gate. It was built by Herod in 24 BCE and it might for all anyone knows be standing over the fortress from which David first saw Bathsheba. Herod was a cruel, murderous ruler but he was also capable of thoughtful gestures like naming towers after a brother (Phasael), a friend (Hippicus) and a wife (Mariamne – whom he later killed). The northeast tower (Phasael's) is erroneously called David's Tower (the view from here is excellent as it's the highest point in the Old City). When the Romans under Titus tore down the city they left this part (always a dominant defence spot) more or less intact.

(Walk No. 1. Bus Nos. 1, 3, 13, 19, 20, 30, 41, 99)

City centre: the commercial heart of the city sits around the triangle formed by Jaffa Road, King George Street and Ben Yehuda Street. The big department stores and many of the restaurants are to be found here. Most of the bus routes include stops in the centre. A large stretch of Ben Yehuda is a pedestrian mall ("midrehov") with outdoor cafes.

(Bus Nos. 4, 5, 6, 7, 19, 15, 18, 21)

City of David and Warren's Shaft: Excavations at this site above the Gihon spring have revealed twenty-five layers of settlement, including the ancient walls built in the 18th century BCE, remains of Canaanite and Jebusite cities, ruins of buildings from the days of the kings of Judah, and the "House of Bullae" – a central archive where 51 clay seals were discovered. Warren's Shaft, named after the explorer who discovered it, is an impressive underground water system dating from the period of the kings of Judah. Open: Sun.–Thurs. 9 a.m.–5 p.m., Fri. 9 a.m.–3 p.m.

***Damascus Gate:** Sultan Suleiman St. (facing the road to Damascus); the largest and most impressive gate – Sha'ar Shechem in Hebrew and Bab el-Amud in Arabic (after a pillar with Hadrian's statue on top, which once stood inside it). Built in 1538. The first gate here was probably built by Herod. About a hundred and fifty years later came Hadrian's construction, which is below today's gate; it marked the northern entrance to his Aelia Capitolina, and part of it can be seen below the present gate. There is a museum in the **Roman Square,** at the beginning of the Cardo, showing the history of the gate. A Roman hall and staircase lead to the top of the gate and the ramparts.

Entrance fee to the museum and to the ramparts which are open from 9 a.m. to. 5 p.m. daily. Down the steps, Damascus Gate Road forks into El-Wad Road (left, leading to the Via Dolorosa and Temple Mount) and Suq Khan Ez-Zeit (right, to the Holy Sepulchre and the heart of the market).

(Walk No. 2. Bus Nos. 1, 23, 27)

Davidka Memorial: Kikar Herut, Rehov Yafo. Mortar designed by David Leibovitch. Used in War of Independence.

(Bus Nos. 5, 8, 11, 13, 18, 20, 21, 23, 27, 31, 32, 39, 40, 50)

***David's Tower** (Migdal David): see **Tower of David, (Museum of the History of Jerusalem)** and also **Citadel.**

***Dome of the Ascension:** a small 13th century structure to the left as you approach the Western Gate of the Dome of the Rock, it serves to remind of Mohammed's ascension to heaven. Visually, it's a remarkable replica of the Byzantine monument commemorating Jesus' ascension on the Mount of Olives.

(Walk No. 2)

***Dome of the Chain:** an interesting 8th century structure located near the Paradise Gate of the Dome of the Rock or behind it if you're facing the Western Gate. Arabs once used the dome to store treasure, and the Crusaders insisted on turning the place into a church. A remarkable feature is that every one of the 17 columns may be seen at once when viewed from any angle.

(Walk No. 2)

***Dome of the Rock:** erroneously also known as the "Mosque of Omar" (which once stood nearby and was reduced to nothing), the Dome is built around the Sacred Rock upon which Abraham was about to sacrifice his son and from which Mohammed ascended on his horse Buraq to Paradise. Both the First and Second Temples stood here. The splendour of the mosque is dazzling and after the gingerbread-cluttered churches the relatively stark simplicity of the intricate mosaics under the golden (bronze) dome cannot but create a strong impression.

Built in 691 by Abd el-Malik as a counter-attraction to Mecca, the octagonal structure has four entrances: the Western Gate (the entrance), Paradise Gate, Judgement Gate and Mecca Gate. The ceiling is inlaid with gold, red and black chips; verses from the Koran are inscribed on the golden frieze at the base; decorations picture fruits or are abstract – no human or animal likenesses; the columns were taken from Byzantine churches – no two are alike and some are marked with crosses. The windows were added in Saladin's time. It is said that David, Solomon, Jesus and Abraham were in the habit of praying at the **Well of Souls** downstairs and that the dead gather here twice a week to pray. Tradition and several maps have it that this is the very centre of the earth. Converted to a church during the Crusades. Open: Sun.–Thurs. 8 a.m.–3 p.m. Museum open Sun.–Thurs. 8 a.m.–12 p.m., 12.30–3 p.m. Closed Fridays and Moslem holidays. Entrance fee (includes El-Aksa Mosque and the Islamic Museum). Tel. (02) 283393.

(Walk No. 2. Bus Nos. 1, 99)

Dominus Flevit (The Lord Wept): About halfway up the Mt. of Olives, on one of the spots where Jesus is said to have stopped to weep over Jerusalem. Planned in the shape of a tear drop by the same Barluzzi who designed the Basilica of the Agony, this Franciscan church includes relics from a Byzantine structure that once stood here in honour of the prophetess Anne (mentioned by the physician Luke). An interesting find on this site was a 3000-year-old Jebusite tomb.

(Walk No. 4)

***Dung Gate:** closest to Western Wall. Overlooking the Ophel. Since 2nd century CE the city's refuse has been carted through this gate to be dumped outside – hence its name.

(Bus Nos. 1, 38)

***Ecce Homo Arch:** spanning the Via Dolorosa, the arch is attached to the **Ecce Homo Convent** of the Sisters of Zion. Built by Emperor Hadrian in 135 CE to commemorate victory over Bar Kochba. Name derives from erroneous belief that Pontius Pilate stood here and proclaimed "Ecce Homo!" (Behold the man!) when presenting Jesus crowned with thorns.

(Walk No. 3)

***El-Aksa:** see Mosque of El-Aksa.

***El-Kas (The Cup) Fountain:** in the courtyard facing El-Aksa, the water comes from subterranean cisterns and is used by the faithful for washing before prayer.

Ethiopian Church: Ethiopia Street (Rehov Ethiopia). Black-domed church serving Ethiopian community. In 1952 an Ethiopian bishop was appointed to Jerusalem. The present community numbers about 250; some of them live in the Old City. It is one of the most exotic sects in the Holy Land. The Queen of Sheba, who visited Solomon in Jerusalem, is thought to have been Ethiopian.

(Close to the route followed on Walk No. 5;
Bus Nos. 1, 11, 17, 35, 39, 40)

E-Tur: Arab village on spine of Mt. of Olives.

Ein Karem: picturesque village on southwestern outskirts of Jerusalem and birthplace of John the Baptist. **Franciscan Church of St. John the Baptist** over Grotto of Nativity of St. John. Open: 8 a.m.–12 noon. and 2.30–5 p.m. Fountain of the Virgin at the base of mosque. **Catholic Church of the Visitation** nearby, at top of hill. Commemorates Mary's visit to John's mother, Elizabeth. Open daily as above. It was redesigned by Barluzzi (Basilica of the Agony, Dominus Flevit, etc.). See the Lower Church and the Upper Church, and perhaps stay in the all-male youth hostel run by hospitable Franciscans. There are several restaurants, studios and art galleries in the area.

(Route No. 4, Bus No. 17)

Exhibition of Musical Instruments: at the Jerusalem Rubin Academy of Music and Dance, Campus Givat Ram; tel: (02)636232. Collection of 250 folk and art musical instruments from all over the world. Open: Sun.–Thurs. 10 a.m.–6 p.m. Entrance free.

(Bus Nos. 9, 28)

Fountain of the Virgin: see Gihon Spring.

Garden of Gethsemane: base of Mt. of Olives. Within courtyard of Basilica of the Agony (Church of All

Nations). Eight fruit-bearing olive trees believed to be so old that they witnessed Christ at prayer for the people of all nations. The Arabs still call it Zerubbabel's Garden. (See "Grotto of Gethsemane.") Open daily 8 a.m. – 12 noon and 2.30 – 6 p.m. (5 p.m. winter).

(Walk No. 4. Bus Nos. 1 and 42 or 43 from Damascus Gate, 64)

Garden Tomb: Schick St., off Nablus Road, one block from Damascus Gate. Gordon of Khartoum made a case for this skull-shaped rock being the original site of Golgotha (Mt. of Skulls), Calvary and the Crucifixion. Its situation and its well-informed caretakers make this a pleasant place to visit; it is frequented by many tourists and pilgrims from every nation and denomination who find it a good place for prayer and meditation. Open 8 a.m. – 12.00 noon and 2.30–5 p.m. daily except Sunday. Group communion services conducted on request on weekdays between 8–11 a.m and 2.30–4 p.m.

(Bus No. 27)

***The Gates** (see also **Ramparts**): The walls surrounding the Old City stretch for more than two miles. Built mainly by Suleiman the Magnificent (1538–41), parts rest on remains of the efforts of Saladin (of Crusader fame) and the greatest builder of them all: King Herod. The most interesting of the eight gates is Damascus (Schechem) Gate, in the northern wall, between New Gate and Herod's Gate. Recently a Roman gate was discovered under the magnificent Ottoman masonry. It is open to the public (entrance fee includes walk along the upper ramparts of the wall).

Seven of the eight gates are open. But the eighth, the Golden Gate, will, according to tradition, open only on Judgement Day (see Golden Gate).

The other four gates are Zion, Jaffa, Dung and Lions' (St Stephen's).

(Walk Nos. 1, 2, 3)

Gihon Spring: Siloam Road, base of City of David, down Kidron Valley. Fresh water underground spring and principal reason for earliest settlement in Jerusalem. David captured Jerusalem by entering the cave and scaling shaft above spring (see Warren's Shaft). Solomon anointed here. King Hezekiah built superb 8th century BCE tunnel from Gihon to Pool of Siloam to channel water within his besieged city. Also known as Fountain of the Virgin as legend credits Mary with drawing its water. Gihon is Hebrew for gushing – water gushes out depending on season and rainfall. You can walk through the tunnel, but expect to get wet. Torch mandatory. (See Hezekiah's Tunnel.) Open: Sun.–Thurs. 9 a.m.–4 p.m., Fri. 9 a.m.–1 p.m. Free.

(Bus No. 1, 42, 43, 99)

***Golgotha:** hill denuded of trees and resembling bald pate or skull during time of Jesus. Name derived from Hebrew word for skull. "Crowned" by Church of Holy Sepulchre. Open: 4.30 a.m.–7 p.m. daily.

(Walk No. 3)

***Golden Gate:** situated roughly in the middle of the eastern stretch of the wall; also called The Gate of Mercy (Shaar Harahamim), it was erected in the 5th century over the traditional (Shushan) entrance to Solomon's Temple and Herod's ironically named Gate of Compassion. If the Damascus Gate is the largest and the most impressive, this one's probably the most beautiful. It was blocked several centuries ago in 1530, some say to prevent the coming of the Messiah, who, it is believed, will enter Jerusalem (and the hallowed Temple Mount area) through this gate. All the dead will be resurrected on the day of the coming. There is a special cemetery on the Mount of Olives which faces the Gate and the Temple Mount – religious Jews are still brought from all over the world to be buried here.

(Walk No. 2)

Great Synagogue: (See Hechal Shlomo)

***Greek Orthodox Patriarchate:** on the road of the same name; a large complex comprising Crusader and more recent accretions. The roof leads to the cupola of the Holy Sepulchre. A new museum across the road contains many archaeological, historical and church artefacts, as well as a library with ancient manuscripts. Small entrance fee.

(Walk No. 3)

Grotto of Gethsemane: located near the **Tomb of the Virgin,** which lies in the **Church of (Mary's) Assumption.** Gethsemane is from the Aramaic **gath-shamnah**, which means oil press (there are traces here of such a press from before the Christian era). In this more-or-less unspoiled grotto Jesus would meet and rest with his disciples. The crypt of the former Abbey-Church of the Assumption of Mary stands next to a 5th century Byzantine shrine over the tomb of Mary, mother of Jesus. The magnificent upper Gothic Church and the Cluny Monastery were razed to the ground after the Crusaders left Jerusalem. In the 18th century, Armenians and Greeks started using the shrine together with the Latins, and to this day various Christian sects and also Moslems have a right of worship here. Altars are dedicated to Mary's husband and parents. Open daily 8.30 a.m. – 12 noon and 2.30 – 5 p.m.

(Walk No. 4. from Damascus Gate, Bus No. 1)

Haceldama (Field of Blood): Hinnom Valley. A Greek convent stands over land bought with the "blood money" that Judas earned for betraying Jesus. The grounds were for a time used as a burial place for pilgrims and other strangers; the Cave of the Apostles is said to be where the Apostles hid during Jesus' trial.

(Bus Nos. 1, 99)

Hadassah–Hebrew University Medical Centre: above village of Ein Karem, southwestern outskirts. World-renowned medical centre whose synagogue is adorned with the famous "Chagall windows" – biblical subjects on stained-glass windows designed by Marc Chagall. Tel. (02)776271/2/9. Sun.–Thurs. 8 a.m.–1 p.m. Guided tours. 2–3.45 p.m. without tours. Call for details of tours in various languages. Entrance fee.

(Bus Nos. 19, 27)

***Haram es-Sharif:** Arabic name – meaning "the Noble Sanctuary" – for the Temple Mount, upon which stand the Dome of the Rock and El-Aksa.

(Walk No. 2 or Bus No. 1)

Hebrew University (Givat Ram campus): Guided tours in English at 9–11 a.m., starting from the Sherman building. Botanical garden. See also Bernard M. Bloomfield Science Museum. Tel. (02)585111.

(Bus Nos. 9, 28)

Hebrew University (Mt. Scopus campus): see Mount Scopus.

Hechal Shlomo: 60 King George Street, facing Independence Park and near the King's Hotel. World religious centre and H.Q. of the Sephardi and Ashkenazi Chief Rabbinate. See the museum, the library and the reconstructed 18th century synagogue from Padua. Sun., Thurs. 9 a.m. – 1 p.m. Fri. 9–11 a.m. Tel. (02)247112.

The **Jerusalem Great Synagogue** adjoining it is open to visitors and is well worth a visit. Open daily 9 a.m. - 1 p.m. On Friday evenings and Saturday mornings, the services feature a well-known cantor and choir.

(Bus Nos. 4, 7, 8, 9, 17, 19, 22, 31, 32, 48)

Herod's Family Tomb: just behind King David Hotel on Abu Sikhra Street. Identified from descriptions in Josephus. Believed to have held bodies of several of Herod's relatives, some of whom he murdered. Rolling stone blocks door.

(Bus Nos. 5, 6, 15, 18, 21, 30)

***Herod's Gate** (also called Flowers' Gate or Bab El-Zahara): facing Saladin Street. It got its name from mediaeval pilgrims who believed that the house of Herod Antipas, where Jesus was sent by Pilate, was located nearby. Antipas's house was probably situated much nearer Mt. Zion, but pilgrims kept coming here and the name stuck.

***Herodian Quarter and Museum:** Hakaraim St. off Hurva Sq. under Yeshivat Hakotel. Open: Sun.–Thurs. 9 a.m.–5 p.m., Fri. 9 a.m.–1 p.m. Entrance fee: Adults IS 3.50, groups 2.50. Tel. (02)283448, 288141.

Herzl Museum: Mt. Herzl, Herzl Boulevard. Herzl's study in Vienna reconstructed, with display of personal belongings and documents. Open: Sun.–Thurs. 9 a.m.–5 p.m., Fri. 9 a.m.–1 p.m. Admission free. Tel. (02)521869, 511108.

(Bus Nos.13, 16, 17, 18, 20, 21, 23, 24, 26, 27, 39, 40)

***Hezekiah's Pool:** off Christian Quarter St. from David St., west of Muristan. Walled in by buildings, also called Almond Pool, Bath of the Patriarchs and Pool of the Towers, it was an important reservoir for Herod's Palace and gardens and surrounding towers. Climb to the balcony of the Petra Hotel near Jaffa Gate to see the Pool. Parts of it can be glimpsed from the top of the nearby Citadel. The Pool is 80 m. long and 49 m. wide and 3 m. below street level.

Hezekiah's Tunnel: cut through rock below the City of David, between Gihon Spring and Pool of Siloam. Built by Judaean King Hezekiah in 8th century BCE. to bring Gihon waters within city walls to withstand Assyrian siege of Jerusalem. Visitors may walk its 600 m. length from Gihon Spring but should take torches and be prepared to get wet up to the knees. Open: Sun.–Thurs. 9 a.m. – 4 p.m., Fri. 9 a.m.–1 p.m. Free. (See Gihon Spring.)

(Bus No. 1)

Hinnom Valley: west of the Old City, linking up in the south with the Kidron Valley below the Pool of Siloam. Called "Gei ben-Hinnom" in Hebrew, the valley was associated with the concept of Gehennah or Hell, due to the terrible rites of Moloch carried out there in biblical times.

(Bus Nos. 13, 20)

Hurva Synagogue: see Synagogues in the Jewish Quarter.

Hutzot Hayotzer: next to the bus stop opposite Jaffa Gate. Arts and crafts centre. Open Sun. – Thurs. 10 a.m. – 5.30 p.m. Fri. 10 a.m. – 2 p.m.

(Bus Nos. 1, 13, 19, 20)

Independence Park: bounded by King George St., Hillel St., and Agron St., the Park may be approached by crossing King George St. from Hechal Shlomo. New Yorkers have been known to refer to it as "Jerusalem's peaceful Central Park." The large reservoir at the tip of the triangle furthest from King George is the **Mamilla Pool** (Bus. Nos. 15, 22) which is thought to have once provided a part of the Old City's water supply by being connected to Hezekiah's Pool and Sultan's Pool. There is a mediaeval Moslem graveyard around the pool.

(Bus Nos. 4, 7, 8, 9, 14, 17, 19, 22, 31, 32, 38)

International Cultural Centre for Youth: 12a, Rehov Emek Refaim. Cultural programmes for youth; exhibits; folklore shows for tourists on Tues. and Sat. nights. Open Sun. and Fri. 9 a.m. – 1 p.m. Mon. and Thurs. 4–6 p.m. Sat. 10 a.m. – 1 p.m.

(Bus Nos. 4, 18)

***Islamic Museum:** see L.A. Mayer Memorial Museum for Islamic Art.

(Walk No. 2. Bus No. 1)

Israel Museum: The largest displays are devoted to Archaeology of the Land of the Bible, Jewish Ceremonial Art and Jewish Ethnography. Other halls and galleries display permanent and changing displays of Israeli Art, Impressionist and Post-Impressionist Art, Paintings before 1900, Pre-Columbian and Ethnic Art, Design, Photography, East Asian Art and Prints and Drawings. Several fine period rooms include an 18th century French Empire Grand Salon which formerly belonged to the Rothschild family; a Venetian rococo room and an English 18th century dining room, all of which show the formality of bygone eras.

Situated close to the entrance is the **Shrine of the Book** which houses the Deas Sea Scrolls. Its white dome resembles the shape of the lids of the jars in which the scrolls were found and contrasts with the black basalt wall nearby, recalling the title of the scroll, "The Sons of Light and the Sons of Darkness," possibly written by the Essenes who lived in the vicinity of Qumran. All of the manuscripts here are some 2,000 years old, ante-dating the fall of the Second Temple during the Roman occupation. The oldest, as well as the longest, of the scrolls is the Book of Isaiah. It is the oldest complete manuscript of a biblical book in existence, over a thousand years earlier than any other known.

The Jewish Ceremonial Art section has the most complete collection of Judaica from all corners of the world where Jewish communities once flourished.

The Department of Ethnography is devoted to the collection, research and disply of material culture and folk art from the different Jewish and non-Jewish ethnic groups currently living in Israel. On disply are examples of costumes such as the attire of a bride from Yemen, ceremonial garments from Morocco and Bukhara as well as jewellery and other objects from Jewish communities, especially from Islamic countries.

The **Youth Wing** offers exciting and challenging exhibitions, changed periodically, which are equally enjoyable for adults and children.

The museum is open 7 days a week: Sunday, Monday, Wednesday and Thursday from 10 a.m.–5 p.m. Tuesday from 4 p.m.– 10 p.m. Friday and Saturday from 10 a.m.–2 p.m. Summer hours are usually extended. Please enquire about special hours on holidays. Entrance fees: Adult NIS 12, child NIS 2, new immigrant NIS 2.

Free guided tours in English are available Sunday, Monday, Wednesday and Thursday at 11.00 a.m. and Tuesday at 4.30 p.m. Special ramps and lifts are available for the disabled to most museum areas. A programme of art films, theatre performances and concerts, for adults and children, continues throughout the year. Tel. (02)708811.

(Bus Nos. 9, 17, 24)

The U. Nahon Museum of Italian Jewish Art, 27 Rehov Hillel. The museum presents all aspects of Jewish life in Italy, both religious and daily, from the Middle Ages to our time. It includes the interior of the 18th century synagogue of Conegliano Veneto, which is still used. Services are held on Friday evenings (20 mins. after candle-lighting) and Saturday mornings (8 a.m.), as well as on festivals. Open: Sun.–Thur. 10 a.m.–1 p.m. Entrance fee: adults — NIS 5, children NIS 3.5. Tel. (02)241610.

(All buses to the center of town)

***Jaffa Gate:** so named because it marked beginning of highway to Jaffa. Inscription says it was built by Sultan

Suleiman 1538–39. General Allenby entered this gate after defeating Turks in 1917. Restored with funds from South African Jewry after Six Day War (it was closed during 1948–67). Today it's the most used thoroughfare into the Old City. It has always been a strategic spot, provoking on occasion pomp and extravagant behaviour. The moat between it and the Citadel was filled up to allow Kaiser Wilhelm II's vehicles to roll in during his celebrated visit at the end of the last century. The road down from here leads to Bethlehem and Hebron.

(Bus Nos. 1, 3, 13, 19, 20, 23, 30)

Jason's Tomb: 10, Rehov Alfasi, Rehavia. Lavish rock-cut tomb in Hellenistic style used by well-to-do Jewish family about 200 years before Christ.

(Bus Nos. 9, 17)

Jeremiah's Grotto (Court of the Prison – Jer. 32:8): Suleiman Street, to the right of the East Jerusalem bus terminus and opposite Herod's Gate. Grotto under sign for "Assalam Panami's Store for Bananas." Legend has it that this is where the didactic, outstandingly virtuous prophet was imprisoned and wrote the Book of Lamentations. An 8th century Moslem saint, Ibrahim el-Adhami, lies buried here. The el-Adhami mosque is at the entrance.

(Bus Nos. 1, 23, 27, 38, 42, 43)

Jerusalem City Museum: see Tower of David.

Jerusalem House of Quality: 12, Derekh Hebron. A centre for the production, exhibition and marketing of products bearing the Jerusalem seal of quality. Free guided tours. Open: Sun. – Thurs. 10 a.m. – 6 p.m. Fri. 10 a.m. – 1 p.m. Information: tel. (02)717430.

(Bus Nos. 5, 6, 7, 8, 21)

Jerusalem Theatre Centre for the Performing Arts: 20 Marcus St., Talbieh. Featuring the best in theatre, music, dance and entertainment from Israel and abroad. Modern architecture, art exhibitions, book store and restaurant. The centre includes the Sherover Theatre, the Rebecca

Crown Auditorium and the Henry Crown Symphony Hall. Tel. (02)667167.

(Bus No. 15)

Jewish Agency Building: corner Rehov Keren Kayemet and King George St. H.Q. of the Jewish Agency and the World Zionist Organization, offices of the Jewish National Fund, the United Jewish Appeal, Keren Hayesod, United Israel Appeals. This is where you'll find the Golden Book of the Jewish National Fund and the Central Zionist Archives. Open: daily 7.30 a.m. – 3 p.m.

(Bus Nos. 4, 7, 8, 9, 19, 22, 31, 32, 48)

***Jewish Quarter:** southeast area of the Old City, bounded by Chain Street to the north, Rehov Ararat to the west, Rehov Batei Mahaseh (which follows the ramparts) to the south, and the Western Wall to the east. Devastated by the Jordanian Arab Legion during 1948–67, synagogues, yeshivas and homes have been built or rebuilt or restored, and archaeological excavations have yielded valuable finds. Several new museums and sites were opened in 1983. During the Maccabean or Hasmonaean dynasty, luxurious palaces made this area an architectural showpiece until 70 CE, when Titus overran Jerusalem and destroyed the Temple and this part of the city. After the 5th century and the advent of the Empress Eudoxia, resettlement was permitted and it probably took place in the vicinity of the Wall. Then came the Crusaders (1099) and it wasn't until Saladin's conquest in 1187 that either Jew or Moslem could safely return to the city. The Jewish Quarter today is larger than the Armenian Quarter but smaller than either the Christian Quarter or the Moslem Quarter.

(Walk No. 1. Bus No. 1, 38)

Kennedy Memorial: at the southwestern outskirts of Jerusalem, the monument is dedicated to the memory of the assassinated President. Fifty pillars (one for each of the states) separated by long, thin glass windows sweep upwards in the shape of a circular trunk that doesn't climb very high when the enormity of its diameter is taken into account. It resembles a truncated tree and symbolizes a life cut short; it's also there to remind one of the late Senator Robert Kennedy. An eternal flame burns at the very centre.

(Bus No. 50 to Moshav Aminadav. Also coach tours)

Kidron Valley: also known as the Valley of Jehoshaphat, sits below the southern Walls between the City of David and the Mount of Olives. From one or two points in the valley, Jerusalem appears as a city rising from an abyss, a mound of houses precariously balanced on a slope. According to the Moslems, the Judgement Day line separating good from evil will stretch over this valley. Most famous sites here are: Tombs of Absalom, Beni Hezir, Zechariah, and the Gihon Spring.

(Bus No. 1)

Knesset (Parliament): Rehov Eliezer Kaplan, opposite Israel Museum. Opened 1966. Giant **Menorah** (seven-branched candelabrum) outside, depicting events of Jewish history, sculpted by Benno Elkan and gift of British Parliament. Entrance gates by late Jerusalemite, David Palombo. Reception hall tapestries by Marc Chagall. Restaurants for members and visitors, and members' synagogue. Government buildings nearby. Guided tours Sun. and Thurs. (when no sittings) 8.30 a.m. – 2.30 p.m. Passport or other form of identity requested.Tel. (02)753333.

(Bus Nos. 9, 24)

L.A. Mayer Memorial Museum for Islamic Art: 2, Rehov Hapalmach. A very attractive museum comprising about 5000 items representing the art of Islamic countries through the ages. There is also an archive and research library. Open: Sun.–Thurs. 10 a.m.–5 p.m., Sat. 10 a.m.–1 p.m. Fri closed. Entrance fee.

(Bus No. 15, Walk No. 2)

***The Latin Patriarchate:** On the road of the same name, between Jaffa Gate and New Gate. Established in the 11th century, its activities were suspended when the Crusaders were banished and the Patriarch went into exile. **St. Saviour's Convent** was built in the mid-16th century following the expulsion of the Franciscans from Mt. Zion. It is a self-contained unit comprising printing press, bakery, wine cellar and so on.

Liberty Bell Garden: Rehov Jabotinsky, across the road from the Montefiore Windmill. Established on the 200th anniversary of U.S. independence, it includes a replica of the Liberty Bell, a puppet theatre, roller-skating rink, and sports facilities.

(Bus Nos. 4, 5, 7, 14, 15, 18, 21)

***Lions' Gate:** named after lions carved in relief on both sides. Built 1538–39. Tradition says Suleiman the Magnificent ordered lions sculpted following his dream that he would be eaten by lions unless he built the Old City walls. Israeli troops first entered Old City through here in Six Day War. Also called St. Stephen's Gate as he is said to have been martyred nearby.

(Walk No. 3. Bus Nos. 1 and 42 or 43 from Damascus Gate)

***Lithostrotos:** An enclosed part of a Roman road within the **Ecce Homo Convent** of the Sisters of Zion. Where Jesus was tried publicly and mocked by Roman soldiers.

(Walk No. 3)

Makhane Yehuda: colourful open market adjoining Rehov Yafo, four streets west of Herut Square. Especially busy on Thursdays, Fridays and holiday eves.

(Bus Nos. 3, 5, 6, 7, 8, 11, 13, 14, 17, 18, 20, 21, 23, 25, 27, 29, 31, 32, 35, 39, 40, 50)

***Mameluke Madrasahs:** Scattered throughout the Moslem Quarter. Islamic theological seminary buildings, some 700 years old.

(Walk No. 2)

Mandelbaum Gate: (also the title of a novel by Muriel Spark); demolished after the 1967 war, it stood at the junction of Shmuel Hanavi, Saint George and Shivtei Yisrael Streets. It was part of an unfortunately situated house (rather than a "gate") which once belonged to a Dr.

Mandelbaum (who sensibly fled the flying buckshot and mortar) and was used as a frontier checkpoint for Christian tourists entering Israel from Jordan. The Israeli convoy to Mt. Scopus prior to the Six Day War passed through here once every two weeks.

(Bus No. 1)

Mea She'arim: The quarter of Jerusalem's ultra-Orthodox communities. North of Shivtei Israel Street, or up Straus Street from the corner of Jaffa Road and King George. Here about one thousand ultra-Orthodox Jews live the life of the Polish shtetl (Jewish village). Some of them do not acknowledge the State of Israel created by Zionists as it could hinder the coming of the Messiah. The entire area is closed to motor traffic on the Sabbath. Visitors should make sure they are modestly dressed (no short pants or sleeveless dresses).

(Walk No. 5. Bus Nos. 1, 3, 11, 29)

Military Cemetery on Mount Herzl: situated on the slope to the north as you walk back along Herzl Boulevard in the direction of the city centre. This is the resting place of Israelis who fell in all the wars since the War of Independence in 1948. Open every day of the year.

(Bus Nos. 13, 16, 17, 18, 20, 21, 23, 24, 26, 27, 39, 40)

***Model of the First Temple:** Rachel Yanait Ben-Zvi Youth Centre for Jerusalem Studies, corner of Plugot Hakotel St. and Shonei Halachot St., Jewish Quarter. Includes a three-dimensional audio-visual show. Open: Sun.–Thurs. 9 a.m.–4 p.m., Tel. (02)286288.

Model of the Second Temple: in grounds of Holyland Hotel, Bayit Vegan. Scale model (1:50) of Jerusalem in 66 CE at beginning of great revolt against Romans. Constructed as far as possible of original materials used at time, including marble, stone, wood, copper and iron. Sources used were Mishna, Tosephta, both Talmuds, Josephus and New Testament. Open: Every day 8 a.m. – 4 p.m. Entrance fee. Tel. (02)788118.

(Bus No. 21)

Monastery of the Cross: Valley of the Cross. Believed

to mark site of tree from which cross was made for Jesus' crucifixion. Sixth century monastery restored in the beginning of the 11th century. Recently re-opened to the public after being closed for several years for complete repair and renovation. Open Mon.–Sat. 9 a.m. – 4 p.m. Entrance fee.

(Bus Nos. 9, 17, 19, 22, 24)

Montefiore's Windmill: This quaint windmill was situated on the Israel-Jordan armistice line between 1948 and 1967. Mill and museum open Sun.–Thurs. 9 a.m–4 p.m., Fri. 9 a.m.–1 p.m. Free.

(Bus Nos. 5, 6, 18, 21)

***Moslem Quarter:** the most densely populated, occupies the northeastern section of the Old City and stretches down beyond the central area. The boundaries are formed by the Walls on the north and the east, Suq Khan e-Zeit on the west, the Street of the Chain all the way to Mt. Moriah in the south. Before the Crusaders this section was Jewish; it was only during the 12th and 13th centuries that the area became a predominantly Moslem one. Includes Temple Mount, start of Via Dolorosa, suqs (markets) and Mameluke buildings.

(Walk No. 2 and start of Walk No. 3)

***Mosque of El-Aksa:** Temple Mount. Islam's holiest shrine after Mecca and Medina, stands on the traditional site of Solomon's Palace and the Palace of the Kings of Jerusalem which was destroyed by the Persians in 614. Built between 710–715 by Waleed, son of Abd el-Malik (who was responsible for the Dome of the Rock), El-Aksa has been shattered twice by earthquake (in 746 and in 1033). Crusaders in 1099 converted the restored structure into a centre for the Knights Templar until Saladin's triumph 88 years later when it was set aside again as a mosque.

A bullet-marked pillar inside the entrance indicates where King Abdullah of Transjordan was assassinated in 1951; the Tombs of the Sons of Aaron to the right are said to contain the remains of the assassins of 12th century Archbishop of Canterbury Thomas à Becket. They came to the Holy Land as pilgrim penitents at the service of the Templars and never made it back. In 1969 an Australian pyromaniac started a fire here and destroyed a priceless ebony pulpit. The south side, facing Mecca, is ahead of you as you walk in; the central nave stands between three aisles on each side (balancing with the seven arched portals outside); white Italian marble was used for the central and left-side pillars; the stained glass windows added by Suleiman in the 16th century give some colour to the gloomy afternoon shadows. Inscription on wall near the main entrance praises the late King Farouk of Egypt for financing repairs. "El-Aksa" means "the distant place" (from Mecca) and is associated in the Koran with Mohammed's night journey. Open same hours as the Dome of the Rock. Closed Friday. Entrance fee includes Dome of the Rock and the Islamic Museum.

(Walk No. 2)

***Mosque of Omar:** see Dome of the Rock.

Mount Herzl: Herzl Boulèvard. Burial place of Theodor Herzl (1860–1904), the journalist, jurist and visionary who enormously inspired the Zionist movement and arranged the First Zionist Congress in Basel in 1897. He died in Vienna but his remains (together with those of his immediate family) were re-interred in Jerusalem in honour of his founding role in the establishment of Israel. Near Herzl's Tomb is the **Tomb of Ze'ev Jabotinsky**, another (re-interred) giant of the early Zionist scene. Golda Meir is also buried here. The **Herzl Museum**, the first building as you approach the memorial area from Herzl Boulevard, is dedicated to the events and some of the objects in Herzl's life (letters, articles, etc., and his reconstructed study).

Down the **Avenue of the Righteous Gentiles** (where all the trees were planted by non-Jews who helped Jews escape from the Nazis) is **Yad Vashem** (see separate entry).

(Bus Nos. 13, 16, 17, 18, 20, 21, 23, 24, 26, 27, 39, 40)

***Mount Moriah:** (see Temple Mount).

Mount of Olives: "And David went up by the ascent of the Mount of Olives, and wept as he went up; and he had his head covered, and went barefoot..." (2 Samuel, 15:30). Associated with Judaism for over 3,000 years, the slopes hold the graves of pious Jews who died with the hope that the Resurrection of the Dead will begin here. Grim, final scenes in the life of Jesus were played out in this area. Of interest here are tombs of the Prophets, Christian shrines and Tomb of Mary, Basilica of the Agony (Church of All Nations), and Garden of Gethsemane, Church of St. Mary Magdalene, Dominus Flevit, Chapel of the Ascension and Church of Pater Noster. From the top of the mount, next to the Seven Arches Hotel, is a breathtaking view of the Old City and parts of the new city.

(Walk No. 4. Bus Nos. 42 and 43 from Damascus Gate)

Mount of Scandal (or Offence): rising on southern side of Silwan village. So named because King Solomon is said to have built temples on it for his pagan wives.

Mount Scopus: North of Mt. of Olives. Here you'll find the Hebrew university's original campus, now rebuilt (—one of its four campuses), the Hadassah University Mount Scopus Hospital and the British WWI military cemetery. The University boasts a classic open-air theatre overlooking the Judaean Desert and the Dead Sea, beautiful panoramas of Old and New Jerusalem from lookout points along the ring road, a computerized central library, an unusual modern synagogue, the Harry S. Truman Research Centre for the Advancement of Peace and a 40-acre botanical garden devoted to Biblical and Talmudic flora and indigenous flora of Israel with a garden for the blind and a rock-hewn, subterrannean Second Temple period tomb, the Nikanor cave. Free campus tours 11 a.m. Sun.–Thurs. from Bronfman Reception Centre, Sherman Administration Building.

(Bus Nos. 4a, 9, 23, 26, 28, 46)

Mount Zion: at southwest corner of Old City outside walls, site of Traditional Tomb of David, Chamber of the Holocaust, Room of Jesus' Last Supper (see Cenacle), David Palombo Museum, Church of the Dormition, House of Caiaphas and various Christian cemeteries. The name "Zion" is thought to have derived from a Jebusite temple or stronghold which stood somewhere here when King David conquered the area. Isaiah prophesied that the law would go forth out of Zion and the word of the

Lord from Jerusalem. The Hinnom Valley below connects with the Valley of Kidron on the eastern side and extends to Yemin Moshe.

(Walk No. 1. Bus Nos. 1, 38)

***Muristan:** quarter adjacent to Church of Holy Sepulchre. Site of 2nd century Roman forum. "Muristan" is Persian for hospital, referring to headquarters here of Crusader Order of the Hospitallers. Kaiser Wilhelm was presented with land here and on it he built (in 1898) the **Lutheran Church of the Redeemer**. The tower of this church dominates the skyline and the view from the top is a good one (fee for ascending tower). See the signs of the zodiac over the gateway, the nearby mediaeval cloister, and the carefully arranged antiquities. There is a Greek bazaar in the area.

(Walk No. 3)

Natural History Museum: 6, Rehov Mohilever. Human anatomy and Israel's fauna. Open: Sun.–Thurs. 9 a.m.–1.30 p.m. Mon. & Wed. 9 a.m.–5.30 p.m. Tel. (02)631116. Entrance fee.

(Bus Nos. 4, 14, 18)

***Nea Church:** Located at the southern end of the Jewish Quarter, the Nea Church is one of the largest Byzantine churches. It was built by the Emperor Justinian (485–565 CE). Open: Thurs.–Sat. 9 a.m.–5 p.m., Fri. 9 a.m.–1 p.m. Tel. (02)228141.

***New Gate:** Rehov Hatzanhanim. Built 1887 by permission of Sultan Abdul Hamid II, to facilitate access between Christian Quarter and Christian properties west of the gate. Closed from 1948 to 1967.

***Old City** (see maps on Southern Sheet): The massive Walls and Gates you see today were constructed by Suleiman towards the middle of the 16th century. Until about a hundred years ago, the enclosed section formed the

city's total inhabited area. It remains divided into four quarters: Moslem (northeast), Christian (northwest), Jewish (southeast) and Armenian (southwest). The Western

Wall, the Church of the Holy Sepulchre, the Dome of the Rock and El-Aksa Mosque are situated here.

(Walk Nos. 1, 2, 3. Bus Nos. 1, 13, 19, 20, 23, 27, 38)

Ophel Archaeological Garden (Yitzhak Ben Youssef Levy Garden): bordering the southern wall of the Old City. These archaeological excavations revealed the administrative complex erected on the Ophel Hill in the First Temple period. Visitors can view remains of structures dating all the way back to King Solomon: the remains of a monumental public building from the First Temple period, paved streets from the Second Temple period, Jewish ritual baths, sections of "Robinson's Arch" from the Second Temple period, and partially-restored Byzantine houses with mosaic floors.

(Bus No. 1)

***Old Yishuv Court Museum:** 6, Rehov Or HaHaim, Jewish Quarter. A house with a courtyard, it was partially destroyed in 1948 and subsequently restored and turned into a museum (in 1976) to reflect the life of the Jewish community of the Old City from the middle of the 19th century until the end of Ottoman rule in 1917. The two-storey museum consists of an Ashkenazi guest room, a Sephardi guest room, a bedroom (showing furniture of the period), a kitchen (with utensils and baking arrangments), and a room for trades and crafts. The house also includes two former synagogues, one Ashkenazi, the other Sephardi. According to tradition "The Ari", Rabbi Yitzhak ben Shlomo Luria Ashkenazi, the famous Kabbalist, was born in one of the ground-floor rooms in 1534. Open: Sun.–Thurs. 9 a.m.–4 p.m. Closed Fri., Sat., eve of Jewish festivals. Entrance fee. Can be reached on foot from Jaffa Gate through St James' Road (see Walk No. 1 for a description of how to get to the Jewish Quarter). Tel. (02)284636.

Pontifical Biblical Institute: 3, Rehov Paul Emile Botta. Archaeological collection including Egyptian mummy. Also library. Visit Mon., Wed., Fri. from 9 a.m. to noon or by appointment. Tel. (02)252843. Admission free.

(Bus Nos. 5, 6, 15, 18, 21)

***Pools of Bethesda:** see Church of St. Anne.

Pool of Siloam: in the Kidron valley. Fed by waters from Gihon Spring. Revered by Christians as site where Jesus cured blind man. Ruins nearby of Byzantine church and Herodian bathhouse. Free.

(Bus Nos. 1, 38)

President's Residence: 3, Rehov Hanassi, Talbieh. Official residence of President of Israel, handsomely ornamented and decorated by leading artists. Open to the public only on special occasions or by previous arrangement.

(Bus Nos. 15, 15a, 99)

Promenade: (see Observation Points, pp.000)

Ramat Rahel: kibbutz on the road to Bethlehem. Entered by way of Talpiot Quarter. This settlement, placed as it was on the pre-1967 border with Jordan, made a target for trigger-happy Arab troops. During the 1948 war, it was alternately lost and re-occupied by Israelis. There is an inexpensive guest house, a swimming pool (open all year round) and tennis courts, also camping facilities, bungalows and a restaurant. There is an archaeological site which includes ruins of an Israelite fort and a Byzantine church.

(Bus No. 7)

Ramparts Walk: There can hardly be a better way to view the city than from the ancient walkway around the Old City. Exit and entry points are located at Lions' Gate, Damascus Gate and Herod's Gate. Open 9 a.m.–5 p.m. Sun.–Thurs.; Fri. 9 a.m.–3 p.m. Entrance fee – adult IS 2.20, child IS 1. Tel (02) 224403.

(Bus Nos. 1, 13, 19, 20, 38)

Rockefeller Museum: near corner of Suleiman St. and Jericho Rd. Originally called the Palestine Archaeological Museum, it was designed by English architect Austin Harrison; the octagonal tower rises over a central courtyard to which the halls and library are connected. Exhibits include the prehistoric Carmel Man, reconstruction of a

Middle Bronze Age tomb, Crusader lintels from the Church of the Holy Sepulchre, and a unique selection of 8th century CE architectural decorative fragments from Hisham's Palace, and coins. There is also a library with thousands of texts on the Holy Land's history, prehistory, geology and geography. Entrance fee. Open: Sun.–Thurs. 10 a.m.–5 p.m. Fri., Sat. 10 a.m.–2 p.m

(Walk No. 3 or Bus Nos. 1, 23, 27, 99)

Russian Compound: off Jaffa Road, near the Main Post Office. Bought by Czar Alexander II and built up in the 1860s, it was in its time a busy centre for Russian pilgrims to Jerusalem; in the 1920s it was the biggest hotel around. See the exterior of the **Cathedral of the Holy Trinity** with its green-domed towers (a fairyland castle floodlit at night). Notice the large unfinished Herodian column across the road from the Cathedral. The Israel government has purchased the compound, which today houses police, law and other administration offices.

(Bus Nos. 3, 5, 11, 13, 15, 18, 19, 20, 21, 23, 29, 38, 40)

Sanhedrin Tombs: in a park near corner Rehov Shmuel Hanavi and Rehov Hativat Harel, Sanhedria. Rock-hewn tombs and caves believed to be burial places of Second Temple judges. Open daily until sunset. You might need a torch. Entrance free.

(Bus Nos. 2, 38)

***Sephardi Synagogue Complex:** see Synagogues in the Jewish Quarter.

***Siebenberg House:** 6 Hagitit St., Jewish Quarter. Display of archaeological remains dating back 3,000 years, which were found under the recently-built home of Theo Siebenberg. Mikves (ritual baths), royal burial vaults, a huge cistern, jars, mosaics, coins and so on were excavated here. Open: Sun.–Thurs. 9 a.m.–5 p.m., Fri. 9 a.m.–1 p.m. Guided tours in English at noon. Entrance fee. Tel. (02)282341.

(Walk No. 1 or Bus No. 1)

Shrine of the Book: see Israel Museum.

Silwan Village: southeast of the City of David. An Arab village across Hashiloah Rd. from the Pool of Siloam. Also known as the Mount of Offence, this is where Solomon built temples to the pagan gods venerated by his many wives. First Temple period rock-hewn tombs are strewn around the village.

(Bus No. 1)

Skirball Museum of Biblical Archaeology at Hebrew Union College: 13 King David St. Open: Sun.–Thurs. 10 a.m.–4 p.m.; Fri., Sat. 10 a.m.–2 p.m. Free. Tel. (02)203333.

(Bus Nos. 5, 6, 18)

Solomon's Quarries: see Zedekiah's Cave.

State Archives: Prime Minister's Office building, Hakirya. Original scroll of Declaration of Independence and other historic documents. Open: weekdays 9 a.m.–1 p.m. Admission free.

(Bus Nos. 9, 24)

St. George's Cathedral: American Colony. Nablus Road. Anglican Church consecrated in 1898.

(Bus No. 27)

St. Stephen's Basilica: (St. Etienne; not to be confused with St. Stephen's Church, below): situated on Nablus Rd. between St. George's Cathedral and the Garden Tomb. A 19th century building over ruins of the first church built by the Empress Eudoxia (5th century), pulled down by the Persians (7th century), rebuilt by the Crusaders (11th century), only to be pulled down again by Saladin (12th century). The Dominican Institute of Bible and Archaeology is situated here. In the courtyard are two large burial caves from the First Temple period. Closed to the public.

(Bus Nos. 42, 43, 64)

St. Stephen's Church: Jericho Rd., diagonally across from the Basilica of the Agony. The first Christian martyr, Stephen, was killed close by, on the steps cut in the rock leading from the Temple Mount to the Kidron Roman bridge.

(Walk No. 4. Bus Nos. 1, and 42 or 43 from Damascus Gate)

***Stations of the Cross:** 14 significant points along the Via Dolorosa. See Via Dolorosa.

(Walk No. 3)

Supreme Court Building: near the Knesset. A superb example of modern architecture, the building was recently opened and has already become a major attraction.

(Bus Nos. 9, 17, 24)

***Synagogues in the Jewish Quarter:** There are many synagogues in this Quarter. The oldest and most interesting synagogues are to be found off Jewish Quarter Road and Bet-El Road. First, the oldest, the **Ramban Synagogue**, was established in 1267 by Spanish rabbi Moshe ben Nahman (known as the Ramban) who remodelled an existing (marble-pillared) Crusader structure. When the Ramban arrived in Jerusalem he found only two Jews (cloth dyers) in the city: the ill-wind of the Inquisition blew more and more Jews to Jerusalem and the Ramban synagogue was at one time used by both Sephardim and Ashkenazim. Late in the 16th century, the synagogue was turned into a mosque. The present structure was built later by the Ashkenazi community and adjoins the old site. Renovated after 1967 it is now used for daily prayers. At the northern wall of the synagogue are the remains of the **Hurva Synagogue**, an impressive and important Ashkenazi devotional centre until 1948 when it was reduced to little more than a wall and rubble by the Arab Legion. Building of the Hurva Synagogue started as long ago as 1700 with money from Sassoon and Rothschild for the Polish followers of Rabbi Yehuda the Hassid; Moslem threats and the death of the rabbi delayed its completion until 1864. A stone arch has been reconstructed above the ruins as a memorial. Open: Sun.–Thurs., Sat. 9 a.m.–5 p.m., Fri. 9 a.m.–1 p.m. Free. Tel. (02)288141. **Four Sephardi Synagogues** (Walk No. 1): down Beit-El Road; built in the 16th century by exiles from Spain, the synagogues were restored to simple elegance and reopened in 1972. Open: Sun.–Thurs. 9 a.m.–3 p.m., Fri 9 a.m.–1 p.m. The **Synagogue of Elijah the Prophet** (Eliahu Hanavi), around a cave supposedly frequented by Elijah, was used as a shelter for goats and other livestock by the Jordanians. Carved hands bless you at the door of the **Istanbuli Synagogue**; the **Synagogue of Rabbi Ben Zakkai,** larger than the other three, was at one point made to look like a mosque to fool intolerant Turks who might have passed by; finally the **Middle (Emtzai) Synagogue** – grew out of the courtyard and ritual bath used by the other three. Money for the improvements came from the patron saints of building and restoration in the Holy Land, the Rothschilds. **The Tiferet Yisrael Synagogue**, on the street of the same name, was one of the largest and most attractive synagogues in Jerusalem before 1948. Today all that remains is an arched facade. The **Habad** and **Bet-El** Synagogues are two other well-known places of worship in this area.

Tax Museum: 32, Agron St. Exhibition relating to history of taxation in Palestine and Israel. Open: Sun., Tues., Thurs. 1–4 p.m. Mon., Wed. 10 a.m.–noon. Admission free.

(Bus Nos. 6, 15, 18, 19, 21, 22)

***Temple Mount (Mount Moriah):** The site of various Jewish sanctuaries throughout the ages, starting with the altar where Abraham prepared to sacrifice Isaac, rebuilt by Jacob during his flight from Esau, and reconstructed by King David when he built the foundations and prepared the materials for the permanent Temple on Mount Moriah. The latter is the name of the natural ridge stretching from the northwest to the southeast. After raising the level of the slopes around the top of the narrow ridge, King Solomon erected the First Temple here.

After the Babylonian exile the ruined Temple was rebuilt by Zerubabel and Ezra. After the Seleucid desecration and partial ruin, the Maccabees did the same. Then a grandiose sanctuary, which served as a huge fortress and national administrative centre and treasury, was erected by Herod the Great in 18 B.C.E., some 2,000 years ago.

This was the Temple mentioned in later religious and historical sources.

The Temple Mount was coveted by innumerable powers and religions: heathens and Christians, Persians and Mongolians and Moslems, Crusaders and colonisers.

Today the Mount is topped by beautiful Moslem edifices: the Dome of the Rock and El-Aksa Mosque. Under them, a mysterious subterranean system awaits exploration: a maze of tunnels, water and drainage conduits, storage rooms and treasure chambers, hide-outs and siege fortifications.

(Walk Nos. 1 and 2)

Third Wall Remains (off Nablus Road at the entrance of the American consulate): what's left of the third city wall (from Jaffa Gate to the West Jerusalem Russian Compound and back to this spot); thought to have been begun by Agrippa, in 41 CE, to enclose the city by then expanding beyond the northern walls.

(Bus No. 27)

Ticho House: Simtat Ticho, off Rehov Harav Kook 7. A branch of the Israel Museum, containing artworks by the late Anna Ticho, and Hanukka lamps collected by her husband, an eye specialist. Open: Sun.–Thurs. 10 a.m.–5 p.m., Fri. 10 a.m.–2 p.m. Admission free. There is a garden restaurant, open from 10 a.m. to midnight during the week, Fri. 10 a.m.–3 p.m. Tel. (02)245068, 244186.

(Walk No. 5 or Bus Nos. 5, 6, 15, 18, 21)

Tomb of David: Mt. Zion. Traditional site of his tomb, as result of erroneous early belief that David's city extended to Mt. Zion. If not in Ophel, as some people believe, David might have been buried somewhere in Bethlehem. However, this enormous, probably Crusader tomb was "identified" as David's by (Spanish) Rabbi Benjamin in 1173, and it has continued to be referred to as such ever since. Open daily 8 a.m. – 5 p.m. Fri. 8 a.m. – 2 p.m.

(Walk No. 1. Bus Nos. 1, 38)

Tombs of Bnei Hezir: Kidron Valley, next to Absalom's Tomb. Hebrew inscription above Doric column indicates tombs of Hasmonaean priestly family. Some Christians believe skeleton found in 4th century was that of Jesus' cousin, James. James may have hidden here after Jesus' arrest. In 15th century, site claimed as Tomb of St. James.

(Bus Nos. 1, 42, 43)

Tomb of Hulda the Prophetess: domed catacomb opposite Church of Pater Noster, Mt. of Olives. Key from officials at nearby mosque.

(Walk No. 4)

Tomb of Jehoshaphat: Kidron Valley, behind Absalom's Tomb. Large hewn alcove decorated with ornately-carved frieze of acanthus leaves. 1st or 2nd centuries CE.

(Bus No. 1, 42, 43)

Tombs of the Kings: Saladin Street. Named erroneously as final resting place of kings of Judah. Actually family tomb of Queen Helena of Adiabene (in Mesopotamia) who came to Jerusalem in the 1st century CE and converted to Judaism. Contained 30 tombs hewn from rock and decorated with symbols of plenty. A rolling stone was used to block the entrance. A torch is necessary.

(Bus No. 27)

Tombs of the Prophets: supposedly Haggai, Malachi and Zechariah, also some later Greek scribblers. Located just off the Mount of Olives Road (from Pater Noster) leading to the Jewish Cemetery and Observation Point. (Use a torch.)

(Walk No. 4)

Tomb of Simon the Just: near Mt. Scopus Road, Sheikh Jarrah quarter. Tomb of 4th century CE scholar, High Priest Simon. Jewish pilgrimages to tomb since 13th century.

(Bus Nos. 2, 25, 27, 40)

Tomb of the Virgin Mary: in Greek **Orthodox Church of the Assumption,** Mt. of Olives. Open: weekdays 6–11.30 a.m., 2–5 p.m. (See Grotto of Gethsemane.)

(Walk No. 4. Bus Nos. 1, 42, 43)

Tomb of Zechariah: Kidron Valley, near Gihon Spring. A massive monument, it was carved out of a single piece of rock, and capped with a pyramid, with pillars on its sides. The name might refer either to the prophet

Zechariah or to Zacharias, father of John the Baptist. It is thought to be a 1st century CE tomb. The controversial scholar-archaeologist John Allegro, following information in one of the Dead Sea Scrolls, excavated around here in the early 1960s in search of Temple treasures hidden from the Romans. A tunnel leads up from here to the Bnei Hezir tombs.

(Bus Nos. 1, 42, 43)

Tourjeman Post: 1 Chail Hahandasa St., near former Mandelbaum Gate. This historic house was restored by the Jerusalem Foundation in 1983. Built in the 1930s on land owned by Hassan Bey Tourjeman, the house served as an Israeli military post on the border with Jordan during the War of Independence and the years of Jerusalem's division. When the city was reunified, the building was partly restored and now features an exhibition of photographs, documents and audio-visual material showing Jerusalem then and now. Open: Sun.–Thurs. 9 a.m.–4 p.m., Fri. 9 a.m.–1 p.m. Tel (02)281278.

(Bus Nos. 1, 11, 27, 99)

***Tower of David** (Museum of the City of Jerusalem): Jaffa Gate. Opened in 1989, this museum relates the history of Jerusalem from the Canaanite period to the present, through archaeological finds and lively exhibits. Also featured is a nineteenth century model of Jerusalem, panoramic viewpoints, and an evening sound and light show. Various tours, including a tour for handicapped visitors, are available. Open: Sun.–Thurs. 10 a.m.–5 p.m., Fri. 10 a.m.–2 p.m., Sat. 10 a.m.–5 p.m. In summer, hours are extended to 7 p.m., subject to change. The sound and light show is presented in Hebrew on Sun., Thurs., and Sat. 7.30 p.m. standard time, in English on Sun., Thurs. and Sat. 8.30 p.m., in German on Sun., Tues. and Thurs. 9.30 p.m. and in French on Mon., Wed. and Sat. 9.30 p.m. Entrance fee.

(Bus Nos. 1, 13, 19, 20)

Tower of the Ascension: the most prominent landmark in the Mount of Olives area. From a rock in what is today a small Russian Orthodox church, Mary watched Jesus ascend to heaven. John the Baptist's severed head was said to have been buried nearby. See Jerusalem and the Dead Sea from the top of the tower.

***Tower of the Storks:** northeast corner of Old City Wall. So named because storks once rested here during their yearly migrations.

***Via Dolorosa** (Way of Grief): If you enter the Old City from Damascus Gate, take the left fork (El-Wad Rd.) and follow it a short distance down until you come to the Via Dolorosa on your left. This is believed to be the painful route taken by Jesus on his walk to crucifixion. Points along the way where he is thought to have stopped or some memorable event occurred have been marked as the 14 Stations of the Cross. Franciscans lead groups in prayer along the Via Dolorosa on Fridays at 3 p.m., starting at El-Omariye School, Moslem Quarter, and ending in the Church of the Holy Sepulchre, Christian Quarter. A pilgrims' reception plaza has been built inside St. Stephen's Gate, where many tours begin.

Station I (Condemnation): in the grounds of El-Omariye School alongside ruins of the South East Tower of the Antonia Fortress (named after Mark Antony by Herod), where Christ was condemned to death.

Station II: across the road, to the left of the gate as you walk into the **Franciscan Bible School and Museum.** A plaque on the wall indicates the spot. **The Chapel of the Flagellation** to the right is an attractive Byzantine structure with striking stained glass windows. An altar here is dedicated to St. Paul who also spent time in the Antonia prison.

The Chapel of Condemnation, at the other end of the courtyard, is where Pilate sentenced Jesus. Also a Byzantine structure, painted effigies inside portray the scenes of the Condemnation and of Mary meeting Jesus (Station IV).

Proceeding along the Via Dolorosa, you come to the **Ecce Homo Arch**. The founder of the Convent of the Sisters of Zion, Ratisbonne, believed (with little justification) that this is where Pilate pointed to the bruised and whipped Jesus and said "Ecce Homo" (Behold the Man). The arch was erected by Hadrian in the 2nd century but it does stand over ruins of the Antonia Fortress as does the **Convent of the Sisters of Zion** where you should see the

Antonia Museum, the **Ecce Home Basilica**, the flagstones (**Lithostratos** – Greek) with games markings, the **Water Conduit**, and so on. Groups are organized from the reception room.

Station III: at the corner of El-Wad and Dolorosa, adjoining the Armenian Catholic Patriarchate and the Polish Biblical and Archaeological Museum. Traditionally, this is where Jesus first fell.

Station IV: a few steps further on, to the left, a small oratory by the Armenian Church of Our Lady of the Spasm. Here Jesus fell exhausted and was first seen by his mother.

Station V: situated across El-Wad Road up the steps to the right in a Franciscan oratory. At this point, the Roman legionnaires forced a Libyan (Simon of Cyrene) to carry Jesus' cross.

Station VI: further along the Via Dolorosa (which has followed roughly an "S" turn) is the Church of St. Veronica, at present kept by the Little Sisters (a Greek order). Traditionally, a noblewoman, Veronica, rushed out on seeing Jesus and wiped his face with a cloth on which his features became imprinted (vera icone – true likeness).

Station VII: at the junction of Suq Khan Ez-Zeit St. and El Khanqa St., two Franciscan chapels where Jesus fell for the second time. The red-tinted column (from Hadrian's time) in one of the chapels gives the exact spot.

Station VIII: across the road from the seventh station, a cross on the wall of the Greek Orthodox Monastery of Charalambos marks the spot where Jesus spoke to the women of Jerusalem and foretold its destruction.

Station IX: off Suq Khan Ez-Zeit Street, steps to the right, a column at the door of the Coptic Convent behind the Holy Sepulchre. Here Jesus fell for the third time. The next five stations are in the nearby Church of the Holy Sepulchre.

(Walk No. 3)

Viri Galilaei: the Latin for Men of Galilee – part of a group that also witnessed Jesus' ascension. Near the above-named Greek church (and closer to the Mount of Olives Road) is a Byzantine chapel commemorating archangel Gabriel's meeting with Mary to tell her that she was about to die.

***The Walls** (see also Ramparts Walk, and maps on

Southern Sheet); nearly two miles of walls were built during the 16th century by Suleiman the Magnificent, the ruler of the Ottoman Empire, to make Jerusalem a "walled city." The British Administration left them standing when it took control 400 years after Suleiman. The Jordanian army used the walls to snipe at people on the Israeli side (1948–1967). Now the municipality has put railings on the ramparts. You can walk from Jaffa Gate to Damascus Gate, and from Jaffa Gate to Zion Gate and Dung Gate along the top of the wall. Open daily from 9 a.m. to 5 p.m. Entrance fee.

Warren's Shaft (see also City of David): in the City of David Archaeological Garden. Shows the underground water system of biblical Jerusalem, connected to the Gihon Spring. Small museum with finds, photographs and model of water works. Open: Sun.–Thurs. 9 a.m.–4 p.m., Fri. 9 a.m.–2 p.m. Entrance fee: adults IS 2, children IS 1.

(Bus No. 1)

***Western (Wailing) Wall (Hakotel):** Temple Mount. Together with southwestern wall, comprises only remains of enclosure of Second Temple. After destruction of Temple by Titus in 70 CE was symbol of lost glory and consequently dubbed "Wailing Wall." Since Jerusalem reunited under Jewish sovereignty in Six Day War it has continued as open-air synagogue; the adjacent plaza is a forum for dancing, singing and meetings.

Large limestone blocks are Herodian. Smaller stones added by Byzantines, Arabs and Turks. Right-hand side for women, left for men. Vaulted arches screened from view on left known as Wilson's Arch, which in Herodian times linked Temple Mount with Upper City. More than 15 metres of wall lie below ground level and length runs past Via Dolorosa.

(Walk Nos. 1 and 2. Bus Nos. 1, 38)

***Wilson's Arch:** excavations next to the Western Wall. carried out by 19th century British explorer, Capt. Charles Wilson. Open: Sun., Tues., Wed. 8.30 a.m.–3 p.m., Mon., Thurs. 12.30–3 p.m., Fri. 8.30 a.m.– noon. Free.

Wolfson Museum: 60, King George Street, within

Hechal Shlomo. Jewish religious and folk art. Religious artefacts, pictures, holiday decorations, embroidery, numismatic collection, ancient maps. Dioramas showing historic scenes from the Bible. Open: Sun.–Thurs. 9 a.m.–1 p.m. Fri. until 12 noon. Entrance fee. Tel. (02)247112.

(Bus Nos. 4, 7, 8, 9, 17, 19, 22)

Wohl Rose Park: located next to the Knesset. 20 acres planted with over 500 strains of beautiful roses. Tours can be arranged by telephoning (02)637233.

(Bus Nos. 9, 24)

Yad Vashem: Mt. of Remembrance, near Mt. Herzl. Memorial to Martyrs and Heroes of the Holocaust. Hall of Remembrance with mosaic floor inscribed with names of 22 largest concentration and death camps under Nazis. Eternal flame and vault with victims' ashes. Synagogue with curtain on Ark and cloth on table salvaged from European synagogues. Permanent exhibition devoted to Nazi anti-Semitism and propaganda under theme, "Remembrance is the Secret of Redemption." Pillar of Heroism, 23 m. high with inscriptions recalling deeds of valour. Central Archives of Holocaust and Jewish Resistance. There is an art gallery of Holocaust works, as well as a synagogue and various sculptures commemorating the martyrs. Avenue of Righteous Gentiles leading to memorial buildings has trees planted in honour of non-Jews who risked their lives to save Jews. Open: Sun.–Thurs. 9 a.m. – 5 p.m. Fri. 9 a.m. – 2 p.m. Entrance free. Tel. (02)531202.

(Bus Nos. 13, 16, 17, 18, 20, 21 ,23, 24, 26, 27, 39, 40 to Mt. Herzl)

Y.M.C.A. (West): Rehov David Hamelekh. One of the consequences of the re-unification of Jerusalem is that the city has two "Y"s. The one in West Jerusalem was constructed in 1933 and is acknowledged as the most beautiful in the world. The bell tower houses the only carillon of bells in the Middle East, and famous carillon-players often give concerts during the summer. Apart from a gymnasium, a swimming pool, and other sporting facilities, it also serves as a moderately priced hotel with a restaurant and a snack-bar. The view of the city from the top of the well-known bell tower, the copy of a second century mosaic map of the city, and the peaceful gardens argue for a visit. Bell tower open: 9 a.m.–2.30 p.m., entrance fee: IS 1.50.

(Bus Nos. 5, 6, 15, 18, 21)

Zedekiah's Cave: This cave acquired its name from the legend that it was used as an escape route to Jericho by King Zedekiah when he attempted to escape the Chaldean army at the time of destruction of the First Temple. It is located below the Old City wall, next to Damascus Gate. The Freemasons call it "King Solomon's Quarries" because they believe it supplied the stone used to build the First Temple. Stones quarried from the cave were in fact used for important public buildings in Jerusalem from the First Temple period, and as recently as the beginning of the twentieth century. The cave is about 1000 metres in circumference. Sealed by the Turks in 1542, it was rediscovered accidently in 1854. Entrance fee. Open: 9 a.m.–1 p.m.

(Bus Nos. 1, 27)

***Zion Gate:** leads to Mt. Zion. Damaged by Palmach in May 1948, when breached to lift siege of Jewish Quarter. Plaque commemorates reopening by Israel Defence Forces engineers after Six Day War. Battle scars preserved to record history of the city.

(Walk No. 1. Bus No. 1)

Zionist Confederation House Cultural Centre: Emile Botta St. (behind the King David Hotel). A historic building which has been restored to serve groups of Israelis and tourists. Programmes consist of lectures, musical performances, poetry readings, etc. Coffee shop and restaurant. Tel. (02)245206.

(Bus Nos. 5, 6, 18, 21)

Zoo: see Biblical Zoo.

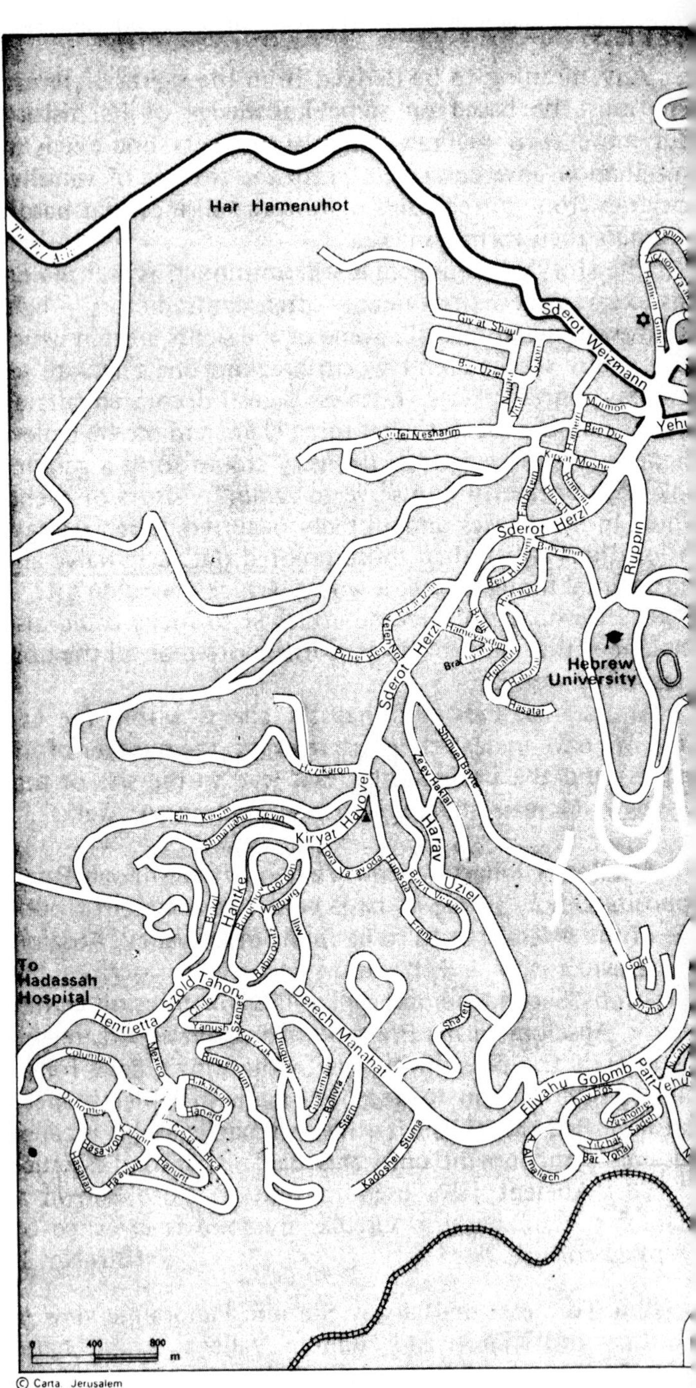
Har Hamenuhot
To Tel Aviv
Sderot Weizmann
Giv'at Shaul
Kanfei Nesharim
Kiryat Moshe
Sderot Herzl
Ruppin
Hebrew University
Hasatat
Shmuel Bayit
Ze'ev Haklai
Harav Uziel
Kiryat Hayovel
Ein Kerem
Hantke
Gordon
Frank
To Hadassah Hospital
Henrietta Szold
Tahon
Derech Manahat
Ringelblum
Bolivia
Stern
Kadoshei Stuma
Eliyahu Golomb
Gold
Sharett
Columbia
Mexico
Hasavyon
Haavivit
Hanurit
Almaliach
Bar Yohai
Yitzhak Sadeh
Hashomer
© Carta, Jerusalem

Hebrew University
Derech Shechem
Nahal Haegoz
Bar Ilan
Har'el
Sderot Eshkol
Shimon Hatzadik
Derech Har Hazeitim
Lohamei Hageta'ot
Hahagana
Paran
Yam Suf
Mea She'arim
Rashi
Yafo
Haneviim
St. George
Suleiman
Hativat Hatzanhanim
Samuel Ben Adja
Derech Yericho
To Jericho
Old City
Mamilla
Agron
King George
Ramban
Keren Hayesod
Hillel
Ben Maimon
Aza
Hativat Yerushalaim
Har Zion
Mishkenot
Jabotinsky
Derech Hevron
Ein Rogel
Emek Refaim
Ben Zakai
Derech Beit Lehem
Chopin
Pinsker
Dubnow
Gedalia Alon
Rahel Imenu
Shimon
Gid'on
Yehuda
Rivka
Metzada
Beitar
Gil'ad
Mekor Haim
Hasadna
Olei Haviv
Ramat Rachel

Walks In Jerusalem

WALK No. 1 – CITADEL, ARMENIAN QUARTER, MT. ZION, JEWISH QUARTER, WESTERN WALL (see Old City map on Southern Sheet).

This comprehensive walk leads you through the Armenian Quarter to the shrines on Mt. Zion, back into the Old City through the Jewish Quarter, and then down to the Western Wall.

Take Bus Nos. 1, 13, 19, 20 or 23 to the **Jaffa Gate** (see Sites).

A **Government Tourist Information Office** is on your left, as you enter the gate.

On your right is the **Citadel**, popularly but erroneously called **David's Tower**. Worth seeing here are the archaeological courtyard and the newly opened Museum of the History of Jerusalem. Also the multi-slide show and a zinc model of Jerusalem made in 1873. Enter the Citadel by climbing the steps off the road curving right. General Allenby announced the liberation of Jerusalem in 1917 from the platform at the top of the steps. The gate behind it was constructed by Suleiman the Magnificent in 1531.

The Citadel was rebuilt by Herod on Hasmonaean foundations with Phasael, Mariamne and Hippicus Towers above the palace fortress. Only Phasael Tower, named after his ill-fated brother, and the Citadel's foundations survive. After the suppression of the Bar-Kochba revolt the Romans stationed their legionnaires in the Citadel. This structure was later added to by the Crusaders and the

Saracens. The upper sections of the walls and all the fortifications were built by the Ottoman Turks.

The moat beyond the gate surrounds the Citadel. Phasael Tower is to your right. Cross a Turkish bridge to the 14th century Mameluke gateway. You may climb the stairs up Phasael. It offers a breathtaking view of the Old City (see "Places to Visit" – Citadel).

The minaret in the southern tower dates back to the 17th century while the southeastern tower is Mameluke. The northwestern tower has Crusader foundations and slits for arrows near the top. As you enter the courtyard you will find excavations from the Hasmonaean and Arab periods. The upper sections of the walls and all the fortifications were built by the Ottoman Turks.

Exit from the Citadel the way you entered. Across the road is the Anglican **Christ Church**. It dates from 1849.

Now go along **Armenian Orthodox Patriarch Road**, past the police station on your right. Turn left into **St. James' Road**, following its curves and then turning left into **Ararat Street**; on your right is Syrian Orthodox Street.

Enter the **Syrian Orthodox Monastery**. (It is only open from 3 to 4 p.m.) These black-robed monks speak and pray in Aramaic, the language in general use during the time of Jesus. Their exquisitely ornamented 12th century church is built over the site of the house of Mary, the mother of St. Mark, where Peter called after being delivered from prison (Acts 12:12–17).

When you enter the church look to your right at the Aramaic inscription on the wall. It states that the church's members were in Jerusalem shortly after the Temple was destroyed. Within the church is a stone baptistry covered with silver. The monks say that Mary, mother of Jesus, was baptised in it. Above this is a painting on leather of the Virgin and the infant Jesus, which the monks claim is the work of St. Luke. Note, too, the hand-carved Patriarchal throne, gilded over near the altar.

As you return to the Armenian Orthodox Patriarch Road , look for the Old Yishuv Museum on Or HaHayim St. (see "Museums"). When you get to Patriarch Road, turn left. Soon you come to the Armenian **Cathedral of St. James.** The church officials will allow modestly dressed visitors within their shrines only during services (see "Places to Visit").

(If you are not allowed in, continue on this road (the **Armenian Museum** is on your left) and walk through **Zion**

Gate, turning right for the Couvent Armenien St. Sauveur.)

The Cathedral is a Crusader building. As you enter there is a chapel on your left. This is claimed to be the spot where thc apostle James was decapitated and where his head is entombed. The other St. James, after whom the church is also named, was the first Christian bishop of Jerusalem and he is said to be buried under the altar.

Access to the **Church of Holy Etchmiazine** is through the Cathedral's southern door. Inside are three stones – from Mt. Sinai, Mt. Tabor and the Jordan – all significant places in Jewish and Christian history.

Close to the entrance to the Armenian compound is a flight of steps leading up to the **Patriarch's residence**. The treasures in here include thousands of priceless works of art and manuscripts. Also within is the sceptre of the last King of Armenia who ruled in the 14th century.

Across the compound is the **Gulbenkian library**. Go down some steps, pass under a gateway and turn right. Here is the **House of Annas** or Convent of the Olive Tree. Jesus is said to have been brought here before being sent to the house of Caiaphas. Jesus is believed to have been tied to the ancient olive tree outside the Convent. The 5th century church within the Convent was renovated in the 14th century. In the recently completed **Armenian museum**, art treasures and antiques are displayed. Entrance is from the main road; a fee is charged.

Exit through Zion Gate (see "Places to Visit") and turn right, soon arriving at the gate with a sign above saying, **Couvent Armenien St. Sauveur**. Beyond the new Armenian church built over the site believed to have contained the House of Caiaphas, and below the paved courtyard, are the tombs of the Armenian Patriarchs of Jerusalem.

Return to Zion Gate, turn right and right again at the fork. Pass the Franciscan **Convent of the Holy Coenaculum**, built in 1936 when the order, banished from Mt. Zion since 1551, was permitted to return.

Bear left and up the steps within the first gate on your left. Cross through the empty room and enter the **Cenacle**, in which Christians, with the exception of the Syrian Orthodox community, say the Last Supper was held. On the top right hand corner near the door are two coloured Crusader coats of arms. The vaulting and hefty pillars also date from the Crusader period. The Moslems damaged this site several times before turning it into the Mosque of the Prophet David, after expelling the Franciscans. They did not allow Jews or Christians to enter.

Return to street level, turn left, walk in to the building, and turn left again. The large stones date from Herod's time. This is the way to the **Tomb of David**; yarmulkas (skullcaps) are available at the entrance.

It is the traditionally accepted site of King David's tomb although it lies well outside the boundaries of the Jerusalem of his time. It is more likely that he was buried on the Ophel but this fact has not deterred pilgrims from coming here to pray, principally Jews on Shavuot, the traditional date of his death.

The silver crowns above the red-velvet covered tomb in the rock cave represent the number of years of modern Israel's independence. Each year another is added. On the right-hand side, as you leave the building, there is the small **King David Museum** established by the Diaspora Yeshiva.

Turn left now to the **Chamber of the Holocaust**. To reach it you must go through the darkened rooms and across the street.

Inside are tattered Tora Scrolls salvaged from the synagogues of Europe, relics of the European Jewish communities under the Nazis and a memorial flame. Tables commemorating individuals and communities destroyed in the Holocaust are attached to the walls.

When you leave, walk opposite the souvenir shop for a visit to the **David Palombo Museum** of welded sculptures. Before his death in 1966, Palombo designed the iron gates to Yad Vashem and the Knesset.

The Diaspora Yeshiva is located next to the Chamber of the Holocaust.

Now retrace your steps to the Cenacle and take the right fork.

You will come to the German **Church of the Dormition**, commemorating the death of the Virgin Mary. Built in 1910 it is supervised by Benedictine monks. Six chapels are built around a huge mosaic floor; a mosaic above the apse shows Jesus and Mary and the Prophets of Israel. On the left, steps lead down to a darkened crypt containing a life-sized effigy of Mary. The church's organ is one of the largest in the Middle East. Concerts are often held here.

Return to Zion Gate, walk through it and turn right. Go down as far as Kikar Tiferet Yerushalayim. From the ancient Turkish walls there is a good lookout over the oldest part of Jerusalem, where David built his capital. On your left is a square, used as a parking lot, built over the remains of a huge Byzantine church. At the eastern end of the parking lot there is the **Metivta Yeshiva**. Take the wooden stairway on your right, down to the most famous synagogues in Jerusalem.

They were originally built in the 16th century by Sephardi Jews expelled from Spain and Portugal. On the same site Rabbi **Yohanan Ben Zakkai**, the 1st century sage, taught his pupils. Here the Sephardic Chief Rabbi, the Rishon LeZion, was consecrated. They were also the centre of Jewish community life. In 1870 Emperor Franz Josef II of Austria was welcomed in the Ben Zakkai synagoguge by the Jewish community. The Jews of the Old City gathered here during the fighting in 1948 and finally surrendered on this spot.

However, the **four synagogues**, sunk three metres below street level, were ransacked and desecrated during the 19 years of Jordanian occupation. It took four years of painstaking restoration work to bring them to their present state. Religious artefacts from old European synagogues have been installed to replace those looted.

The **Ben Zakkai Synagogue** (Sephardic), has twin Arks above which is a blue and gold mural with a Jerusalem motif, echoing the opulence the synagogue had known in former days.

The **Eliahu Hanavi Synagogue** is the oldest. It takes its name from an ancient belief that here Elijah the Prophet once made up the minyan (quorum) during a Day of Atonement service in Jerusalem. A chair near the door replaces the ancient one he is said to have sat on. Note the 16th century wooden Ark brought from Italy. It is now an Ashkenazi synagogue.

The **Emtzai (Middle) Synagogue** is the smallest of the four. Next to it is the **Istanbuli Synagogue**, which had a congregation made up principally of young people, craftsmen and small shopkeepers. Its name derives from the many worshippers who came from Turkey. It has a gilded 17th century Ark from Ancona, Italy and a four-columned bima (platform) from Pesaro. This is used mainly by students from the Metivta Yeshiva, and on Saturdays by a largely English-speaking congregation who follow the Spanish and Portuguese rite.

Return now to Kikar Tiferet Yerushalayim and turn left down **Batei Mahase Road**, parallel to the Old City wall.

Silwan Village is on your right (in the valley below) and the Mt. of Olives is ahead on the horizon.

Turn left in the doorway at the sign mentioning Yeshivat Hakotel. You may wish to go down the steps facing you and visit the **Writers' Club**, if it's open.

Now walk down to the courtyard of the yeshiva on your right and take the steps leading left. The large arcaded building on your left is **Beit Rothschild**. Inside are the offices of the Company for the Reconstruction and Rehabilitation of the Jewish Quarter. The relics of capitals and column bases in the forecourt were unearthed in the Jewish Quarter and date to the 2nd and 3rd centuries BCE.

Walk to the far end of Beit Rothschild and turn left down the lane at its end. The **I.D.F. monument** on the right is dedicated to the Jews who fell in the Old City during the War of Independence.

Turn right into **Rehov HaGaled**, under the arched tunnel and into **Rehov Beit El**. You are facing an ancient Kabbalist centre called **Beit El**. The high arch on your left towers over the ruins of the most famous synagogue in the Jewish Quarter, the **Hurva**. This synagogue was built with borrowed money and destroyed by Moslem money-lenders in 1721 when a debt was not repaid. Rebuilt in 1857, the Hurva was destroyed again by Jordanian soldiers in 1948. (See "Places to Visit").

Steps leading down from the Hurva bring you to another ancient house of prayer called the **Ramban** synagogue. The renowned Jewish scholar Nachmanides established this synagogue in 1267 and described in a letter to his son the pillars that are the structure's central architectural feature.

As you stand at the edge of the square you can't miss the 500 ft.-long **Cardo,** which was the main street here in Roman times. It was used for parades and religious processions. This Cardo ran through Aelia Capitolina, the Roman town built after the destruction of the Second Temple (1st century CE). The structures along it date to the **Byzantine** 5th century C.E. It was 22 metres wide with a central strip for horses and chariots. Now restored, it includes archaeological exhibitions and a shopping centre.

On Rehov Plugat Hakotel nearby is the **Israelite Broad Wall**, dating back to the First Temple, and next to it, on Rehov Shonei Halachot, is the **Israelite Tower** (10 metres underground).

Continue walking east to Rehov **Tiferet Yisrael**. Steps leading up will bring you to an arched facade, all that remains of a four-storey, 19th century synagogue, **Tiferet Yisrael** or **Nissan Beck** synagogue. To the west is the entrance to the Karaite synagogue, which reportedly dates back to the 11th century. This historic site is located underground, and only if you remove your shoes will you be permitted to enter. In the basement of 10, Karaite St. is a newly restored Herodian quarter of impressive dimensions with mikvaot (ritual baths), frescos, colourful mosaic floors and so on.

Return to Rehov Tiferet Yisrael and continue walking under the multi-arched arcade which leads to the wide steps descending to the Western Wall (Kotel). On your left is the **"Burnt House,"** which was burnt on the day the Temple was destroyed. On your right is the chief study hall of **Yeshivat HaKotel**. Halfway down the steps on your right is the newly rebuilt **Porat Yosef Yeshiva,** designed by architect Moshe Safdie. On your left are the ruins of a Crusader church and hospital. The **Western Wall** is approached through a plaza. Christian visitors might consider a detour to the **Nea Church** which is situated below Yeshivat HaKotel (entrance through Rehov Nehamu, near **Siebenberg House,** with its finds from the First Temple period and later).

Walk across the plaza towards the **Western Wall**. Women pray on the right, men on the left. To the right of the women's section is Moors' Gate leading into the **Temple Mount.** To the right of this ramp is an archaeological site which has yielded relics of the First Temple period.

When you come close to the wall, notice the many scraps of paper pressed into the crevices. They are the written wishes and prayers of worshippers continuing an ancient tradition.

Observe the tell-tale sign of the Herodian masons. No mortar was used to pack these finely cut blocks of stone.

On your left, you will find a dark archway. Go in and follow the tunnel that leads to the excavations under Wilson's Arch at the northern corner of the wall. Named after a 19th century British excavator, it is part of a bridge that once linked the Temple Mount and the Jewish Quarter, formerly the Upper City. It is also Herodian. Inside Wilson's Arch are more areas for prayer. Note also the illuminated shaft that shows how far down the stones of the Western Wall reach. You will come out at the men's praying section of the Western Wall.

You may now walk to Dung Gate to catch Bus No. 1 or 38 for the ride back to town, or climb up the stairs and walk through the bazaar or Jewish Quarter to Jaffa Gate.

WALK No. 2 – MOSLEM QUARTER AND THE TEMPLE MOUNT, OLD CITY (see Old City map on Southern Sheet).

This walk covers the Moslem part of the Old City, taking you through the fabled bazaars, past choice examples of Mameluke architecture, past the Western Wall and onto the Temple Mount. (A description of the Western Wall is provided at the tail end of Walk No. 1 because there it is the culminating attraction of a walk through the Jewish Quarter.)

Take a bus – 1, 23, 27, 42 or 43 – to **Damascus Gate** (see "Places to Visit").

The Arab name for it is Bab el-Amud (Gate of the Pillar), referring to the pillar from the Roman period from which the distance to Damascus was measured. On the level below the main gate is the Roman Gate, which once led to a square and a column with Hadrian's statue on top; there is now a small museum here devoted to the history of the gate. Once inside Damascus Gate, the most ornate of all the Old City gates, you will find yourself enveloped in the world of Arabia.

The steps of **Damascus Gate Road** lead past shops and cafes crushed together. A thousand and one sights greet you. Pause to watch the Arab men smoking from the hookas, tobacco pipes with long tubes to draw smoke through a jar of water.

Five roads lead off the base of the steps. Continue along **El-Wad Road,** stopping to scrutinize, admire or purchase from the stalls showing metalware, leatherware, baskets, olivewood carvings and other handicrafts. The stalls peter out along the brief stretch of the winding **Via Dolorosa** when you pass Stations III, IV and V of the Cross (see Walk No. 3).

Continue straight on, turning right into **Takiyeh Street.** Walk up until you come to a building on the left, whose facade is distinguished by black basalt, pink marble and white limestone stripes. This was a theological seminary when built in 1540 and contains features of both Mameluke and Ottoman architecture. Known as the **Madrasah Resaiya,** it is still a school.

Climb the steps to the **Takiyeh Convent,** a little way up on the left. Once a palace, it is now a Moslem orphanage. It was built in 1398 by the Princess es-Sit Tunshuq, who is buried in the handsome building opposite.

The next building up on the left houses a large carpentry shop. Some authorities believe it was a Moslem soup kitchen established by the wife of Suleiman the Magnificent in the early 16th century.

Return to **El-Wad Road** and cross over into **Ala 'Uddin (Aladdin) Street.** An arched doorway on the left once led to another **Madrasah.** The inscription honours the Mameluke Inspector of Buildings who erected the first Saracen buildings after the defeat of the Crusaders.

Further up on the left and right is the **African Quarter** of the Old City. No one knows with any degree of certainty when or how their forefathers arrived in Jerusalem. Some knowledgeable people hold that these are the descendants of 16th century pilgrims from Chad and Somalia. Others claim the Africans arrived as slave labourers. Their quarter is dank and squalid. On the left they are housed in the 13th century **Madrasah Hsaniya** which the Ottomans later converted into prison cells for condemned men. It has the oldest Mameluke doorway in Jerusalem. On the right they are quartered in the 13th century hospice.

Continue up, past the marble columns from the Madrasah. Ahead of you is the **Bab el-Nadir** or Prison Gate, leading onto the Temple Mount. The blue and green tiles are from a 14th century school. The steps lead up to the offices of the Moslem Supreme Council.

Return to El-Wad Road and turn left. Go under the arch and turn left into **Bab el-Hadid Road.**

You cannot fail to notice the 15th century **Madrasah Muziriya** on the right. The decorations above the arch are typical of that period.

Go back to El-Wad Road, and stop at the entrance to a long darkened "tunnel." This was the **Souq el Qattanin** (Cotton Market), built in 1329, after which it was a flourishing cloth market.

Turn left into **Bab el-Silsileh Road** (Street of the Chain) and proceed until you come to the **Gate of the Chain,** leading onto the Temple Mount.

With your back to the gate you can see one of the fountains built by Suleiman the Magnificent. Its base is actually a Roman sarcophagus. The flower-shaped relief is from Crusader times. On your left is a court of the Chief

Rabbinate, in a 14th century building formerly housing the **Madrasah Tankiziya.** The shell-shaped niche and black calligraphic designs date from 1329.

Walk back, cross over El-Wad Road to Chain Road, and, just before the turning left to Western Wall Road, take a peek through the iron bars of the windows on your left. The three **tombs** inside belong to the 13th century Emir Turbat Barakat Khan and his sons. Overlooking this sepulchral courtyard is the **Khalidiya Library,** a collection of ancient and priceless manuscripts held by the Khalidiya family.

Continue up Bab el-Silsileh (Chain) Road until you see, on your right, the numbers 0182 above the entrance to a side-street. Turn in here and arrive at the **Khan e-Sultan.** Erected in the late 14th century as an inn, with stables below, it later housed the Sultan's harem. Alas! the hand of fate . . . where the nymphs once frolicked the donkeys now bray.

Return to the main street and turn right; you'll soon find yourself at the busiest intersection in the Old City. Eight market streets merge here, dazzling you with everything you can wish to buy. If you go left, down **Souq el-Hussor,** the Straw Market, you will see an ancient arch at the entrance. It is part of the Gate of the Gardens, and was here during Second Temple times.

Push your way back to Bab el-Silsileh Road and walk down, turning right into Western Wall Road.

In a few seconds you will be standing before the Herodian slabs of rock that make up the mighty Western Wall. For a full description see the last part of Walk No. 1.

Walk diagonally across the plaza and climb the steps above the excavation site to the Moor Gate.

There are signs here quoting the Chief Rabbinate as saying it is forbidden to enter the Temple Mount. Religious Jews will not enter the Mount; as the exact site of the Holy of Holies is unknown, they might inadvertently step on sacred ground.

The **Islamic Museum** is on the right of Moors' Gate. You can buy tickets here to the Dome of the Rock and the Mosque of El-Aksa. Visitors of both sexes must be modestly dressed; no cameras or large bags allowed in the mosques.

The next site on your right is a small domed building known as **Qubat Yusef** or the Dome of Joseph, built in 1191 by Saladin. Further along is the Women's Mosque, access to which is permitted only to Moslem women.

The grey-domed **El-Aksa Mosque** was built at the beginning of the 8th century by Caliph al-Waleed, son of the builder of the more imposing Dome of the Rock. However, earthquakes damaged it often and much of what you see dates from 1034 when it was restored by Caliph al-Zahir. He was responsible for building the dome and seven northern doors of the present rectangular house of worship, but Saladin decorated the dome with the mosaics. The mosque can hold 5,000 people. It gets its name from a passage in the Koran where Mohammed is described as being transported by night from the Sacred Temple in Mecca to the Distant Temple (in Jerusalem). Aksa is Arabic for distant (see "Places to Visit").

King Abdullah of Jordan, grandfather of King Hussein, was assassinated at the entrance to this mosque by an Arab extremist in 1951.

As you leave the mosque, take a look at the far corner on your right. Christians claim this site is the Pinnacle of the Temple, where Satan tempted Jesus. The small building here is the entrance to **Solomon's Stables,** where the Crusaders stabled their horses. However, unless you can get someone from the Supreme Moslem Council to open it, you will not be able to enter.

Between the El-Aksa Mosque and the Dome of the Rock is a fountain known as **El-Kas** (The Cup). Moslems sit on the stone seats and wash themselves before entering the mosques to pray.

The stone coverings on the esplanade to your right conceal huge underground halls, networks of tunnels and passages, as well as intricate systems for storing water which probably date back to First and Second Temple days.

Ascend the steps under the arches, also known as Mawazin (scales). It is said they will balance the souls of men on the Day of Judgement. On the left of the top step is a summer pulpit, intricately designed in 1456.

The **Dome of the Rock** was erected by Caliph Abd el-Malik in 691 around the rock upon which Abraham is believed to have intended sacrificing Isaac. Both Solomon's Temple and the Second Temple stood here (see "Places to Visit").

When Caliph al-Ma'moon renovated the Mosque in 813 he altered the plaque, trying to show that he had built it. But his workmen neglected to change the date!

The golden dome rises 36m. and is 26m. in diameter. It is made of aluminium from Italy.

This mosque was also damaged by earthquakes and substantially restored and improved by successive generations. Suleiman the Magnificent replaced the windows in the dome with stained glass of floral design painted in gold. He also placed the Persian tiles on the outside walls. The exterior is also decorated with verses from the Koran.

Inside you will see the sacred Rock enclosed by a fence. It owes its origins to the iron gate of the Crusaders who had to put an end to the pilgrims' practice of chipping bits off and taking them home as souvenirs. On the right-hand corner is a small enclosure in which is the legendary footprint of Mohammed, left when he ascended from here to heaven. It also contains some hairs from his beard.

Another mark on the scarred rock is said to be the handprint of the Archangel Gabriel, who held the rock down during Mohammed's ascent.

If you walk around the rock you will come to some steps leading down to a cave where the souls of the dead are said to meet in prayer.

Exit from the mosque and look to your right. The larger domed structure is the **Dome of the Ascension,** and the other is the **Dome of the Prophet.** Walking further to your right you see the **Dome of the Chain,** dating from the 8th century.

Cross the stairway ahead of you towards the Mt. of Olives and follow the path to the blocked-up arches of the **Golden Gate.** Tradition holds that the Messiah will come through the Golden Gate. The Moslem cemetery, located on the other side of the gate, was probably put there to prevent his entry, since in Jewish law a priest is not allowed to walk through a cemetery.

Ascend the steps leading to the ramparts for a marvellous view of the Mt. of Olives opposite and the Kidron Valley below. The northeastern corner of the Temple Mount has a Herodian tower near the Gate of the Tribes, leading through to Lions' Gate.

Return now to the entrance of the Dome of the Rock and walk towards the steps facing the entrance. Beside the steps is the **Dome of the Spirit** where Moslems claim Mohammed will call the faithful on the Day of Judgement.

On the left of the steps is the **Dome of St. George.** On your right, at the bottom, is another domed structure known as the **Throne of Jesus.** Towering over the northwest corner, to the left, is the **minaret of el-Ghawanimeh.** A gate of the same name leads to the Via Dolorosa.

The cloisters on your left have a number of gates leading to the Moslem quarter. You have seen the other side of several of them at the beginning of this walk. All the gates are clearly signposted. Next to the **Iron Gate** you can look through the barred window and see the huge tomb of King Hussein ibn Ali, great-grandfather of King Hussein.

Walk south to the **Cotton Gate**, at the end of the "tunnel" you could not enter earlier. Once more you can see the marvellous colouring of the Mameluke structures.

The **Ablution Gate** is opposite the ornate **Sabeel Qait Bey,** a fountain built in 1455.

Before you reach the **Gate of the Chain** you pass by the square **Madrasah Sultaniya** and the **Madrasah Ashrafiya.** By now you should recognise their distinctive styles.

Opposite the Gate of the Chain is an early 13th century building on a raised platform. It is the **Qubat en-Nahawiya,** where Arabic literature was studied.

Continue to Moors' Gate and leave the way you came in.

If you wish to take a bus back to town you may catch a No. 1 outside **Dung Gate**. Alternatively, you can walk back to **Damascus Gate** and catch one of the following buses: 1, 23, 27.

WALK No. 3 – VIA DOLOROSA, OLD CITY (see Old City map on Southern Sheet).

The **Via Dolorosa** (Way of Grief) is the traditionally accepted last route trodden by Jesus when led to his crucifixion. Altogether there are 14 Stations of the Cross marking significant events along the route. It begins in the northeastern section of the Old City. The road was re-paved recently and includes resting areas for pilgrims.

Take a bus to the **Rockefeller Museum** (No. 1, 23, 27, 42 or 43). Walk downhill towards the Mt. of Olives, turn right into **Jericho Road** and then first right up to **Lions' Gate** (see "Places to Visit").

The second building on the right is the Crusader **Church of St. Anne,** built over the birthplace of Mary and named after her mother. Walk down the steps on the right to the very cool, stone-walled crypt, the actual site of the birth.

To the northwest of the church you'll see ruins dating to the time of Jesus. They include the two **Pools of**

Bethesda where Jesus is believed to have cured the paralytic. The remains of a Byzantine basilica are here. Also among the ruins are a ritual bath and caverns dating from Hasmonaean times.

Continue along **Al-Mujahideen Road,** turning into **King Feisal Street,** second on the left.

This is off the Via Dolorosa but there are two fine examples of 13th century Mameluke Madrasahs. The first is the **Madrasah el Dawadaria.** Note its double vaulted gate. The other is the **Madrasah e-Salania.** Observe the decorations suspended above the coloured facades. Looking like hardened putty-work, it is the characteristic feature of the Mameluke theological seminaries.

Return to the main road and walk up the stairs to the **El-Omariye School.** This is the **1st Station** of the Cross on the **Via Dolorosa.** Open only at 3 p.m. on Friday afternoons for the Franciscan procession along the Via Dolorosa.

The colossal **Antonia Fortress** stood here and Pontius Pilate was living in it when Jesus was brought before him for a private trial in the courtyard. If you climb up the steps to the building on the south you will get a fine view of the Temple Mount through the bars of the windows.

It is from Station I that the Franciscan fathers begin their weekly pilgrimage along the Via Dolorosa at 3 p.m. on Fridays.

Station II is opposite the school back on the Via Dolorosa. Walk inside the **Franciscan monastery.** On your left is the **Chapel of the Condemnation**, with Roman flagstones thought to be from the **Antonia Fortress** and four huge columns inside. On your right is the **Chapel of the Flagellation** where Jesus was scourged. There is a beautiful stained glass window behind the altar. In the courtyard there is a model of Jerusalem that includes the Second Temple. Between the two chapels is the Franciscan Faculty for Biblical and Archaeological Studies.

The next street on the left, **Bab el-Ghawanim Rd.**, takes its name from the gate opening onto the Temple Mount at the end.

After the junction of these two streets come to the **Ecce Homo Arch** and the **Convent of the Sisters of Zion** on your right. Early tradition held that Pontius Pilate stood here and thundered "Ecce Homo!" ("Behold the Man!") However, we now know that the arch was constructed by the pagan Emperor Hadrian to commemorate his victory over the Jews led by Bar-Kochba.

The Church inside has part of this triple-arched triumphal gate behind the altar. See the model of the Antonia Fortress in the lecture hall. Below the convent is the **Lithostrotos,** where Jesus was publicly tried and where the Roman soldiers mocked him as a false king and prophet. The low vaulted arches rise above the great stones of the Antonia pavement. The blocks of stone were grooved to prevent horses from slipping – it is a "Via Romana," perhaps the true Via Dolorosa. They also bear the scratchings by Roman legionnaires playing "the game of the king."

Before you get to the Lithostrotos have a look at the giant water cisterns below the paving. They hold water, just as they did during the days of Jesus. Flavius Josephus gave us their name: **Strouthion.**

Adjacent to the convent is the **Greek Orthodox Praetorium,** with a sign over the door reading, "Prison of Christ." Steps lead down to the grottos where Jesus is said to have been imprisoned.

The Via Dolorosa leads into **El-Wad Road,** a main Old City artery that eventually leads to the Western Wall. Turn left and, almost immediately, on your left, you will see **Station III.**

This is where Jesus fell for the first time. The small Polish chapel marking the spot has a relief sculptured above the door. Carved by Thaddeus Zielinsky, it portrays Jesus falling under the weight of the Cross.

The small oratory near the entrance to the Armenian Catholic **Church of Our Lady of the Spasm** marks **Station IV,** where Jesus met his mother, Mary.

As you walk round the corner, to the right, following the Via Dolorosa, there is a small **Franciscan Oratory.** This is **Station V,** where Simon of Cyrene helped Jesus carry the Cross. Notice the deep impression on the wall near the door. Legend attributes it to the handprint of Jesus, who supported himself here.

The Via Dolorosa now climbs steeply towards Calvary. Pass **El-Beiraq** leading left and just before the overhanging arch arrive at **Station VI,** the **Church of St. Veronica,** on the left. Here Veronica wiped the face of Christ. The Church has a candelabrum above the stone altar. Below are the remains of a Byzantine monastery.

As you arrive at the junction with the bustling Souq Khan e-Zeit, observe **Station VII** notched above the entrance to a Franciscan chapel facing you. This marks the place where Jesus fell the second time. There was a city gate here 2,000 years ago, and Christians call this entrance Judgement Gate, following the tradition that Jesus' death notice was posted to it.

Walk uphill along **Khanqa Street** until you reach **Station VIII** opposite the **"Station VIII Souvenir Bazaar."** There is a Latin cross on the peeling yellow walls of the **Greek Monastery of St. Charalambos,** built over the site where Jesus consoled the women of Jerusalem.

Retrace your steps, turning right into the Souq Khan e-Zeit. Most of the shops along here date from Crusader times.

Ascend the stairway on your right. You will soon come to a Roman column resting against a wall behind some steps. The pillar is over **Station IX,** where Jesus fell for the third time.

On your right is the Coptic Orthodox **Queen Helena Church.** Ahead of you is the **Coptic Orthodox Patriachate** within the **Monastery of the Sultan.** The community has occupied this site since 1219. Beyond the steps on your left is the **Ethiopian Compound.** It is a flat terrace and is on the roof of the Chapel of St. Helena, within the Church of the Holy Sepulchre below. The African huts are inhabited by Ethiopian monks. The olive tree enclosed by a wall is claimed by the monks to be the bush where Abraham found the ram caught in a thicket.

Return to the Souq Khan e-Zeit. A few steps away, to the right, is the **Russian Church of Alexander Nievsky,** with excavations dating to Herod's time. Ring the bell. There is an entrance fee. When you leave the church, turn right into Dabbagha Road and left into **Muristan Road.** A few metres down is the Lutheran **Church of the Redeemer,** built in 1898 in the Crusader style. The view from the bell-tower is one of the best in the Old City.

Back on Dabbagha Road you will see an arcade on your left. This is the **Muristan** (Persian for "hospital"), where the Crusader Order of the Hospitallers, the Knights of St. John, had their hospital and headquarters. This is now a Greek bazaar known as Souq Aftimos, with an ornamental fountain in the middle built by the Greek Orthodox in the 19th century. It is a good place to buy leatherware and embroidered bags and Oriental dresses.

After browsing around, return to its entrance and turn left to the **Church of the Holy Sepulchre** for the remaining five Stations of the Cross.

This holiest shrine in Christendom stands over the hill

of Golgotha, derived from the Hebrew word for skull, because 2,000 years ago it resembled a skull or bald pate, with no trees on its summit.

The Empress Helena built a church here in 335 CE, over the ruins of Hadrian's Temple of Venus.

It was destroyed by the Persians in 614, restored, attacked a number of times under Moslem rule, and rebuilt by the Crusaders; wrecked by the Khwarizms, the 13th century Egyptian mercenaries, it was also damaged by fire in the 19th century. It has been restored on various occasions, right up until the present. The facade and bell towers were built by the Crusaders.

As you enter notice the red slab of stone on the floor, facing you. It is the **Stone of the Unction** and covers the spot where the body of Jesus was anointed.

Turn right, past the stone benches that remain from the tombs of Crusader kings. Further on is the **Chapel of Adam** where the cleft in the rock is said to have been rent by the earthquake when Jesus died (Matthew 27:51).

Retrace your steps and turn right, up the stairs to the top of **Calvary.** On the right hand side are **Stations X** and **XI,** where Jesus was stripped of his garments and nailed to the Cross. This is the **Chapel of the Franks.**

On the far left is the Greek Orthodox chapel around **Station XII.** This is the place of the crucifixion and is richly decorated with precious metals, statues and suspended lamps. If you put your hand through the silver disk below the altar you can feel the top of the rock of Calvary.

Jesus' body was taken off the cross at **Station XIII,** marked by the small Franciscan **Altar of Stabat Mater Dolorosa,** between the two chapels. The wooden statue was fashioned in the 17th century and sent from Lisbon in 1778.

Descend to ground level and bear right. Go down 13 steps, past the crosses carved on the walls by Christian pilgrims. The **Chapel of the Discovery of the Cross** is reputed to be the place where St. Helena discovered the original cross during her stay in Jerusalem. The bronze statue of St. Helena is on the left-hand altar.

Working your way around the right hand side of the church, you arrive at another flight of steps leading down to the Armenian **Church of St. Helena.** Byzantine pillars support the Crusader vaulting.

Back at ground level you will see the **Chapel of the Division of the Raiment** on your right, next to the steps. The legionnaires distributed the clothes of Jesus here. Continue right of the steps and curve left. Pass the seven arches, remains of the Byzantine Church, and then turn left to **Station XIV,** the **Holy Sepulchre**.

The 19th century edicule is the focal point of the church. It is topped by an onion-shaped cupola. The vestibule is the first of two chambers. This is known as the **Chapel of the Angel.** Here an angel is said to have sat on a stone and proclaimed the resurrection. **The Sepulchre** is through an arched doorway. A marble slab covers the burial place of Jesus in a chamber only 2 metres square.

When you exit, turn to your left and pass the Stone of the Unction near the entrance to the church.

After leaving the church, turn right, up **St. Helena Road** and right again along **Christian Quarter Road.** This is a good place to buy religious handicrafts and trinkets. Turn right into **Khanqa Street** and left into **Souq Khan e-Zeit.** It is one of the main thoroughfares in the Old City and a fascinating place to bargain and buy from the crowded stalls of the bazaar.

Souq Khan e-Zeit leads into **Damascus Gate Road** and out of the Old City. If you turn right at Christian Quarter Road, and right at David St. you will come out at Jaffa Gate.

WALK No. 4 – THE MOUNT OF OLIVES
(see map on Southern Sheet).

There is a sense of pilgrimage for anyone going by foot up the sacred **Mt. of Olives.** On its slopes is the holiest **Jewish graveyard** in the world, where for centuries people have bought burial plots in advance of their death as it is said the Messiah will walk through the Golden Gate, facing the Mount, on Judgement Day.

Christians revere the hill because of its association with the life of Jesus, particularly the days preceding his crucifixion.

The road up is steep and we recommend the entire walk only for persons who are physically fit. Or, to take it in reverse from uphill, down. However, the route as far as the onion-domed Russian Orthodox Church of St. Mary Magdalene may be walked by persons of any age.

To reach the starting point take Bus. No. 1, 23, 42 or

43 to the **Rockefeller Museum** and walk downhill, turning right into Jericho Road. Just after the turn-off to the Lions' Gate, take the left-hand fork. Cross the Kidron Valley bridge and go down the steps, left, to the Greek Orthodox **Church of the Assumption,** also known as the **Tomb of Mary.**

Descend the 44 steps to the darkened, rock-cut church. Half way down are two chapels. On the right, in a niche, are the remains of the builder of the church, Millicent, daughter of Baldwin II, the Crusader monarch. The open sarcophagus lies at the bottom, on the right, under a great dome of rock.

When you leave the church turn left immediately. A door leads to the **Grotto of Gethsemane,** where Jesus is believed to have been arrested. There are rock paintings on the walls from Crusader times.

Walk up to Jericho Road and up the tarred road on your left; through the gate on your right is the **Garden of Gethsemane.** The eight olive trees are so old that experts say they were here when Jesus prayed in the Garden before his arrest.

The Basilica of the Agony (Church of All Nations) was built in 1919–1924. The brilliant mosaic of C. Bargellini on its facade makes it one of the outstanding churches in Jerusalem. Its focal point inside is a slab of rock before the altar. On it Jesus prayed. In 380 CE it was cut by the Emperor Theodosius for the first church built here. The Persians destroyed it and the Crusaders erected a small chapel. However, Saladin wrecked this. In 1666 the Franciscans regained possession of the site.

The church has 10 columns and 10 wall-pillars supporting 12 cupolas.

Turn right up the hill. The Russian Orthodox **Church of St. Mary Magdalene,** built by Czar Alexander III in 1888, is on your left. The onion-shaped domes and the general style reflect the architecture in Moscow during the 16th and 17th centuries.

The Grand Duchess Elizabeth Feodrovnya, sister of the Empress Alexandra, is buried in the crypt (see "Places to Visit").

The road steepens now. To your right is the **Jewish cemetery.** The Jordanians used tombstones from here for building materials from 1948 to 1967.

The next church uphill, on your left, is **Dominus Flevit** (The Lord Wept). It was built in 1954 over the place where

Jesus wept over the imminent destruction of Jerusalem.

The small church, supervised by Franciscans, is designed in the shape of a tear-drop. When it was built, the remains of a Byzantine church were unearthed, including the large mosaic to the left of the church door.

Ancient tombs uncovered in the gardens date back to the late Canaanite period. The ossuaries span the period from the Hasmonaeans to the Byzantines.

Further up the Mt. of Olives you will pass by the graves of 48 Jews – civilians and soldiers – who fell in the Old City during the War of Independence and who were reinterred here after the Six Day War.

Higher up, a gate leads to the **Tombs of the Prophets** Haggai, Zechariah and Malachi, and their disciples. A guide is on hand to lead you down to the candle-lit rock cave, with burial niches all around. It is refreshingly cool below.

Only a few steps remain between this point and the road at the base of the Seven Arches Hotel. Now is the time to bring out your camera for the grandest view of the Old City and parts of new Jerusalem.

Walk up the main road, with the Seven Arches Hotel on your right. Turn right and enter the gate to the **Church of Pater Noster** and the **Basilica of the Eleona.** They are built over the place where Jesus is said to have taught his disciples the Lord's Prayer. For this reason you will see the walls of the entrance and cloister decorated with porcelain panels, on which the Lord's Prayer is written in 44 languages.

Just before the cloisters is the tomb of the Princess de la Tour d'Auvergne. She bought the neglected site and built the monastery and chapel for the Carmelite Sisters in 1874. An urn near the window above the monument contains the heart of her father. Walk through the cloisters down to the **Grotto of the Pater Noster.** Christians say that Jesus often came here. Eusebius, writing in the 4th century, noted that the Empress Helena built a church over this grotto. It was sometimes referred to as the Eleona (Greek for "the olive grove"). The Persians destroyed it but the Crusaders erected a new chapel. Saladin put the Mt. of Olives out of bounds to Christians and the grotto was lost in the rubble. Excavations by the Princess failed to locate it but in 1910 archaeologists found the grotto below the Basilica of St. Helena.

Opposite the Pater Noster, next to the minaret, is the domed **Tomb of the Prophetess Hulda.**

Retrace your steps to the main road, turn right and right again just before the **minaret.** Pay the Moslem gatekeeper a small consideration and he will open the gate to the walled compound enclosing the **Chapel of the Ascension.** This octagonal chapel marks the spot from where Christians claim Jesus ascended to heaven. The enclosed rock on the floor, in front of the "mihrab" (Moslem prayer niche), is said to be marked with the Footprint of Jesus. The lower walls and doorway are Crusader while the cupola is Saracenic. Grappling hooks on the walls outside are used to partition tents when Christians camp here during the holy day of Ascension.

The (Russian) **Tower of Ascension** is the most prominent landmark here.

Retrace your steps to the road below the Seven Arches Hotel.

WALK No. 5 – MEA SHE'ARIM

(see map on Southern Sheet).

This walk can take you as little as 45 minutes. It leads through Mea She'arim, the quarter in which the veteran members of Jerusalem's ultra-Orthodox religious community live, work, study, and pray.

A word of caution. **Do not drive** through during the Sabbath, from mid-Friday afternoon until Saturday evening. If you do, your vehicle is likely to be stoned as the residents will regard your actions as a desecration of the holy Sabbath. In addition, women should, every day of the week, wear dresses that reach below the knees and make sure their sleeves cover their elbows. Men should wear something on their head on entering the market place, and should also try to avoid wearing shorts.

The people who live here let their hair grow long over the ears, in obedience to the biblical command not to "round the corners of your heads." These side-curls are called "peyot." They also wear the black garb, with long frock-coats, black or white stockings, black homburgs or the variations of fur hats known as shtreimels, which is how Polish merchants dressed in the 18th century. Being a conservative community the ultra-Orthodox kept this mode of dress to the present day.

Mea She'arim was founded in 1875 and was the second area settled by Jews outside the Old City walls. Its name translates as "one hundred gates" or "a hundredfold." It derives from the passage in Genesis 26:12, where "Isaac sowed in that land, and reaped in the same year a hundredfold."

Many of the buildings in the quarter have small balconies with iron grilles that overhang the cloistered lanes, streets and alleys. There are patios and courtyards and the general atmosphere is that of the lost "shtetls" of eastern Europe, from where their forebears emigrated. Everywhere there is the sing-song sound of Yiddish, the tongue spoken by many who regard Hebrew as a holy language to be used only in prayer.

Naturally, Mea She'arim is a quarter filled with shops selling religious artifacts. You will find silverware, candelabra, mezuzot, yarmulkas (skullcaps), tallithot (prayer shawls), tefillin (phylacteries) and many other items for sale.

The quarter abounds in synagogues, mikvaot (ritual baths) and scribes who write the long Tora Scrolls by hand. Scores of yeshivot (Talmudic academies) hum with the recitations of students. Many of the residents group themselves around rabbinical leaders, some of whom owe their leadership to dynastic right.

There is also the extremist sect, the Neturei Karta, which does not recognize the State of Israel as its proclamation was not preceded by the coming of the Messiah. Some of this extremism is manifested in slogans which are spray-painted on walls.

Start the walk at **Kikar Zion** in Rehov Yafo. Walk northeast, away from the Old City, and turn right into **Rehov HaRav Kook.** Follow it uphill (**Ticho House** is on your left) proceed into **Rehov Hanevi'im** (Street of the Prophets). Throughout this area are some of the first houses to have been built outside the Old City Walls at the turn of the century.

The **Avraham Chaba Exhibition**, at the **Yad Sara** headquarters on Rehov Hanevi'im 43, displays over 300 works of miniature Judaica, portraits of world renowned political figures and scriptures written on eggs, straw and small pieces of parchment.

Cross the road and bear right down the hill. Pass the **Ethiopian Consulate General** with the mosaic of a lion on its facade. Turn left into **Rehov Devora Hanevia.** The castle-like building on your right, behind the huge white building, is the **Ministry of Education and Culture.** It was formerly the Italian Hospital.

Turn right at **Rehov Rabbi Shmuel Salant.** Now, as you walk down to the junction with **Rehov Mea She'arim**, you get your first view of the charming narrow streets where the frail upper balconies meet to form a kind of arcade.

Turn left at Rehov Mea She'arim. If you want to buy some religious artefacts, now is the time. After a hundred metres you arrive at the entrance to the **market-place** on the left. The sign above the gate makes it unequivocally clear how modest your dress should be "so as not to offend the residents of the quarter." The main residential area is across the road from the market.

We feel it is better to let you roam around here without guiding you along any particular streets. Beyond the stalls with fish, meat, vegetables and other produce are more warrens of lanes that lead you into areas with houses resembling those on Rehov Salant.

Return to the market entrance and continue left on Rehov Mea She'arim. Further on, turn left into **Rehov Nathan Straus** up the hill and pass, on your right, modern office blocks; more Mea She'arim homes are on your left.

Cross Rehov Hanevi'im and walk down the road to Rehov Yafo. Turn left and walk one block to **Kikar Zion,** where this walk began.

New in the Old City

Archeological excavations continue in the Old City and "new" sites are being turned up all the time. Some of the most recent and fascinating finds are the Herodian Quarter, an exclusive residential neighbourhood from the time of the Second Temple period, and, in excavations along the Western Wall, the bedrock of the Temple Mount. We suggest the following tour for those who are interested in the First and Second Temple periods.

Starting at Jaffa Gate (which you can reach by buses 1, 13, 19, 20, or 23), take the first right onto Armenian Patriarch Road, turn left into St. James' Road, and follow its curves past Ararat Street. Keep going straight on Or Ha'haim St., cross over the remains of the Byzantine Cardo, then cross the large square in the centre of the Jewish Quarter, towards the Mizrahi Bank and take Rehov Tiferet Yisrael which leads you to the Burnt House.

You can buy a combined ticket that gains you admission to the Burnt House and the Herodian Quarter, both from the Second Temple period, and to the Israelite Tower, from the First Temple period.

The Burnt House, so-called because it was discovered under a layer of ashes, was destroyed by fire at the end of the great revolt against the Romans in 70 C.E. (a month after the Temple was destroyed).

It was owned by a family of priests, the Katroses, who may have used it to prepare incense for service in the Temple. You can see the remains of the ritual baths, and glass and stone vessels (which were used by priests because they don't conduct ritual impurity). The Katros family is mentioned in the Talmud in an unfavourable light: "Woe is me from the House of Katros, woe is me from their pens." (The implication is that the family used its priestly position for personal gain.)

The single most impressive find here was a human forearm, from the finger tip to the elbow joint, the only skeletal remains from the Second Temple period discovered in the Jewish Quarter. According to Prof. Nahman Avigad, the archaeologist responsible for the Jewish Quarter, the bone belonged to a 21-year-old woman. Nearby, a metal spearhead was found, probably the weapon of Jewish defenders who tried unsuccessfully to stave off the Roman onslaught.

Since the bone is almost certainly of a Jewish woman, it was buried in accordance with Jewish law, but pictures are on display.

Nearby, archaeologists found a drainage tunnel. According to the historian Josephus, some of the last Jewish rebels to hold out against the Romans hid in tunnels such as this. (More than 1,900 years later, during the Warsaw Ghetto uprising, Jewish rebels hid in the sewage system).

The Burnt House has a 12-minute slide presentation that explains its history, and provides background information on the Herodian Quarter as well. The English soundtrack runs at 9:30 and 11:30 a.m. and 1:30 and 3:30 p.m. A German soundtrack is available on request (call 288141).

Allow about 30 minutes for the Burnt House.

Leaving the Burnt House, turn right and return to the Mizrahi Bank. Turn left and then left again at the first alleyway, Rehov Hakara'im. About 10 metres down this road, on your right, is the entrance to the Herodian Quarter (Wohl Archeological Museum).

This site, which was only recently opened to the public last year, is a 30,000 square foot area that was known as the upper city of Jerusalem. It was the exclusive residential neighbourhood of the city during the Second Temple and was destroyed by fire in 70 C.E., on the eighth day of the Hebrew month of Elul, the same day that the Burnt House was destroyed.

The remains of at least six villas were uncovered here, each with its own ritual bath, implying that the residents of the Upper City were religiously observant Jews. It is also likely that some of the residents were priests.

The largest home, aptly called "The Mansion", covers 600 square metres and may have had a second floor, which increases its size to about 1,000 square metres.

On the mansion's mosaic floor archaeologists found real and immediate evidence of the second destruction of Jerusalem. On the floor are charred wooden roofing beams which fell during the fire. They lay undisturbed for 1,900 years until excavated by Israeli archaeologists.

Among the other findings are two plaster fragments that when fitted together show about two-thirds of a Menora (candelabrum) carved inside. This may be the most accurate image of the candelabrum that existed in the Temple.

Allow about 45 minutes for the Herodian Quarter.

You'll exit the Herodian Quarter on the Rabbi Yehuda Halevi stairs. Turn left, walk up, turn left at the top of the stairs, Rehov Misgav Ladach, continue to an alleyway called Rehov HaGitit, turn left, walk down the stairs to the Siebenberg House. Thre is an entrance fee. Tours are conducted at 12:00 p.m.

More fascinating than the archaeological treasures here, is the story of how they were discovered. Theo and Miriam Siebenberg bought the house in 1970 and Theo was convinced that it was built over significant archaeological remains. But archaeologists were sceptical, so he conducted and financed the excavations himself (including construction of steel-reinforced concrete buttresses to reinforce the street). The Siebenbergs, or one of their employees, will guide you around the royal burial vaults, jars, mosaics and coins, some dating back 3,000 years and present a slide show.

Allow 45-60 minutes for the Siebenberg House.

Leaving the Siebenberg House, return to Rehov Misgav Ladach, and make your way back to the Mizrahi Bank at the large square. Turn right on Rehov Bonei HaChomot, walk to Rehov Shonei Halachot, turn left. On your right is the entrance to the Israelite Tower, believed to be the place where the Babylonians breached the wall surrounding Jerusalem in 586 B.C.E. On your left, you have Yad Ben Zvi, and its model of the First Temple period of Jerusalem (entrance fee).

Come at noon or 4 p.m. and you can hear a presentation on the era.

Allow 45-60 minutes.

Another fascinating new site is the Western Wall.

Archaeologists have dug along the northern continuation of the Wall and have reached the bedrock of the Temple Mount.

Guided Walking Tours (Old City, City of David)

In addition to the Society for the Protection of Nature tour mentioned earlier, there are walking tours of the Old City that begin from the courtyard of the Citadel.

Walking tours are conducted every day from the Sheraton Plaza Hotel. Contact the hotel for details.

It is possible to walk along the top of the ramparts of the Old City Wall from gate to gate, except from Lions' Gate to Dung Gate, every day from 9 a.m. to 5 p.m. A small fee is charged.

There are tours of the Ophel Garden excavations, (southern wall) daily except Saturday at 9 a.m., 1 p.m., and 2.30 p.m. Tickets may be purchased near Dung Gate. Wear comfortable shoes. Additional details from Government Tourist Offices.

Free guided tours of the Old City begin at 10 a.m. every Saturday from the Municipal Tourist Office, 17 Jaffa.

Bus Tour Of The Main Sites

Bus 99 leaves from the bus terminal below Jaffa Gate every hour on the hour weekdays and passes most of the main tourist spots in the capital. You can do the round tour or stop at any point along the route, catching the next bus when it comes along. The round trip lasts about 90 minutes. You can buy a full-day pass and a two-day (consecutive) pass.

Tours from Jerusalem

ROUTE No. 1 (Map: Northern Sheet K, L, M 17–22)

Jerusalem – Jericho (28 km.) – Qumran (48 km.) – En Feshkha (51 km.) – En Gedi (93 km.) – Massada (109 km.) (Start on Road No. 1 and join Road No. 90.)

(Distances in brackets refer to start of route.)

Don't be fooled into thinking that these 109 km. can be zipped up in a couple of hours. You will be visiting places where civilization fermented, where man first settled in an urban society and where he penned some of the greatest literature the world has ever known. In addition, you are sure to want to swim at one or two of the four oases along the route.

Some may want to return to Jerusalem at the end of the sightseeing. But this is a good route to link up with trips radiating from Beer Sheva, and you may decide to sleep over in the capital city of the Negev, or in Arad.

The abrupt descent from 835 m. above sea level in Jerusalem to 250 m. below sea level at Jericho makes for stupendous vistas of rolling scenery.

Before starting off it is advisable to take along a spare

can of gasoline and water as these facilities are scant in the parched Wilderness of Judaea. In addition, guard against the possibility of a pounding sunstroke and a roasting suntan by wearing some form of head covering.

Road No. 1 to Jericho crosses the **Kidron Valley** and curves round the base of the **Mount of Olivès,** leaving behind a trail of villages on Jerusalem's periphery, including **Bethany,** where Jesus raised Lazarus from the dead.

About 1 km. later there is a turn-off left to a deserted military camp constructed by the Jordanian Arab Legion out of tombstones uprooted from the Jewish cemetery on the Mt. of Olives between 1948 and 1967. After 3 km. you come to the newly built town of **Ma'ale Adumim.**

A few kilometres away is **Mishor Adumim,** an industrial suburb of Jerusalem.

About 17 km. from Jerusalem the road rises sharply to an old caravanserai. Enclosing a deep well, it is regarded as the **Inn of the Good Samaritan,** immortalized in the parable recited by Jesus (Luke 10:30–37). This is the original Ma'ale Adumim ("red ascent").

Ruins of a **Crusader castle** peek out from the red earth nearby. Iron oxide is responsible for this scarlet tint.

When you reach the fork in the road 4 km. later, with signs to Mitspe Yericho and Wadi Qelt, turn left along the old road to Jericho, for an hour's detour into the deep gorge of **Wadi Qelt.** Drive the next 5 km. until you reach the lip of the gorge. Park here and take the path winding down for a half hour walk.

WADI QELT (Map: L17)

The Greek Orthodox **Monastery of St. George** perches precariously half-way up the gorge. Tiny caves pockmarking the cliff-face are used as cells by several of the reclusive monks during many days of isolated prayer. On the other side of the wadi, a green-belted canal rushes down with the pull of gravity from springs further up.

Built near the site where tradition has it that the prophet Elijah was fed by ravens, the church includes some frescoes and decorated floors that have survived from the original 6th century monastery.

As with most Christian places of worship, the original was almost completely destroyed by the Persians. Evidence of their orgy of violence can be seen in a cave about 100 m. from the monastery. It contains the skulls and bones of Christians who were herded here to be slaughtered en masse.

The monks point out the Tomb of St. George within the monastery in spite of the fact that most authorities hold that the tomb of the patron saint of England is located in the church bearing his name in Lod.

Other sites include a cave-cum-chapel where Elijah is said to have lived for a while, and a large aviary overlooking the wadi.

The Monastery of St. George is open seven days a week from 8 a.m. – 4 p.m., but it is inadvisable to visit on Sundays, when the monks are continually at prayer.

You could drive down the road another 5 km. to Jericho.

Return to the highway and 5 km. further on you begin to drop below sea level. Your ears may even pop during the rapid descent. There is a road sign indicating the fact that you're at sea level.

A road to the right leads to the mosque of **Nebi Mussa,** over the place where Muslim legend claims Moses is buried. The biblical account holds that "Moses died in the land of Moab, ...but no man knows the place of his burial to this day" (Deuteronomy 34:5–6).

As you leave the mountains, turn left for Jericho on Road No. 90. The road ahead leads to Qumran and Massada.

JERICHO (Map: M16)

Jericho is the oldest and the lowest city in the world. Carbon 14 tests date its beginnings to approximately 11,000 years ago.

The life-giving spring at the foot of the ancient tel or archaeological mound brings seasonal wonders with orange-flowered poinciana trees, evergreens, palms and hibiscus. The oasis is the secret of Jericho's endurance. Fed from a rocky underground basin that traps the winter rains from the Judaean highlands, the spring surfaces at the foot of the tel. It is known as **Elisha's Spring** following his miraculous treatment of its waters (2 Kings 2:19–22).

In keeping with all Arab towns in Judaea and Samaria, Jericho also has an appealingly low-level skyline. However, the humble, makeshift and deserted refugee camps at its southern and northern ends are a grim reminder of current, unsolved problems.

History

When the late British archaeologist Kathleen Kenyon excavated the tel from 1952–58, she electrified the world by claiming that "Jericho has provided evidence of the transition from man as a hunter to man as a member of a settled community."

She found the earliest defensive walls known to mankind and the earliest pottery unearthed in the Holy Land. Most remarkable of all is the mysterious **round tower** of Jericho dating back to 8000 BCE. It has puzzled scholars the world over and none can say what its purpose was. Some 10 m. in diameter, it has steps leading down from an opening in the top. Twelve bodies were found at its entrance when it was uncovered.

By the time Joshua crossed the River Jordan with his trumpeting tribesmen, the men of Jericho had long experience in techniques of survival. Yet "the wall fell down flat" and the Israelites were off to an auspicious start on their conquest of the Holy Land.

Joshua's curse on anyone rebuilding Jericho (Joshua 6:20–27) was as harmless as David cursing Mt. Gilboa.

However, thc oasis did become impure shortly after Elijah was swept to heaven on an incandescent chariot at the city boundaries. It remained for the prophet Elisha to sprinkle the water with salt, making it "wholesome to this day" (2 Kings 2:4–22).

Jericho fell to the Babylonians in 587 BCE but Jews returning from exile in the same century rebuilt it. With the arrival of the Greeks and then the Romans, the resort city was moved slightly west. King Herod built himself a winter palace here; it has recently been excavated and can be visited.

Jericho again rose to prominence during the life of Jesus. The site of his baptism by John the Baptist is traditionally set by the banks of the Jordan on the eastern boundary of Jericho (Matthew 3:13–15).

The soaring **Mount of Temptation,** atop which New Testament accounts say Jesus was tempted by the devil for 40 days and 40 nights, broods over the western edge of Jericho (Matthew 4:1–4).

The ancient city was razed during the 1st century war

against the Romans. Several centuries later it was moved to its present location by the Byzantines. But the 6th century synagogue in the north shows how extensive its boundaries were.

It experienced a flash of regal glory when Caliph Hisham Ibn Abd el-Malik, ruling in Damascus, constructed a winter palace in 743. Disaster struck only four years later when an earthquake destroyed the city and the palace.

Jericho capitulated to the Crusaders in 1099, after which they constructed sugar mills at the foot of the Mt. of Temptation, using Herodian water systems. Saladin ousted the Christians in 1147, following which Jericho was almost deserted. The Egyptians burned down the buildings when they retreated from the country in 1840. At the close of World War I it surrendered to General Allenby.

Since 1967, when it was taken by the Israel Defence Forces, Jericho has been administered by a locally elected council, while the Israel Civil Administration has the final say.

Sites

Ancient Synagogue: north of the tel. Colossal mosaics on floor of 6th century synagogue, below private Arab house, illustrations include menora, lulav, etrog and Aramaic inscription, "Peace unto Israel," also extolling the memory of those who made the mosaic. Open: daily 8.30 a.m. – 3 p.m. Entrance free.

Baptism of Jesus: east of Jericho on banks of Jordan River. Out of bounds to tourists indefinitely as close to ceasefire line.

Crusader Sugar Mills: at foot of Mt. of Temptation. When in use in 11th century, were driven by Herodian water systems. To get there take left turn just before Tel Jericho, then second left along bad road. Walk remaining 200 m. to huge stone millwheel.

Farm School: 4 km. east of Jericho. Founded by Palestinian Arab in 1951 for refugee boys and orphans. Saline soil treated with sweet water. Funded by Ford Foundation and others.

Hisham's Palace: 3 km. north of tel. Remains of winter palace of Caliph Hisham Ibn Abd el-Malik of Damascus. Destroyed by earthquake in 747 CE, four years after completion. Brilliant mosaics, ruins of mosques, heated bathing rooms, double-storey residences. Maintained by National Parks Authority. Open: daily 8 a.m. – 4 p.m. (5 p.m., Apr. – Sept.). Entrance fee.

Monastery of the Temptation: Greek Orthodox monastery halfway up the vertical cliff of the Mt. of Temptation, on western border of city. Where Jesus fasted 40 days and nights while being tempted by the Devil (Matthew 4:1–4). Access off road to Ramallah.

Tel Jericho: mound 20 m. high and 65 dunams in area, northwest of market place, where relics from first city in the world date back to 9000 BCE. Round tower of unknown purpose, dates back 10,000 years. Earliest building of its size in the world. Spring of Ein es-Sultan (Elisha's Spring) rises at base of tel. Open: daily 8 a.m. – 5 p.m. Entrance fee. There is a special parking lot – you are not allowed to stop on the main road.

The 20 km. drive from Jericho to Qumran on Road No. 90 takes you deeper into the bleached terrain before you get your first view of the Dead Sea. The road runs parallel to it before the turn-off to the monastic ruins and celebrated caves of Qumran. (For description of the Dead Sea area, see Route No. 22.)

QUMRAN (Map: M18)

A nimble Bedouin boy, scrambling up these gaunt cliffs in search of a lost goat, found the first of the Dead Sea Scrolls in 1947. Since then fragments of every book of the Old Testament, apart from the Book of Esther, have been plucked from the caves at Qumran.

They are the oldest known biblical manuscripts in the world. The Book of Isaiah, containing all 66 chapters in Hebrew, was written on parchment in about 100 BCE, making it the oldest and the largest of the seven original scrolls.

They were written in the scriptorium of the ruins of Qumran where a sect, generally believed to have been the ascetic Essenes, once lived. Josephus wrote of them as "communists to perfection," adopting simple dress and adhering to strict rules of membership, with some remaining celibate while others took wives merely to propagate their kind.

Professor Yadin believed that the Essenes joined the defenders of Massada in the final holdout against the Romans. A sectarian scroll discovered on Massada is identical to one found in the Qumran caves.

Qumran, which was first settled during the 8th century BCE, was settled some six centuries later by the Essenes. It was abandoned by the sect in the reign of Herod, during which an earthquake wrecked the area, splitting the walls and cracking the cisterns.

When the band returned, some 30 years later, they prepared for the end of the world, which they described in one of their scrolls, "The War of the Sons of Light Against the Sons of Darkness." Their end came when the Romans burned their collective settlement in 68 CE.

During the Bar Kochba rebellion a Roman garrison was stationed at Qumran but it was abandoned from then until 18 centuries later when the site was excavated following discovery of the scrolls.

The National Parks Authority maintains the site. Notable among the ruins are the ritual bath, scriptorium (where pottery inkwells were found), a potter's workshop, kitchen, assembly and dining hall, laundry, water systems, a stable and the adjacent cemetery where some 1,200 graves were found. The members of the tightly-knit sect apparently lived in surrounding huts, tents and caves.

Open: daily (Apr. – Sept. 8 a.m. – 5 p.m., Oct. – Mar. 8 a.m. – 4 p.m.). Entrance fee. Cold drinks and sandwiches are served in the air-conditioned cafeteria at the entrance to the park.

Descend to the main road and 3 km. further south arrive at the oasis of **En Feshkha** (Einot Zukim).

This natural sweet-water spring gushes out of the desiccated earth close to the **Dead Sea** shore. It slices through the land as a tree-shaded canal and fills two huge artificial pools with its refreshing waters, only metres from the salty Dead Sea.

En Feshkha is a popular spot during the weekend, when it is normally as packed as the Tel Aviv beaches. The National Parks Authority has installed changing and washing facilities. Light meals and cold drinks are available. Open: 8 a.m. – 5 p.m. summer, 8 a.m. – 4 p.m. winter.

Those who arrive within 30 minutes of closing time may find it difficult to be admitted. Entrance fee.

Continue along Road No. 90, opened on Independence Day 1971. It runs above the level of the Dead Sea, but always in line with its shore, making it a motorist's dream.

If you feel like driving to the summit of this mountainous road for a truly panoramic view of the Sea, take the turn-off to the **field school, Mesoque-Deragot,** or, further on, to **Kibbutz Mitzpe Shalem**.

The highway passes by some rock sculptures, installed by the Public Works Department to mark the construction of the road from En Feshkha to En Gedi. From here it is a short distance to the kibbutz and oasis of En Gedi.

EN GEDI (Map: L21)

For the fourth time along this route the dry wilderness is irrigated by the waters of an oasis. At En Gedi (Fountain of the Kid), cascading waterfalls and limpid pools are bordered by luxuriant trees and wild flowers.

Little has changed since the poet was moved to write in the Song of Songs, "My beloved is to me a cluster of henna blossoms in the vineyards of En Gedi" (Cant. 1:14).

In this region David fled the wrath of the jealous King Saul and stealthily "cut off the skirt of Saul's robe" in a cave (I Samuel 24:4).

Anxious to preserve this heritage, the Nature Reserves Authority has proclaimed it a nature reserve and visitors are reminded that it is forbidden to pick the flowers or hunt the wild life that includes ibex. Open: daily 8 a.m. – 4 p.m. Entrance fee.

A trail leads up to the heights of the Nature Reserve on the north of the kibbutz, crossing the stream at many points. You pass a series of pools and small waterfalls until you get to **David's Spring** and a 35 m.-high waterfall with a shallow pool below it.

A fenced-off historical site in the kibbutz's date groves includes the mosaic floor of an ancient synagogue. The remains of a Chalcolithic temple are an hour's walk away. Here, too, Jews lived in prosperity until they fled to the caves of Nahal Hever, further south, when the Romans encamped at En Gedi during the revolt of Bar Kochba.

The flourishing kibbutz is fragrant with fruit and vegetables and shaded by scores of trees. There is a guest house within the kibbutz. Night hikes to the spectacular caves below Massada are sometimes organized when there is a full moon – enquire at the kibbutz.

If you wish to swim in the Dead Sea, En Gedi is the place because fresh water showers are installed on the beach to wash off the sticky salt afterwards. There is a self-service restaurant here.

The 18-kilometre stretch between En Gedi and Massada is close to the shore, providing endless opportunities to study the bizarre, lunar-like landscape. Driftwood is bent into tortured shapes and baked white by the sun.

Four km. from En Gedi pass by the hot sulphur springs with modern buildings – **Hamei Mazor** (see Health Resorts).

Nahal Hever, less than halfway to Massada, has a series of caves secreted within steep cliffs. From the bat-filled interiors, Professor Yadin's expedition recovered the unique **Bar Kochba letters,** glassware, jewellery, fragments of clothing, coins and legal documents. They are displayed in the Shrine of the Book at the Israel Museum in Jerusalem.

The Roman camp, perched at the top of the cliff and in the surrounding area, made escape impossible for the Jews who fled here during 132–5 CE.

Cross **Nahal Tze'elim,** which becomes a torrent of water during the few hours of sudden winter rains.

The turn-off to Massada is clearly signposted close by. (For a description of Massada see Route No. 22.)

ROUTE No. 2 (Map: Northern Sheet K17 to F23)

Judaea (The West Bank)

Jerusalem – Bethlehem (8 km.) – Gush Etzion (19 km.) – Hebron (36 km.) – Beer Sheva (79 km.) (Road No. 60.)

(Distances in brackets refer to start of route.)

Whether you go all the way through to Beer Sheva is immaterial but visits to Bethlehem, Gush Etzion (the Etzion Bloc) and Hebron should rank high in anyone's itinerary of the Holy Land. Each, in its own way, strikes a religious or nationalistic chord, with several points along the way providing added attractions.

The road to Bethlehem is a clear, straight run immediately after the Jerusalem railway station. It is idyllically rustic with olive groves and the gently sloping hills adding to the scenic attraction beyond.

On the way to Bethlehem is the **Biblical Resources Pilgrim Centre.** It boasts a Scripture Garden with reconstructions of items from the biblical world, such as a wine press, a threshing floor and water systems. There are also magnificent views across to Bethlehem and the Judaean Desert, and a cafeteria. You can even enjoy a 4-course Biblical Meal in a Roman villa! Open: Mon.–Sat. 8.30 a.m.–5 p.m. (summer), 8.30 a.m.–4.30 p.m. (winter). Biblical Meals by appointment. Entrance fee (children under 5 free). Tel. (02)767361.

Some minutes after leaving Jerusalem, on your left, is the Greek Monastery, **Mar Elias**, named after the prophet Elijah. Built in the 6th c., it was destroyed by an earthquake and rebuilt in the 14th c.

Bethlehem's church-steepled skyline appears; but such is the enchantment of this city that there seems to be no separation between its perimeter and the countryside.

Bethlehem is a town so grey with tradition that it was prominent in the Jewish mind some 1,600 years before the birth of Jesus, when Rachel, wife of the patriarch Jacob, was buried here. Rachel's tomb is on your right, before the turning (left) to Bethlehem. The road ahead is to Hebron.

BETHLEHEM (Map: J18)

It parts from the lips like a whispered prayer and echoes around the world as the birthplace of Jesus.

Your every expectation will be fulfilled on seeing the **Church of the Nativity** and **Manger Square,** despite their ritual exposure to television cameras on Christmas Eve.

Down in the dimly-lit **Grotto of the Nativity** the pungent smell of incense lingers over the ancient manger. And outside is **Shepherds' Field,** where the heavenly host sang, "Glory to God in the highest, and on earth peace among men."

Christianity's shrines are tucked within the town's low, grey stone buildings, bordered by terraced vineyards and pastoral olive groves that have not changed these past 2000 years.

It is a town of steeples and spires, of Franciscan monks

Bethlehem

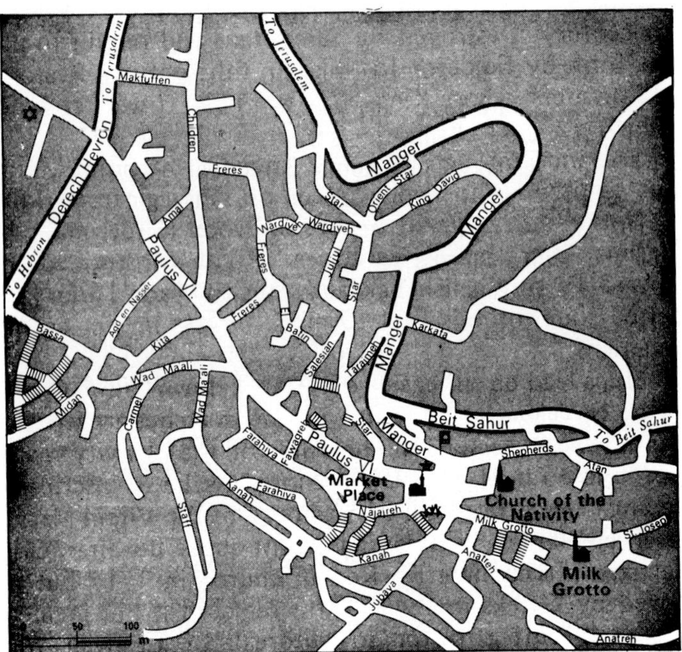

in brown habits and sandals and Greek Orthodox priests cutting stately figures in long black robes. There are pealing church bells and scenes reminiscent of biblical times, with overburdened donkeys struggling up the cobbled lanes.

During the period of the Judges, the biblical romance of Ruth and Boaz was played out in the fields on the eastern side of the town.

King David was born in Bethlehem. The Bible relates how the Philistines were garrisoned within, yet David's warriors stealthily drew water from the town's wells for their monarch.

Bethlehem is awesomely lovely, with narrow streets and cool stone structures. It is ideal for meandering at whim through the lanes and alleys, into the souq for the aura of the Orient, and out past the elders sitting on stools as they draw on hookahs or sip strong coffee.

About 25,000 people live in Bethlehem, of whom slightly more than half are Moslems, the remainder being Christian Arabs.

Tourist Information Office: Manger Square, diagonally opposite the police station. Tel. (02) 742591.

Sites

Church of the Nativity: dominating Manger Square. One of most revered sites in Christendom as it marks place of Jesus' birth. First church built by Empress Helena in 4th century. Destroyed by Samaritans and rebuilt in present form by Emperor Justinian in 6th century. Restored by Crusaders, two of whose Kings, Baldwin I and II, were crowned within.

Entrance through very low "door of humility," built thus to prevent Moslem horsemen intent on sacrilege from riding in. Notice many carved crosses on wood inside, made by pilgrims over many centuries. Roof constructed by Edward IV of English oak and tons of lead. Turks later melted some of this lead to make bullets in war against the Venetians.

Steps lead on either side of the altar down to the Grotto of the Nativity. Bronze doors in marble arches are work of Crusaders. Silver star on the Altar of the Nativity marks spot where Jesus was born, denoted by Latin inscription reading, "Here Jesus Christ was born of the Virgin Mary." Seventeen lamps burn day and night above the altar. Original star placed here by Roman Catholic church in 1717 but removed by Greeks in 1847. Turks replaced it but incident was contributing factor to outbreak of Crimean War.

Catholics are forbidden to use the Altar of the Nativity, but may burn incense over the star. They use the Altar of the Manger, a few metres away, which is marked by a Latin inscription saying that the newborn Jesus was placed here (by the Virgin Mary). On Christmas Eve, the Latin Patriarch takes a wooden image of the infant Jesus from the adjacent Franciscan **Church of St. Catherine** and solemnly places it on the **Altar of the Manger**, where it remains until Epiphany.

Background notes: rights in the Basilica and Grotto are held jointly by the Greek Orthodox, Armenians and Latins (Catholics). Rivalries during the past centuries led to fisticuffs between the religious orders. The intricate status quo has been adhered to here (as in the Church of the Holy Sepulchre in Jerusalem) since compromises were worked out by a British District Commissioner. Peace is maintained only through the three communities strictly observing tight schedules. For instance, the Greeks must finish censing the Altar of the Nativity by 4.30 a.m., when the Catholics hold their first mass. The Armenian mass begins at 8 a.m., after which the Grotto is open for private prayer and to the general public.

David's Wells: King David Street, off Manger Street. Three large cisterns from which King David longed to drink while Philistines were garrisoned in Bethlehem (2 Samuel 23:13–17). Byzantines built church and convent here 4th–6th centuries. Monks serving in church buried in catacombs and names of several still seen on some of the 80 tombs.

Field of Ruth: east of Milk Grotto, with Judaean desert unfolding towards Dead Sea. Where Ruth, the Moabite, gleaned barley from the field of her husband-to-be, Boaz (Ruth 2).

Milk Grotto: Milk Grotto Street, short walk southeast of Church of Nativity. Franciscan church over cave where tradition says Virgin Mary spilt milk while nursing Jesus. The drops turned black stones milk white. Packets of this powdery white stone sold to pilgrims, allegedly with power to increase flow of mother's milk.

Rachel's Tomb: at northern entrance to Bethlehem, on Jerusalem Road. Traditional burial place of matriarch Rachel, wife of Jacob (Genesis 35:19–20). Ancient domes and pillars enclosed in 18th century and renovated by Sir Moses Montefiore in 1841 (see inscription on marble tablet within). Visited by devout on new moons, during month of Elul and on 14th Heshvan, traditional anniversary of her death. Headcovers available at entrance. Open: Sun-Thurs. 8 a.m. – 6 p.m. Fri. 8 a.m. – 1 p.m. Closed Sat. Admission free.

Shepherds' Field: idyllic terraced fields with olive trees on left of eastern entrance to city. Where angel appeared to shepherds to announce birth of Jesus (Luke 2:8-20). There are two churches here, one Roman Catholic and the other Greek Orthodox.

Suq: few minutes' walk west of Manger Square. Better bargains and greater variety of wares than in Manger Square although quality sometimes not as good. Fine opportunity to see colourful dress of Arabs from

Bethlehem and neighbouring villages selling fruits and vegetables in an open-air market.

Sites near Bethlehem

Herodion: palatial fortress 9 km. southeast of Bethlehem along well-signposted road (No. 356). Herod artificially raised height by piling debris on summit of hill. Built palaces inside in 1st century BCE. Josephus described it as resembling woman's breast. Had 200 white marble steps leading up to circular wall and towers. Commanding view of Jerusalem suburbs, Dead Sea, Bethlehem and Judaean Desert. Herod buried here with great pomp. Seized by Romans after destruction of Second Temple and used by Bar Kochba as district headquarters.

Remains include stone benches from synagogue and mikve (ritual bath). Also ruins of 5th–6th century Byzantine chapel. Recent finds, near base, of Herodian town with palace, hippodrome and pleasure garden.

The National Parks Authority provides parking facilities and toilets. Open 8 a.m. – 4 p.m. (5 p.m. in summer). Entrance fee.

Mar Saba Monastery: 14 km. east of Bethlehem (partly along Roads Nos. 3717 and 398). Most spectacular of all Holy Land monasteries, clinging to walls of canyons of Kidron Valley. Reclusive monks, some of whom have been in caves for years without communicating even with each other. Monastery destroyed and pillaged many times since Byzantine era. Present structure built by Russian government in mid-19th century. Women forbidden to enter. Road from Ubeidiya leads to monastery.

Return to Bethlehem and follow Road No. 60 to Hebron past hills solid with grey slabs of rock, around several neat villages where vines and olives are plentiful and then, one kilometre after the village/refugee camp of Dahiche and stone quarries, swing left for **Solomon's Pools.**

These three gigantic, rectangular-shaped cisterns, surrounded by tall trees, were attributed to King Solomon, but are known today to date from Herod's time, when they formed part of a magnificent water system for Jerusalem. Even today they hold hundreds of thousands of gallons of opaque-green water.

Opposite are the ruins of a Crusader fortress, which guarded this important water source. Remnants of water conduits may also still be seen.

Continue on this side-road for one kilometre, along a road that has been shaved on the side of a steep hill leading down to the valley. The road leads into the small Christian-Arab village of Artas. Down below in the valley is the **Monastery of Hortus Conclusus,** stretched across the base of a mountain and set at the edge of huge gardens. Hortus Conclusus is Latin for locked garden and is inspired by a passage from the Song of Songs, attributed to Solomon: "A garden locked is my sister, my bride, a garden locked, a fountain sealed" (Song of Songs 4:12).

Return to the highway and almost immediately notice the plaque on the right hand side. It is a memorial to 10 Jews mown down by Arabs at this spot in December 1947, only 11 days after the United Nations had voted to partition Palestine into Arab and Jewish states.

Continue over the Judaean hills for another 12 km. before reaching the religious settlements grouped together under the banner of Gush Etzion (Etzion Bloc). Turn right into Road No. 367.

GUSH ETZION (ETZION BLOC) (MAP: J19)

Gush Etzion is a tract of denuded hills only 13 km. north of Hebron. It comprises **Kfar Etzion, Migdal Oz** and **Rosh Zurim** (which breed turkeys, produce candles and metal parts, and grow carnations), **Moshav Elazar** and the rural centre of **Alon Shvut** with its Har Etzion Yeshiva and apartments for young people who live here but work in Jerusalem and other nearby places. There is also a museum and a Field School in Kfar Etzion. No entrance on Shabbat.

The first Jewish settlement here in modern times opened in 1927 when Orthodox Ashkenazi and Yemenite Jews set up an agricultural unit called Migdal Eder. But they disbanded after the slaughter of Jews in Hebron in 1929.

A second attempt at Jewish settlement was made by Shmuel Holtzman, a citrus grower from Rehovot, who started a settlement in 1935 and called it Kfar Etzion. But the crops and properties were destroyed by Arabs in 1937.

In 1943 some young members of Hapoel Hamizrahi returned to the area, planted orchards and crops, introduced light industry and built a synagogue. Other kibbutzim were established nearby. In May 1948, after months of siege, during which they suffered casualties, the defenders could no longer withstand the numerically superior forces of the Arab Legion. Their end came a day before Independence was proclaimed in Israel.

The Arabs massacred the 127 defenders, raising the total number of dead at Gush Etzion to 240, and then set about uprooting the trees. The defenders and those who died trying to lift the siege showed incredible valour.

There were the 14 Jews who blew themselves up in their armoured car when they saw no possibility of escape from swarms of Arabs attacking them on their return from Kfar Etzion to Jerusalem. Then there were the famous 35, killed to a man while on their way through the Valley of Elah to lift the siege (see Route No. 6). Finally there were the 20 women and youngsters entombed in the cellars of a building dynamited during the final battle. Their bodies were recovered and reinterred when Israeli troops recaptured Gush Etzion in 1967.

Those who survived the 1948 massacre founded Kibbutz **Nir Etzion** near Haifa, Kibbutz **Ein Tzurim** in the south, **Beerot Yitzhak** and a new **Massuot Yitzhak** in the heart of the country. Kibbutz **Revadim,** just off the Jerusalem-Beer Sheva road, was also in the pre-1948 Etzion Bloc. With the end of the Six Day War many of the survivors, together with the children who had been evacuated from Kfar Etzion, returned to rebuild the Etzion Bloc. A new town named **Efrat** is located on the eastern side of the **Etzion Bloc** across the main road, and further east, in the Judaean Desert, are the settlements of **Tekoa** and **Ma'ale Amos.**

Sites

Last stronghold of 1948: ruins opposite museum in Kfar Etzion. Former summer home of Benedictine Fathers in Jerusalem. Twenty women and children entombed for 19 years after the building was dynamited in 1948.

Field School Igloos: at Kfar Etzion. Youth hostel and dormitories for students.

Museum: pictorial display of history of settlement in the area. Names of slain defenders inscribed on one wall. Memorial candle in wax-filled upturned soldier's helmet. Open: Sun.–Thurs. 8.30 a.m. – 4 p.m., Fri. 8.30 a.m. – 3 p.m. Winter: 10 a.m. – 4 p.m. weekdays, 10 a.m. – 2 p.m. Fri. Closed Sat. Entrance fee.

Back on Road No. 60, drive past typical examples of the profuse viticulture of the Hebron area, with small Arab villages hugging the roadside. The road rises slightly and peaks at just over 1,000 m. above sea level near Hebron.

Turn left in **Halhul** for a look at the traditional Tombs of Gad and Nathan, set behind a courtyard of a private Arab house.

During the remaining 4 km. to Hebron you will pass by several open-air glass factories that have made Hebron famous. You can stop and watch the entire process from treatment in the red-hot furnaces to the art of glass-blowing. The wares sold at these factories and stalls are much cheaper than the identical jars, vases, plates and other glassware offered for sale in the heart of the city.

HEBRON (Map 12, HJ20)

One of the four cities holy to Jews, Hebron is inextricably bound up with the fabric of Hebrew history. It is sanctified in Jewish eyes because the patriarchs, Abraham, Isaac and Jacob, are buried in the **Cave of Machpelah** with their wives Sarah, Rebecca and Leah, and because David was anointed king in Hebron and ruled here at the beginning of his reign.

The massive structure built by Herod over the Cave of Machpelah dominates this city of hills. Everything, from the bustling souq to the stone villas in the suburbs, seems to radiate from it.

Hebron is essentially an introverted city, wrapping itself in the solitude of its vines and holding within its bosom the shrines that pilgrims and tourists visit regardless of the efforts of the townspeople.

Apart from the characteristically heavy and colourful glassware – a trade believed to have been introduced by Jewish immigrants from Venice after the Crusaders – Hebron seems content to rest on its laurels of chance association with biblical figures.

However, if you drive to the fenced, hill-top Jewish settlement of **Kiryat Arba,** you will soon appreciate the latent passions that Hebron evokes. These Orthodox Jews were held at arm's length after the Six Day War. But their insistence on being allowed to live in Hebron won them the initial right to live within the Military Government compound. Their settlement, complete with synagogue and yeshiva, has been expanding geographically and includes about 3,000 Orthodox and secular Jews.

History

Some 3,600 years ago Hebron was a Canaanite town that had not yet changed its name from Kiryat Arba to Hebron (Joshua 14:15). At about this time Abraham and Sarah pitched their tent by the Oaks of Mamre. Through divine appearance they were promised the birth of Isaac (Genesis 18).

When Sarah died in Hebron, Abraham bought the Cave of Machpelah, with the trees and the field adjoining it, in the first recorded transaction involving a Hebrew purchaser of real estate in the land of Canaan (Genesis 23).

About 700 years later, Moses sent men to spy out the land as he prepared to advance on the Promised Land. They visited Hebron which, they reported, was occupied by giants and was well fortified. But when they came to the nearby Valley of Eshkol, "they cut down from there a branch with a single cluster of grapes, and they carried it on a pole between two of them" (Numbers 13:21 – 24). Ever since, this image has represented the bounty of the Promised Land.

Hoham, King of Hebron, was slain by Joshua at the battle of Ayalon during the conquest of Canaan (Joshua 10:3).

About 250 years later King David ordered the assassins of Saul's son, Ish-bosheth, hanged beside the pool at Hebron, after their feet and hands were cut off (2 Samuel 4:12).

Jews were expelled after the destruction of the First Temple and again 1,700 years later when the Crusaders converted the mosque and synagogue around the Cave of Machpelah into a church.

The Hasmonaean John Hyrcanus took the city at the end of the 2nd century BCE. During the war against the Romans the Jews captured it, only to lose it later when the Romans burned it down.

The Byzantines erected a church over the cave of the patriarchs. This was adapted as a mosque with the Moslem conquest. Henceforth Hebron was known as Khalil al-Rahman, "The beloved (Abraham) of (God) the merciful."

It became a district capital under the Mamelukes. Their harsh decree in 1266 forbidding the Jews to enter the Cave of Machpelah was enforced by various conquerors and authorities until June 1967. Before then, the closest Jews could get was to the seventh step of the staircase leading up to the mosque.

In all its turbulent history, Hebron has seldom witnessed such chilling, xenophobic murder as the pogroms of 1929, when its Jewish community was literally decimated in a few hours.

When the town was captured in the Six Day War the Jewish quarter and cemetery were found almost completely destroyed.

Sites

Beit el-Khalil (House of the Friend): signposted at northern entrance to Hebron. The Hebrew name is **Alonei Mamre** (Oaks of Mamre). This is where Abraham built an altar (Genesis 13:18). An ancient well, more than 5 m. in diameter, is referred to as Abraham's Well. Perhaps also where David reigned, as archaeological excavations show signs of towers and walls from Davidic kingdom and early monarchy. Two-metre-thick stone wall enclosing area 60 m. wide and 83 m. long constructed by Herod, possibly as place of worship or walled compound serving later as market place or caravanserai. Hadrian chose site to sell remnants of Bar Kochba's army into slavery. Ground reconsecrated by Constantine with Basilica of the Terebinth of Mamre, foundations of which are still visible. Desolate since Arab conquest in 7th century.

Cave of Machpelah: burial cave of Adam and Eve, Abraham, Isaac and Jacob and their wives, Sarah, Rebecca and Leah. Cave purchased by Abraham, according to Genesis 23, for 400 silver shekels. Base of Herodian wall below additions by Crusaders. Entrance to cave sealed and denoted by brass plate below small dome in same room containing cenotaph to Isaac and Rebecca. Formerly synagogue and Byzantine chapel. Church of St. Abraham under Crusaders. Mosque since 13th century. A synagogue was re-established there in 1967. Walls decorated with quotations from Koran. Cenotaph to Joseph in separate room across courtyard. For opening hours, call (02) 962166.

Kiryat Arba: Jewish settlement on northern perimeter of city. Founded by religious Jews who spent Passover 1968 living in the Park Hotel in Hebron and later moved to the Military Government compound before being permitted to establish permanent housing.

Municipal Museum: Main Street. Pottery, glass and other objects depicting artifacts in daily use in Hebron and vicinity during successive centuries. Open: daily 7.30 a.m. – 2.30 p.m. Entrance fee.

Oak of Abraham: 2 km. south of turn-off to Well of Abraham. Ancient oak tree within grounds of Russian monastery. Held by some to be the tree under which Abraham was visited by three men and told of the impending birth of Isaac (Genesis 18). However, others claim that the original was at Beit el-Khalil and was torn away in pieces by early pilgrims seeking souvenirs.

Suq: close to Cave of Machpelah. Good bargains in jewellery, trinkets, metals and curios with Oriental dazzle.

Tomb of Abner: opposite entrance to the Cave of Machpelah. Gloomy cave lit by candles. Abner was slain in Hebron by David's jealous commander-in-chief-to-be, Joab (2 Samuel 3:27), and was mourned by King David as "a prince and a great man."

The road to Beer Sheva is pleasantly dappled with vines and stone terraces for the first quarter, after which it opens up into grass-covered hills.

At a point 12 km. south of Hebron turn left if you wish to visit the ruins of the 4th century CE synagogue in the Arab village of **Samua,** formerly the biblical town of Eshtemoa. The detour is only 7 km. and is worthwhile because it leads to the first ancient synagogue discovered south of Jerusalem. There are fine examples of carved lintels and mosaics; the most impressive sight of all is the double Tora shrine with a deep niche that held the sacred scrolls.

Return to Road No. 60. A further 23 km. brings you to

flatter wastes and the turn-off to Arad. Then pass **Omer,** the beautiful suburb town known colloquially as "millionaires' row" by the citizens of Beer Sheva.

Continue along the main highway, passing (on your right) the strange concrete **memorial** to the men of the **Negev Brigade** who liberated the region during the War of Independence. Worth stopping to look at.

A branch road leads left to the remains of biblical settlements on **Tel Beer Sheva** and, close by, in **Tel Sheva,** where you can see modern housing built for Bedouin who have forsaken their nomadic way of life.

Entry to Beer Sheva is through an industrial site. For a description of the city see the chapter on Beer Sheva.

ROUTE No. 3 (Map: Northern Sheet K17 to L14 and G14)

Samaria or Shomron (The West Bank)

Jerusalem – Nebi Samwil (5 km.) – El Jib (10 km.) – Ramallah (19 km.) – Ofra (26 km.) – Ma'ale Ephraim (50 km.) – Rosh Ha'ayin (92 km.) (Road Nos. 437, 60, 3, 458, 505.)
(Distances in brackets refer to start of route.)

The highway through Shomron (Samaria) is a trail into antiquity, traversing the heart of the biblical Kingdom of Israel. It is also the "West Bank" that was conquered by the Kingdom of Jordan in 1948 and fell to Israel in the Six Day War (1967). This is the contested area. In its western part live about 750,000 Arabs. Its eastern half is empty. Israelis are divided on the issue of the West Bank's future: the "doves" hold that the densely populated western part should be incorporated by Jordan, thus forming a Palestino-Jordanian state, or that it should become an independent Palestinian state; the eastern and empty part can be loosely settled. The "hawks" point out that the West Bank is less than 15 km. from the sea and looms over the most densely populated area of Israel. Should it be held by enemies, it would endanger Israel's very existence.

The easiest way of getting here from the northern part of Jerusalem is from the Central Bus Station towards Ramat Eshkol. It is 5 km. to Nebi Samwil, heading northwest on the Golda Meir Road. This road passes the newly built suburb of Ramot Allon, named after the late Yigal Allon. Head in the direction of the prominent minaret of Nebi Samwil.

NEBI SAMWIL (Map: J17)

Set on top of the highest hill overlooking Jerusalem, this is the traditionally accepted burial place of the Prophet Samuel (Nebi Samwil in Arabic), although, as with many supposed biblical locations, controversy surrounds this site.

The Crusaders caught their first view of the eternal city from these heights and consequently dubbed it Mont Joie (Hill of Joy).

In 1730 the Turks built a mosque over the tomb after sealing the cave. They forbade Jews to enter and pray. The present mosque was built when the earlier one was destroyed in World War I.

One of the high-ceilinged rooms contains a carpet-covered tomb but the rest of this place of worship is empty. However, stairs lead to the roof of the mosque for an excellent view of Jerusalem, with the Dome of the Rock and other landmarks clearly visible. Towards the north you see Givon and several new settlements. Open: daily 8 a.m. – 4 p.m. winter; 8 a.m. – 5 p.m. summer.

Leaving Nebi Samwil, take the first turning to the right and after 1 km. turn right again. On the plain before you there are a few new settlements. On your left is **Hadasha;** ahead of you is **Givon;** further away, to the northwest, is **Givat Ze'ev.** Pass Givon and turn right to the Arab village of **El Jib**. In the centre of the village turn right, and drive up the small hill until you get to **Gibeon,** the site of an ancient biblical city. Archaeological excavations have revealed a rock-hewn pool with spiral steps leading down into it. A tunnel connects the pool to a spring. All the holes in the rock next to the pool were used to store wine, grains, oil, etc. Gibeon is mentioned several times in the Bible (e.g. Joshua 9:3; 2 Samuel 2:13).

Return to Road No. 437 and turn right for a short drive past the Atarot industrial centre. Then turn left onto Road No. 60 and pass Atarot airport.

The antennae of Ramallah's broadcasting station stand beacon-like above the city.

RAMALLAH (Map: J16)

Because of its bracing climate, Ramallah has long been a sought-after winter resort for wealthy Jordanians and Arabs from other countries. King Hussein was a frequent visitor when on vacation in the northern Judaean hills.

The clean, wide streets of Ramallah make it one of the most pleasant cities in the West Bank.

Ramallah's twin town of El-Bira gives it a mixed Moslem-Christian population.

You drive along the main road that seems to tend towards the right, and as you leave **El-Bira** you find a sign indicating "Ofra" to the right along Road No. 3. You will pass the Arab village of Birge Bitin on your right. This is the site of biblical **Beit El** where Jacob had his dream (Gen. 28:19), and Samuel offered sacrifices to God (I Sam. 10:3,8). The site has been dug many times since 1927, revealing important remains. It was covered up in 1960, and has since been built over. As you drive on you pass Arab villages; note the amount of building going on here as on the Ramallah Road – mostly with money sent by young Arabs working in the Gulf states, Saudi Arabia and Jordan.

You then pass the new settlement of **Ofra.** About a hundred religious families live here, maintaining themselves by working at a variety of occupations from agriculture and carpentry, to silk-screen printing and computer services. There is also a Field School here.

About 17 kms. from Ramallah you reach the **Allon Road** (No. 458) that cuts through Eastern Shomron from north to south.

You now have three alternatives: 1) If you drive south you will reach the impressive gorge of Wadi Qelt (see Route No. 1) and a few kms. beyond it, the Jerusalem-Jericho highway (Road No. 1). 2) Driving straight on you reach Jericho by a secondary but scenic old road (No. 3). Turning left onto the Allon Road again you follow the ridge of the Shomron hills, an arid mountain area.

Following the Allon Road north (your left) you will pass the settlements of **Rimmonin, Kohav HaShahar**, and **Givat Adumma** before you get to **Ma'ale Ephraim,** a townlet that offers a view of the Jordan Valley; you either drive down Road No. 507 to the Jericho-Tiberias Rd. (No. 90), or drive west, through the densely populated western side of Shomron (Road No. 505). Driving back the way you came for a few kilometres, you reach a fork signposted "Nablus." You take this excellent new road until you get to the Jerusalem-Nablus Road. To your right: **Nablus,** the biggest town in Shomron, with the impressive remains of the Roman (2nd century CE) town of Sebastia (Route No. 8), 15 kms. to the north of Nablus. To the left (south) leads the winding old road (No. 60) back to Ramallah and Jerusalem.

If you drive straight on along Road No. 505 you will cross the West Bank from east to west. On the way you will pass the new Jewish settlements of **Tapuach, Ariel, Barakan** and **Elkana,** as well as many Arab villages, hugging the hilltops, surrounded by tilled fields and olive groves. After passing the settlement of Elkana you will see on your right the village of **Kafr Kassem,** and the biblical site of **Izbet Sartah,** where the some of the earliest alphabetic inscriptions have been found (Proto-Canaanite, from the 2nd millennium BCE). This, until 1967, was the eastern border of Israel. If you stop here for a moment and look in front of you, you will see Israel's "soft underbelly": the most densely populated part of the country; and only some 15 kms. away, the western border of Israel, the Mediterranean. It was here that Jordan had strong artillery forces and tanks massed along a 30 km. front until 1967, threatening to cut the country in two, through Israel's narrow coastal strip. Turn left (into Road No. 444) to **Rosh Ha'ayin** (Route No. 7), drive through the town, and turn right towards the crossing of Road No. 40, where you can choose between **Tel Aviv** and **Jerusalem.**

ROUTE No. 4 (Map: Northern Sheet K17 and J17–18)

The Judaean Hills

Jerusalem – Bet Jalla (10 km.) – Batir (18 km.) – Mevo Beitar (24 km.) – Ein Karem (50 km.) (Road Nos. 60, 375, 386.)

(Distances in brackets refer to start of route.)

This route takes a few hours and leads through scenic countryside surrounding Jerusalem, on to the last stronghold of Bar-Kochba and then to the village where John the Baptist was born. Be careful on the narrow mountain roads.

Follow Route No. 2 to Bethlehem; after Rachel's Tomb turn right to the Christian hamlet of **Bet Jalla.** Ascend to the peak of **Mt. Gilo** and follow the signs to **Deir Kremizan Monastery.** This picturesque Silesian monastery trains men for the priesthood but is more famous for its delightful wines and for the ancient tombs on the slopes of the terraced hill.

On leaving the monastery turn right up the hill. Next to the Everest Hotel you will see a former British army and Arab Legion camp, now the Field School and settlement of **Har Gilo**. At the entrance you'll find a Roman mausoleum and ancient agricultural implements. From the observation tower, there is a magnificent view of southern Jerusalem and Beit Jalla, Bethlehem and the Judaean Desert.

Drive onto the main road, No. 375, turn right and then left. Now you are in open, rocky country. At the fork veer right for the Arab village of **Batir,** where Bar-Kochba made his last stand on the hill at the edge of the square known as Kasr al-Yahud (Jews' Fortress). This was the ancient site of Beitar. It fell to the Romans in 135 CE after a protracted siege.

Parts of the ancient walls form supports for the terraces in the village. While here note the remains of two Roman siege camps on the southern side and an inscription close to the village spring, commemorating the presence of the two Roman legions.

Return to the main road and take the right fork. Pass the village of **Hussan** and soon after it the remains of concrete tank barriers erected by the Jordanians near the pre-June 1967 borders.

Drive on, passing moshav **Mevo Beitar** and the houses of **Zur Hadassah** built on grey concrete bomb shelters. Parts of Jerusalem are visible most of the time. Drive straight on past **Nes Harim** and one of Keren Kayemet's (JNF) tree-planting centres. On your right you will see a sign for the **Soreq Cave** in the **Avshalom Nature Reserve**. Well worth a visit, it was discovered in 1968 and opened to the public 10 years later. You can see superb stalactites and stalagmites, including a rare formation known as 'Cave Corals'. Other impressive formations have been nicknamed 'City of Pagodas', 'Mexican Hats' and 'Elephant Ears'. For opening hours, call (02)911117.

Return past Nes Harim, and at the road junction to Qiryat Gat and Ashqelon turn towards Jerusalem, taking Road No. 386. Down the hill, the road eventually crosses the stream of **Nahal Soreq,** close to the railroad linking Jerusalem with the coast.

Pass **Even Sapir,** with the **Hadassah Medical Centre** perched above the valley. The road leads into the village of **Ein Karem,** just inside the Jerusalem city limits. (See Jerusalem "Places to Visit" for visiting hours in the churches.)

Close to the centre of the village is the Franciscan **Church of St. John the Baptist,** built in 1885. The Byzantines built the first church over this site in the 5th century. A stairway leads down to the Grotto of the Nativity of St. John.

On leaving the church cross the main road running through the village and arrive at the **Fountain of the Virgin** below the minaret.

You will have to climb the hill to reach the Catholic **Church of the Visitation** on the summit. The Magnificat, etched in 42 languages in the courtyard, commemorates Mary's visit to Elizabeth, mother of John the Baptist (Luke 1:46).

From here you return to Jerusalem.

The Coastal Plain

(Map: Northern Sheet C10 to C19)

The Coastal Plain is the most densely populated area of Israel. It is also a microcosm of Israeli society because it contains the wheels of industry and great stretches of the pastoral. Few sand wastes remain and cities like Tel Aviv, Ashdod, Ashqelon and Netanya rise up like mirages along the long-neglected strip.

The heavy industries revolving around the ports account for much of the activity, but all credit for the mesmerizing beauty of the cultivated fields is due to the kibbutzim and moshavim that fill in the gaps between the cities and towns.

Proof that colonizers with great civilizations once inhabited the Coastal Plain has been unearthed at many points. The Philistine presence is conspicuous in Ashdod but excavations in Tel Aviv have revealed one of their temples within the grounds of the Eretz Israel Museum. The most spectacular finds, however, are those of the Roman amphitheatre and Crusader city at Caesarea.

The Coastal Plain is a sportsman's paradise. Its Mediterranean beaches include remote, sandy playgrounds where you can soak up the sun far from the beaches with all modern trappings. The country's only golf course cuts a green swathe through the dunes of Caesarea while tennis courts abound at sports clubs and alongside hotels.

The Coastal Plain is the envy of the other regions when it comes to national parks and camping and picnic sites. They are well spaced, with a 160–km.–long broad highway slicing through scenery cornucopic with banana plantations, orange groves and vineyards.

Jaffa (Yafo) is the undisputed queen of the night-owl scene. Strolling down Dizengoff Street in Tel Aviv or Herzl Boulevard in Netanya on a Saturday night has become an essential part of growing up Israeli-style.

Tel Aviv-Jaffa

(Map: Northern Sheet E,F14)

With its easy informality, its warm Mediterranean beaches and outdoor cafes, Tel Aviv is easily the most sophisticated of Israel's cities.

The city's character can best be explained by comparing it to Jerusalem, only 45 minutes, but in some ways 2,000 years, away.

Jerusalem is timeless and awe-inspiring; a city of golden stone and layered history. Free-wheeling Tel Aviv is where people go for business, shopping, sand, fun and whatever happens to be IN at the moment. It's the country's financial, fashion, media and commercial centre and arguably its cultural centre too, though some would say Jerusalem deserves that title.

By the time Jerusalem has closed up for the night, Tel Aviv is just beginning to warm up. As in Manhattan and London, a visitor to Tel Aviv has the feeling of being right where everything is happening.

Today Tel Aviv has a population of some 357,000, but that only includes central Tel Aviv and Jaffa. Including the surrounding cities of Ramat Gan, Holon and others which adjoin or are very near, the total population reaches over a million and a half. That makes Tel Aviv by far the largest conurbation in Israel.

HISTORY

Considering its size and importance today, it comes as a surprise that Tel Aviv was nothing but a sand dune 100 years ago.

Tel Aviv.

The view from Jaffa.

Tel Aviv actually began as a suburb of Jaffa, the adjoining city with which it melded in 1950. Jaffa (meaning "beautiful") is an ancient and venerable town which is mentioned in both the Old and New Testaments.

According to Jewish tradition, Jaffa was first established after the Flood by Noah's son Japheth, from whom the town took its name. Jonah, it is said, was swallowed by a whale after he left the port of Jaffa, and Peter performed the Miracle of Tabitha here. In Greek mythology, Andromeda was chained to a rock in Jaffa port.

First inhabited 4,000 years ago, Jaffa was once a Philistine town. Later King Solomon used the port to bring cedars from Lebanon which were used for the great Temple in Jerusalem.

Though King Herod built Caesarea to replace Jaffa as his main port, Jaffa became important again under Moslem and Crusader rule. The town then declined until the nineteenth century, when it began to grow in size and influence.

So crowded did Jaffa become that a group of Jews decided to leave Jaffa's lively, noisy and dirty environs to create a garden suburb which would become Tel Aviv. They bought uninhabited sand dunes north of Jaffa, formed an association called "Ahuzat Bayit" and divided property into parcels of land by drawing lots.

The romantic name Tel Aviv ("Hill of Spring") was chosen for the new community in 1910 partly because of its associations with rebirth and revitalization, and partly because it recalled the vision of Ezekiel. In the biblical Tel Aviv of Babylon, the exiled prophet saw the vision of animated dry bones, which drew him back to Israel. Yet another association is with Theodor Herzl's visionary book "Alteneuland". "Tel Aviv" is the free Hebrew translation of that title.

It is amusing today to think that Tel Aviv's founders once banned commercial enterpise in the city. That ban, of course, did not last long; after the First World War (during which the settlers of Tel Aviv were dispersed), the town took enormous commercial strides. In 1921 it became a separate township and the first modern Jewish city in the world. By 1924 Tel Aviv had a respectable population of 35,000, which was to grow to over 200,000 by 1948.

Tel Aviv's most significant moment in modern history came when David Ben-Gurion proclaimed the state of Israel on May 14 1948, in the home of mayor Meir Dizengoff.

ORIENTATION

Tel Aviv, on the Mediterranean coast 95 km south of Haifa and 62 km northwest of Jerusalem, is a sprawling city with several centres of attraction.

Many of the city's luxury hotels are located on **Hayarkon St.**, along the **Beach Front**, which also features a pleasant walkway, a marina and a number of cafeterias and restaurants. Following the curve of the coast south is **Jaffa**, still full of old-world charm, with its meandering cobbled streets of galleries, quaint shops and markets.

Dizengoff is the principal shopping, strolling and people-watching street, and a pause at one of its many pavement cafes to enjoy the passing show, particularly on Friday afternoons, is not to be missed. At the south end of Dizengoff lies Dizengoff Circle with its flamboyant and controversial revolving statue by sculptor Agam. In recent years, the action has moved further north. Many of Israel's glossy fashion boutiques and popular restaurants now lie around the Dizengoff-Yirmiyahu area.

Two other main shopping streets are **Ben Yehuda**, between Dizengoff and Hayarkon, worth exploring for its art galleries and souvenir shops, and **Ibn Gvirol**, with its new glossy shopping centre, Gan Ha'ir, next to city hall. At the end of Ben Yehuda lies **Allenby Street**, once the centre of Tel Aviv shopping and now older and shabbier, but still interesting. Many historical areas lie off Allenby, as do the bustling Carmel and Bezalel Markets. All areas can be reached by bus from the **Central Bus Station**. This area comprises a gaggle of Mid-Eastern style small streets crowded with bargain merchandise, fast food and produce stalls.

ACCOMMODATION

See also general Accommodation section.

Tel Aviv has more than 6,000 hotel rooms and other accommodation of all grades.

HOTELS

Dan Tel. (03)5202525. 99 Hayarkon St.
Hilton Tel. (03)5202222. Independence Park.
Carlton Tel. (03)5201818. 10, Eliezer Peri St.

Tel Aviv street scenes.

Kikar Kedumim, the centre of Old Jaffa where the most frequented cafes and night clubs are to be found.

Mediterranean
Sea
Dolphinarium
Charles Clore Park
Old Jaffa
Jaffa
Beit Bialik
Shalom Tower
Kikar Magen David
Hayarkon
Ben Yehuda
Allenby
Eilat
Kibbutz Galuyot
Sderot Yerushalayim
Japhet
Ben Zvi
Herzl
To Bat Yam
To Ramla

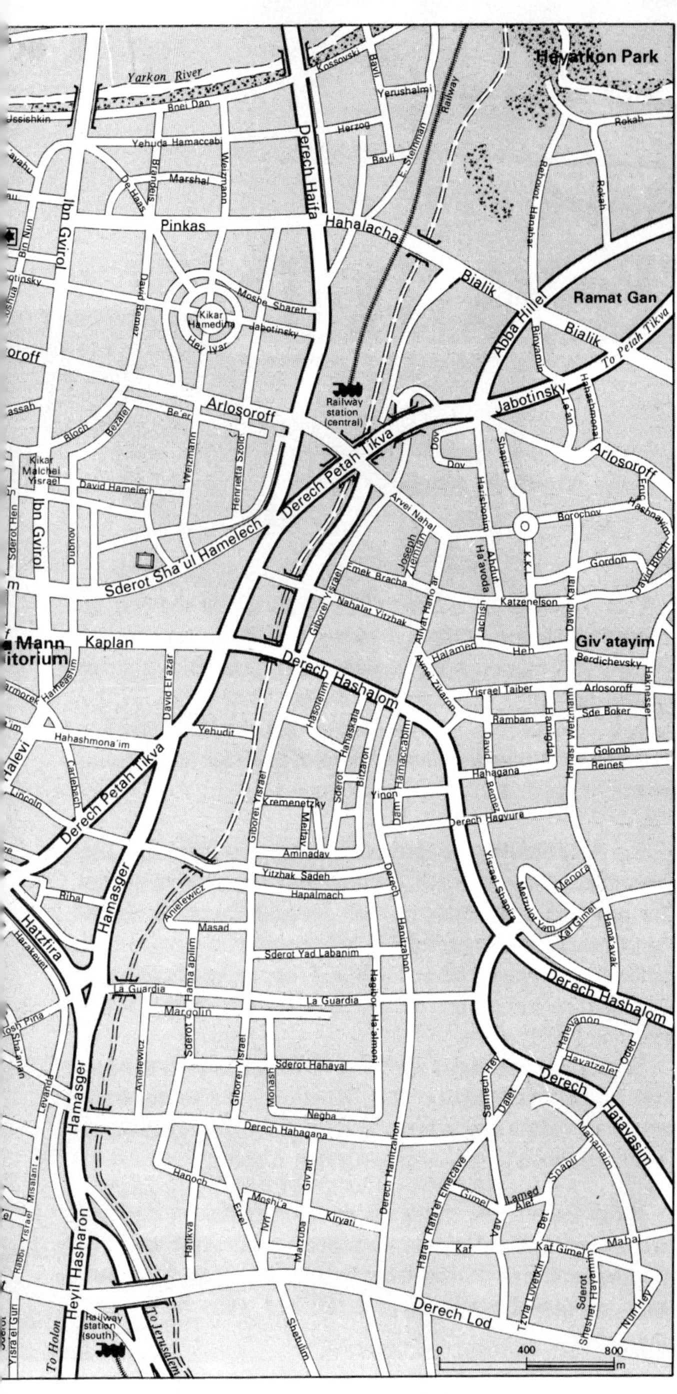

Hayarkon Park
Yarkon River
Ramat Gan
Giv'atayim
Railway station (central)
Railway station (south)
Kikar Hamedina
Kikar Malchei Yisrael
Mann Auditorium
Derech Haifa
Ibn Gvirol
Pinkas
Hahalacha
Bialik
Abba Hillel
Jabotinsky
To Petah Tikva
Arlosoroff
Derech Petah Tikva
Sderot Sha'ul Hamelech
Kaplan
Derech Hashalom
Hamasger
Hatzfira
Heyil Hasharon
Derech Lod
Derech Hatayasim
Derech Hahagana
Derech Hamitzahon
To Holon
To Jerusalem
Railway
0 400 800 m

The Jaffa Flea Market: a must for bargain hunters. (Below) Tel Aviv.

Tel Aviv

The Bahai Temple, Haifa.

Haifa Port.

Ramada Continental Tel. (03)5272626. 121 Hayarkon St.
Dan Panorama Tel. (03)5190190. 10 Kaufman St.
Moriah Plaza Tel. (03)5271515. 155 Hayarkon St.
Sheraton Tel. (03)5211111. 115 Hayarkon St.
Avia Tel. (03)5360221. Near Ben-Gurion Airport. Savyon.
Astor Tel. (03)5223141 . 105 Hayarkon St.
Grand Beach Tel. (03)5466555. 250 Hayarko St.
Ramat Aviv Tel. (03)6990777. 151 Derekh Namir.
Sinai Tel. (03)5172621. 15 Trumpeldor St.
Tal Tel. (03)5442281. 287 Hayarkon St.
Ambassador Tel. (03)5103993. 56 Herbert Samuel St.
City Tel. (03)5246253. 9 Mapu St.
Florida Tel. (03)5242184. 164 Hayarkon St.
Maxim Tel. (03)5173721. 86 Hayarkon St.
Shalom Tel. (03)5243277. 216 Hayarkon St.
Basel Tel. (03)5244161. 156 Hayarkon St.
Adiv Tel. (03)5229141. 5 Mendele St.
Ami Tel. (03)5249141. 152 Hayarkon St.
Armon Hayarkon Tel. (03)455271. 268 Hayarkon St.
Imperial Tel. (03)5177002. 66 Hayarkon St.
Moss Tel. (03)5171655. 6 Ness Ziona St.
Bell Tel. (03)5177011. 12 Allenby St.
Miami Tel. (03)5103868. 8 Allenby St.
Tamar Tel. (03)5286997. 8 Gnessin St.
Aviv Tel. (03)5102784. 88A Hayarkon St.
Country Club Tel. (03)6990666. Derekh Namir, Glilot
Deborah Tel. (03)5278282. 87 Ben Yehuda St.
Habakuk (apartment hotel) Tel. (03)6042222. 7 Habakuk St.
Yamit (suites hotel) Tel. (03)5171111. 79 Hayarkon St.

YOUTH HOSTELS

Tel Aviv Youth Hostel Tel. (03)5441748. 36 Bnei Dan St.

HOSTELS

There are about 10 hostels along the esplanade, in Hayarkon St. and in Ben Yehuda, Bograshov and Dizengoff Streets.

CHRISTIAN HOSPICE

Immanuel House, 8, Auerbach St., Jaffa. Tel. (03)821459. P. O. B. 2773.

HERZLIYYA

Daniel Hotel and Spa. Tel. (09)544444. Herzliyya on Sea.
Dan Accadia. Tel. (09)556677. Herzliyya on Sea.
Sharon. Tel (09)575777. Herzliyya on Sea.
Tadmor. Tel. (09)5723213. 38, Basel St.
Eshel. Tel. (09)570208, Herzliyya on Sea.

USEFUL ADDRESSES AND NUMBERS

Tourist Information – Israel Government Tourist Office – 5 Shalom Aleichem St., tel. (03)660259. Open: Sun.–Thurs. 8:30 a.m.–5 p.m. and Fri. to 2 p.m. The tourist information centre at Ben-Gurion airport is open around the clock, tel. (03)9711485.

Police – Tel. 100. Stations are located at 221 Dizengoff St., Kikar Namir and at 14 Harakevet St. near the Central Bus Station.

Ambulance and first aid services – Tel. 101. The central office of Magen David Adom is at 2 Alkalai St., next to the Fire Department.

Medical Services – Ichilov Hospital, Weizmann Blvd. – casualty ward daily and on Sun., Tues., Thurs. and Sat. nights. Hadassah Hospital, Balfour St. – casualty ward daily and Wed. and Fri. nights. Hotels can arrange for doctors.

Chemists – duty roster for nights and sabbath can be obtained from the newspapers and on the front doors of chemists.

Post Offices – Main post offices are at 132 Allenby St. and 12 Mikve Israel St. Tel. (03)5228009.

Akko. The Old City.

Akko. Mosque of Ahmad Jazzar.
Fishing boats in the Marina.

CULTURE AND ENTERTAINMENT

Art

As well as having several museums, Tel Aviv is a centre for all Israeli artists. Many galleries are concentrated around Gordon, Ben Yehuda, Shenkin and Bograshov Streets as well as in the artist's quarter of Jaffa. Galleries are usually open from 10 a.m. to 10 p.m.

Theatre and Music

Tel Aviv audiences are sophisticated and enthusiastic, and the city's many concerts and theatres are well attended. Main performances are held at the Mann Auditorium, on Huberman St., which is home to the Israel Philharmonic Orchestra; at Habima Theatre in Habima Square; the Cameri Theatre, 101 Dizengoff St.; Beit Lessin Theatre, 34 Weizmann St.; Neve Zedek Theatre, 6 Yehieli St.; Hasimta Theatre, 8 Mazal Dagim St. and others. The Israeli Opera is based at 95 King Solomon St. See newspapers for listings of events.

Pubs and Nightclubs

Tel Aviv is the centre of the country's night life. Tel Aviv and Jaffa have some 50 nightclubs, many with an oriental flavour, and some traditionally elegant. They are generally found in the Old Jaffa area, in the big hotels, along Dizengoff St. and in the Hayarkon-Yirmiyahu neighbourhood. Fashionable pubs wax and wane in popularity and can be found all over central Tel Aviv and Jaffa.

SPORTS AND OUTDOOR LIFE

(See also general section on sports)

Tel Aviv's largest park is Hayarkon Park on Rokach Blvd. with thousands of dunams of gardens, lawns, a rare exotic garden, a lake and a miniature railway. Other areas of greenery include Park Hadarom in South Tel Aviv, Gan Meir in King George St., Gan Hakovshim in Hakovshim St. and Gan Yaakov in Tarsat Blvd.

The Sportek on Rokach Blvd. offers a large variety of sports fields and facilities including a jogging track. Other sports include rowing and kayaking on the Yarkon River, tennis on courts at Rokach Blvd. and in Jaffa on Yefet Street. The Hilton and Ramat Aviv hotels also have tennis courts.

Tel Aviv beaches are well known for their warm Mediterranean water, though the calm waters can be deceiving. Do not swim without the supervision of lifeguards, who are generally on duty at public beaches until 4 p.m. in summer.

Swimming pools are available at hotels, at Gordon Beach and in Ramat Aviv at the university. Tel Aviv has two marinas, near Atarim (Namir) Square, where boats and wind-surfing equipment can be hired, and at Jaffa Port.

SHOPPING

Tel Aviv is a wonderful centre for both local and international goods. Main shopping centres and stores include Dizengoff Centre at Dizengoff Square, Gan Ha'ir on Ibn Gvirol St., and the Canion Ayalon in Ramat Gan, which are all modern malls; Kikar Hamedina (State Square) for elegant, expensive boutiques; and stores in the Dizengoff, Ben Yehuda, Allenby and Ibn Gvirol areas.

Markets include the large and colourful Carmel (Shuk Ha-Carmel) market for fruit, vegetables, clothing and sundries off Allenby Road and the Flea Market (Shuk Ha-Pishpishim) in Jaffa for copper, leather, furniture and just plain junk.

TRANSPORTATION

Bus

Tel Aviv's Central Bus Station is located in the heart of the city and can be reached by bus lines 4, 5, 26 and many others. Best for tourists is line 4 which picks up passengers along Ben Yehuda St. and Allenby St. or line 5, which picks up passengers along Dizengoff St. and Rothschild Blvd. at frequent intervals.

Most urban bus lines are operated by the Dan Company. For information, call (03)7543333. Inter-urban lines are operated by Egged, tel. (03)5375555. Buses do not run on Friday evenings or Saturday. They begin running again after the Sabbath on Saturday evenings. Most urban lines run from 5.30 a.m. to midnight.

Tiberias; the old and the new.

Tiberias. The synagogue of Rabbi Meir Ba'al Haness, a 2nd century miracle worker.

The Sea of Galilee.

Taxi

Sherut (joint) taxis which hold 7 passengers operate along bus routes Nos. 4 and 5 to the Central Bus Station. They can be flagged at the bus stops and cost about the same as the bus. Regular taxis operate from about 20 ranks around the city. They can be ordered by telephone (see the telephone book or Yellow Pages) or flagged down on the street. Make sure the driver uses the taxi meter. Inter-urban taxi rides are charged according to fixed prices, rather than by meter.

Train

The train station is at Arlozoroff St., tel. (03)5421515, but trains are less frequently used than buses in Israel. The main train service operates from Tel Aviv north to Herzliyya, Netanya, Haifa, Nahariyya and other towns en route. The train to Jerusalem leaves from the Bnei Brak station. Buses which run to the railway station include lines 12, 32 and 73.

Air

Internal air flights from the Tel Aviv area leave from Dov airport at the northern entrance to the city. Daily flights leave for Eilat, Jerusalem, Haifa and the Upper Galilee.

Car

Most major international car hire firms, and some local firms, operate in Tel Aviv.

Parking can be difficult in Tel Aviv, though there are some 130 public parking grounds. Parking is prohibited wherever road signs indicate, along sidewalks painted with red and white or red curbstones, and of course at intersections, pedestrian crossings and bus stops. Parking cards for street parking at permitted areas (painted with blue and white) can be purchased at bookstores and news-stands, and are hung on the car window. Unlawfully parked cars are liable to be towed away or locked with Denver boots.

WORSHIP

Synagogues

(Times of service may be found in the Friday edition of newspapers and on the synagogue notice boards.)

The Great Synagogue – 110 Allenby St. (Ashkenazi) Bus no. 4. Tel. (03)5604905.
Ihud Shivat Zion Synagogue – 86 Ben Yehuda St. (Ashkenazi) Bus Nos., 4, 62 Tel. (03) 5234337.
Ohel Moed Synagogue – Shadal St. (Sephardi). Bus Nos. 5, 12. Tel (03) 5609764.
Recanati Synagogue – Ibn Gvirol St., behind Shekem Store (Sephardi).
Tiferet Zvi Synagogue – Herman HaCohen St. (Ashkenazi).
Kedem Synagogue – 20 Carlebach St. (Progressive Reform).
Kehillat Sinai – 10 Kaplan St. (Conservative) Bus Nos. 12, 19.

Churches

Protestant:
Scottish Church of St. Peter – 21 Yefet St., Jaffa. Bus Nos. 10, 25, 41, 46.
Emmanuel Church (Lutheran) 1 Nevi'im St., Bat Yam. Tel. (03)5519138.

Roman Catholic:
St. Peter's Monastery – Jaffa. Bus Nos. 10, 25, 46. Tel. (03)822871.
St. Michael Church – between Hadumim Square and the Port, Jaffa.
St. Antonio Latin Parish Church – 51 Yefet St., Jaffa. Bus Nos. 10, 25, 41, 46.

PLACES TO VISIT BY AREA

Ramat Aviv – Beth Hatefutsoth (Nahum Goldman Museum of the Jewish Diaspora), Eretz Israel Museum, Tel Aviv University, the Planetarium.

Around Allenby St. – Bialik House, Rubin House, Museum of the City of Tel Aviv, Central Library for Music, Eliahu Golomb House, Carmel Market, Shalom Tower Wax Museum and Observatory.

Around Ben-Gurion St. – David Ben-Gurion house, beaches.

North Tel Aviv – Harry Oppenheimer Diamond Museum.

Around Rothschild Blvd. – Independence Hall, Bible Museum, Eliahu Golomb House.

Rosh Haniqra, Israel's northernmost point.

Rosh Haniqra.

Around Habima Square – Tel Aviv Museum, Helena Rubinstein Museum, Mann Auditorium, City Hall.

Jaffa – Museum of Antiquities of Tel Aviv – Jaffa, Old Jaffa, Flea Market, Israel Experience.

PLACES OF INTEREST

Ben-Gurion House: 17 Ben-Gurion Blvd., tel. (03)221010. David Ben-Gurion, first prime minister of Israel, lived in a house overflowing with books in many languages, but otherwise quite modest. The family kitchen even lacked an oven. See how he lived, and all the family mementos in his well-preserved house, now a museum with a research and study centre. The library has 20,000 volumes.. Short film show. Open: Sun.–Thurs. 8 a.m.–3 p.m., Mon. 8 a.m.–5 p.m., Fri. 8 a.m.–1 p.m. Entrance free.

(Bus No. 4)

Bialik House: 22 Bialik St. Tel. (03)651530. Formerly the home of Israel's national poet, Haim Nahman Bialik, this house, which is right down the street from Rubin House, includes a museum, archives and a library. Closed for repairs until early 1990.

(Bus Nos. 1, 4, 5. Walk No. 1)

Bible House (Bet HaTanakh): 16 Rothschild Blvd. Tel. (03)657760. Books, manuscripts and paintings related to the Bible are exhibited here in the former home of Tel Aviv's first mayor, Meir Dizengoff. On the ground floor you'll find **Independence Hall Museum** where the independence of the state was proclaimed. Exhibits deal with various stages in the history of Zionism. Open: Sun–Thurs. 9:00 a.m.–1:30 p.m.

(Bus Nos. 4, 5. Walk No. 1)

Carmel Market: Corner of Allenby and Hacarmel Sts. This is the place to visit to experience the lively sights, sounds and smells of the Middle East, and perhaps pick up a bargain. You won't find tourist souvenirs in this market, but you will find the freshest produce, the latest clothing fads and the hottest fresh-baked pita bread in town on sale.

(Bus Nos. 1, 2, 4, 10, 90. Walk No. 1)

Central Library for Music: 26 Bialik St. Tel. (03)658106. Exhibition of musical instruments from all over the world. Open: Sun.–Thurs. 2 p.m.–6 p.m., Mon., Tues. and Thurs. 10 a.m.–12 noon.

(Bus Nos. 1, 4, 5)

City Hall: Though not architecturally distinguished, Tel Aviv's 12-storey City Hall in handsome Kikar Malkhei Israel (Kings of Israel Square) provides fine views of the city from the top.

(Bus Nos. 8, 10, 1, 55. Walk No. 2)

Dizengoff Square: The Piccadilly Circus of Tel Aviv, this square is the centre of action for Tel Aviv people-watchers. Dizengoff Centre features a busy indoor mall to the south and a raised pedestrian plaza with a controversial sculpture by Yaakov Agam. More an entertainment than a work of art, the sculpture revolves and spews fire and water to the sound of music for a short period each day.

(Bus Nos. 1, 2, 5, 21, 61, 90)

Eliahu Golomb House (Beit Hagana–Israel Defence Forces Museum): 23 Rothschild Blvd. Tel. (03)623624. This museum tells the history of Jewish defence from the Hashomer organization till the creation of the Israel Defence Forces. Open: Sun.–Thurs. 8 a.m.– 4 p.m., Fri. 8 a.m.–12.30 p.m. Entrance fee.

(Bus No. 4. Walk No. 1)

Eretz Israel Museum: (formerly Ha'aretz Museum). Ramat Aviv. Tel. (03)6415244. Recently expanded, this museum complex sprawls over a large area and includes a number of separate pavilions. Included are a ceramics museum, a glass museum, the Kadman Numismatic Pavilion with an excellent collection of ancient coins from the area, the Nechustan pavilion of mining and metallurgy, a museum of ethnography with Jewish costumes and artefacts, and a demonstration of traditional workshops. The **Tel Qasile Excavations** of a Philistine settlement are also on the grounds. Open: 9 a.m.–2 p.m. Sun.–Thurs., Tues. 4–7 p.m. also, closed Fri., Sat. 10 a.m.–2 p.m. Near the museum is the **Planetarium**. Tel.

The Mt. Hermon Ski Resort.

(03)6415244 with hourly performances Sun.–Fri. from 10 a.m. Entrance fee.

(Bus Nos. 24, 25, 27, 74)

Etzel Museum: Herbert Samuel Promenade, Tel. (03)652044. History of the Etzel underground pre-state movement. Open Sun.–Thurs. 8.30 a.m.–3 p.m., Fri. 8.30 a.m.–noon. Entrance fee.

(Bus No. 46)

Flea Market (Shuq HaPishpeshim): Jaffa, near Hagana Square. A melange of copper, fabric, leather, antiques and plain junk on sale. Bargaining is part of the game.

(Bus Nos. 10, 46. Walk No. 3)

Harry Oppenheimer Diamond Museum. 1 Jabotinsky St., in the Israel Diamond Exchange, Ramat Gan. Tel. (03)5751547. A small but interesting museum showing the history and technique of diamond production, with a film. Revolving exhibitions, on subjects such as jewellery and stamps with a diamond theme, are also held here. Guided tours available. Open: Sun.–Thurs. 10 a.m.–4 p.m. Tues. 10 a.m.–7 p.m.

(Bus Nos. 50, 51, 54, 60, 61, 81, 86)

Helena Rubinstein Pavilion of Contemporary Art: 6 Tarsat Blvd. Tel. (03)5287196. An extension of the Tel Aviv Museum of Art, the Pavilion shows temporary exhibitions of contemporary art, and houses the Helena Rubinstein Collection of Miniature Rooms.

(Bus Nos. 5, 6)

Israel Experience: 4 Pasteur St. Old Jaffa Mall. Tel (03)836106 or 813205. A one-hour multi-media show on a 20 metre wide screen using 51 projectors. The subject is Israel in all its aspects – from kibbutz life to religious joys of Jerusalem, to history. A good introduction to the country. Open every day, with shows in English, Hebrew, Spanish and French. English, German and Spanish performances at noon 6, 8 and 9 p.m. Hebrew and French at 7 p.m., but times vary with the season.

(Bus Nos. 10, 46)

Israel Theatre Museum: 3 Melchet St. Tel. (03)292686. Theatrical props and items from the history of Jewish theatre, both in Israel and the diaspora. Open: Sun.–Thurs. 9 a.m.–2 p.m.

(Bus No. 5)

Jabotinsky Institute: Metzudat Zeev, 38 King George St. Tel. (03)75287320. Museum, archives and library dedicated to the Zionist leader Zeev Jabotinsky and the National Movement. Open: Sun.–Thurs., 8 a.m.–3 p.m., Fri., Sat. 8 a.m.–1 p.m. Entrance fee.

(Bus No. 5)

Lehi Museum: 8 Yair Stern St. Tel. (03) 820288. History of the Lehi pre-state underground movement. Open: Sun-Thurs. 9 a.m.–1 p.m.

(Bus Nos. 41, 85, 86)

Luna Park: Exhibition grounds, Rokach Blvd. Tel. (03)6423070. An amusement park with a variety of rides, including a roller coaster. Open from 5 – 11 p.m. in summer.

Museum of Antiquities of Tel Aviv-Jaffa: 10 Mifratz Shlomo St., Jaffa. Tel. (03)6957361. Archaeological finds and records illustrating the history of Tel Aviv-Jaffa. Open: Sun.–Thurs. 9 a.m.–1 p.m., Tues. also 4–7 p.m, Sat. 10 a.m.–2 p.m.

(Bus Nos. 41, 46, 90, 10)

Museum of the History of Tel Aviv-Jaffa: 27 Bialik St. Tel (03)653052. Located on one of the most charming streets in old Tel Aviv, this museum features documents and artefacts relating to the city's founding and history. An audio-visual presentation titled "24 Hours in the Life of a City" can also be seen. Open: Sun.–Thurs. 9 a.m.–2 p.m. Entrance free.

(Bus. Nos. 1, 4, 33. Walk No. 1)

Namir (Atarim) Square: A complex of restaurants and shops located at the corner of Hayarkon St and Ben Gurion Blvd.

(Bus No. 4)

Old Jaffa: picturesque old city. Its most historic portions have been restored as an artistic and cultural centre. The Arab architecture, ancient excavated sites, churches, mosques, museums, cobbled lanes, studios and galleries, clubs and restaurants make it a leading tourist centre. Liveliest by night.

(Bus Nos. 10, 46. Walk No. 3)

The Nahum Goldmann Museum of the Jewish Diaspora (Beth HaTefutsoth): Tel Aviv University Campus. Tel. (03)6462020. Generally acknowledged to be one of the world's great museums. This should not be missed. A presentation – by means of dioramas, models, murals and slide- and film-shows – of the main aspects of Jewish life, and the story of the survival of Jews in the lands of the dispersion during the 2,500 years from the destruction of the First Temple to the establishment of the State of Israel. The permanent exhibits are arranged thematically rather than chronologically or geographically and are divided into "Gates" or sections: Family, Community, Faith, Culture, Among the Nations, and Return. In the Chronosphere, about 50 people can watch a 25 minute, multiprojector audio-visual display on the history of the migrations of the Jewish people. There is also an auditorium and special study areas. A computer has been programmed with information on thousands of family names – visitors can address the computer in English or in Hebrew and request information which is presented in the form of a print-out. The dairy cafeteria serves light meals. Guided tours in several languages, but must be arranged in advance. Open: Sun., Mon., Tues., Thurs. 10 a.m. – 5 p.m. Wed. 10 a.m. – 7 p.m. Fri. closed; Sat. closed. Entrance fee.

(Bus Nos. 13, 24, 25, 27, 45, 49, 74, 79, 86, 274, 572, 604)

Rubin House: 14 Bialik St. Tel. (03)5103230. This charming house, now a gallery, museum and library, was home to one of Israel's best known painters, Reuven Rubin. He painted scenes of early life in Israel and particularly Tel Aviv, many of which can be seen here. His studio has been preserved exactly as he left it. A short film show on his life can also be seen. Open: Sun., Mon., Wed., Thurs. 10 a.m.–2 p.m., Tues. 10 a.m.–1 p.m. and 4–8 p.m., Sat. 11 a.m.–2 p.m.

(Bus Nos. 1, 4, 33. Walk No. 1)

Safari Park: Ramat Gan, near Kfar Hamaccabiah. Tel. (03) 776181. Cruise around in your car or, in summer, a bus and look at the wild animals in a nature reserve-like atmosphere. Then visit the attractive zoo. Cafeteria and picnic area. Open: 9 a.m.–4 p.m. every day, in summer 9 a.m.–5 p.m. Near the Safari is the **Human and Animal Museum**, tel. (03)775509, which shows exhibits relating to the evolution of man, animals and flora. Open: Sun.–Thurs. 9 a.m.–2 p.m., Fri. 9 a.m.–1 p.m., Sat. 10 a.m.–4 p.m. Entrance fee.

(Bus Nos. 30, 35)

Shalom Aleichem House: 6 Berkowitz St. Tel. (03)6956513. Small museum dedicated to the Yiddish writer's works, letters and belongings. Open: Sun., Tues. and Thurs. 10 a.m.–2 p.m. Entrance free.

(Bus Nos. 9, 18, 22, 28, 32, 70)

Tel Aviv University: Ramat Aviv. An attractive, quiet green campus for one of Israel's largest and most prestigious universities. Call (03)6408111 for information on guided tours.

(Bus Nos. 13, 24, 25, 27, 79)

Tel Aviv Museum of Art: 27 King Saul Blvd. Tel. (03)6957361. Israel's largest fine arts museum features an impressive collection of international and Israeli art. Lectures, concerts and films are also held in the museum. The Helena Rubinstein Art Library is housed here. Open: Sun. –Thurs. 10 a.m.–9.30 p.m., Fri. 10 a.m.–2 p.m., Sat. 10 a.m.–2 p.m., 7–10 p.m. Entrance fee: NIS 10.

(Bus Nos. 9, 18, 28, 70, 82, 91)

Wax Museum: In the Shalom Tower, Tel Aviv's tallest

building. 9 Ahad Ha'am St. Tel. (03)5177304. More than 100 of Israel's famous personalities immortalized in wax. Open: Sun.–Thurs. 9 a.m.–6.30 p.m., Fri. 9 a.m.–1.30 p.m.

(Bus Nos. 1, 4, 12, 25, 61)

Yarkon Park: Tel Aviv's largest park with 1,250 acres along the banks of the Yarkon River. Among its attractions are a tropical garden, a small lake with boats for hire and a children's railway. Occasionally free outdoor concerts are held here.

(Bus Nos. 21, 28, 48)

WALKS IN TEL AVIV-JAFFA

WALK No. 1 – ALLENBY ROAD TO THE SEA

This walk can be done in leisurely style if a morning is set aside and if you wish to break for lunch before ending, do a bit of shopping en route, and also take your time browsing in four museums. However, the walk can be completed in a few hours if you take care to schedule no more than a few cursory glances inside the museums and if you refrain from shopping.

The route starts on busy Rehov Allenby, named after the British general who conquered Palestine from the Turks in World War I. Take a bus number 3, 4, 16, 17, 32 or 33 and get off at the stop just before or immediately after the junction of **Rehov Allenby and Sderot Rothschild.**

Turn left (south) and within a few seconds you will arrive at **Bet Eliahu Golomb**, the Israel Defence Forces Museum at 23, Sderot Rothschild. It is located inside the original apartment owned by the late Eliahu Golomb, a founder of the Hagana, the pre-State defence forces. Golomb's two-roomed apartment, which was never discovered by the British, is preserved in its original state. Extensions to the building have provided four floors of exhibits. Weapons, photographs and uniforms trace the struggle of the Jews to settle the land, defend themselves, assist Jews from the Diaspora to sneak in illegally, and control their own destiny in their own homeland. Girl soldiers are available as guides.

Almost opposite, in the middle of the road, is a fountain and **Founders Monument**, a sculpture that depicts in relief the development of Tel Aviv.

Facing you, on the other side of the boulevard, is **Bet HaTanakh** (Bible House). Opened in 1973 to house an exhibition of books, manuscripts, paintings and other objects relating to the Bible, this building was at one time the home of Meir Dizengoff, Tel Aviv's first mayor. It was in this building that David Ben-Gurion assembled the leaders of the Jewish community in the Hall of Independence for the historic proclamation of the State of Israel on 14 May 1948.

Turn left, cross **Nahlat Benyamin** and turn right (west) at **Rehov Herzl.** The tallest building in the Middle East, the **Migdal Shalom** (Shalom Tower), faces you. Soaring 140 metres above Tel Aviv, this 37-storey building is a complex of offices, wax museum, amusement park, parking garage, restaurants, post office and banks. The elevator takes you to the observatory at the top for a tremendous view of Tel Aviv and its surrounding suburbs. A fee is charged.

Back on ground level, walk two blocks up **Rehov Ahad Ha'am**. At the corner of Rehov Allenby, on your left, you will see the **Bet HaKnesset Hagadol** (Great Synagogue). Recently renovated, it is where the Ashkenazi Chief Rabbi of Tel Aviv is ceremonially installed in office.

Turn left and stroll down **Rehov Allenby**, passing numerous fashion boutiques, jewellery shops and cafes. When you reach a point where six streets come together at Rehov Allenby, you are in **Kikar Magen David** (Shield of David Square). There are underground pedestrian passages to every connecting street.

The first street to your left is **Nahlat Binyamin** and along it is a pedestrian mall.

Turn left into **Rehov HaCarmel**. The babble of noise that greets you comes from Tel Aviv's largest, most colourful open-air market, **Shuq HaCarmel** (Carmel Market). This is a world in itself, with vendors ad-libbing lyrics to their songs of praise about their wares. Everything under the sun seems to be up for sale: beads, belts, balloons, strawberries, clocks, cameras, enamelware, scarves, travel bags and radios. The salty smell of fresh fish mixes with the fragrance of ripe fruit and vegetables. There are bargains galore.

Weave your way back through the throngs but keep moving in a westerly direction, parallel with Rehov

Allenby. You will now find yourself in an entirely different neighbourhood, **Kerem HaTeimanim** (Yemenite Vineyard). There is a quiet charm within these narrow streets and blocks of white and pink-faced old buildings. The Kerem (vineyard) is famous for its numerous restaurants that serve Yemenite delicacies.

Get back to Rehov Allenby by walking north. Cross over to the other side and walk along Rehov Bialik, stopping at number 14 for the **Rubin Museum** (see "Places of Interest") and then at number 22, **Bet Bialik**, which was the home of the Hebrew national poet, the late Haim Nahman Bialik. The double-storey house, set within a quiet residential area, has been converted into a museum. It contains many of his manuscripts and writings translated into other languages, his voluminous library and his sombre study complete with inkwells, stiff leather couch and period furniture. Exhibits include the diploma conferring a doctorate in Hebrew Literature from New York's Jewish Theological Seminary of America, the poet's pocket Bible that he always carried with him, and his watch, which stopped at the moment he died in 1934.

Close by, at 27, Rehov Bialik, is the former City Hall that is now the **Museum of the History of Tel Aviv-Jaffa.** The comprehensive exhibits depict the growth of today's metropolis from wind-swept sand-dunes as recently as 1909, when the first lots were parcelled out. Photographic displays tell much of the story. Be sure to see the office used for many years by Meir Dizengoff. A 30-minute slide show illustrates the history of the city.

Return to Rehov Allenby and turn right. The juncture of Allenby Road and Ben Yehuda Street is officially called **Kikar Bet BeNovember** (Second of November Square). It commemorates the publication in 1917 of the Balfour Declaration promising a "national home for Jews in Palestine." The square is commonly referred to as **"Mugrabi"** the name of a cinema/theatre no longer in use.

Continue west toward the sea along the curved part of Allenby.

The last building on your right, at the end of Rehov Allenby, was the home of the **Israel National Opera**. It was once the Knesset (Parliament) of Israel and the square at the bottom of Allenby is still known as **Kikar HaKnesset** (Parliament Square). The newly opened **Opera Tower** "canion" includes designer boutiques, cinemas and cafes. Shopping hours are 10 a.m. to 10 p.m., and Fridays till 2 p.m. There are cafes and restaurants on both sides of the promenade. The "Jerusalem Beach" is nearby.

WALK No. 2 – KIKAR DIZENGOFF – HABIMAH – CITY HALL

The walk starts at **Kikar Dizengoff** (Dizengoff Circle), which lies in the heart of Tel Aviv's smartest shopping area. Named after Zena Dizengoff, wife of the first mayor of Tel Aviv. The Circle was reconstructed a couple of years ago in order to solve the traffic problems that previously plagued it. Tens of thousands of vehicles now use the underpass daily and more people than ever appear to be frequenting the cafes. Note the colourful sculpture by Yaakov Agam over the underpass.

Walk down the southern end of **Rehov Dizengoff**,away from the crush of coffee houses, pizzerias and shops and follow the winding road to Rehov Hamelekh George. At this junction you will see the shopping mall known as **Dizengoff Centre**, which has risen on an area that housed wooden shacks not so long ago.

Cross over **Rehov Hamelekh George** and continue uphill along Rehov Dizengoff until it is bisected by **Sderot Tarsat**. Facing you, on the right hand side, are three buildings that form the cultural centre of Tel Aviv. On the left hand corner is the **Helena Rubinstein Pavilion** of the Tel Aviv Museum. Exhibitions by local and international artists are held within its two floors. Behind this building is the beautifully landscaped **Gan Yaacov** (Jacob's Garden). You may want to sit within its cool confines and contemplate the changes that have taken place in this area. It was to this very site that the early settlers converged to rest on the Sabbath and to water their camels from a nearby well.

On the right of this garden is the sumptuously renovated **Habimah National Theatre**, where Hebrew plays are staged, and sometimes translated simultaneously into English.

Immediately behind Gan Yaacov is the **Mann Auditorium**, home of the Israel Philharmonic Orchestra and venue for concerts and conventions.

Continue the walk by getting back to Rehov Dizengoff. Follow it right and downhill, turning left into **Rehov Ibn Gvirol**. Had you continued across Ibn Gvirol into Rehov Kaplan you would have arrived at **Bet Sokolov**,the journalists' centre on the right, and the headquarters of the **Jewish Agency** in the huge modern building on your left. Further on is the **Kirya,** a complex of IDF and government offices.

Of particular interest to English-speaking tourists is **Z.O.A. House** at the corner of Rehov Ibn Gvirol and Rehov Daniel Frisch. It is on the left-hand side of the road, a few seconds after you turn right at the corner of Ibn Gvirol and Dizengoff. The occasional Oneg Shabbat programme on Friday night includes Israeli folksinging and folkdancing. English theatre and plays in several East European languages are produced here. Z.O.A. House was founded by the Zionist Organization of America and there is a photographic display of all the presidents of the U.S.

Continue north along Ibn Gvirol, turning right into Sderot Shaul Hamelekh (King Saul Boulevard). The **Tel Aviv Museum,** lauded by France-Soir as "one of the most beautiful modern museums in the world," is on your left. Note the sculpture by Henry Moore in front of the entrance. The permanent collection includes art treasures from many periods, particularly by the greats of the impressionist and post-impressionist schools. There are also tapestries and examples of kinetic art. Weekly concerts, lectures and films are presented in the Kaufmann Hall and the Recanati Auditorium.

Reverse direction and return to Ibn Gvirol, turning right at the corner of Sderot Shaul Hamelekh. Walk past the shops until you see a large square, dominated by a multi-windowed building. This is **Kikar Malkhei Israel** (Kings of Israel Square) and the **City Hall**. The plaza is a favourite gathering place for families on the main holidays and festivals, particularly on Purim, when thousands of children congregate here in fancy dress costumes, and on Independence Day, when the lamp-posts and trees are decked with coloured lights, and fireworks displays add to the merriment.

West of City Hall, on the right-hand side of Sderot Ben-Gurion, stood the old Zoo (now moved to the **Safari Park** in Ramat-Gan. See Tel-Aviv "Places of Interest").

Walk up **Sderot Ben-Gurion** until you reach Rehov Dizengoff. Turn left, pass the numerous sophisticated boutiques, jewellery shops, art galleries, book stores and sidewalk cafes until you reach the starting point of this walk at Kikar Dizengoff. (If you want to visit **Ben-Gurion House,** don't turn left at Dizengoff but walk on for a couple of blocks till you get to 17, Sderot Ben-Gurion.) Ahead of you, as you face the sea, is Kikar Namir.

WALK No. 3 – OLD JAFFA

Exotic Jaffa is a must for every tourist's itinerary. It is far more than a promontory studded with quaint artists' studios and galleries, jewellery shops, boutiques and curio stores. It is also a **nightclub capital**, with everything offered from striptease to Israeli folkdancing. In addition, Jaffa is rich in history and legend (see "History").

Old Jaffa is a 40-minute stroll from the promenade at Tel Aviv's shorefront along Retsif Herbert Samuel. Alternatively, you can take a bus number 10 from Rehov Hakovshim, or bus number 46 from the Central Bus Station.

You will pass the **Charles Clore Park** adjacent to the shore. (The closed down Dolphinarium is where the park ends on the Tel Aviv side.) Opposite is a large-scale urban renewal project. When completed it will be an exciting stretch of riviera, complete with office buildings, hotels, shops, widened roads and broadened beaches.

Get off the bus near the clocktower at the entrance to Jaffa. This is **Kikar Hahagana** (Hagana Square). The tower was built in 1906 by a Turkish Sultan, Abdul Hamid II, to mark the 30th anniversary of his accession to the throne. Its ornamental bars and stained-glass windows, each of which depicts an episode in Jaffa's history, are the work of a kibbutz member from Ashdot Yaacov.

Turn left into **Rehov Bet Eshel** at the southern end of the square (the bus approached from the north). One block down, on your right, you'll find the beginning of the sprawling, cacophonic **Shuq Hapishpeshim** (Flea Market). A sample of the range of wares offered includes Oriental jewellery, Persian carpets, beaten lead and copperware, ivory carvings, Victoriana, pots and pans, ancient maps and bizarre lampshades. A word of advice: don't buy the first object you like for the first price quoted. Accept the blandishments and coaxings of the vendors as part of the colour and "chutzpah" of the shuq. Bargaining is the order of the day and you need not be embarrassed to suggest a drastically reduced price and then happily settle for something slightly more reasonable.

After you've had your fill of this district return to Kikar

Hahagana and cross the main road into **Rehov Mifratz Shlomo**. The minaret on your right soars over the **Mahmoudiya Mosque**,whose cloisters are a magnificent sight of vaulted ceilings.

The kiosks and open-air cafes that you pass now offer all the sweet pastries common in the Middle East, such as Baklawa, Chadif, Zlabiya and Malfuf. This is the authentic background to sample a plate of kebab, or fresh fish, with Arabian-style salads, and then to sip Turkish coffee. Prices are reasonable.

The first of Old Jaffa's nightclubs are on your left. A few seconds later, also on your left, is the **Museum of Antiquities of Tel Aviv-Jaffa**. The archaeological collection comes from chance finds and excavations in the Tel Aviv – Jaffa area. Marble columns and capitals outside the museum are from the 1st century BCE and were brought from Caesarea during the last century.

Continue up Rehov Mifratz Shlomo. The panorama of the Tel Aviv shoreline opens up spectacularly below. The black cluster of rocks in the sea are called **Andromeda's Rocks**. Greek legend holds that the maiden Andromeda was chained to one of them when Perseus swooped down on his winged horse, slew the sea monster and rescued her.

After passing several cafes you come to the orange-coloured **Church of St. Peter, Holy Land**, administered by Franciscan fathers. Several wood carvings inside are exquisite.

The flight of steps leading downhill, just before the church, takes you to the area of the old port where fishermen bring in their daily catch. But this detour should be taken at the end of the walk.

Enter **Kikar Kedumim**,the focal point of Old Jaffa, by walking up the stone steps opposite the church. This square is almost ringed by nightclubs and cafes, shops and studios. In the centre of the square are excavations of buildings dating back to the 2nd century BCE. Explanatory signs and recorded descriptions are available at the site.

The first turning left at the far end of the square takes you to a site of archaeological excavations and a bird's-eye view of Tel Aviv. Follow the tarred road up the hill and veer right before the road goes downhill. The view from the summit is breathtaking.

Return to the square, walk down the flight of steps on your left and turn left into a paved alley, **Simtat Mazal**

Dagim (Pisces Lane). This is the first of many streets named after the signs of the Zodiac. It is best to shop where your fancy leads you.

Make your way back to Simtat Mazal Dagim and Kikar Kedumim. Cross the stairs to the other side of the square and descend the steps along **Rehov Shimon Haburski** (Simon the Tanner). Facing you at the bottom of this street is the huge wooden door of the **house** that tradition says belonged to Simon the Tanner. It was here that St. Peter stayed after miraculously restoring Tabitha to life, as recorded in Acts 9:36–43. Inside the courtyard you can see a well that was used in Jesus' time, and a stone-sculptured coffin which is believed to have been made during Simon's time, and which the conquering Moslems refashioned into a wash-stand to purify themselves before prayer. The minaret dates from these times; the walls of the mosque previously enclosed a Crusader church. The floor, however, is from earlier times.

Simtat Mazal Keshet (Sagittarius) leads off to the right just before Simon the Tanner's house. It descends past the decorative facades of private residences. Veer right at the bottom and walk along **Netiv Hamazalot** (Lane of the Zodiac). There are more shops and galleries on your right, and glimpses of the sea can be caught on your left.

From the Church of St. Peter you can either take the steps to your left, downhill through the park to the harbour and sea wall, or continue down Rehov Mifratz Shlomo to the clocktower for the return trip to Tel Aviv.

BAT YAM

Aptly named "daughter of the sea," Bat Yam is a city of 180,000 on the seafront five and a half kilometres south of Tel Aviv. Although a close neighbour of Tel Aviv, the city has a character of its own, and plenty to offer visitors in its own right.

Bat Yam, which was originally named "Bayit va-Gan" (House and Garden) was founded in 1926 by a small group of religious families. Forced to leave in the 1929 Arab riots, the settlers returned to the town in 1931 and were soon joined by others. The town grew rapidly after 1948 – from some 10,000 in 1953 to more than 60,000 in 1967. It became a city in 1958. One of its most famous residents was the Yiddish writer Sholem Asch, whose house is now a museum.

Bat Yam's main attraction, of course, is the sea. As a holiday resort, the city offers three and half kilometres of golden beach with calm, warm waters, under lifeguard supervision during the April through mid-October swimming season. One beach is reserved for observant religious bathers, with separate swimming times for men and women during the summer. An attractive new promenade along the beach, lined with many seaside restaurants and cafes, provides a pleasant place for a stroll.

Other amenities include two swimming pools on the beach, an aqua slide, sports centre, hang-gliding facilities, health club, an ice skating rink (a rare attraction in Israel) and several museums.

USEFUL NUMBERS

Municipal Tourist Information Bureau – 43 Ben Gurion Ave. Tel (03)5072777. Fax: 972-3-596666.
Police – 21 Gilbert St. Tel. (03)5514444.
Fire – 12 Haavoda St. Tel. (03)5514444.
First Aid – (Magen David Adom) – 4 Rabinovitch St. Tel. (03)5511111.
Main Post Office – Migdal Nahum, Hameginim Square. Tel. (03)592309.
City Hall – 2 Yehuda Halevy St. Tel. (03)5552555.

ACCOMMODATION

Sunton: Tel. (03)5527796. Fax (03)5527796. 136 Ben-Gurion Ave. Opening soon.
Colony Beach Apartment Hotel. Tel. (03)5551555. Fax (03)5523783.
Armon Yam Tel. (03)5522424. 95 Ben-Gurion Blvd.
Bat Yam Tel. (03)864373. 53 Ben-Gurion Blvd.
Via Maris Tel. (03)5060171. 43 Ben-Gurion Blvd.
Sarita Tel. (03)5529183. 127 Ben-Gurion Blvd.
Mediterranean Towers (senior citizens) Tel. (03)5553666. 2 Hayam St.

WORSHIP

Tachkemoni Synagogue – (Ashkenazi) 58 Herzl St.
Heichal Yaakov Synagogue – (Sephardi) Yerushalayim and Sokolov Sts.
Merom Israel Synagogue – (Ashkenazi) 16 Ha'azmaut St.
Machzikey Tora – (Sephardi) 23 Ha'azmaut Blvd.

TRANSPORTATION

Many buses connect Bat Yam with Tel Aviv, a distance of about 15 minutes. Numbers 81, 83, 85 and 86 arrive at the Tel Aviv Central Bus Station. Numbers 406 and 404 drive to Jerusalem hourly. Number 144 goes to Ben-Gurion airport.

PLACES OF INTEREST

Municipal Museum: 6 Struma St. Ramat Yosef. Tel. (03)591140. Various art exhibitions by Israeli and foreign artists are held here. Open: Sun.–Thurs. 9 a.m.–1 p.m.; 4–7 p.m.; Fri. & Sat. 9 a.m.–1 p.m.

(Bus Nos. 85, 86, 18, 8, 42)

Ryback Museum: Hadadi St. Ramat Yosef. Tel. (03)5068645. Permanent exhibition by the late artist Issachar Ryback. Open: Sun.–Thurs. 9 a.m.–1 p.m.; 4–7 p.m.; Fri. 8–11 a.m.

(Bus Nos. 85, 86, 18, 42)

Shalom Asch Museum: 50 Arlozoroff St. Tel. (03)5064536. Permanent exhibition of the works of the famous Yiddish writer and his private art collection. Open daily for groups by appointment.

(Bus Nos. 25, 83, 85, 86, 87, 88)

Ice Skating Rink: Next to Sports Centre. Tel. (03)5526655 Open 10 a.m.–midnight.

(Bus Nos. 1, 86, 90, 92, 98)

Bat Yam Sports Centre (Country Club): Hakomemiut St. Includes four swimming pools, ten tennis courts and stadium. Tel. (03)5517063.

(Bus Nos. 40, 42, 28, 18, 2, 9, 86, 1)

Yacht Club: Sea Palace Beach. P. O. B. 121. Tel. (03)599895.

Agur Hang-Gliding Club: Sea Palace Beach. Tel. (03)580144.

Tours from Tel Aviv

ROUTE No. 5 (Map: Northern Sheet E14 to K17)

The old road to Jerusalem

Tel Aviv – Ramla (19 km.) – Latrun (35 km.) – Jerusalem (61 km.) (Road Nos. 44, 424; Highway No. 1.)

(Distances in brackets refer to start of route.)

The Tel Aviv-Jerusalem expressway (No. 1) – not to be confused with the road taken on Route No. 5 – was completed in August 1979. The distance between the two cities is now 60 km. From city centre to city centre it is approximately 63 km. Travelling time has been cut to about 55 minutes (assuming that one keeps to the legal speed limit).

Access to the new Netivei-Ayalon four-lane divided highway that runs from the vicinity of the Tel Aviv South Railway Station to Sha'ar Hagai is via interchanges only – at Gannot, Shapirim, (near Beit Dagan), Ben-Gurion Airport, and Latrun. These exit and entry points are marked in the following order on the drive from Jerusalem: Ramallah, Ashqelon; Ramla, Lod, Petah Tikva; Beit Dagan; Haifa; Jaffa, Holon.

The distance between Tel Aviv and the airport on the expressway is 12 km. Those who use this road to Jerusalem will see an altogether different stretch of country to what they might remember from Route No. 5, the old road.

Distances for Route No. 5 are calculated from the junction of Geha Road, **Mehlaf HaShiva'a**. You will know when you have reached this busy intersection because the headquarters of the **Meteorological Service**, with conspicuous antennae, are on its southeast corner (on your right).

Four kilometres later, on Road No. 4, you arrive at the turn-off (left) to **Kfar Habbad**, an interesting agricultural settlement with a yeshiva. It is one of the best-known Hassidic villages because of the annual Bar Mitzvah services, in the presence of the Chief of Staff, for children of soldiers killed in action.

The Habbadniks' spiritual leader is the Lubavitcher Rebbe who lives in Brooklyn, New York. They welcome visitors and this is a good opportunity to see the day-to-day life of students at a Talmudic academy.

Five kilometres later the road forks (right) for Ramla.

RAMLA (Map: F16)

Ramla was the only town founded by the Moslems during their long rule in Palestine. It was built by Caliph Suleiman in the 8th century on what was a strategic site on the south-north route from Egypt to Syria and on the west-east route from Jaffa to Jerusalem. Nearby Lod, which had previously fulfilled this function, had been destroyed by the Arabs in 700 CE.

Ramla is also believed to have been the site of Arimathea, from where Joseph came seeking Jesus's body, from Pilate, for burial.

The Crusaders camped here, as did Napoleon.

Today it is a city of between 40,000 and 45,000 people, many of whom are of North African origin.

Sites

Church of St. Nicodemus and St. Joseph: just off main road, Rehov Herzl, in town centre. Easily recognisable by high bell tower. Built in 1902 over site of ancient hospice of same name where Napoleon set up staff headquarters in 1799. Supervised by Franciscan fathers. Stained-glass windows above altar donated by Spanish Government.

The White Tower: near junction of Rehov Herzl and Rehov Herzog. Thirty-metre-high minaret built in the 13th century by Sultan Beibars. Four faces adorned by arched windows. Climbed by Napoleon.

At foot of tower are remains of Suleiman's 8th century mosque and ruins of fountain and tombs. Stone steps lead to underground vaulted rooms, once part of mosque. Ruins at southern and eastern ends of compound are from mediaeval inn serving pilgrims to Jerusalem.

When you leave Ramla for Jerusalem on Road No. 424 you drive past settlements that formed the front line for two decades. One of them, **Kfar Shmuel**, is named in honour of the late American Zionist leader, Stephen S. Wise.

A road on the right leads to **Kibbutz Gezer**. Three kilometres further another branches right to historic Tel Gezer. You may like to detour here for the 10-minute drive over a bumpy, secondary road.

TEL GEZER (Map: G16)

The ruins of biblical Gezer are being excavated just past the goat-skin tents of a number of Bedouin.

With a commanding view of the strategic highway to the coast, Gezer was fortified by King Solomon after it was given as a dowry for an Egyptian princess he married. Already excavated are the stone pillars of a Canaanite temple. Other finds, on display in the Rockefeller Museum, Jerusalem, include 5,000-year-old household utensils, bracelets, knife blades, glassware, limestone containers for cosmetics and other objects from the 15th century BCE.

Return to the main road; pass **Mishmar-Ayalon,** and very soon, before you take the downward-winding road over the bridge, the **Ayalon Valley** opens up in one of the most dramatic vistas in Israel.

This was the biblical pass leading to the Judaean hills. It was the battleground where Joshua bade the sun to stand still (Joshua 10:12), and where Saul and David defeated the Philistines. Here Judah Maccabee defeated the Greeks to control the roads to Jerusalem.

The Crusaders and Saladin traversed this wide bowl

and the allied armies grouped here for their march on Jerusalem during World War I.

In 1948 the British turned over the **Latrun Police Station**, ahead of you, to the Arab Legion. Repeated attacks by the Israelis, under Lt. Col. Yitzhak Rabin (who was Prime Minister from 1974 to 1977 and was again elected in 1992), failed to dislodge them.

Another road to Jerusalem was built further south and out of sight of the Arab machine-gunners. To your left you see Highway No. 1 to Jerusalem.

At the end of the valley is Latrun.

Nearby, along a dirt road that begins opposite **Kibbutz Nahshon,** is **Neve Shalom,** a Jewish-Arab settlement inspired by a Dominican monk whose ideal is religious coexistence.

LATRUN (Map: G17)

The **Monastery of Latrun** peers down on the road and is surrounded by vineyards. It was founded in 1890 by a group of Trappist monks from France. Between 1948 and 1967 it was in no-man's-land between Israel and Jordan and supervised by the UN. The monks are contemplatives following the rule of St. Benedict. Their time is divided between manual labour, prayer, and study of the Bible and other religious books. The monks support themselves making choice wines and liqueurs.

On the heights of the hill on which the monastery stands are the ruins of the 12th century Crusader road-fortress of Le Toron des Chevaliers. It was wrecked by Saladin to stop Richard the Lion-Heart's advance on Jerusalem, but the English king nevertheless lodged here in 1191 and 1192 before abandoning his march. Traces of the wall can be seen; there is a well-preserved gate to its west. There are three rows of halls on the north side, partially repaired by a Jordanian garrison which also dug the slit trenches before the Six Day War.

Across the road, opposite the monastery, is a **Memorial** and **Museum of the Israel Defence Forces Armoured Division.**

To the left of the monastery is Road No. 3 (passing under Highway No. 1) leading to Ramallah. A short way down is **Imwas**, associated with the Maccabean rebellion and revered by Christians as Emmaus, the site of Jesus' manifestation before his disciples after the crucifixion. A church is built above the mosaic floor of an ancient house of worship.

At the first right turn you are back on Highway No. 1 toward Jerusalem, and the route soon broadens into two lanes each way. During the War of Independence it was a narrow pass and here, at **Shaar Hagai** (Bab el-Wad in Arabic), armoured Jewish convoys fought their way through with supplies for besieged Jerusalemites in 1948. The rusted hulks of the vehicles that did not get through line the roadside, with the dates of the attacks marked on boulders.

Up the hill, a road to the right leads to **Shoeva** and **Shoresh**. The latter is a moshav with a popular club and swimming pool.

High up on a hill to the left is a silver-spiked monument to those who gave their lives trying to break the siege of Jerusalem. There is a good view of the Judaean hills from the parking area and picnic site.

After one kilometre, the road flattens out; a signpost points left to Abu Ghosh. Try to include this detour in your itinerary.

ABU GHOSH (Map: J17)

Some 3,800 Arabs, predominantly Moslems, live in this quiet village on the slopes of hills. Until Highway No. 1 was completed, it lay on the main route to Jerusalem. It gets its name from a 17th century sheikh who imposed toll taxes on all travellers passing through to Jerusalem. The villagers cooperated with Jewish defence forces before and during the War of Independence.

Abu Ghosh is on the site of biblical Qiryat Yearim, where the Ark rested before being taken to Jerusalem. The **Monastery of the Ark**, built on top of the mountain above the village in 1924, stands over the traditional site of the house of Abinadab, where the Ark of the Covenant was kept (2 Samuel 6:3). Its colossal statue of St. Mary holding the infant Jesus may be seen from far off.

The Crusaders slept in Abu Ghosh the night before they marched on Jerusalem in 1099. Four decades later they built one of the most beautiful Romanesque churches in the holy land, confusing Abu Ghosh with the site of biblical Emmaus.

The **Crusader church** of today's **Benedictine Monastery** rises above the ruins of a 1st century CE Roman fort. A stone embedded in a wall is inscribed with the name of the Roman Tenth Legion. The Moslems used the church as a mosque and then as a stable before the French restored it and reconsecrated it in 1907. It is located on the lower part of the hill.

If you continue through the village you will come to three interesting settlements. The first is **Qiryat Yearim**,a children's village financed by Jews from Switzerland.

Nearby is **Ma'ale Hahamisha** (Ascent of the Five). This kibbutz has a popular guest house with tennis courts and a swimming pool. The kibbutz is named in honour of five men slain by Arabs while planting trees in 1938.

Qiryat Anavim is another kibbutz with a guest house and swimming pool. It is 700 m. above sea level and has a striking memorial to the men of the Harel Brigade who fell in the mountains of Jerusalem during the War of Independence.

Whether you drove through Abu Ghosh or by way of the shortcut, you turn off (right) to the picnic and camping site of **Aqua Bella** (En Hemed). The remains of an ancient oak forest, as well as fig and olive trees, are spread around the landscaped gardens near the running brook. Dominating everything are the double storey ruins of a 12th century Crusader structure that experts believe was a manor house. Others claim it was a nunnery, but there are no traces of a chapel.

Of particular interest are two of the three ground-floor rooms around the courtyard. They are dug into the ground because of the slope. All the rooms at this level are barrel-vaulted. The outer walls are two metres thick while the whole structure is 40 m. by 30 m.

An entrance fee is paid at this picnic site. There is also a popular camping site next to the park, at Bet Nekofa.

Return to Highway No. 1, where a hill soon looms on the right. This is **Castel,** with the ruins of a Roman fortress clamped to it. Bitter fighting raged here during 1948. Now it is a national memorial site.

The road dips sharply. Take care to change into low gear and drive slowly as Motza Bend, at the base of the decline, is treacherous, even in the dry summer months.

After climbing and curving for several minutes you round a corner with Jerusalem facing you.

ROUTE No. 6 (Map: Northern Sheet E14 to F20 and G18)

The Shephelah (Lowlands)

Tel Aviv – Rishon LeZion (10 km.) – Rehovot (15 km.) – Qiryat Gat (60 km.) – Bet Govrin (78 km.) – Bet Shemesh (113 km.) – Ramla (139 km.) (Road Nos. 44, 4, 412, 40, 35, 38.)

(Distances in brackets refer to start of route.)

This route should appeal to those with a feel for biblical history and a yearning for the open countryside of the Holy Land. It leads through parts of the fertile coastal plain, across the Shephelah, or lowlands, where you can explore cathedral-sized limestone caves, and goes on to the Valley of Elah where David slew Goliath, and back to Tel Aviv.

Start the route by following the signs south to Ashdod (Road No. 4). Some 12 km. further on, follow the signs over the bridge and enter Rishon LeZion along Rehov Jabotinsky.

RISHON LEZION (Map: E15)

Established in 1882, Rishon LeZion (or LeZiyyon) was the first settlement founded by pioneers from outside Israel. The beginnings were hard as the farmers had to bring water in on the backs of camels from Mikve Yisrael, just south of Tel Aviv. Baron Edmond de Rothschild came to their aid with money and distilling equipment for a winery.

Today Rishon LeZion is foremost among our wine exporters and a visit to the **Carmel cellars** is recommended for those with time on their hands. (The other cellars are in Zikhron Yaaqov.) Free guided tours. Open 8.30 a.m. – 3 p.m.

Rishon also boasts a number of "firsts" in modern Israel. It was here that the country's first Jewish kindergarten, elementary school and all-Jewish wind orchestra were established. Here, too, the poet Naphtali Herz Imber read a poem to the settlers in 1882. Soon after, another settler at Rishon, Samuel Cohen, set it to music. Today it is the country's national anthem, known as "HaTikvah" – The Hope.

A new college providing higher education towards a B.A. has been opened. Near the town are some splendid beaches.

Continue along road No. 412 to reach Rehovot.

REHOVOT (Map: F16)

Israel's scientists and presidents have made this city famous. The country's first head of state, **Chaim Weizmann,** founded the Sieff Institute in 1934, and it now ranks among the leading scientific research institutes in the world under its present name of the **Weizmann Institute of Science**.

It was while Professor Ephraim Katzir was working here that he was elected Israel's fourth president (1973–78).

The **Levi Eshkol Faculty of Agriculture**, directly opposite the Weizmann Institute on Rehov Herzl, is named after the late Prime Minister of Israel and is a faculty of the Hebrew University of Jerusalem.

For information about free guided tours, tel. (08)481275.

Rehovot was founded in 1890 when immigrant farmers planted vineyards and almond trees here. Citrus fruits followed and today the city prospers with food processing, chemical and other plants, in addition to being a centre for mixed farming and citrus plantations.

Sites

Citrus Packing Houses: at the northern entrance to the town and around it. Open during the season.

Weizmann Institute of Science: open from 8 a.m. – 3.30 p.m. Film on Institute's research activities 11 a.m. and 2.45 p.m. For further information, call the Visitors' Section of the Public Affairs Office, Tel. (08)483597.

Weizmann House: the official residence of Chaim Weizmann, the first president of the State of Israel. Open: Sun.–Thurs. 10 a.m.–3.30 p.m. Closed on Friday, Saturday and holidays. Entrance fee: NIS 5. Tel. (08)343328, 343230. Group tours should be arranged in advance.

At the end of Rehov Herzl (Road No. 412) you arrive at the Bilu junction of three roads. On Road No. 40, follow the signs to Beer Sheva on the right and pass by Israel's largest kibbutz, **Givat Brenner.**

Now drive through **Gedera**, a pleasant agricultural community, with picturesque, red-roofed houses on the hill, founded by the Bilu settlers in 1884.

You begin to feel the whiff of country air as the landscape eases into lazy orchards and wheat fields.

Turn left in the direction of Qiryat Gat (Road No. 40) and soon pass by the religious **Kibbutz Hafetz Hayim**, noted for the packed kosher meals that you find in Israeli supermarkets. It, too, boasts a fine guest house, with a swimming pool.

The fields stretch for dozens of kilometres and now and again you see clusters of settlements far off the eucalyptus-lined road. Suddenly the development town of **Qiryat Gat** looms ahead as you turn left.

QIRYAT GAT (Map: E19)

Qiryat Gat is the heart of an extraordinarily successful settlement scheme. The population has grown to about 30,000; its industrial expansion includes major enterprises such as textiles, cotton and sugar processing.

Around it, in the Lakhish area, are more than 40,000 people in 63 villages. The settlers came from nearly 40 countries. Qiryat Gat is the capital of the Lakhish region.

When the plans for settlement were drawn up, the odds were weighted heavily against seeing them materialize. The Lakhish area measures over 1,000 sq. km., of which only half is arable. Water was scarce. Adding to the problems were the proposed settlers themselves, who were generally unskilled and from diverse cultural backgrounds.

They were divided up into groups according to background to form villages of basically the same pattern and way of life. Immediate social problems were thus minimized. A network of services was placed within easy reach of each group of villages; for additional government services the settlers had only to go to nearby Qiryat Gat or Ashqelon.

Continue along the main road skirting the northern

perimeter of Qiryat Gat. Just before the city cemetery a gravel road leads to the foot of the historic site of Tel Erani (biblical Gat has not yet been found). This was one of the Philistine cities and may well have been the birthplace of Goliath. Many ancient stone walls can be seen on its western slopes while the view of the lowlands from the summit is exhilarating.

Past Tel Erani are the **Hazan Caverns**, man-made caves and tunnels used as hiding-places by Jews at the time of Bar-Kochba's rebellion. The site had earlier been used for producing olive oil (a subterranean oil-press has been found), but with the preparation for the Revolt, it was turned into a secret hideout from the Romans.

The road (No. 35) passes through dozens of hills covered with feathery pines. This is the **Hamalakhim (Angels) Forest** and you can detour off left where the signpost points to the Sam Gutlin Observation Post.

A couple of kilometres later the signpost directs you to Road No. 3415 (right) to **Kibbutz Lakhish** and the fortified heights of the adjacent battle site of biblical times. Continue along the road leading up to the kibbutz orchards and stables. Then turn second left up the gravel road to the beginning of the ancient fortifications.

LAKHISH (Map: F20)

Traces of habitation on this hill have been found dating back 5,000 years, but Lakhish is first mentioned in the Bible when Joshua slew all its inhabitants and hanged its king at nearby Makkedah (Joshua 10:22–32).

As it guarded the route from the lowlands to Hebron and Jerusalem it was a natural look-out post that had to be fortified. Solomon's son, Rehoboam, included it in a string of surrounding cities that he built in defence of Judah (2 Chronicles 11:9).

In 701 BCE the Assyrian King, Sennacherib, rolled through Judah, finally laying siege to Lakhish.

In 1935 the famous "Lakhish letters" were discovered, throwing much light on the subsequent capture and destruction of Lakhish by the Babylonian, Nebuchadnezzar, who later went on to destroy Solomon's Temple in Jerusalem.

Lakhish rose again under the Persians in the 5th century BCE and was captured by Alexander the Great in 332

BCE. The site was abandoned shortly after the 2nd century BCE.

Ambling through the ruins the visitor can see remnants of the double walls, a gate, the residence of the Persian governor, leftovers of a Sun Temple and several rooms.

10 kms. further south are the Caves of Hazan.

Return to Road No. 35 and turn right. Drive down the hill and stop before turning right opposite the Crusader ruins at **Kibbutz Bet Govrin**.

BET GOVRIN (Map: G19)

Bet Govrin (or Guvrin) was the centre of the largest region in the land during the Roman occupation. That its citizens were affluent in the 3rd and 4th centuries can be seen from the scattered, ornate tombs they built and from mosaics of hunting scenes found in several houses. The mosaics are in the Israel Museum, Jerusalem.

The many ruins here are from the Frankish settlement and castle, built to protect the kingdom from raiding Egyptians based in Ashqelon. Saladin destroyed the castle in 1191 to prevent the Christians from repossessing it.

Having turned right opposite the Crusader ruins, take the first tarred road left leading up to a parking lot. Walk a few metres down to the first of the enormous **limestone caves**, some 20 m. high.

Their origin is uncertain but they may have been dug by Philistines to build their cities on the coastal strip. There are hundreds of these chalk-white and beige limestone caves dug below the surface of the earth in this region. In time they were used as churches. Notice the Byzantine and Crusader-order crosses carved on the walls. The inscriptions include ancient Hebrew and Greek as well as the inevitable scrawls of recent visitors.

The weird and wonderful shapes resemble basilicas, with the opened domed tops throwing in streams of sunlight.

Exiting from the parking lot, turn left, past the shell of the 12th century Crusader **Church of Saint Anna** built on the ruins of a Byzantine church.

There is a rusted iron gate on the left. There are many more caves down here, near the gate, but they are not easily accessible and visitors should take care to keep to the rocks as the area is dotted with open holes that drop to great depths.

The most interesting caves here are immediately ahead of the gate. Stone steps lead down to three adjoining limestone caverns and the walls are moist with moss and lush with ferns. Note the steps circling the cave on the left and leading down to the bottom of what was obviously once a cistern.

Cross over to a tarred road leading within a few metres to a parking lot on your left. Immediately ahead, and seemingly covered by a bush, is the entrance to the famous **Sidonian Tombs**. The several dozen niches comprised the final resting place of a wealthy family from Sidon and have been dated to the 3rd century BCE.

Walk now along the double-tracked path to what is popularly dubbed "**The Colonel's Tomb**," in honour of the officer who was in charge of the region during British Mandate times and who saw that they were made accessible after their discovery. These tombs are identical to the Sidonian Tombs.

Back out of the "tombed" area, turn left, stopping opposite the summit of **Tel Maresha**. The panoramic view from here accounts for its strategic importance and it, too, was fortified by Rehoboam (2 Chronicles 11:8). It capitulated to Sennacherib after the fall of Lakhish. In 163 BCE Judah Maccabee took it but yielded it to the Syrians the following year. It reverted to Jewish control when the Hasmonean, John Hyrcanus, captured it in 125 BCE, forcibly converting its Idumaean population to Judaism to ensure their loyalty.

After Pompey's conquest of the Holy Land, Maresha became an autonomous city under a Roman pro-consul in Syria, but it was razed by the Parthians as Herod fled to safety across the Dead Sea in 40 BCE.

Return to the main road, turning left and almost immediately driving across Road No. 343. Turn right and pass **Kibbutz Bet Nir** on your left.

The vineyards and crops of **Moshav Luzit** open up. Take the gravel road on the right, directly opposite the kibbutz signpost. After some 300 m. you arrive at the entrance to even more wondrous limestone caves. Soaring as high as the previous caves, they are more enigmatic because parts of their walls are honeycombed with niches that no one has yet been able to find a reason for. Note the inscriptions and the Christian crosses, many of which are high up on the sun-illuminated walls.

Continue along the main road, turning right at Agur,

passing densely wooded hills. Take the left turn to Sha'ar Hagai at the crossroad.

Within minutes you will be in the biblical **Valley of Elah**. The partly denuded hill on your left is **Tel Azekah** where the Philistines grouped as they faced the wavering Israelites. It was in this valley that David came forward with his sling and a bag of stones and slew the giant Goliath (1 Samuel 17:1–5).

This is the valley where 35 men of the pre-State Haganah were ambushed by Arabs and slain to a man as they were on their way to help the besieged settlers at Gush Etzion on 16 January 1948 (see Route No. 2).

Continue straight on, past **Kfar Zekharya**, a village founded in 1950 by immigrants from Iraq and Kurdistan. The mosque is a leftover from the former Arab village. Stop up the hill, just past the village, for a look back at the marvellous beauty of the Elah Valley.

The terrain becomes very rocky and dotted with olive trees. A signpost directs you right up an accessible – but very rough – road to the Silesian monastery of **Beit Jimal**, founded in 1873. The monks teach Arab orphans and boys from impoverished homes. The white and red dry wines from the vineyards are very good and very cheap.

When foundations were being dug for the church atop this peak, 5th century mosaics, together with a cross and a tomb, were discovered. As a 5th century priest wrote that he had found an urn here containing the remains of the 1st century Jewish sage, Rabbi Gamliel, there is speculation that this may indeed have been his final resting place, although a large domed tomb at Yavne is also pointed out as the tomb of the rabbi. The small, open tomb may be seen near the crypt below the beautifully decorated church. The mosaics hang on the wall outside.

As these are the last hills before the plain it is possible, on a clear day, to see the power station chimneys at Ashdod and the Shalom Tower in Tel Aviv.

Continue past **Bet Shemesh**, a development town named after the ancient town where the Ark of the Lord once rested. (The ancient Tel Bet Shemesh is off the main road as you enter the town.) Nearby (crossing Bet Shemesh and passing Mahseya) is the Avshalom Stalactite Cave (see below). Cross the railway line and the small bridge; after 3 km. you are at the Shimshon Junction; turn left for Ramla (Road No. 44). The road to Jerusalem is straight ahead.

Soreq Stalactite Cave: Avshalom Shoham Nature Reserve, Bet Shemesh (about 20 kms. southwest of Jerusalem, 2 kms. from Nes Harim). A 5,000 sq. m. cave with a wide variety of stalactites and stalagmites, discovered by chance in 1968 and opened to the public in 1977. Special lighting brings out the incredible beauty of the mineral formations, which grow at the rate of about 0.2 millimetres per year. Open: Sun. – Thurs. and Sat.: 8 a.m. – 4 p.m. Fri. and eve of holidays 8.30 a.m. – 1 p.m. Enquiries on a postcard to Soreq Cave, P.O.B. 251, Bet Shemesh. Tel. (02)911117. Entrance fee. Bus No. 413 from Jerusalem or Bet Shemesh. Egged and United Tours include a visit to the cave in their regular tours. You can also take Bus No. 413 from Jerusalem or Bet Shemesh.

This is the **Valley of Soreq**, where Samson lived. The Bible mentions that Samson "loved a woman in the valley of Soreq, whose name was Delilah" (Judges 16:4).

Long before reaching Ramla you pass the wooded picnic sites at **Eshtaol** and **Ta'Oz**. Then there is the Mitzpe Harel observation tower next to **Kibbutz Harel** for a comprehensive view of the entire valley.

For a description of Ramla and the remainder of the journey to Tel Aviv see Route No. 5 in reverse.

ROUTE No. 7 (Map: Northern Sheet E14 to G14 and G16)

The Sharon

Tel Aviv – Petah Tikva (14 km.) – Rosh Ha'ayin (20 km.) – Ben Shemen (32 km.) – Lod (37 km.) (Road Nos. 443, 444, 453.)

(Distances in brackets refer to start of route.)

[For details of Highway No. 1 between Tel Aviv and Ben-Gurion Airport (Lod), see preliminary note to Route No. 5.]

Route No. 7 will take you a couple of hours at the most, during which you will visit two forts, a gigantic Roman mausoleum, the Tombs of the Maccabees, historic Lod and countryside around Tel Aviv.

The easiest way of starting is to get onto the Haifa Road and turn right into **Rehov Arlosoroff** and then, after passing the Tel Aviv North Railway Station, veer left into **Rehov Jabotinsky** in **Ramat Gan**. Follow this road past the 28-storey **Diamond Exchange Centre** for several kilometres. After crossing the Geha junction you will come to **Beilinson Hospital** and then **Petah Tikva**.

This mother of 19th century Jewish agricultural settlements was founded in 1878. The stone arch on the right-hand side of Rehov Rothschild is in memory of Baron Edmond de Rothschild who assisted the early settlers with finance.

Near the exit follow the right-hand fork eastwards at the petrol station.

Pass Kibbutz Givat HaShlosha and within a few minutes you'll see the remains of a mighty fortress standing on the hill on the left hand side of the road. It is **Antipatris** (Tel Afek), brooding over the springs that form the source of the **Yarkon River**. It guards the western flank of the biblical Pass of Afek, a strategic site on the Via Maris.

The fortress includes remnants of the Crusaders' "Fort at Deaf Springs," with Mameluke and Turkish additions. In earlier days, Herod had built a fortress here in memory of his father, Antipater – hence the name.

Many battles were waged at the pass. The Philistines overran the Israelites in about 1066 BCE and St. Paul was led through in captivity on his way from Jerusalem to Caesarea and Rome.

The nearby town of **Rosh Ha'ayin** is populated by some 12,700; a large number of them immigrated from Yemen shortly after the War of Independence.

Continue along the road for about another 3 km., past Kibbutz Einat.

Ruins of the 12th century Crusader fortress of **Mirabel** (Migdal Afek) are on top of the hill facing you. It is a few kilometres west of the pre-1967 border.

Byzantine Christians had lived here earlier and a stone above a door to the right of the entrance is inscribed. in Greek, "Martyrion of Saint Kerykos." Kerykos was a young martyr put to death with his mother by the Romans in the 4th century CE.

The Crusaders fortified this hill, about 2 km. west of the Samarian hills, because it formed the eastern flank of the Pass of Afek.

In 1152, a rebel Crusader army, loyal to Queen Mother

Melisande, surrendered in the fortress to troops loyal to Baldwin III. Later, Saladin conquered it and used it as a base for raiding the coastal plain. Before the end of the century the Moslems destroyed it as part of their scorched-earth policy.

Arab villagers lived within these baronial-sized rooms when it was part of the village of Migdal Tzedek, prior to the 1948 war.

Four kilometres further south along Road No. 444 you'll see on your left the **Roman Mausoleum**, unchanged since it was built in the 2nd century CE. Two Corinthian columns help support the stone roof. Many of the stones measure more than a metre long. The niche inside is a mihrab, cut by Arabs who at some later stage converted it into a mosque. They named it Nebi Yehia – Arabic for the prophet John.

The road (No. 444) to **Ben Shemen** passes several quarries – which supply stones to the region – before reaching a junction 12 km. from Rosh Ha'ayin. It forks right (Road No. 453) for Ben-Gurion Airport.

Continue along the other road to **Ben Shemen Woods**. Near Moshav Hadid the road cuts through pine woods forming part of the **Herzl Forest**. There are many tables and log benches for picnickers.

An amphitheatre nearby is used during the summer months for entertainment. The observation tower helps the forest rangers spot fires while also providing visitors with a chance to scan the hill country where the Maccabees launched their revolt.

Drive on, following the signs to the **Tombs of the Maccabees** at **Modiin**. They are cut in the rock on the slopes of a hill, near a memorial to the Israel Defence Force.

Return now on the same road and continue westwards until you arrive at Lod.

LOD (Map: G15)

Lod was settled by the Canaanites and then by the Benjaminites. The exiles returning from Babylon also built houses here. During the rule of the Maccabees it was purely Jewish, but in 43 BCE the inhabitants were sold into slavery.

The New Testament relates that St. Peter visited it when it was known by its Greek name of Lydda. A few decades later, the Romans burned it to the ground before destroying Jerusalem.

The most famous settlers were the Crusaders. Much of the church they built in the 12th century survives and the Greek Orthodox community set up the **Church of St. George** within part of its ruins in 1874. Inside you can see the right hand apse, two bays of the nave and the northern aisle of the Crusader structure.

Down in the crypt of the church is the **Tomb of St. George,** the patron saint of England, who is said to have been born in this town in the 3rd century. Note, too, the sculptured portrayal of St. George slaying the dragon above the entrance to the church.

Modern Lod has a population of 47,800, many of them immigrants from Russia who work at the nearby **airport**.

Lod is 2 km. northeast of Ramla. However, just before entering Ramla, turn right for the road back to Tel Aviv, along Route No. 5 in reverse. Alternatively, you could return towards Ben-Gurion Airport and take Highway No. 1 to Tel Aviv or Jerusalem.

ROUTE No. 8 (Map: Northern Sheet E14 to K12 and F11)

Northern Sharon and Western Shomron

Tel Aviv – Kfar Saba (22 km.) – Kalkilya (26 km.) – Nablus (56 km.) – Sebastia-(Samaria) (66 km.) – Tulkarm (84 km.) – Netanya (99 km.) (Road Nos. 2, 5, 4, 55, 57, 60.)

(Distances in brackets refer to start of route.)

This fascinating circular route takes you to the heart of Samaria, through bucolic countryside, to towering Mt. Gerizim, where Samaritans (see "Communities") celebrate their Passover and where Joshua assembled the tribes of Israel. Close by is Sebastia (Samaria) where the biblical kings of Israel had their capital after Judaea was separated from the other tribes.

The trip requires an entire morning, but can only be attempted if the army has not closed off part of the area due to intifada violence. Extreme caution should be exercised in the territories.

Leave Tel Aviv on the Haifa Road (Highway No. 2), turning right opposite the Country Club at the 10 km. peg (Road No. 5). Continue along this road until you come to the fork that directs you right to Jerusalem and left along Road No. 4 to **Kfar Saba**, founded as an agricultural settlement in 1905 and today a town of some 40,000.

At the next junction take the right fork and, turning immediately left, follow the signpost to Kfar Saba, crossing the town eastwards and then the pre-1967 cease-fire line with Jordan on Road No. 55 until you reach **Kalkilya**, which you pass through.

The road to Nablus is clearly signposted in this small town. After you leave Kalkilya and its citrus plantations, the beauty of **Samaria** opens out in all its still simplicity. The road leads through rolling countryside with grey stones splattered on the faces and summits of the hills. The tarred road is lined with many olive and citrus groves and there are lush orchards. The pace of life in Samaria is indicated by the familiar sight of mule-driven carts.

When passing through the Arab villages notice how splendidly the stone buildings blend in with the surrounding landscape. These houses are set on several mounds and the road winds past cypress trees, fine, symmetrically lined rock terraces, olive groves, goat herds and sprays of wild flowers and thistles that are a lovely feature of Samaria.

You pass the settlements of **Maale Shomron, Karne Shomron** and **Kedumim,** as well as the town of **Emanuel** established by Orthodox Jews.

The road tacks round the side of a mountain and suddenly, with wide-angled-lens grandeur, the city of Nablus comes into view, its profusion of grey stone houses dwarfed by biblical **Mt. Gerizim** on the right and **Mt. Ebal**, scarred by modern quarries, on the left.

Enter the city and follow the signposts up Mt. Gerizim for a look at many of the principal sites and for a bird's-eye view of Nablus and the Mountains of Ephraim.

NABLUS (SHECHEM) (Map: K12)

The area around modern **Nablus** featured prominently in the lives of the Patriarchs for there was a settlement here called **Shechem** (its ruins have been uncovered on the eastern edge of the town).

It was here that Abraham built an altar after God had promised this land to his descendants (Genesis 12:7). Here, too, Jacob bought land from the Canaanites, pitched his tent and also built an altar (Genesis 33:18-20). Joseph's body was brought here from Egypt and buried in Jacob's plot (Joshua 24:32).

After the conquest of Canaan, Joshua fulfilled Moses' command and assembled the Israelites here, encouraging them to keep their faith by relating the blessings that would follow, and warning them of the curses that would befall them if they transgressed the Mosaic laws (Joshua 8:30-35).

Abimelech was crowned king here during the period of the Judges (Judges 9:6), and the country split into the kingdoms of Israel and Judaea when the northerners at Shechem rejected Solomon's arrogant son, Rehoboam, and seceded from the kingdom (I Kings 12:19–20).

Biblical Shechem was destroyed by the Assyrians in the 8th century BCE but became a powerful city when the Samaritans built their Temple on Mt. Gerizim in the 4th century BCE. Their shrine was converted into a Temple to Zeus by Antiochus II in 170 BCE, and this and the city were razed and levelled several decades later by the Hasmonaean leader, John Hyrcanus.

Modern Nablus, which since 1987 has been under curfew more often than not, derives its name from the Roman town founded in 72 CE close to the ruins of biblical Shechem. Known as Flavia Neapolis, its name was corrupted to Nablus following the Arab conquest in 636 CE.

The Crusaders renamed it Naples in the 12th century when they built a palace and a citadel and raised its status to the second capital of their kingdom.

Jews had lived in Nablus during many periods but they abandoned the town after the 1929 riots. The Samaritans, however, clung to this area and their present quarter lies at the foot of Mt. Gerizim.

Nablus today is famous for its soap manufacturers. It is also an administrative centre, being the largest town in Samaria.

Sites

Mt. Gerizim: 881 m. above sea level. Tarred road well

signposted to summit. Sacred to Samaritans for at least 2,300 years and site of their Passover pilgrimage for ritual slaughter of sheep.

Sites on summit include modern Samaritan synagogue; fenced-off slab of rock said by Samaritans to be site over which Abraham intended sacrificing Isaac; stones marking Samaritan version of place where Joshua built an altar (the Bible says this was Mt. Ebal); ruins of octagonal Byzantine church; tomb of 12th century Sheikh Ghanem, built over one of several mountain lookout posts erected by Samaritans to signal each other with bonfires to warn of approaching enemies.

Jacob's Well: near eastern base of Mt. Gerizim. Believed to have been dug by the Patriarch Jacob. Also the site where Jesus talked with the Samaritan woman. Modern Greek Orthodox church stands over the site. Open: 7 a.m. – 12 noon, 3–6 p.m.

Joseph's Tomb: just north of Jacob's Well and clearly signposted. Domed tomb set behind huge mulberry tree.

Samaritan Quarter: west of Mt. Gerizim. There are only a few hundred Samaritans today. Synagogue contains Samaritan Torah Scroll said to date from 13th year of settlement of Israelites in Canaan.

Shechem: ruins of biblical cities on mound west of, and close to, Joseph's Tomb, in village of Balata. Remains of defensive wall from time of Patriarchs, 3,600-year-old Hyksos temple, and relics from Israelite occupation during period of Judges and of Kings of Israel.

As you drive west along Road No. 60 out of Nablus towards Sebastia (Samaria), note the broad, clean streets of the city, with stone houses that are often inviting to the eye because of their coloured wooden shutters, wrought-iron work, red-tiled roofs and vines growing over patio roofs.

After a short while take the fork to the right that leads north on Road No. 60. A short distance later, on your left, is the new settlement of **Shavei Shomron;** take the road to the right that skirts the ancient hill of Sebastia.

The road leads through the Arab village of **Samaria**. The situation permitting, you may want to stop outside the open-air cafe and walk over to the adjacent **mosque** in a 12th century Crusader cathedral. It was built here because early Christians associated this site with the burial-place of the head of John the Baptist.

Inside the courtyard you will find steps leading down to a darkened room with four slits for windows. Pilgrims in the Middle Ages trekked here to see what were described as the tombs of the prophets Obadiah and Elisha. However, there are no tombs to be seen nowadays.

Continue through the narrow village streets until you reach the entrance to the National Parks site of Sebastia. It is open daily 8 a.m. – 5 p.m. (4 p.m. in winter). An entrance fee is paid.

SEBASTIA (SAMARIA) (Map: J12)

This conspicuous hill, now fruitful with quiet olive groves, was settled during the Bronze and Iron Ages. However, its importance dates from biblical times when, in the early 9th century BCE, Omri, King of Israel, bought it for two talents of silver. "He fortified the hill and called the name of the city which he built, Samaria, after the name of Shemer, the owner of the hill" (I Kings 16:24). It is easy to see why the Kings of Israel maintained their capital here.

Samaria, or Shomron in Hebrew, means "watchtower." It rises 100 m. above the fertile plain. From the fortified palace complex that Omri and his son and successor, Ahab, built on the summit, it was possible to see the Sharon Valley and the coast on the west, and the Jezreel Valley with its strategic pass at Megiddo to the north.

Omri and Ahab are known to us through the Bible as men who "did more evil in the sight of the Lord than all who were before them." Ahab married the notorious Jezebel and under her influence built a temple to Baal at Samaria. He also overlaid many of the fixtures and fittings of his palace with exquisitely carved ivory, earning for himself another biblical epitaph as the monarch who built "the ivory house" (1 Kings, 22:39). The Hebrew prophets continually upbraided the rulers of Samaria for their sins, with Isaiah delivering a tongue-lashing against the "drunkards of Ephraim" (Isaiah 28:1).

In 722 BCE, the Assyrians conquered Samaria after a three-year siege and deported most of the vanquished. Those they brought in as colonizers gradually intermarried with the few Israelites who remained, giving birth, according to popular belief reinforced by the Bible (2 Kings 17), to the first generation of Samaritans. Samaritans deny this and claim they were a separate group before the exile.

The Samaritans courted the favour of Alexander the Great during their political rivalry with the Jews in Jerusalem. But after the Samaritans' great temple was completed on Mt. Gerizim in 332 BCE, they burned alive Alexander's prefect for the area.

The result was the merciless slaughter of the fleeing Samaritans and the occupation of their city at Samaria. The remnants of this community fled to the foot of their sacred mountain. Re-settlement of Samaria and the region was carried out by 6,000 Macedonians. However, the Hasmonaean, John Hyrcanus, destroyed much of the hill city in the 2nd century BCE.

Samaria rose to greatness again under the vigorous rule of Herod the Great. He named it Sebastia in honour of the Roman Emperor Augustus (Sebastos is "Augustus" in Greek).

The final destruction came at the hands of the Persians.

Sites

Byzantine Church: below the acropolis. Dates from 5th century. Walls up to 4 m. high remain.

Forum: many columns standing from about 30 BCE when built by Herod.

Hellenistic Tower: huge blocks of stone cut for round tower. Erected during 4th century BCE.

Israelite Gate: 9th century BCE, on eastern slope. Stones retain scratch marks of hinges of doors to the gate.

Israelite Wall: built in 9th century BCE. Surrounded perimeter of city. When fortified with towers, bastions and casemates it was 10 m. wide and enclosed 5 dunams.

Israelite Walls on Acropolis: finely cut stones set on deep foundations.

Roman Amphitheatre: 1st century BCE. Facing north. Most of the stones are still in place.

Roman Basilica: 3rd century CE. Many columns still standing.

Roman Temple: dedicated to Emperor Augustus by Herod and mounted by huge steps.

Street of Columns: on southern base of hill. Main thoroughfare during Herodian period.

Return left to Road No. 60 with the signpost directing you right to Tulkarm and Netanya (Road No. 57), taking care not to follow the road leading past the tank as this goes north to Jenin. **Tulkarm**, an Arab town, offers the traveller a market place where fresh fruit and vegetables are sold alongside trinkets, curios and pita. Be careful. You could become the target of stone-throwing youths.

Back in your car, you will soon cross a railway line. It was so close to the cease-fire lines before June 1967 that Israeli train passengers used to rib one another: "Don't lean over the border!"

There are a number of agricultural villages and settlements between this point and the Haifa-Tel Aviv Road.

You may either cross the main road that is a few hundred metres from the centre of Netanya, or take the left turn and continue straight on to Tel Aviv for the remaining 30 km. on Highway No. 2. For a description of this last part of your journey see Route No. 12.

ROUTE No. 9 (Maps: Northern and Southern Sheets E14 to E19 and E,F23)

To the Negev capital by way of the Shephelah

Tel Aviv – Rishon LeZion (16 km.) – Rehovot (22 km.) – Qiryat Gat (60 km.) – Beer Sheva (107 km.) (Road Nos. 44, 4, 264, 412, 40.)

(Distances in brackets refer to start of route.)

This route leads through many of the settlements founded by Zionist pioneers in the late 19th century, and enters the northern Negev where much of the fighting was carried out during the War of Independence.

To get to Qiryat Gat take the road leading to Rishon Lezion as detailed in Route No. 6, then continue along this route on Road No. 40 until you reach the northern perimeter of Qiryat Gat.

The junction is known as the Plugot Crossroads, with the right fork (Road No. 35) going to Ashqelon. It was at **Faluja,** on your immediate right, that the Israeli Army encircled an Egyptian brigade during the War of Independence. The second in command of the invaders was none other than the late Gamal Abdel Nasser.

Follow the signpost to Beer Sheva, detour round Qiryat Gat and then take the left fork down to Beer Sheva on Road No. 40 to the south.

Drive on past the string of settlements with cotton and wheatfields and then stop for a closer look at the imposing concrete memorial on your right.

This is the **Yiftach Brigade Memorial**, commemorating the Yiftach Palmach brigade that saw action in the Galilee and in the centre of the country before shifting south to rout the Egyptians in the "Faluja Pocket." Large concrete steps lead up to the austere memorial inscribed with the names of valiant men. The lawns and trees that surround it are near tables and benches set here for picnickers.

At **Tzomet Qama** there are two roads (Nos. 264 and 40) to Beer Sheva. (No. 40 is the shortest route to the northern part of Beer Sheva.) No. 264 passes many settlements, set on undulating hills, that gallantly withstood attacks from Egyptian armour and infantry in 1948. Twelve kilometres from Beer Sheva, the road joins up with the highway coming in from Gaza, Yad Mordechai and Netivot (Road No. 25).

The remaining part of the trip is outlined at the end of Route No. 10.

ROUTE No. 10 (Maps: Northern and Southern Sheets E14 to B20 and E,F23)

To the Negev capital along the ancient "Via Maris" (Sea Road)

Tel Aviv – Ashdod (31 km.) – Ashqelon (55 km.) – Yad Mordechai (64 km.) – Beer Sheva (115 km). (Road Nos. 44, 4, 25, 250).

(Distances in brackets refer to start of route.)

There are several routes from Tel Aviv to Beer Sheva but this one is recommended above all others because it covers some of the most glorious beach resort areas along the Mediterranean, passes through an heroic kibbutz at Yad Mordechai, and cuts through a typical example of a development township at Netivot. There is also a detour from Yad Mordechai through Gaza to Netivot (Road Nos. 44, 4).

Take the same road out of Tel Aviv that starts Route No. 6. Instead of turning left to Rishon LeZion, continue straight along the motorway (No. 4) to Ashdod.

If you want to visit Yavne, leave the motorway at signpost 26 (on Road No. 42, about 6 km. from the Meteorological Station). **Yavne** is a new immigrant town on the site of the famous biblical Yavne. When the Second Temple was destroyed in 70 CE, Rabbi Yohanan Ben Zakkai obtained permission from Titus to set up a centre for religious studies here. A dome-topped building to the west of Yavne is considered by some as the tomb of Rabbi Gamliel, the great 1st century CE sage who lived here. Walk from the tomb across the main road and up the hill facing you. The remains of a **mosque**,dating back to the Mameluke period, and of a **Crusader castle**,stand on the summit.

Continue along the highway, turning right into Road No. 41 at the entrance to Ashdod.

ASHDOD (Map: D17)

This vigorous young town is destined to overtake Haifa as the country's major port and has been planned for 350,000 people, which will make it the third largest centre in Israel.

Founded in 1957 on windswept sand dunes close to the ancient Philistine city, Ashdod now numbers more than 80,000 people. While its sandy beaches justify plans to turn it into a leading resort area, Ashdod is at present principally a port city with burgeoning industries. More than 1,000 vessels weigh anchor here every year and the industrial site in the north includes electronics plants, wool processing facilities, cosmetics factories, truck and bus assembly plants, and citrus packing, as well as synthetic fibres (rayon and nylon thread) plants. The two power stations provide almost half the electricity consumed nationally.

Drive up the Yaffa Ben-Ami Memorial Hill in front of the conspicuous lighthouse for an all-embracing view of the harbour and the beaches.

Note: photography is forbidden from this site as it is close to a military area.

Back on Highway No. 4, to your right, heading south, after a few kilometres you cross the bridge called **Ad Halom.** It was at this point that the Givati Brigade routed the Egyptian invaders on a June night in 1948, after Egyptian reconnaissance units had already reached Yavne.

Drive on towards Ashqelon; you might want to turn right to the **Nitzanim Youth Village** and the **Queen Juliana Maritime School.** The road there turns right, through the demolished buildings of a former British army camp. Nitzanim is a model village where immigrant and deprived youth are helped to become integrated Israelis. Much of the funds come from Jews in the United States and Europe.

Return to the highway and continue south until the signpost directs you right to Ashqelon.

ASHQELON (Map: C18,19)

In our opinion this charming city, 65 km. south of Tel Aviv, is pre-eminent among the beach resorts along the Mediterranean coast. It offers a variety of attractions, notably a sprawling park with camping site and picnic area adjacent to the sea, long stretches of clean beaches, sports facilities, nightclubs, pubs and many historic sites. Organized tours of the surroundings are also available during summer months.

Tourist Information Office: Afridar Centre, tel. (07) 770111. Open: weekdays 8.30 a.m. – 1 p.m.; Tues. 8.30 a.m. – 12.30 p.m.; Fri. and Sat. closed.

History

Ashqelon, one of the five principal cities of the Philistine Kingdom, is associated with Samson and Delilah, and it is easy to believe that the beach was a favourite playground of theirs.

Ashqelon was the Philistine harbour and a centre of their culture. After the Philistines killed King Saul, David cried out, "Publish it not in the streets of Ashqelon...lest the daughters of the Philistines rejoice" (2 Samuel, 1:20).

Ashqelon was later captured by Alexander the Great and became a centre of Hellenistic culture. Under the rule of the Roman lackey, King Herod, it became an important cosmopolitan centre, and remained so under Moslem rule until the city was destroyed in the thirteenth century during the Crusades. The National Park is situated on the site of ancient Ashqelon.

Some one hundred years ago, the village of **Majdal** (today Migdal) was founded by Arabs in the Ashqelon area. Following the establishment of the State of Israel, other communities sprang up around it, including **Afridar**, founded by South African Jewry, which won the acclaim of many town planners. Together with the **Barnea, Givat Zion** and **Samson** districts, they were amalgamated into a town called Migdal Ashqelon, which was granted city status as **Ashqelon** in 1955.

Today Ashqelon is a restful holiday resort (pop. 60,000–plus) with gardens and shady boulevards leading to a seemingly endless stretch of golden beach, bordered by cliffs. The weather here is warm throughout the year, with rain falling during a few days in winter.

Sites

Byzantine Church: on the cliff-top in the Barnea Quarter. Ruins from 5th or 6th century.

(Bus No. 5).

Mosaic Floor: Barnea Quarter about half a kilometre northwest of Byzantine church. Also from Byzantine period.

National Park: south of Afridar beach, set amidst thousands of trees, Crusader ruins and sculptures of Atlas, Nike, Eirene, goddess of peace and others. Log tables and benches for picnicking, spacious lawns. Entrance fee. Open seven days a week, all hours, because there's a camping site here. Entrance fee to the camping site does not include entrance to the park.

The Sarcophagi: in December 1972, two 3rd century CE Roman sarcophagi were discovered while foundations were being dug for a villa. The subjects carved on the sides were taken from Roman mythology. They are on view in Afridar. Open daily 8.30 a.m. – 4.30 p.m. and Fri. 8.30 a.m. – 2.30 p.m. Closed Sat. Admission free.

The Ashqelon Khan is situated in Atzmaut Square in the north of the Migdal district. The area has been restored and in one section is the Museum of Modern Ashqelon. Open Sun.–Thurs. 9. a.m.–1 p.m., 4 p.m.–6 p.m., Fri. 9 a.m.–1 p.m., Sat. 10 a.m.–1 p.m.

Ashqeluna Watersport Park: On the Delilah beach is the largest water-sport park in the country. Beautiful lawns, five gigantic water-chutes, a water carousel and three swimming pools – one specially designed for toddlers.

Take the main road out of Ashqelon and turn right onto Road No. 4 which takes you to Yad Mordechai, passing through harder landscape abounding with cacti. The entrance is on the right, about 8 km. south. (About four-and-a-half kilometres south of Ashqelon is the **Hey Daroma** drive-in restaurant.)

YAD MORDECHAI (Map: C19)

The spirit of Israel and the Jews is synthesized at this remarkable kibbutz founded in 1943 and named in honour of Mordechai Anilewicz, who died fighting the Nazis while commander of the Jewish Fighters' Organization in the Warsaw Ghetto.

The first signpost within the kibbutz leads to a giant **statue of Anilewicz** clutching a grenade. It is set on a hilltop in front of the dislodged water tower that was shelled during the Egyptian attack in 1948.

The second signpost takes you to another hill which overlooks the reconstructed scene of bitter fighting during the War of Independence. Life-sized, blackened cut-outs with helmets and rifles represent the advancing Egyptians, reinforced with tanks set around the hill. Obsolete weapons of the defenders are in position in slit trenches on the hill. Recorded explanations of the battle, the retreat of the heavily outnumbered Israelis, and the eventual recapture of the kibbutz six months later, are given in all major languages. Open: Sun. – Thurs. (summer) 8 a.m. – dusk. Fri. 8 a.m. – 5 p.m. Sat. all day. Tel. (07)720529. Entrance fee includes visit to the museum.

Visit the **museum** in the kibbutz devoted to pictorial and weapons displays showing the kibbutz under fire and European Jewry under the Nazis. The haunting music and laments follow you around as you tread the cobbled floor in the darkened interior, coming face to face with a simple inscription: "There were one and a half million children."

From Yad Mordechai continue straight for Beer Sheva, via Netivot (on Roads 34 and 25).

Twenty kilometres after leaving Yad Mordechai on Road No. 34, travelling southeast, you reach **Netivot** on your right. It is well worth taking a few minutes to drive round this embryonic settlement as it is a sterling example of how the arid Negev is being brought to life.

Continue towards Beer Sheva on Road No. 25, noticing how, in spite of the parched, cracked earth, fields have been cultivated. The **Sharsheret Forest** appears like a mirage in this landscape. Cross Nahal Gerar and the turn-off right to **Ofakim**, another development township. Five kilometres later the road swerves left to join up with Route No. 9.

Continue past a tree nursery of the Jewish National Fund, avoiding the turn-off to Jerusalem and Tel Aviv. You are now 12 km. from Beer Sheva. Notice how, as you approach the capital of the Negev, the mass of apartment blocks seem to reach out for the eroded wastes that lie beyond them.

ACCOMMODATION ON ROUTE No. 10

(See also general "Accommodation" section.)

HOTELS

ASHDOD
Miami Tel. (08) 522085. 12 Nordau St.
Orly Tel. (08) 565380. 22 Nordau St.

ASHQELON
Shulamit Gardens Tel. (07) 711261. 11 Hatayassim St.
Samson's Gardens Tel. (07) 736641. 38 Hatamar St.

ROUTE No. 11 (Map: Northern Sheet E14 to G10 and N6

The Valley of Jezreel

Tel Aviv – Megiddo (78 km.) – Afula (90 km.) – Mt. Tabor (105 km.) – Nebi Shu'eib (125 km.) – Tiberias (132 km.) (Road Nos. 2, 65, 7266, 77, 7717)

(Distances in brackets refer to start of route.)

Covering a few hours, this trip cuts across some of the most fertile areas of Israel and includes the site where the New Testament claims that Armageddon, the last great battle of the world, will be fought. It also includes biblical Mt. Tabor and the Horns of Hittin – holy to the Druze community.

Take the northern highway (No. 2) out of Tel Aviv, following Route No. 12 until you turn right at the turn-off to **Hadera**, 40 km. from Tel Aviv, a malarial swamp before settlers arrived here in 1891. The museum is located in an old Khan. Proceed along Rehov Herbert Samuel in Hadera. A signpost directs you left to Afula. Then go first right, along Rehov Weizmann and continue until another signpost points ahead to Afula (Road No. 65). (If you want to avoid passing through **Hadera**, take the bypass by driving on the highway (No. 2) a few kilometres and turn right into Road No. 65, which takes you direct to Afula.)

Drive past the orange groves of **Kibbutz Gan Shmuel.** The road passes stately cypresses and rounds a corner into open fields and rolling countryside.

The Irron Forest is on your left and double-storey houses of a number of Arab villages cling to the slopes of hills.

The road suddenly rises and you should pull over to the shoulder for a beautiful view of the flat and chequered fields of the **Jezreel Valley** below.

Its springs made it a habitable place from time immemorial, and the Bible and archaeological discoveries this century point to the prosperity of its former residents. But at the turn of the century it was a forsaken swamp.

The Jezreel Valley was also the scene of countless battles because it lay on the Via Maris – the Way of the Sea – and was the thoroughfare for armies and caravans making their way between Assyria and Egypt.

Today it is abundant with fruit, vegetables and wheat. There are many fine National Parks within its expansive boundaries and several museums in the kibbutzim that display ancient finds together with modern art.

When you reach the crossroads for Haifa, left, Givat Oz and Samaria, right, and Afula straight on, turn left into Road No. 66 and drive for 2 kms. to the hill of Megiddo.

MEGIDDO (Map: J8)

As it commanded the Via Maris it was a strategic site from the time that man first lusted for power and conquest.

Archaeologists have unearthed the remains of 20 cities at Megiddo. They include buildings from shortly after the time when King David conquered the hill and fortifications constructed by his son, Solomon (I Kings 9:15). The oldest discoveries date back some 4,000 years and form a **Canaanite Temple**, complete with a limestone altar.

While here you must see the 9th century BCE shaft and tunnel built by the Israelite King Ahab. The 60 m. shaft linked up with a 120 m.-long tunnel to the source of water lying just outside the fortifications. This ingenious engineering feat enabled those inside to withstand protracted sieges. Notice how the tunnel bulges irregularly in one section. This is the result of two teams of workmen digging through the rock and limestone from opposite ends and meeting up only after hacking in wrong directions. Steps and lights have been installed in the tunnel for visitors.

The New Testament holds that this is the place where the last battle of the world will be fought (Revelations 16:16); Armageddon is a corruption of Har Megiddo ("the hill of Megiddo" in Hebrew).

Note: This National Parks site has a **museum** and a restaurant and it is advisable, for better understanding, to see the scale model of the site in the museum prior to walking around the ruins.

Museum: Sat. – Thurs. 8 a.m. – 5 p.m. Fri. 8 a.m. – 4 p.m. **Site:** April–Sept. 8 a.m. – 5 p.m. Oct. – March 8 a.m. – 4 p.m. Closes one hour earlier Fri. and eve of holidays.

Water Tunnel: 8 a.m. – 4.30 p.m. During winter the tunnel may be closed to visitors. Entrance fee.

AFULA (Map: K8)

Return to the crossroads and continue (left) to Afula on Road No. 65. This town serves as the commercial, transportation and administrative centre for the Jezreel Valley. On Succot there is a Harvest Festival and horse race in Afula.

On reaching Afula turn first right and first left, passing the Central Bus Station. Follow the road uphill, turning right towards Mt. Tabor and Tiberias. The left fork (Road No. 60) leads to Nazareth and Haifa.

Continue on Road No. 65, climbing the hill, past the hospital, with more spectacular views of the Jezreel Valley on your right.

The road passes **Givat HaMoreh** with Afula's newest suburbs, then the sunflower fields of Nein. A gas station and restaurant stand at the entrance to **Daverat**. Mt. Tabor looms on the left while the smooth-coloured fields form a carpet of colour in the depths of the valley.

Pass Tamra and then turn left into Road No. 7266, over the stream where cattle and sheep graze. Swing right at the entrance to **Dabburiya**, a pleasant Arab village at the foot of Mt. Tabor.

Ignore the left fork to Kfar Shibli and continue up Mt. Tabor, taking care to drive slowly because, although the road is tarred all the way to the summit, there are scores of hairpin bends.

MT. TABOR (Map: L7)

At 588 m. above sea level, Mt. Tabor towers above the Jezreel Valley and is similar in shape to Sugar Loaf Mountain overlooking Rio de Janeiro. Scattered here and there are encrusted remnants of **Crusader fortifications**.

It was here that the prophetess Deborah assembled the tribes in the period of the Judges for the battle against Sisera the Canaanite (Judges 4:6). Here, too, Josephus Flavius raised fortifications before he deserted the Jews rebelling against the Romans in 66 CE.

Mt. Tabor is sacred to Christians as the "high mountain apart," upon which Jesus was transfigured before Peter, James and John (Matthew 17).

The miraculous event is the reason why several churches were built on the summit. The first one, at the end of the first turning left near the top, is supervised by Greek Orthodox monks. The date above the bell tower shows that it was built in 1911.

The Franciscans built the **Church of the Transfiguration** higher up, on the ruins of Byzantine and Crusader churches, in the 1920s. The Latin inscription above the entrance is taken from the account of the transfiguration, according to Matthew 17. A mural of the transfiguration is set behind the altar of this beautifully decorated church. Their monastery is close by. The basilica is open daily 8 a.m. – 12 noon and 3 p.m. – sunset. Pilgrims can stay at the hospice run by the Franciscans (see "Accommodation" for this route).

Descend to the main road (No. 65) and soon pass **En Dor** where, according to I Samuel 28:7–25, King Saul consulted a witch shortly before his death on nearby Mt. Gilboa.

Turn left at Moshav **Kfar Tabor**, founded in 1902. There are wheat fields and lucerne, then the **Kadoorie Agricultural School** on the left. At Kfar Tabor, stop at the **Farmer's Yards Museum** (tel. 06–765844), which features a reconstructed pioneer farm. Grouped around a stable, sheep pen and chicken yard are an authentic farmer's house, which gives a picture of the life of Israel's pioneer families and an exhibition hall and craftsmen's quarters, including a working smithy and harness-making operation. There is a pleasant dairy restaurant on the premises. Open 8.30 a.m.–6 p.m. every day. At the side of the road close by are the massive ruins of a **traders' inn**, built by the

Turks in 1588. At **Tzomet Golani** (where there is a memorial and museum dedicated to the Golani Brigade) turn right to Road No. 77.

Kibbutz Lavi's Guest House is nearby. Descend the hilly region, avoiding the right fork to the Kinneret. The (upper) western suburbs of Tiberias begin to take form, and when you round a corner you come face to face with another of those superlatively beautiful views in Israel. There, below, to the left, is the northern part of the harp-shaped Sea of Galilee.

Turn right to the observation point for a breathtaking view of the Sea of Galilee and the Golan Heights framing the eastern bank. There is a giant telescope here for a closer look at sites below.

Now take the road (No. 7717) leading left, directly opposite the Lake View Restaurant turn-off. You are in the **Arbel Valley**, wedged between the **Horns of Hittin** on your left and **Mt. Arbel**,with its sheer cliff face, on your right.

Pass the Moshav Shitufi of Kfar Hittin, then the wheat fields, vineyards and cow pastures of Moshav Arbel. Turn left up the hill. The road very shortly comes to a dead end before the Tomb of Jethro.

NEBI SHU'EIB (Map: M6)

Jethro, the father-in-law of Moses, is held in great regard by the Druze who believe that his tomb is located here. It lies at the foot of the **Horns of Hittin**, an extinct volcano bolstered with enormous slabs of stone. This is also where Saladin, leading the Moslems, finally defeated the Crusaders in 1187.

The **Tomb**, set in a mosque-like domed hall, is the site of annual pilgrimages by Druze from all over the country during April.

Visitors wishing to go inside the prayer hall in the same room as the Tomb must first remove their shoes and cover their heads with a hat, shawl or handkerchief. The interior is muffled with dozens of Persian carpets; the raised Tomb is also covered by colourfully woven carpets.

Drive back to Moshav Arbel, turn left and take the road leading close to the grapefruit orchards. Within a few minutes you will be near the cleft in the cliff face at the northern edge of the fields. There are caves on the slopes of Mt. Arbel.

Return to the main road, turning left for Tiberias. Very soon you pass a sign informing you that you are exactly at sea level. **Tiberias** is ahead of you.

As you drive down the hill (in low gear) you are treated to a fabulous view of the Sea of Galilee, which lies 212 m. below sea level. For a description of Tiberias see the chapter on the Galilee.

ACCOMMODATION ON ROUTE No. 11

(See also general "Accommodation" section.)

HOTELS (See Tiberias)

KIBBUTZ GUEST HOUSE

LOWER GALILEE
Lavi Tel. (06)799450. Kibbutz Lavi.

CHRISTIAN HOSPICE
Franciscan Convent of the Transfiguration
Mt. Tabor Tel. (06)567489 P. O. B. 16 Nazareth.
For pilgrims only. Closed in winter.

ROUTE No. 12 (Map: Northern Sheet E14 to G6)

Along the sea road to Haifa

Tel Aviv – Netanya (25 km.) – Caesarea (51 km.) – Zikhron Yaaqov (65 km.) – En Hod (85 km.) – Haifa (98 km.)(Road Nos. 2, 4, 652.)

(Distances in brackets refer to start of route.)

This is the main route to Haifa; Highway No. 2 ranks among the best in the country. However, towards the end of the trip the route follows the narrower road that used to be the old road to Haifa, taking you to the wine-cellars at Zikhron Yaaqov and the artists' village of En Hod.

Finding the way out of Tel Aviv to Haifa is simple. If

you are anywhere within 2 km. of the sea shore, drive east, away from the sea, and you will soon come to Derekh Haifa. Turn left and from this point on it is easy going.

The Haifa Road passes the bulbous **Lasky Planetarium** and the **Eretz Israel Museum complex** on the right, and then forms the border between the suburb of Ramat Aviv on the right and so-called "L-Plan" suburb on the left.

Pass the **Country Club**,opposite the turn-off to Jerusalem, and soon come to another set of traffic lights. To the left is **Herzliyya Pituach** (next to the sea) while the right fork leads to **Herzliyya** town proper.

At the next set of traffic lights the road turns right for the plush quarter of **Kfar Shemaryahu** or left to more villas in Herzliyya Pituach, overlooking the Mediterranean. These two areas boast some of the most luxurious homes in the country.

Turn left for the site of **Apollonia** (Tel Arshaf), a port dating back to Hellenistic times, where the remains of a Crusader castle may still be seen. The shrine of **Sidna Ali**, a Moslem commander during the time of the Crusades, is found nearby.

Thousands of emerald-green blobs of smooth glass, each the size of a brussels sprout, can be seen on the beach below the Crusader ruins. They are believed to be rejects from a glass factory in operation on top of the cliffs between the 4th and 8th centuries CE. A large kiln and slabs of glass were discovered above a 4th century CE cemetery on the cliffs.

The ubiquitous orchards of the fertile **Sharon Plain** swamp the roadside nearly all the way to **Netanya**,but as you get closer to this resort city you can see sand dunes, the likes of which covered this whole stretch some 60 years ago.

The outlying suburbs are anything but aesthetic. However, once you have turned left at the traffic lights you will realize why this resort city has become known as "The Pearl of the Sharon."

NETANYA (Map: F11)

Fittingly, the emblem of this top tourist resort is the lily of the Sharon, recalling the Song of Songs, "I am a rose of Sharon, a lily of the valley" (Cant. 2:1).

Originally planned as a citrus-growing centre and named in honour of the American philanthropist Nathan

Netanya

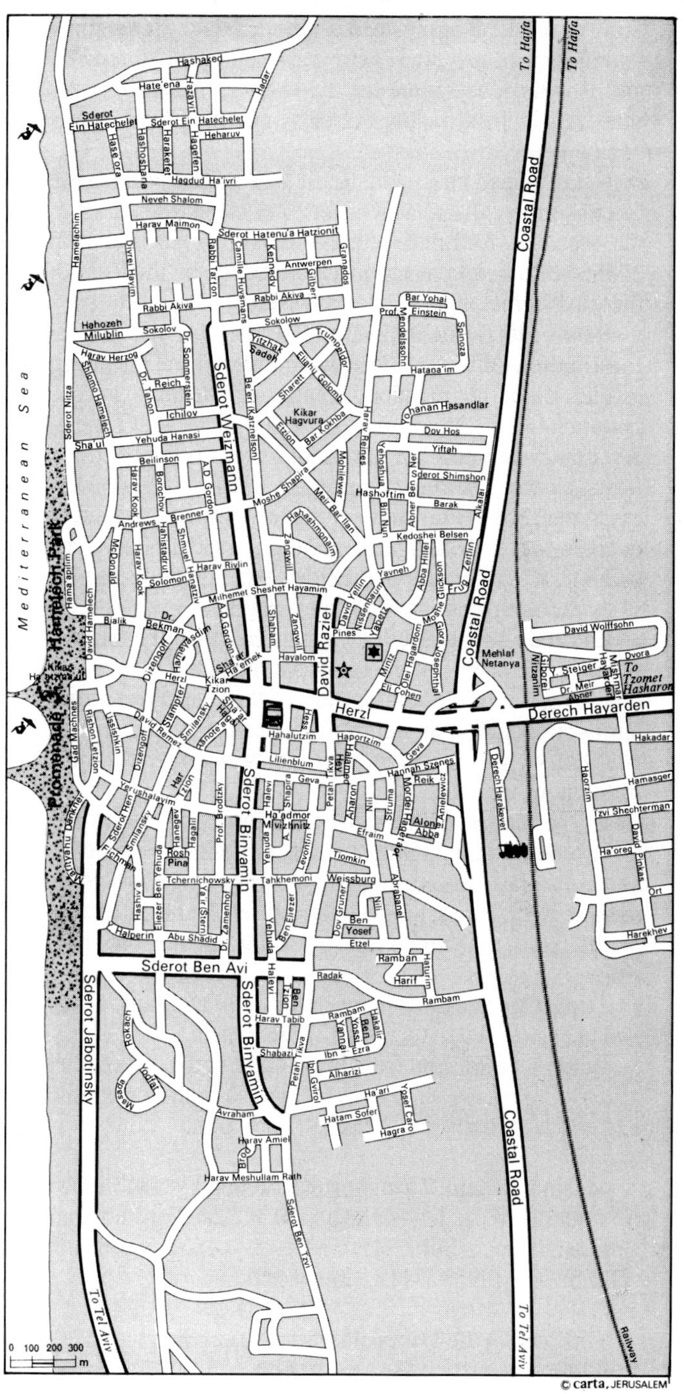
Mediterranean Sea
Hamelech Park
Promenade
Coastal Road
To Haifa
To Tel Aviv
Railway
Herzl
Derech Hayarden
Sderot Weizmann
Sderot Binyamin
Sderot Jabotinsky
Sderot Ben Avi
Sderot Ben Tzvi
David Raziel
Kikar Hagvura
Kikar Tzion
Kikar Ha'atzmaut
Mehlaf Netanya
To Tzomet Hasharon
Hashaked
Hate'ena
Hazayit
Hadar
Sderot Ein Hatechelet
Sderot Ein Hatechelet
Heharuv
Hase'ora
Hashoshana
Harakefet
Hagefen
Hagdud Ha'ivri
Neveh Shalom
Harav Maimon
Sderot Hatenu'a Hatzionit
Hamelachim
Divrei Hayim
Rabbi Tarfon
Camille Huysmans
Kennedy
Antwerpen
Gilbert
Granados
Rabbi Akiva
Rabbi Akiva
Hahozeh Milublin
Sokolov
Sokolow
Bar Yohai
Einstein
Prof. Mendelssohn
Spinoza
Hatana'im
Yohanan Hasandlar
Trumpeldor
Yitzhak Sadeh
Eliyahu Golomb
Sharett
Harav Herzog
Shlomo Hamelech
Dr. Sommerstein
Reich
Dr. Tahon
Ichilov
Be'eri (Katznelson)
Etzion
Bar Kokhba
Harav Reines
Dov Hos
Yiftah
Sderot Shimshon
Hashoftim
Barak
Alkalai
Yehoshua Bin Nun
Abner Ben Ner
Kedoshei Belsen
Sderot Nitza
Sha'ul
Yehuda Hanasi
Beilinson
Harav Kook
Borochov
A.D. Gordon
Moshe Shapira
Meir Bar Ilan
Mohilewer
Hahashmona'im
Andrews
Brenner
McDonald
Harav Kook
Histadrut
Shmuel Hanatziv
Harav Rivlin
Solomon
Zangwill
Yavneh
Abba Hillel
Glickson
Zerlin
Frug
Milhemet Sheshet Hayamim
Hama'apilim
David Hamelech
Bialik
Dr Bekman
Hameyasdim
A.D. Gordon
Sha'ar Ha'emek
Shaham
Zangwill
David Yellin
Nissenbaum
Yabetz
Pines
Moshe Hagardom
Giora Josephthal
Hayalom
Mintz
Olei Hagardom
Eli Cohen
Dizengoff
Herzl
Stampfer
Smilansky
Gad Machnes
Ussishkin
Rishon Letzion
David Remez
Hanote'a
Hess
Hahalutzim
Haportzim
Geva
Lilienblum
Hannah Szenes
Reik
Anielewicz
Dizengoff
Har Tzion
Yerushalayim
Sderot Herzl
Smilansky
Petah Tikva
Halevi
Shapira
Geva
Aharon
Nili
Struma
Morderai Hagetaot
Ha'admor Mivizhnitz
Alonei Abba
Efraim
Levontin
Yehuda Halevi
Hanegev
Hagalil
Prof. Brodetzky
Rosh Pina
Fichman
Yehuda
Tiomkin
Weissburg
Abrabanel
Tchernichowsky
Tahkhemoni
Hashiv'a
Eliezer Ben Yehuda
Ya'ir (Stern)
Dr. Zamenhof
Ben Eliezer
Dov Gruner
Nili
Ben Yosef
Etzel
Halperin
Abu Shadid
Ramban
Hatturim
Harif
Radak
Rambam
Rambam
Ben Tzion
Harav Tabib
Hakalir
Ben Yossi
Yannai
Ibn Ezra
Shabazi
Alharizi
Ibn Gvirol
Ha'ari
Yosef Caro
Hatam Sofer
Hagra
Avraham
Harav Amiel
Harav Meshullam Rath
Hokach
Yodfat
Massada
Derech Harakevet
David Wolffsohn
Dvora
Y. Steiger
Dr. Meir
Abner
Nitzanim
Gibborei
Hakadar
Hamasger
Horzim
Tzvi Shechterman
David Pinkas
Ha'oreg
Ort
Harekhev
0 100 200 300 m
© carta, JERUSALEM

Strauss, Netanya has instead developed on the strength of its inherent beauty. It is extremely popular with tourists and Israelis. They come for the invigorating sea breezes that waft in from below the cliffs on which Netanya is perched.

Netanya also boasts the finest landscaped promenade in the country, from which flights of steps lead down to the beaches with breakwaters that have broken the strip of sand into quiet bays, artificially curved by the force of the waves breaking on stone walls out at sea.

Rehov Herzl, the main street, leads up to the Tourist Information Office, the sleek war memorial and the promenade; it is the magnetic centre of Netanya and is crammed with restaurants (Oriental, European, Chinese, Sea Food, etc.) and boutiques and shops offering exotic fruits, clothing, jewellery and so on. Part of it is a pedestrian mall. On Friday and Saturday nights it is packed to overflowing as Netanyanites indulge in their favourite pastime of strolling down the sidewalks. Visitors also take rides in colourful horse-driven carriages.

Located on the Mediterranean coast of the **Sharon Plain**, 25 km. north of Tel Aviv, Netanya enjoys sea breezes and a gentle sun for most of the year. Winters are temperate and not as wet as in the north. Its population, 130,000, is greatly augmented by vacationers, almost throughout the year.

As the seat of the regional government, Netanya has attracted a number of industries, notably diamond cutting and polishing. This is a good opportunity to see the craftsmen at work as guided tours are offered and at certain places reductions are given for on-the-spot factory purchases.

Tourist Information Office: Kikar Ha'atzmaut, at the end of Rehov Herzl, tel. (09) 827286. Open: Sun. – Thurs. 8.30 a.m. – 3 p.m., and from May till the end of September also 4 – 7 p.m. Fri. 8.30 a.m. – 2 p.m. Winter hours: 8.30 a.m. – 2 p.m. daily. Fri. 8 a.m. – 12.30 p.m.

Moshav Avihail, 2 km. north of Netanya, was founded by veterans of the Jewish Legion of World War I and has a **museum**. Open: Sun. – Thurs. 8 a.m. – 2 p.m. Fri. 8 a.m. – 1 p.m. Tel. (09) 823118. Entrance fee.

The Pearl of the Tribes of Israel (Pninat Shivte Israel). Folklore centre of Yemenite culture. Kikar

Ha'atzmaut 11 (3rd floor). Tel. (09) 331325. Open Sun.–Fri. 10.00 a.m. – noon.

The Iris Reserve. From end of January till end of February. Ben-Gurion Blvd. (southern exit centre of Netanya, 1 km. after "Bet Goldmintz").

Wingate Institute for Physical Education and Sport: (6.5 miles from centre of Netanya). Israel's National Centre for training national teams and visiting sports groups from abroad. It has an indoor Olympic-size swimming pool, a stadium with a 400 metre running track, five gymnasia, sports fields, halls of residence, sports hotel, computerised library, dinimg rooms and cafeterias. The Institute also houses the Israel Archives of Physical Education and Sports and the International Sports Hall of Fame.

Botanical Garden (Chavat Hanoy): Near the agricultural school "Midreshet Ruppin" (6 miles from centre of town). Tel. (09) 688103. Open Sun.–Thur. 7.00 a.m.–4.00 p.m. Fri. till 1.00 p.m. Bus 26.

Back on the highway, you'll find that the cultivated area bordering the road suddenly gives way to sand dunes and the sea appears very soon. Pass **Mikhmoret**, where there is a fish restaurant by the roadside and a good bathing beach, and then, 46 km. away from Tel Aviv, follow the signpost directing you right for Caesarea. The road makes a U-turn and leads under the bridge of the Haifa Highway No. 2 towards the sea.

Take care to drive slowly as the sand dunes are as thick as any in the Negev and the sea breezes frequently blow sand across the road, making skidding a certainty.

The road leads to the entrance of Caesarea's National Park and Kibbutz **Sedot Yam** (fields of the sea) founded in 1940. The kibbutz has beach facilities and guest rooms at its resort centre "Kayit Ve'Shayit" (tel.(06)364111).

CAESAREA (Map: G9)

Once a proud Roman port-city and Crusader bastion, Caesarea has assumed a dreamy, faraway character amid thick sand dunes in the shelter of huge banana plantations.

The monumental amphitheatre and hippodrome where Roman legionnaires frolicked, and the powerfully constructed Crusader fortifications, are in a good state of repair.

The romantic spell is so strong in this wonderfully quiet place that the very rich and the illustrious, Baron James de Rothschild among them, have in recent years built themselves luxurious villas next to the tapering Roman aqueduct.

Sportsmen and picnickers are in their element in this balmy Mediterranean resort. The country's only **golf course**, adjoining the five-star Dan Caesarea Hotel, has no water hazards; but the rough is dotted with pistachio bushes and carob trees.

The sandy beaches are all the more enticing for the buried treasure they hold and many an Israeli has felt cock-a-hoop on discovering ancient coins and pottery below the sand wastes or beneath the shallow waters. There is an entrance fee to the beach. The bathing facilities are excellent, though swimming when there isn't a lifeguard can be dangerous. There is also a harbour for sailing boats.

It is worth timing your visit to Caesarea to coincide with lunch for epicurean delights await you at several restaurants behind the Crusader moat. Then, sated with Mediterranean fish and Oriental salads, you can meander along the harbour and drop in at a number of art galleries, studios, jewellery and curio shops.

History

Caesarea made a modest entry into history as a small anchorage built by the Phoenicians in the middle of the 3rd century BCE. They called it Straton's Tower.

At the end of the 2nd century BCE it was incorporated into the Hasmonaean kingdom by Alexander Jannai.

When Pompey captured Jerusalem, Caesarea was still a place of limited importance. It rose to greatness under Herod who took 12 years, from 22 BCE, to build the port city he named in honour of Caesar Augustus. He built palaces, a temple, an amphitheatre, public buildings, a market place and a deep sea harbour.

Writing 50 years later, the historian Josephus enthused over the buildings, "all constructed in a style worthy of the name which the city bore". Caesarea became one of the leading maritime cities. Such was its splendour that in 6 CE it became the seat of the Roman procurators of Judaea.

In 66 CE violence broke out between Caesarea's Jewish

and Syrian communities, sparking the nationwide Jewish revolt against the Romans. The Roman victors brought many Jewish captives to be fed to the lions here while the rest were shipped to slavery in Rome. Vespasian gave it the status of a Roman colony.

With Jerusalem razed, Caesarea became the capital of Palestine for almost 500 years. Jews gradually returned. Excavations close to the aqueduct show remains of a synagogue and tombstones from the 2nd to the 4th centuries. In the 12th century Benjamin of Tudela reported about 200 Jews living in Caesarea.

It also figured in the development of early Christianity. It was here that St. Peter baptised the centurion (Acts 10), and that St. Paul was imprisoned (Acts 23); and it was from Caesarea that St. Paul set sail for Rome (Acts 27). In the 3rd century the scholar Origen established the famous school of Caesarea. The tradition was continued by his renowned pupil, Eusebius.

With the Arab conquest in 640 the town declined in importance and Herod's splendid harbour decayed. In 1101 it fell to the Crusaders and in 1187 to Saladin. It changed hands a number of times, returning to Christian domination in 1228. Louis IX's "impregnable" walls were raised in 1251 but Caesarea was taken by Sultan Beibars in 1291, and destroyed by the Mamelukes.

In 1884, a fishing village was founded on the site by Muslim refugees from Bosnia. It was later taken over by the Arabs and abandoned in 1948.

The area was developed with the help of the Rothschilds, and it has become a leading resort area and retreat for the affluent.

Sites

Crusader City: bordering beach. Fortified in 12th and 13th centuries. French King Louis IX built moat, 10 m. wide and 15 m. deep, and massive walls. Restored bridge to main gate, close by remains of 10-m.-high defensive tower. Ruins of Cathedral of St. Paul built on rubble of Caesar's temple. Crusader harbour, atop Byzantine and Roman ports, is west of Crusader city. Open daily. Entrance fee (includes a visit to Roman Amphitheatre).

Hippodrome: north of Street of Statues. Entrance through stone gate decorated with cross off main road.

Roman horse-racing course 320 m. long and 60 m. wide. Three conical blocks were polished to reflect sun and excite the horses.

Roman Amphitheatre: south of Crusader city near Sedot Yam beach. Built in 2nd century and excavated and restored by National Parks Authority in 1961. Rivalled only by Roman amphitheatre at Bet Shean in size and state of preservation. Mid-summer concerts held here.

Roman Aqueduct: north of Crusader city above sand dunes on beach. Built in 2nd century to conduct fresh water from Carmel mountain range for Caesarea residents.

Street of Statues: east of Crusader city. Within 5th century Byzantine forum. Giant headless statues, one of white marble from 2nd century, the other in red porphyry of 3rd century, uncovered by chance in 1954. Greek inscription in mosaic floor.

To continue to Haifa drive along the road at right angles to the Crusader City, pass the golf course and hotel and, at the junction with the old road (No. 4) to Haifa, turn left.

The development town of **Or Aqiva**, named after the 2nd century Rabbi Akiva who was martyred at Caesarea, is built near this junction. It houses many immigrants who came to Israel in the fifties and who lived in makeshift tents and shacks at Caesarea.

This is vineyard territory and the Sharon Valley becomes a mass of green during the season. There are also many banana plantations.

Pass **Binyamina** and **Beit Hananiya**, keeping track with the railway lines between the main highway (No. 2) and Road No. 4, which you are on. A signpost points right to Zikhron Yaaqov, 3 km. further up the hill on Road No. 652.

ZIKHRON YAAQOV (Map: G9)

Nestling enchantingly on the heights of a mountain overlooking the sea, Zikhron Yaaqov is the heart of wine country and the home of the famous **Carmel wineries** (there are also cellars in Rishon LeZion).

You should avail yourself of the guided tours of the plant in English and French offered all year round. However, the best months to stop over at Zikhron Yaaqov ("In memory of Jacob") are August and September, when the vineyards are heavy with grapes and when you can nibble on bunches while watching them being crushed and taken off to ferment.

The success story of the verdant fields compares remarkably with the trials of the pioneers who arrived in 1882. They would assuredly have gone bust had it not been for the patronage of Baron Edmond de Rothschild, after whose father the town is named. He brought in a wine-press in 1886 and provided the financial support to sustain the farmers.

His dying wish in Paris in 1934 was to be buried in the Holy Land and 20 years later he was reinterred in Ramat Hanadiv, nearby.

The proud little town, with fourth and fifth generation farmers, gained additional fame as the Palestinian headquarters of the World War I "Nili" spy ring. The Jewish group's founders included the famed natural historian Aaron Aaronsohn, his brother, Alexander, and his sister, Sarah. They fed the British with military secrets on the enemy Turks.

On learning of their exposure, Sarah ordered her colleagues away from the town and remained alone. She was captured and subjected to four days of brutal torture. Then she shot herself to death in the Aaronsohn home which had been the ring's headquarters. The home and the period pieces within it have been preserved as a national memorial and museum.

Sites

Aaron Aaronsohn Picnic Site: alongside mountain road leading from coast into Zikhron Yaaqov. Dedicated to the noted agronomist, discoverer of emmer wheat in the Galilee, and founder of the Nili spy ring.

Bet Aaronsohn: 40, Rehov Hameyasdim, north of the same road to Ramat Hanadiv. Compound includes museum with memorabilia of Aaronsohn family and Aaron's library. Living quarters, decorated with original furniture, include bedroom where Sarah died, and trapdoor concealing "Nili" spies' hideaway. Guided tours:

Sun. – Thurs. 9.30 a.m. – 1 p.m., Fri. 10 a.m.–12 noon. Film included.

Carmel Oriental Wineries: on eastern slope of town. Guided tours of the wineries, which have been operating for over 100 years; Sun. – Thurs. 9 a.m. – 3 p.m., Fri. 9 a.m. – noon. Concludes with wine-tasting. Fee: adults NIS 7, children NIS 5.

Ramat Hanadiv: "Heights of the Benefactor." On southern outskirts of town, along Rehov Hameyasdim (Road No. 652 from Binyamina to Zikhron Yaaqov). Lavish park overlooking coastal plain and sea. Stately tomb of Baron Edmond de Rothschild and his wife, Baroness Adelaide, within crypt of memorial gardens. All financed by James A. de Rothschild, son of Baron Edmond. Entrance to park through gates adorned with Rothschild crest. Crypt open: Sun – Thurs. 9 a.m. – 4 p.m. Fri. 9 a.m. – 2 p.m. Closed Saturday. Gardens open daily 8 a.m. – 4 p.m. Admission free.

Yad LaMeyasdim: north of Ramat Hanadiv, along Rehov Hameyasdim. Scroll-shaped edifice depicting in relief the founding of Zikhron Yaaqov and neighbouring villages. Surrounding lawns have display of agricultural tools used by early settlers.

To get to En Hod follow the old road (No. 4) northwards, close to the Carmel mountain range, past banana plantations, until a signpost directs you right. The artists' retreat is about one kilometre past the olive groves.

EN HOD (Map: G7)

The merit of this slight detour is immediately evident. En Hod is one of those dreams come true . . . a picturesque retreat nestled against the hillside of the Carmel overlooking the blue Mediterranean. It beckons to the visitor with its peace and beauty.

Here painters, sculptors, ceramicists, potters, weavers, photographers, print-makers, writers, dancers, and musicians work and make their homes.

After the War of Independence (1948) this ruined and deserted (Arab) village was earmarked for demolition. The painter Marcel Janco implored the government to allow him and other artists to resettle it as an "artists' colony." The request was granted, and with the help of the City of Haifa, the area was turned into a garden-spot not only for those who live there but for all who visit. The ruined Arab houses were restored with additions fashioned in the stone of the area so that, from a distance, the village seems to be one with the landscape. The **Janco-Dada Museum** is dedicated to Janco and includes a permanent exhibition of 50 of his works. Tel. (04)842350.

A visitor can stroll through the village and see two well-preserved oil presses and visit the communal Gallery-Bazaar in which the works of the resident artists are displayed for sale. The Gallery-Bazaar is open every day, all year, from 9.30 a.m. Closing time is 5.30 p.m., except on Fridays when it's 4.30 p.m. Entrance fee.

During the summer, there is a programme of music or other entertainment in the amphitheatre. The restaurant-cafe is open to all and it serves as a meeting place for the villagers. It is often the scene of impromptu parties and get-togethers.

The village also has student classes in painting, sculpture, drawing, ceramics and allied arts, and enquiries are welcomed.

Further enquiries may be made by telephoning (04)942029.

A word of caution: the ruins of the Crusader castle at Athlit, on the seashore, which can be seen from En Hod, are closed to the general public as they lie within a military area.

From En Hod there are three choices open to you to continue to nearby Haifa.

You may get back onto the main highway (No. 2), although this seems unnecessary in view of the proximity of Haifa. Or you can turn right and drive along the old road (No. 4).

A longer, but more scenic, route takes you over the Carmel range, past an ancient Roman quarry and "Little Switzerland" (see Route No. 13), so that you approach Haifa from its suburbs on the heights of Mt. Carmel. To follow this route, return to the old road, turn right and very soon right again (on Road No. 721) for the 7 km. stretch to Kibbutz **Bet Oren**. However, just before reaching Bet Oren, take the right fork, and shortly afterwards, the left fork. This road (No. 672) will take you past Haifa University and, eventually, into the heart of Haifa.

ACCOMMODATION ON ROUTE No. 12

(See also general "Accommodation" section.)

HOTELS

NETANYA
Seasons Hotel Tel. (09) 618555. 1 Shderot Niza.
Blue Bay Tel. (09) 337475. 37 HaMelachim St.
Galil Tel. (09) 624456. 18 Shderot Niza.
Goldar Tel. (09) 338188. 1 Ussishkin St.
Grand Yahalom Tel. (09) 624888. 15 Gad Makhnes St. K.
Park Tel. (09) 623344. 7 David Hamelekh St.
Galei Hasharon Tel. (09) 623430. 42 Ussishkin St.
Galei Zans Tel. (09) 624717. 6 HaMelakhim St. (Shabbat observing). K.
Palace Tel. (09) 620222. 33 Gad Makhnes St.
Residence Tel. (09) 623777. 18 Gad Makhnes St.
Margoa Tel. (09) 624434. 9 Gad Makhnes St.
Ginot-Yam Tel. (09) 341007. 9 David Hamelekh St.
Hamelech Koresh Tel. (09) 613555. 6 Harav Kook St.
King Solomon Tel. (09) 338444. 18 HaMaapilim St.
Mitzpe Yam Tel. (09) 623730. 4 Karlebakh St.

CAESAREA
Dan Caesarea (Golf Hotel) Tel. (06) 362266. K.
Mediterranean Nueiba Tel. (09) 93113. Michmoret Beach.

ZIKHRON YAAQOV
Baron's Heights & Terraces P. O. B. 332. (06) 300333. K.
Bet Maimon Tel. (06)390212/3/4.

The Galilee

(Map: Northern Sheet)

The Galilee is the northern region of Israel. Stretching from a line just below Haifa all the way up to the Lebanese border, it is flecked with villages and farms and ethnic communities rooted in the soil.

Its rolling hills, specked with grey stone and pine forests, are dream-like and distant, beckoning all who crave the quieter, purer life.

In spring it is ablaze with wild flowers that rock the imagination. The summer air is cool and light in this open countryside. Winter is chilly and snow often blankets the high-lying kibbutzim in the Upper Galilee.

Sun-worshippers and water sports enthusiasts can take their pick of resort towns or quiet nooks along the Mediterranean coastal border and around the Kinneret.

The rolling hills hold many historic sites with ancient synagogues, mosaics from early churches and archaeological excavations.

Our driving routes also lead you over the rolling hills to many Arab and Druze villages where the only movement appears to be in the spreading vines and rustling olive groves.

Within this agrarian picture are a number of cities that stand out as beacons: Haifa, Tiberias, Zefat, Akko, Nahariyya, Nazareth and Karmiel.

We have carved the Galilee into western and eastern sections. Haifa serves as the base for the west while Tiberias is the hub of the eastern flank and the gateway to the Golan Heights. By using this arrangement you can cut down several days of driving time.

Haifa

(Map: Northern Sheet G, H6)

The gateway to the northern region, Haifa sprawls between sea and mountain. Arguably Israel's prettiest city, with more than a passing resemblance to San Francisco and Cape Town, Haifa is also a city of contradictions.

On one hand, the city is green and verdant as it climbs the slopes of Mt. Carmel. On the other, Haifa is a blue collar metropolis of a quarter of a million, home to burgeoning petrochemical, oil and computer industries. Though a city of beautiful beaches and mountains, Haifa also suffers at times from air that is more polluted than many other parts of the country.

There are other contradictions too. Haifa has survived riots and hostilities over the centuries, but today, it is one of Israel's most tolerant cities, where Arab and Jew, Christian and Bahai, observant and secular live together in relative harmony. It is the only city in Israel where buses run on the Sabbath.

With its impressively large number of museums, its attractive scenery and its sandy beaches, Haifa is well worth a visit.

HISTORY

Like most Israeli cities, Haifa is rooted in the past. Recent digs at Tel Shiqmona, on the coast just south of Haifa, have brought to light buildings from the First Temple period down to Seleucid times.

Haifa's rich history stretches back millennia. Discoveries from as far back as the Bronze Age show that a small port was located near this site. The area was also settled in Roman and Greek times.

Biblical references to the Mt. Carmel region include a mention of Elijah's cave and Mt. Carmel itself, where the prophet Elijah challenged the pagan priests of Ba'al. The Talmud does not neglect the area either; it tells us that the shellfish from which the purple dye for the traditional tallit or prayer shawl was made came from the coast around this area.

After the Crusader invasion and conquest, when the town's Jewish defenders were slaughtered, Haifa began a slow decline. Other conquests followed: by Saladin in 1187, by the Mamelukes in 1265. But for hundreds of years, Haifa remained an insignificant, impoverished backwater.

By the seventeenth century, Haifa had begun to revive and develop again. Destroyed once again by a local leader to prevent its capture by the Turks in 1761, Haifa was re-established at its present site.

At the beginning of the nineteenth century, Haifa had about 4,000 inhabitants, many of whom were Christian Arabs. The German Templar settlers who arrived in the mid 1800s made important contributions to the town's growth and industrialization.

Haifa received real impetus for growth when it was linked by rail with Damascus and Egypt in the period before the First World War, making the town an important waystation. Later, when the British wrested control of Palestine from the Turks, the port was further expanded and developed and Haifa became a significant maritime centre.

When Jews returned to Israel, Haifa became a major target of settlement; indeed Theodor Herzl urged Jews to develop Haifa, which he called "the city of the future." During the early years of the twentieth century, the population grew in great leaps: from 20,000 in 1914 to 50,000 in 1931, to 150,000 (of which Jews made up a third) in 1948. Many of the city's Arabs subsequently left when the British evacuated the city that year.

Haifa became a centre for Jewish immigration in the period of Nazi oppression, when thousands entered through the port. It continued to develop and grow, and today, with a quarter of a million residents, is headquarters to the Israeli Navy, Israel Railways, the Israel Electric Company and the giant contracting firm Solel Boneh. It

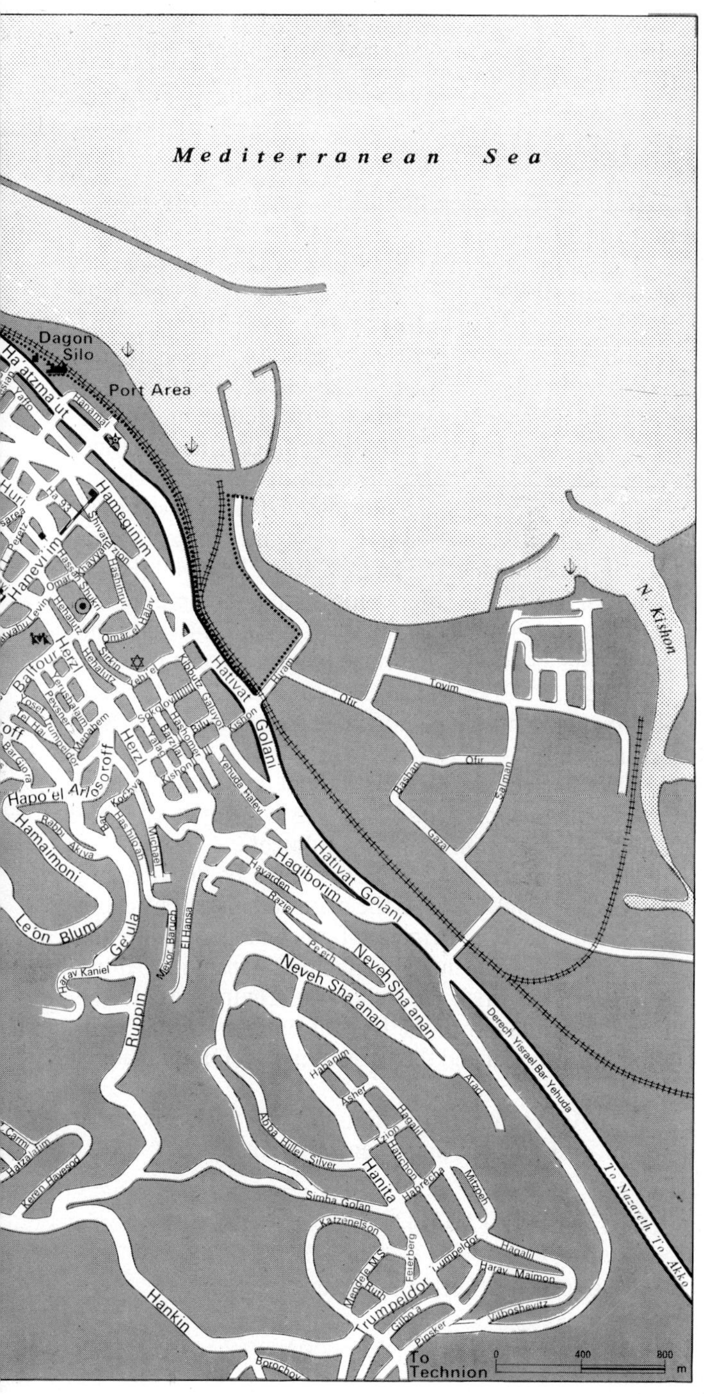
Mediterranean Sea
Dagon Silo
Port Area
N. Kishon
Hativat Golani
Hagiborim
Neveh Sha'anan
Derech Yisrael Bar Yehuda
To Nazareth
To Akko
Hameginim
Herzl
Balfour
Hanevi'im
Ha'atzma'ut
Hapo'el
Arlosoroff
Hamaimoni
Le'on Blum
Ge'ula
Ruppin
Hankin
Trumpeldor
Hanita
Simha Golan
Abba Hillel Silver
Ofir
Toyim
Gazal
Salman
Katzenelson
Harav Maimon
Mitzpeh
Hagalil
To Technion
0
400
800
m

is also the world centre of the Bahai sect, with its remarkable gold-domed sanctuary and magnificent gardens on the slopes of Mt. Carmel.

ORIENTATION

Haifa is located on the Mediterranean coast, 98 km north of Tel Aviv and 44 km south of the Lebanese border.

Topographically, the city winds around the bay and climbs the slopes of **Mt. Carmel**, which offers spectacular views. Down below, where the attractive buildings of the Dagon Grain Silo tower over the dockyards, the port provides employment for many of the city's blue collar workers, as do the chemical, petrochemical and oil industries.

Slightly higher up is the **Hadar** central business district. Today slightly shabby, the district still retains the charm and style of an earlier day. Further up still lie residential neighbourhoods, crowned at the top by the **Carmel Centre**, with its luxury hotels and houses. Along Yefe Nof (Panorama) St. there are observation posts looking over the wide sweep of the bay all the way to Akko, 24 km to the north. Higher still lie luxurious homes, the campuses of the **Technion** and **Haifa University** and the **Carmel Nature Reserve**. The unusual **Bahai Shrine** with its lovely gardens lies halfway up.

The Carmelit subway runs straight up Mount Carmel, linking the sectors of the city. It has recently been renovated, and runs from 6 a.m. to midnight.

Hadar Hacarmel, with its tree-lined boulevards and scores of sidewalk cafes, is the main shopping centre, but in recent years, a number of ultra-modern shopping centres have sprung up. These include Hanevi'im Centre, in Hadar Hacarmel; the Panorama Centre, next to the Dan Panorama Hotel; the Horev Centre on Horev St. in the Ahuza district and the pedestrian mall ("midrachov") on Nordau St.

Two Arab communities in Haifa are **Wadi Nisnas**, near Hadar, and **Kababir**, in the central Carmel area.

ACCOMMODATION

(See also general "Accommodation" section)

HOTELS

Dan Panorama Tel. (04)352222. 107 Hanassi Ave.
Dan Carmel Tel. (04)386211. 87 Hanassi Ave.
Nof Tel. (04)354311. 101 Hanassi St.
Shulamit Tel. (04)342811. 15 Kiryat Sefer St.
Beth Shalom Carmel Tel. (04)377481. 110 Hanassi St.
Dvir Tel. (04) 389131. 124 Yefe Nof St.
Ya'arot Hacarmel Health Resort Tel. (04)323111. Mt. Carmel.
Marom Tel. (04)254355. 51 Hapalmach St.
Nesher. Tel. (04)620644. 53 Herzl St.

CHRISTIAN HOSPICES

Stella Maris Monastery (Italian) P.O. Box 09047. Tel. (04)523459.
Bethel Hostel 40 Hagefen St. Tel. (04)521110
St. Charles Hospice 7 Meir St. Tel. (04)523705.
St. Maximus Mt. Carmel Tel. (04)381274.
Stella Carmel (Evangelical Anglican, British) P.O. Box 7045 Tel. (04)391692.

YOUTH HOSTEL

Carmel Youth Hostel Tel. (04)531944. South approach to Haifa, Hof Hacarmel.

USEFUL NUMBERS AND ADDRESSES

Tourist Information: 20 Rehov Herzl, Tel. (04)666521.
The Haifa Tourism Development Assoc., Ha-Nasi Blvd. 106. Tel. (04)374253.
Main Post Office: 19 Palyam Blvd. Open 7 a.m.–6 p.m., Fri. until 2 p.m. All-night cable service. Tel. (04)304130.
Bus information: Tel. (04)549131. The **Central Bus Station** is located at the entrance to Haifa.
Railway: Bat Galim. Tel. (04)564564.

EMERGENCIES:

Police: 82 Ha'azmaut Rd. Tel. 100.
Magen David Adom – Emergency first aid. 10 Itzhak Sadeh St. Kiryat Eliezer. Tel. 101.
Fire: 102.

WORSHIP

SYNAGOGUES

Central (Ashkenazi) – Herzl St. Hadar Hacarmel.
Eliahu Hanavi (Ashkenazi) – 16 Sinai Blvd. Mt. Carmel.
Hechal Netanel (Sephardi) 43 Herzl St.
Moriah Congregation (Conservative) 7 Horev St. Ahuza.
Progressive Congregation 142 Hanassi Blvd. in Beit Rothschild.
Sha'ar Hashamayim – 8 Bialik St.

CHURCHES

Roman Catholic:
Catholic Church – 80 Hameginim Blvd.
Carmelite Monastery – Stella Maris Blvd.
Greek Catholic – 23 Ein Dor St.

Protestant:
Scandinavian Seamen's Church (Lutheran) – 43 Hagefen St.
St. Luke's (Anglican) 4 St. Luke St.

Bahai:
Bahai Shrine – Hazionut Blvd.

MOSQUE

El-Istanqlal Mosque – Faisal Square.

CULTURE

Haifa has a symphony orchestra which performs regularly, and a theatrical company said to be the best in Israel. There is also a cinematheque showing the best in serious film.

PLACES OF INTEREST

Bahai Shrine: Hazionut Blvd. The magnificent gold dome of the Shrine of the Bab is an unmistakable landmark in Haifa. The building houses the Mausoleum of the Bab (Mirza Ali Muhammed). It is part of a complex of monumental structures and gardens in Haifa and Akko which make up the World Centre of the Bahai faith. The Versailles-style gardens surrounding the building are beautifully kept. Visitors must be modestly dressed and smoking and eating are not allowed in the shrine or arcade. Cameras are forbidden in the shrine, open 9 a.m.–noon daily. The gardens can be explored from 8 a.m.–5 p.m. Tel. (04)358358.

(Bus Nos. 22, 23, 25, 26, Walk No. 3)

Bat Galim Cable Car: From the Stella Maris Carmelite Monastery on Mt. Carmel down to the Bat Galim Promenade and back. Operates Sun.–Thurs. 10 a.m.–5 p.m., Sat. 10 a.m.–6 p.m. Shorter hours in winter. Tel. (04)510509.

Beaches: Haifa has a string of municipal beaches, including Bat Galim, which has facilities for observant Jews.

(Bus Nos. 41, 42, 43, 44, 45)

Carmel National Park: Encompassing 22,000 acres, this area on the crown of Mt. Carmel is one on the beauty spots of Israel. Twenty-five recreationn areas provide facilities for picnics and fun. Although parts were destoyed by fire in 1989, the area is being replanted. It is easiest to travel to the park by car, but you can take a bus to Haifa University and then walk, or take buses 91 and 92.

Carmelite Monastery: Derekh Stella Maris. Principal sanctuary of the Discalced Carmelite Order. Cave associated with prophets Elijah and Elisha. Impressive church and small antiquities collection. Open daily 6 a.m.– 1.30 p.m., 3–6 p.m.

(Bus Nos. 25, 26)

Clandestine Immigration and Naval Museum: 204, Allenby Rd. opposite Elijah's Cave. Illegal immigrant ship, "Af-al-pi-khen," which ran British blockade, exhibited in grounds. Maps, mementos, dioramas, photographs and other exhibits of "illegals" period and modern navy. Also surrender flag of Egyptian frigate captured while shelling Haifa Bay in 1956. Open: Sun., Tues. 9 a.m.–4 p.m., Mon., Wed., Thurs. 9 a.m.–3 p.m. Fri. 9 a.m.–1 p.m. Sat. closed. Entrance fee. Tel. (04)536249.

(Bus Nos. 3, 5, 44, 45, 46, 47, 49 [direct].)

Dagon Silo Archaeological Grain Museum: Plumer Sq. by the port. The history of grain-handling and storage in ancient Israel, with working models. Guided tours every day except Sat. at 10.30 a.m. or by appointment. Open to public only at time of tour. Free. Tel. (04)664221.

(Bus Nos. 10, 12, 122, Walk No. 1)

Elijah's Cave: off Derekh Allenby, below Stella Maris lighthouse and Carmelite Monastery. Believed to be the resting place of the prophet before his encounter with the false prophets of Ba'al. Revered by Jews, Christians and Moslems. Christian tradition holds that the Holy Family sheltered here on return from Egypt. Jews of Oriental background gather here first Sunday after Tisha B'Av, recite Isaiah 40 and invoke the prophet's intercession to better their fate, cure their illnesses and bless their offspring. Open Sun.–Thurs 8 a.m.–4.45 p.m. in winter, 5.45 p.m. in summer. Fri. 8 a.m.–12 p.m. Tel. (04)527430.

(Bus Nos. 43, 44, 45, 49)

Gan Ha'em (Mother's Park): Central Carmel. Beautiful park and promenade with small zoo and Museum of Prehistory.

(Bus Nos. 21, 22, 23)

Haifa Museum of Ancient Art, Modern Art, Music and Ethnology: 26 Shabbetai Levi St. **Museum of Ancient Art**: archaeological collections of Mediterranean cultures from the beginning of history until the Islamic conquest in the 7th century CE. Outstanding collections of Graeco-Roman culture, Coptic art, painted portraits from Faiyum, rare collections from Israel – coins of Caesarea and Akko, terracottas of all periods. Antiquities of Haifa – finds from the Shiqmona excavations, and from the seabed. **Museum of Modern Art**: collection of paintings and sculptures of Israeli artists. Print cabinet: works of Israeli and foreign artists. A library and collection of slides and reproductions are open to the public. Lectures and projection of art films or slides are given in the evenings. **Museum of Music and Ethnology**: musical instruments (folk and classical). Coins and medals on musical subjects. Artefacts of Jewish ceremonial and folk art and ethnographic collections from all continents. Open: Sun.–Sat.

10 a.m.–1 p.m., Tues., Thurs. and Sat. also 5–8 p.m. Entrance fee. Tel. (04)523255.

(Bus Nos. 10, 12, 22, 23, 25, 26, 28)

Haifa University: Derekh Abba Khoushy, Mt. Carmel. Self-governing after nine years of tutelage by Hebrew University of Jerusalem. It is a liberal arts and social science oriented institution. At the Visitors' Centre, films are screened and explanatory talks are given. Visitors should ask to see the **Reuben and Edith Hecht Museum** and the two art galleries, one of which contains a unique collection of works by Jewish artists who perished in the Holocaust. Free guided tours Sun.–Thurs. 9 a.m.–12 noon or by arrangement including the Hecht Museum. The museums only are open on Sat 10 a.m.–1 p.m. Tel. (04)240111. (See Route No. 13).

(Bus Nos. 24, 36, 37, 37a, 92)

Israel Oil Industry Museum: Located in the Shemen oil factory in Kishon port area. Housed in the restored old "Atid" factory building, this museum shows ancient as well as more recent items connected with the edible oil industry in Israel. Open: Sun.–Thurs. 8.30 a.m. – 2.30 p.m. Tel. (04)670491, 670237.

(Bus No. 2)

Japanese Art Museum (Tikotin Museum of Japanese Art): 89 Hanassi Blvd. Central Carmel. Founded in 1959 through donation of private collection of Swiss citizen, this museum contains more than 6,000 items including drawings, prints, painted fabric screens, illuminated books, lacquerwork, statues and metalwork. Also Japanese rock garden. Temporarily closed. Tel. (04)383554.

(Bus Nos. 22, 23, 31, Walk No. 3)

Kababir: A village at the end of Kadima St. on Mt. Carmel populated by Moslems of the Ahmadiya sect, founded in India in 1889.

(Bus Nos. 9, 34)

Mané-Katz Museum: 89 Yefe Nof Street. Collection of Katz's works plus his chiefly Jewish antiques in the late artist's studio, which the Municipality has turned into a museum. Open: summer – Sun.–Thurs. 10 a.m. –1 p.m.,

4–6 p.m., Fri., Sat. 10 a.m.–1 p.m.; winter – Sun.–Thurs. 10 a.m.–3 p.m., Fri., Sat. 10 a.m.–1 p.m. Entrance free. Tel. (04)383482.

(Bus Nos. 22, 23, 31. Walk No. 3)

National Maritime Museum: 198, Derekh Allenby. Display of 5,000 years of maritime history, including Egyptian, Phoenician, Jewish, Greek, Roman, medieval and modern seafaring. Special sections deal with marine mythology; ancient anchors; coins; fish and dolphins in art; scientific instruments; amphoras; the Mediterranean, its islands and ports; cartography, marine philately; naval battles; marine ethnology. Specialized library. (6000 volumes.) Open: Sun.–Thurs. 10 a.m.–4 p.m., Sat. 10 a.m.–1 p.m. Fri. closed. Entrance fee (includes entrance to six Haifa museums). Tel. (04) 536622.

(Bus Nos. 3, 5, 43, 44)

National Museum of Science, Design and Technology: Balfour St., in the old Technion campus. Focus is on the secrets of science and technology and the advances of Israeli science-based industry. Open: Mon., Wed., Thurs. 9 a.m.–5 p.m. Tues. 9 a.m.–7 p.m. Fri. 9 a.m.–1 p.m. Sat 10 a.m.–2 p.m.

(Bus Nos. 12, 21, 28, 37)

Panorama Observation Points: Along Yefe Nof (Panorama) St., where it is possible to see the city and its bay, Akko, Rosh Haniqra and sometimes Mt. Hermon. Also Gan Ha'em (see above) and Bat Galim along the waterfront. Wilhelm's Obelisk, where Kaiser Wilhelm observed a majestic view of Haifa in 1898, is along the Yefe Nof Panorama.

Prehistory Museum (Stekelis Museum of Prehistory): 124 Hatishbi St. on Central Carmel, entrance through Gan Ha'em. Palaeolithic artefacts and finds from the Carmel Caves. Open: Sun.–Thurs. 8 a.m.–3 p.m., Sat. 10 a.m.–2 p.m. Tel. (04)371833.

(Bus Nos. 3, 5, 20, 21, 22, 23, 28, 31, 37)

Railway Museum: in the old East Railway Station, Derekh Ha'atzmaut. Documents and artefacts connected with the railways since their inception in 1882, as well as two diesel locomotives from the '50s, three cabooses and five passenger and cargo cars. Open: Sun., Tues., Thurs. 9 a.m.–12 noon. Entrance fee. Tel. (04)564293.

(Bus Nos. 41, 42)

Reuben and Edith Hecht Museum: Main building, Haifa University, Mt. Carmel. Archaeological exhibits on the theme of "The People of Israel in the Land of Israel." Art wing with exhibition on "Impressionism and the Jewish School of Paris." Open Sun.–Thurs. 10 a.m.–4 p.m., Fri. 10 a.m.–1 p.m., Sat. 10 a.m.–2 p.m. Tel. (04)240577. Entrance free.

(Bus Nos. 24, 36, 37, 37a, 93)

Sculpture Garden (Gan Hapesalim): Opposite 135 Hazionut St. A public garden overlooking Haifa Bay, which features eighteen bronze statues by Ursula Malbin.

Shiqmona: An archaeological site (tel) south of Haifa on the coast below Carmel Cape. Buildings from King Solomon's time down to the second century BCE Seleucid period have been uncovered, as well as a mosaic now on display in the Museum of Ancient Art. The tel is named after the shikma (sycamore) tree that once grew in this area.

(Bus No. 42)

Technion (Israel Institute of Technology): Neve Sha'an, Mt. Carmel. Israel's world-renowned Institute of Technology offers degrees in engineering, science, architecture and town-planning, medicine and other subjects. The largest research centre in the country and Israel's first university. More than 100 buildings on a 300 acre campus. Among them are the Churchill Auditorium, dedicated by Anglo-Jewry and friends of Sir Winston Churchill and Ohel Aharon (Tent of Aaron) campus synagogue with Galilean marble and roof in shape of inverted pyramid. View of Mt. Hermon on a clear day. Information and slide show at Coler-California Visitors' Reception Centre. Open: Sun.–Thurs. 8 a.m.–2 p.m. with 20 minute film every hour until 1 p.m. Fri. 8 a.m.–noon. Tel. (04)293863.

(Bus Nos. 17, 19, 31)

Zoo: Educational zoo in Gan Ha'em on Central

Carmel. Open: Sun.–Thurs. 8 a.m.–4 p.m.; Fri. 8 a.m.–1 p.m., Sat. 9 a.m.–4 p.m. In July and August, Sun.–Thurs. 8 a.m.–6 p.m. Entrance fee. Tel. (04) 377019.

(Bus No. 27)

WALKS IN HAIFA

WALK No. 1 – DEREKH HA'ATZMAUT

Start the walk at Kikar Paris, the town terminus of the Carmelit, Haifa's underground railway, to **Derekh Ha'atzmaut**, where you turn left.

Derekh Ha'atzmaut is an active, lively street, often filled with the passengers of a cruise ship stopping for a few hours. Here, the shops do not take a noon-time break but remain open until 3 or 4 p.m. At night, it becomes a popular sailors' area.

Derekh Ha'atzmaut reflects the dual nature of Haifa's port area. When the port area was constructed, land was reclaimed from the sea and the shaded office buildings lining the left (northeast) side of Derekh Ha'atzmaut were erected. The right (southwest) side of Derekh Ha'atzmaut has both new buildings and older buildings pre-dating the port, going back to when this was the waterfront street of Haifa.

Derekh Yafo, one block before Derekh Ha'atzmaut, reflects the waterfront atmosphere with its many small shops, oriental cafes and restaurants.

At **Sha'ar Palmer** (Palmer's Gate) look northeast towards the **harbour**. It is possible to visit the harbour on presentation of a passport. While the harbour itself does not have proper facilities for visitors, Ogen Boat Tours operate launch tours of the harbour in spring, which give a fascinating seaside view of the city on the Carmel.

Back on Derekh Ha'atzmaut, a few minutes' walk brings you to **Kikar Plumer**. Overhead, a ramp leads directly to the passenger shed in the port. The old West Railway Station linking Haifa with Tel Aviv, Jerusalem, Beer Sheva, Akko, Nahariyya, etc., is also located here. The new Railway Station is near the Egged Central Bus Station in Bat Galim, further west.

Just past Kikar Plumer you come to the dominating **Dagon Silo** on the right. The Silo houses an archaeological collection illustrating grain storage and handling since prehistoric times. The activities of this most up-to-date Silo are explained by means of electromechanical models. (See "Places of Interest".)

Back on Derekh Ha'atzmaut, turn left into Rehov Salesian, then right into Derekh Yafo and follow this street to Sderot Ben-Gurion. There turn left on the pleasant boulevard lined with red-roofed stone houses of the old "German Colony."

Further up, turn into Rehov Hagefen till you get to Rehov Shabbetai Levi and the new museum centre at No. 26. Retrace your steps to Sderot Ben-Gurion. Unless you are exceptionally fit, and feel able to climb these steps, this is where your walk around Haifa's port ends. (See the Bahai Shrine on Walk No. 3.)

You can take bus no. 44 and visit **Elijah's Cave**, and the **Maritime Museum** and the **Clandestine Immigration and Naval Museum**. All of them are near the western entrance to the city.

WALK No. 2 – HADAR HACARMEL

If the port area is the commercial heart of Haifa, **Hadar HaCarmel** is the shopping and cultural centre of the city. Nestling halfway up Mt. Carmel, it boasts fine shops, cafes, cinemas, theatres, museums, etc.

Start the walk at **Kikar Masaryk** on Rehov Hanevi'im. It can be reached by taking the Carmelit subway to the Hanevi'im station or by taking a bus to "Armon." This area is popularly called "Armon" after the large cinema of that name just north of Kikar Masaryk.

Turn into Rehov Shabbetai Levi and visit the Haifa Museum Centre at No. 26.

Return to Rehov Hanevi'im and proceed northeastwards. There are crowds of people, numerous cafes, cinemas and kiosks. Many local and suburban buses have their terminal in the area. If you haven't yet tasted a felafel, the Israeli "hot dog" substitute made from fried balls of chick peas soaked in spices and vegetables and eaten in a pita (a sort of flat roll), this could be an opportunity to do so. Arab sweetmeats, too, are found in this part of town, which is only a few streets away from an Arab quarter.

Walk downhill on **Rehov Hanevi'im**, as far as **Kikar Solel Boneh**. This 15-storey "skyscraper" on the left houses the Haifa offices of Solel Boneh, the Labour

Federation's industrial complex. Opposite Solel Boneh Building is the new Hanevi'im Tower Shopping Mall with boutiques, restaurants and cafes. Turn right, into Rehov Hassan Shukri, which soon brings you to the pleasant **Gan Hazikaron** with an observation point enabling you to look down at the port below and out over the Bay of Haifa and the Plain of Zebulun. Opposite is the **City Hall**.

Passing the City Hall, turn right at the corner into Rehov Bialik.

Walk (southwest) along Rehov Bialik to Rehov Hekhalutz. Turn left onto **Rehov Hekhalutz** in a southwesterly direction. Rehov Hekhalutz, and Rehov Herzl, one block above the former, are popular shopping centres. Rehov Herzl is more elegant and expensive than the other.

Reaching the corner of Rehov Hekhalutz and Rehov Bilu, turn right, go one block uphill and turn right into **Rehov Herzl**.

Walking along Rehov Herzl in a northwesterly direction, you will see Haifa's **Great Synagogue** on the left. A block past the synagogue is the intersection of three streets. Turn left into **Rehov Arlosoroff**. **Gan Binyamin** is on the right.

Retrace your steps along **Rehov Arlosoroff** to **Rehov Mikhael** and turn left into the latter, which leads to **Gan Binyamin**. Above the garden stands the **Haifa Municipal Theatre**, a fine structural achievement. Leave by the lower end of the garden, turn left into **Rehov Nordau** (which is being converted into a pedestrian mall), and walk in a northwesterly direction. Rehov Nordau, now the main shopping street of Hadar HaCarmel, has a number of fine shops, shaded by trees. One more block to the north (lower down the hill) is Rehov Herzl, previously the main shopping street of the area. Pedestrian lanes connect the two streets. Walk down one of them to Rehov Herzl, and continue along the latter, walking left, to **Rehov Balfour**. There you cross by way of the underground passage to **Bet Hakranot** – the large block of shops, cafes, etc., the heart of Hadar. Here you will also find the premises of the Government Tourist Office.

Walk along Rehov Balfour, climbing steeply up the mountain to the **Technion** – the Israel Institute of Technology – on the right. This is the "old" Technion which was originally built in 1912. It was the first structure erected in Hadar HaCarmel but was not used for this purpose until 1925. Today it is called the "old" Technion to distinguish it from the "new" Technion City on Mt. Carmel. The former is also the National Museum of Science and Technology.

Retracing your steps on Rehov Balfour to the corner of Rehov Herzl, downhill this time, turn left at Bet Hakranot and walk along Rehov Herzl. You soon reach Kikar Masaryk where this walk began.

WALK No. 3 – GAN HA'EM, SCULPTURE GARDEN AND BAHAI SHRINE (down Mt. Carmel on the west side)

There are two particularly well-known sights in Haifa: the first, the view of the city, bay, hills and valleys as seen from the crest of Mt. Carmel; the second, the lovely gardens of the Bahai Shrine and the golden-domed shrine itself. This walk includes both.

The walk starts at the highest station of the Carmelit, Gan Ha'em, on Mt. Carmel. Start by visiting **Gan Ha'em** (Mother's Park), next to the Carmelit's exit. The park contains a **Zoo**, and the **Museum of Prehistory** (Opposite Gan Ha'em is the Panorama Tower with its chic shopping mall and coffee-shops.)

After visiting Gan Ha'em and its museums, walk to **Sderot Hanasi** (Weizmann Blvd.), the main street of the neighbourhood, where the Carmelit exit is located. Walk towards the crest of Mt. Carmel, in a northeasterly direction. Sderot Hanasi turns left, but continue straight ahead, following **Sha'ar Halevanon** until you come to **Rehov Yefe Nof** (Panorama Road), which runs along the ridge of the hills affording a lovely view of Haifa, the bay, the plain of Zebulun and the hills of Galilee. Turn to the left, and you will come to observation points with extensive views. Visit the **Mane Katz Museum** at 89, Yefe Nof.

Pass the Dan Carmel Hotel, with its "Rondo" restaurant. On **Rehov Daphna** turn left and walk up to Sderot Hanasi. Turn left and at No. 89 you come to the **Museum of Japanese Art**.

Leaving the museum, follow Sderot Hanasi downhill and, reaching its end, turn right. Walking downhill again, turn right on Sderot HaZionut, and walk down to No. 135 and the beautiful **Sculpture Garden** overlooking Haifa Bay and from there continue down to the **Bahai Shrine** and gardens, one of the showpieces of Haifa.

The gardens extend above and below the road, with the golden dome of the shrine in the lower part, and the Parthenon-like Bahai Archives in the upper part. Geometrically landscaped gardens surround the two buildings, creating a world of their own, serenely remote, encouraging meditation.

The Bahai Shrine houses the remains of the Bab Mirza Ali Muhammad, who was executed by the Persian authorities in 1850 after declaring himself a prophet of the new religion (see "About Israel – Religions"). The interior is a small room adorned with fine carpets, tapestries and crystalware (you must remove your shoes before entering). The gold shingles of the dome were donated by Bahai believers from all over the world.

After arriving at the eastern end of the Bahai Gardens, take the first turn left into **Rehov Shifra**. This leads to a flight of stairs which goes downhill to Rehov Abbas. Turn right at Rehov Abbas, then left at the first turning into Rehov Haparsim, leading to Rehov Hagefen. The new museum complex is nearby. Less than a block away is the Arab-Jewish Cultural Centre at 2, Rehov Hagefen. Follow Hagefen for two blocks west to Sderot Ben-Gurion; turn right and walk to the German Colony.

WALK No. 4 – DOWN MT. CARMEL TO THE CENTRE

Exploring Mt. Carmel is not as difficult as it may seem – if you walk down the steps cut into the mountainside. This walk "downstairs" provides a quick and interesting cross-section of the city. (There is nothing to stop the energetic walker from doing this walk in the other direction.)

Start from the Gan Ha'em station of the **Carmelit** underground train on Mt. Carmel. Leave the station and turn left, north; walk downhill to **Rehov Yefe Nof (Panorama).** It is so called since it runs along the edge of Mt. Carmel, affording a breathtaking view of the city below, its harbour, and the surrounding plains and mountains. This view is one of the highlights of a Haifa tour, and should not be missed, either by day or by night.

Turn right and walk along this street until you see a flight of stairs on the left, called **Madregot Gedera**, where the descent of the mountain begins. There are no hand rails, so be careful.

At the bottom, turn right into **Rehov Hahashmonaim** and then left again into **Sderot Wingate**, past Bet Harofeh and Rothschild Hospital, and down **Madregot Spinoza. Bet Harofeh** houses Haifa's Medical Assocation, located at 2, Sderot Wingate.

Madregot Spinoza descends past **Rehov Hess** and **Rehov Bar Giora**, leading to Rehov Arlosoroff and to the top of **Rehov Balfour**. Follow the latter downhill and in a few minutes you reach the **Old Technion**. Continue as far as the intersection of Rehov Balfour and Rehov Herzl, in the centre of **Hadar HaCarmel**.

If you are still not tired and want to continue all the way down, turn left into **Rehov Herzl** and walk to **Rehov Hanevi'im;** following it downhill, pass **Kikar Solel Boneh** to **Madregot Hanevi'im**. Follow the stairs past a turn until they lead to **Kikar HaHagana**. Here turn right into **Rehov Hiat** (Khayat) which leads to **Palmer's Gate**, the entrance to the port.

Tours from Haifa

ROUTE No. 13 (Map: Northern Sheet G6 to H7 and H6)

The hills of Carmel

Haifa – "Little Switzerland" (7km.) – Isfiya (13 km.) – Daliyat el-Carmel (16 km.) – Mukhraka (21 km.) – Nesher (41km.) – Haifa (44 km.) (Road Nos. 672, 721.)

(Distances in brackets refer to start of route.)

No time limit can be set on this outing as you may wish to spend between a few hours and a full day motoring into the many shaded picnic spots and observation points atop the **Carmel** range.

Assuming that you start the route just after **Gan Ha'em** in the **Central Carmel**, drive uphill along **Sderot Moriah**, past villas and flats with individual character. Follow the bends of this wide thoroughfare into **Rehov Horev** which passes through the suburb of **Ahuza**.

It then leads straight into **Derekh Abba Khoushy** (Road No. 672), where the sea soon comes into view on the right hand side.

If you intend visiting the **Technion – Israel Institute of Technology,** turn left into Rehov Dr. Biram just before the

Sonol gas station on your left. Dr. Biram leads into Rehov International. Then turn right into Rehov Borochov, right into Rehov Malal and arrive at the gates of this scientific centre.

The **Haifa University** campus is 1 km. after the Sonol station, along Derekh Abba Khoushy. And once more, along this stretch, you pass by many luxurious villas.

Just before the turn-off to the Nesher Cement Works, and immediately in front of the tall radio antenna, there are two roads leading right. The first of these leads to some of the most scenic views on the Carmel, in an area justifiably dubbed "**Little Switzerland**." Here you can soak in all the virgin purity of the **Carmel woods**. The road weaves and turns, offering many choice picnic sites.

The second turn right off the main road leads to a picnic area complete with log tables and benches.

At a point 2 km. past the Nesher turn-off, the road (No. 721) forks right to **Kibbutz Bet Oren** and its popular Guest House.

If you want to visit the artists' village at **En Hod** (see Route No. 12), take the left fork on the way to Bet Oren, pass the ancient Roman quarry, and 5 km. later you are at the bottom of the Carmel where a signpost directs you (left, and, after a km., left again) to the village close by.

From the turn-off to Bet Oren it is only 4 km. to the first of all the Druze villages, **Isfiya**.

Many centuries ago there was a village populated by Jews at this site but it was destroyed by the Crusaders. It is easy to see why people have always yearned to live here. Isfiya overlooks the Jezreel Valley from a height that provides a bird's-eye view of the terrain.

The **Druze** (see "Communities") are renowned for their warm hospitality, and if you stop to ask one of these villagers for directions you may be invited into his home for some Turkish coffee.

Drive on for 3 km. to the second Druze village on the mountain, **Daliyat el-Carmel**. This resembles Isfiya in nearly every respect except that the main street has a number of shops selling Druze handicrafts. These include straw baskets, chairs and tables, multi-coloured carpets and jewellery. Friday is the day of rest and all shops are closed.

The road travels up and over the hilly region and 2 km. later forks left to Muhraka. There is a parking lot 3 km. further on, at the top of the mountain.

Muhraka, or **Keren Carmel**, is believed to be the site on Mt. Carmel where Elijah the Prophet triumphed over the prophets of Baal, only to incur the wrath of Jezebel (1 Kings 18:20–46, 19:1–3). The **Carmelite Monastery of St. Elijah**, built in 1883, is located here, 482 m. above sea level. There is a magnificent view of the Jezreel Valley and the area around Mt. Carmel from the roof of the monastery. Open: daily 8 – 11.45 a.m., 1 – 4.45 p.m. Fri. 8 – 11.45 a.m.

Return to the main road (No. 672) and backtrack as far as the turn-off to the **Nesher Cement Works** to the right.

When you drive down this winding road it is advisable to change into low gear as the descent is steep.

At various points along the road you will drive under the giant metal cups being hauled by pulley up and down Mt. Carmel, from the quarries to the Nesher plant below. This route back to Haifa also provides superlative views of the Zebulun Valley and the bay area. From Nesher it is a few minutes' drive back to Haifa, through its southeastern suburbs on Road No. 75.

ROUTE No. 14 (Map: Northern Sheet G6 to J3 and L4)

Western Galilee

Haifa – Akko (24 km.) – Nahariyya (34 km.) – Rosh Haniqra (44 km.) – Peqi'in (107 km.) – Yehiam (124 km.) – Haifa 176 km.) (Road Nos. 4, 899, 864, 89, 70, 85, 8833.)

(Distances in brackets refer to start of route.)

This route circles the western section of the Galilee and is considered by many to be the most beautiful part of Israel. There are afforestation and land reclamation schemes in this mountainous region. There are also throwbacks to history, with Crusader castles and vine-clustered villages inhabited by Jews, Moslems and Druze. It is a day-long trip.

Getting out of Haifa on the road to Akko is quick and trouble-free. Drive onto **Derekh Ha'atzmaut** – the road along which stands the fortress-like **Dagon Silo**. Then drive southeast (on Road No. 75) to the large junction **Tzomet HaQeriyot** with a signpost pointing left for Akko (Road No. 4).

Very soon you cross the **Kishon River**, where Barak defeated the Canaanites in the time of Deborah the Prophetess (Judges 4:12–13).

The road to Akko is dull from a tourist's point of view as it is hemmed in by industrial premises and uninspiring blocks of flats.

There is no chance to see the graceful curve of the Haifa Bay area or to appreciate the fertility of the **Zebulun Valley** through which you are driving. But the return part of the trip affords countless opportunities for such views from higher ground.

Pass by **Kfar Masaryk** (15 km. from the junction), a kibbutz founded by Czech immigrants and named after the first president of that country.

Akko comes into focus when you drive near some very tall and slender palm trees. The oblong shape of the Turkish Khan el-Umdan streaks above the skyline. Fork left for the Old City of Akko.

AKKO (ACRE) (Map: H5)

Time is trapped and beauty captured for posterity in Akko, where the Mediterranean waves break against the solid city walls. When you walk along these 18th century parapets you look down on a cluster of spired minarets and bubbly mosques, and a nest of churches, all appearing to float above the indigo blue sea.

Secreted within the walled perimeter is a labyrinth of alleys and winding streets. The smells of the bazaars mix with the sea air. The shouts of children punctuate the steady stream of market music.

This is Akko, city of a thousand sensations. It is the most dramatic leftover of history in all Israel because its allure extends underground to the restored **Crusader City.** This holds all the colour of the Middle Ages. Rambling through its cool and musty-smelling rooms you feel the strength of the hefty pillars and vaulted roofs that characterize their fervid builders.

The **Mosque of Ahmad Jazzar** is the most beautiful in Israel outside of Jerusalem, while the **Citadel-Museum of Heroism** brings you face to face with the gallows on which Jews were hanged during the British Mandate.

Akko (Acre)

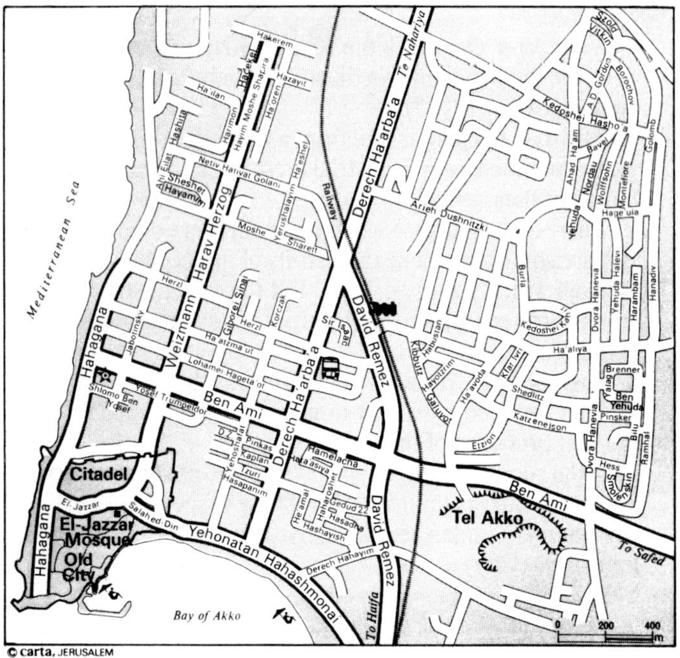

Location: Akko is a promontory on the northern end of Haifa Bay, 24 km. from Haifa and 20 km. south of the Lebanese frontier. It lies on the border between Upper and Lower Galilee.

Climate: pleasant breezes from the sea and the Galilean mountains relieve the summer heat. Winter is wet and damp rather than cold.

Population: About 40,000, of whom a quarter are Moslems, Druze, Christians and Bahais.

Tourist Information Office: El-Jazar Street, tel. (04)911764.

History

Akko was for long a Canaanite city, just east of the present Old City. It was conquered by several pharaohs but the Israelite invaders from the tribe of Asher failed to dislodge the inhabitants and it remained a Phoenician city (Judges 1:3).

It fell to Sennacherib, the Assyrian, and after the Persian conquest it was used as a naval base in the campaigns against the Egyptians.

It was during Ptolemaic rule that its name was changed to Ptolemais, by which it was known right up until the Arab conquest.

With the Roman conquest of Palestine it became a port, being used as a base by Vespasian in his Galilean campaigns.

Christians lived in Akko soon after the crucifixion and St. Paul landed here on returning from Tyre (Acts 21:7). About 2,000 Jews were butchered in the city at the outbreak of the war against the Romans, but they returned after the conflict and have lived here almost continuously ever since.

Akko fell to the Persians, the Byzantines and eventually the Moslems in 636.

When Baldwin I, assisted by the Genoese fleet, captured Akko in 1104, it became the headquarters of the Knights of St. Jean and was revived as an important commercial centre. They lost it to Saladin but Richard the Lion-Heart joined in its capture in 1191 when, known as **St. Jean d'Acre**, it became the capital of the Crusader kingdom.

Exactly 100 years later the Mamelukes seized it amid a bloody slaughter of the Christian and Jewish populations.

Not until the period of Ottoman rule did Akko recover from its forsaken state to enter a glorious era under the governorship of Pasha Ahmad Jazzar (1775–1804). He built the outer city walls, the majestic mosque that bears his name, and the bath-house in which the modern museum is located.

During this period, in 1799, the defences of Akko withstood a two-month siege by Napoleon, who was considerably weakened after the British fleet captured his siege guns. The stand at Akko thwarted his hopes of an eastern empire.

Akko began to lose importance with the growth of Haifa port, especially as the latter had deeper waters.

The Turks lifted the ban on building outside the Old City when, at the turn of the century, they allowed a new suburb to be developed in the north. After the War of Independence, another new quarter was built east of the Old City.

Akko was notorious during the British Mandate when Jewish underground fighters were held in the citadel. Some were hanged here. It mada international headlines when Jewish commandos breached its walls in 1947.

The city fell to the Israelis two days after the proclamation of the State of Israel.

Today it is the world centre (together with Haifa) of the **Bahai** faith; it also has a number of Roman Catholic and Maronite churches, in addition to mosques and synagogues.

With the re-opening of the subterranean Crusader City and its enduring charm as a fishing harbour, Akko is thriving as a tourist mecca. And its new marina can only attract more visitors.

The Israel Fringe Theatre Festival takes place here during Succot (Sept./Oct.). Most of the performances for a fee are in Hebrew. The Vocalisa (Vocal Music Festival) takes place during Passover (April).

Places of Interest

Bahai Gardens (El Bahja): Located just beyond the northern outskirts of Akko are the imposing formal gardens which surround the central shrine of the Bahai world, the building housing the remains of the founder of the faith, Bahaullah. The building is the focal point of the worldwide Bahai community which now numbers some five million adherents. Visitors must be modestly dressed; smoking and eating are not allowed in the shrine or its precincts. Photographs may be taken in the gardens, but not within the shrine itself. The building is open on Friday, Saturday, Sunday, and Monday from 9 a.m. until noon, and the gardens from 9 a.m. to 4 p.m. every day. Tel. (04) 358358.

Bazaar: narrow, winding streets of the Old City; interesting shops and stalls. Open on working days.

Burj es-Sultan: Crusader watchtower. Contains guardroom and dungeon. There is a restaurant here.

Citadel – Museum of Heroism: built by Jazzar Pasha in 1785 on Crusader foundations. Top-security prison under British Mandatory authorities. Museum commemorating

Jewish freedom fighters imprisoned here by British. Museum includes original death cell with red garments of condemned men, gallows, and photographic display recalling mass break-out in 1947. Open: 9 a.m. – 5 p.m. Fri. and eve of holidays 9 a.m. – 12 p.m. Entrance fee.

City Walls: access to top by steps near Law Courts. Old cannons stand in position. Spectacular view of Mount Carmel and Haifa, Galilee and Old City.

Fishing Harbour: remains of Crusader harbour. Boats for hire and boat tours. Tourist arcade with shops, galleries and restaurants opposite pier. Diving centre and boat ride along the walls of Akko.

Khan el-Franj: called "Franks' Inn," having served European merchants during Turkish rule. Original mediaeval gate still standing. Seventeenth century St. Francis Monastery located here.

Khan el-Umdan (Inn of Columns): built in 1785 as a caravanserai. Plans to turn it into tourist hotel. Soaring clocktower built in 1906.

Mosque of Ahmad Jazzar: built in 1781 on ruins of the Cathedral of the Holy Cross. Most beautiful mosque in the Galilee. Box in fenced-off area upstairs contains hairs of beard of prophet Mohammed, shown to public only on 27th day of month of Ramadan. Tombs of Ahmad Jazzar and Suleiman Pasha outside. Sun-dial in garden. Recently opened underground water reservoir. Open: daily 8 a.m.-12.30 p.m., 1 – 3.30 p.m., 4 – 7.30 p.m. Entrance fee.

Subterranean Crusader City: entrance opposite Mosque of Ahmad Jazzar. Includes magnificent examples of Crusader architecture; entrance halls, Knights' Halls, Grand Manoir, Crypt, tunnel and Al-Bosta. Also, display of mediaeval columns, capitals and tombstones. Open: Sun. – Thurs. 8.30 a.m. – 4.45 p.m. Fri. 8.30 a.m. – 1.45 p.m. Sat. 8.30 a.m., – 4.45 p.m. Entrance fee includes a visit to the Turkish Bath.

Tel Akko: Canaanite city east of the present town. Crusaders called the tel "Toron." From this hill Napoleon shelled Akko in 1799, so it is also known as "Napoleon's

Hill". Archaeological finds from the Bronze Age and on.

Turkish Bath (formerly Municipal Museum): in 18th century former Turkish bath-house built by Ahmad Jazzar. Contains relics from the region dating back to Canaanite times. Also exhibits illustrating Arab and Druze folklore. Pillars, floor and part of elevated seating in former steam room are covered with Roman marble from Caesarea and Tyre. Open: Sat. – Thurs. 8.30 a.m. – 4.45 p.m. Fri. 8.30 a.m. – 1.45 p.m. Entrance through subterranean Crusader City.

A Walk In Old Akko

The massive walls surrounding the Old City enclose bygone eras and all the main sites to see in Akko. Our recommended walking tour will take about three hours to complete, including ample time to browse through the museums.

Enter the Old City on **Rehov Ben-Ami**, and, from it, **Rehov Weizmann**. There is a parking lot at the end of Rehov Weizmann.

The Mosque of **Ahmad Jazzar,** on your left, is typical of the style of the Ottomans towards the end of the 18th century. Beautifully decorated with blue and brown murals inside, it has wall-to-wall Persian carpeting. The women's galleries are upstairs, on either side of the building. In the yard of the mosque you can see the underground water reservoir.

On leaving the Mosque compound, cross the street and enter the restored subterranean **Crusader City** by going through the gates of a former Turkish building. These cool and vaulted rooms were crafted by the Crusaders and used by them as their living quarters and administrative centre before and after they made Akko the capital of their Holy Kingdom.

The entrance halls are a mixture of architectural styles, with Turkish structures built on top of the Crusader bases. Descend a few steps to another hall. The upper arches of Crusader columns that protrude from the floor show that it is about four metres above the original Crusader level.

Move to the **Knights' Halls**, intact for more than 700 years. This was the fortress of the **Hospitallers**, the Order of the Knights of St. John. One of the halls down here is used periodically for concerts and entertainment.

The ceiling of the hall next to this has a patch of concrete. This was covered up during district excavations and marks the same spot where Jews, imprisoned in the Akko Citadel by the British in 1947, tunnelled through. At that time the hall was filled with rubble. The prisoners escaped later by more daring means.

A gate situated directly opposite the entrance to the Knights' Halls leads to more halls that were known in the mediaeval period as the **Grand Manoir**. This was an administrative centre.

A passage descends to the lowest level of the fortress and to the famous **Crypt**. It was given this name because of its unusual depth. This spacious hall actually served as a dining room and ceremonial reception hall. Tradition holds that Marco Polo was received here during a stopover on his historic voyage to China. Four entry gates on three sides of the hall point to the key location of the Crypt within the fortress.

You have to lower your head now for a walk through the 65 m. long narrow **tunnel** that the Crusaders used in times of emergency. It connected the fortress with the open quarters of the Knights of St. John at a place called **Al-Bosta**. This may have been a hospital or an assembly place for pilgrims. Its six halls feature cylindrical cross-vaulted roofs and gates that open on one side only. Near the exit you will see a display of some of the finds made by the excavators, including a 13th century tombstone, Latin text on marble and many fragments of Crusader capitals and columns.

Follow the signposts to the **Municipal Museum** close by. Located in an opulent, 18th century former Turkish bath-house, the museum contains relics of this region dating back to Canaanite times. The pillars, floor and part of the elevated seating are covered with Roman marble, brought here by Jazzar Pasha from Caesarea and Tyre.

Out in the open air again, walk back past the Great Mosque, veer right and then left and walk straight down past the shops. The grandiose stone steps leading up to the top of the walls are on the left of the **Law Courts**. The **walls** date back to Da'hr el-Omar and Jazzar Pasha, both of the 18th century. From one side you get a kaleidoscopic view of Haifa Bay, from the other you see **Tel Akko** (Napoleon's Hill) and the Galilee. Note the huge ammunition stores and shooting posts on one corner known as **Burj el-Commandar**.

Return to the Law Courts and turn left. Facing you is the old, enormous **city gate**, strengthened with bolts.

To continue our walk, turn back and take the second turning on the left to the **Khan e-Shawarda**. This is a courtyard surrounded by workshops. When Akko was conquered by the Mamelukes in 1291, this was the site of a convent of Franciscan sisters. Tradition says they preferred suicide to dishonour when the city was conquered.

Opposite, on your left, is **Burj es-Sultan**, the last of the Crusader watchtowers still standing at its original height. The ground floor is now a nightclub; the building contains a guardroom and a dungeon where prisoners were confined. It was surrounded by water on three sides when it was built. The reclaimed area dates back to the Turks, when the walls were completed.

If you continue walking along the walls you will arrive at the **fishing harbour**. You can take a boat ride along the walls. Turn right and then left to get to the most graceful complex of buildings in Akko. This is the **Khan el-Umdan** (Inn of Columns). The original shape of this spacious inn has been preserved. The granite columns that surround the courtyard of the caravanserai were brought from Caesarea. The rectangular **clock tower**, built in 1906, soars over the Khan, and if you walk up the spiral stairs to the top you will get a breathtaking view of the spires and domes of the Old City below.

Exit from the Khan on the side opposite the clocktower and continue right along the sea wall. **Abu Christo's** seafood restaurant is on your left. This is a good place to stop, select a live lobster in the kitchen, and have a meal a few metres from the sea and the ruins of the Crusader port.

There is a new tourist centre at the Pisan Port.

Continue north along the sea wall, passing by craftsmen fashioning copper and other metals in their shops. The **lighthouse** and **St. John's Church**, built on Crusader foundations, are on your left. Notice the remains (under the lighthouse) of a fortress with storage space for weapons and ammunition.

Our walk leads along the western wall lining the Mediterranean. On the right are Arab houses and street scenes that are almost biblical in their simplicity.

A few minutes from the lighthouse is the **Citadel – Museum of Heroism** that dominates the entire city. Built in 1785 by Jazzar Pasha on Crusader foundations, this fortress was used by the British Mandatory authorities as a top-security prison. Many Jews who fought for the liberation of Israel in pre-State days were imprisoned here. The mass break-out in 1947 brought the fortress international publicity.

The Citadel is now a museum to commemorate the Jewish freedom-fighters and their exploits. The most poignant scene is the death cell, where we can see the red garments worn by the condemned men. Nearby, are the original gallows, with a frayed noose and an open trapdoor.

You will be led to the rooftop of the fortress. The view from here is unsurpassed anywhere in Akko. You can see as far as the border with Lebanon, south to Haifa and Mount Carmel and far into the Galilee.

From the Citadel you can either retrace your steps or cut across the city through the maze of alleys, taking in the sounds of the Orient and the squeezed **bazaars** that are so colourful and so uniquely Akko.

In the summer you can enjoy the lovely beaches of Akko. Recommended: the Argaman beach, located on the road to Haifa. Akko has a song festival in April and a theatre festival in October.

Return to the main road (No. 4) and turn left for Nahariyya. Pass by some squalid-looking flats, cross the railway line, and soon arrive at the ornate, wrought-iron gates of the **Bahai Gardens**. Entry is through the second gate, a few seconds' drive north, to your right.

The founder of the Bahai faith, Baha'u'llah, lived and died here. His shrine is adjacent to the mansion. As with the Bahai Shrine in Haifa, this holy place is surrounded by clipped lawns, trees and gardens with Versailles-like dimensions. It is open to the public on Sun., Mon., Fri., Sat. 9 a.m. – 12 noon. Admission free.

Drive on for a couple of kilometres and turn right into the grounds of **Kibbutz Lohamei HaGhettaot** ("The Ghetto Fighters"). Founded in 1949 by survivors from the Jewish ghettos in Nazi-occupied Poland and Lithuania, the kibbutz maintains a museum dedicated to the Holocaust and Jewish Resistance. The galleries contain many photographs that speak for themselves, and models of ghettos and concentration camps. The museum is also the repository of many paintings and sculptures by Jewish artists who languished in concentration camps. Tel. (04) 820412.

Open: Sun. – Thurs. 9 a.m. – 4 p.m. Fri. 9 a.m. – 1 p.m. Sat. 10 a.m. – 5 p.m. There is a buffet close by. Admission free.

An amphitheatre adjacent to the museum looks down on the **aqueduct** built by Ahmad Jazzar to bring the Kabri spring waters to Akko.

Drive on two kilometres and leave the main road at Regba. Passing between this moshav and the Arab village Mazra'a, four kilometres on through avocado orchards, you'll reach the kibbutz-like settlement **Nes Ammim**. It was founded in the 60s by Christians, who wished to develop a new relationship between Christians and the Jews of Israel, based on trust, respect and solidarity.

Europeans and Americans work together, and take part in a study programme about current events in Israel and the relations between Christians and Jews. Visitors can receive a basic explanation about Nes Ammim and can see one of the biggest rose-growing enterprises in Israel. People with more time can take part in the learning-activities of the village, which has a three star guest house.

Continue to Nahariyya, passing by the moshav shitufi and rest resort of **Shavei Ziyyon** ("Those who return to Zion").

Enter **Nahariyya**, 10 km. north of Akko, either by crossing the road and the railway line and driving through the southern suburbs, or by turning left at the traffic light on the main road ahead.

NAHARIYYA (Map: H4)

The slow-pedalling cyclists of Nahariyya epitomize the even-tempered, unharassed attitudes of the people of this resort town. Founded by Jews from Germany fleeing Europe in 1934, Nahariyya has ever since been characterized by its neat and tidy houses and the politeness of its shopkeepers. During the last few years it has earned a reputation as a night-life centre for U.N. troops stationed across the Lebanese border. Nahariyya has some 30,000 inhabitants. In 1980 it achieved global recognition of sorts when an international windsurfing competition was held here. The sailing centre is north of the beach.

The main street is **Sderot Ga'aton**, spliced down the middle by the Ga'aton River and thickly overlaid with the branches of spreading eucalyptus trees. The town derives its name from this brook as the Hebrew for river is "nahar." One of the delights of staying here is to amble down Sderot Ga'aton; sit at one of the sidewalk cafes and munch on the creamy confectionery that is so popular. Another popular pastime is to take a ride on the horse-carriages, colourfully bedecked for the benefit of honey-mooners and other vacationers.

Sderot Ga'aton leads directly onto the **Galei Galil Beach**. There is a heated, closed swimming pool on the beach, next to an Olympic-sized open pool and the children's pools.

At the end of the main street is a new promenade, overlooking the sea. There the visitor can find restaurants, pubs, and children's amusements, besides sea sports such as sailing and surfing.

But all the surface calm masks the industrious nature of the residents. Down in the industrial sector there are plants for dairy products, machine parts, and asbestos, as well as a spinning mill.

Before leaving Nahariyya, make sure to visit the roof of the **Town Hall** for a fine view of much of the Western Galilee. This shows how marvellously situated it is, close to Akko, Rosh Haniqra, the Crusader castles at Montfort and Yehiam, and the hills of Upper Galilee.

In the same building there is also a **Museum of Archaeology and Modern Art** and a **Museum of the History of Nahariyya.** Open: Sun. – Fri. 10 a.m. – noon. Sun. – Wed. 4 – 6 p.m. Admission free.

The remains of a fine Byzantine church can be seen in Bielefeld St., near the Katznelson School.

Nahariyya's climate is a delightful mixture of sea breezes and mountain air during the summer, making it a favourite holiday resort teeming with vacation crowds.

Tourist Information Office: Sderot Ga'aton near Central Bus Station, tel. (04) 929800. Open: Sun. – Thurs. 9 a.m. – 1 p.m., 4 – 7 p.m. Fri. 9 a.m. – 1 p.m. Closed Sat. Anyone wishing to meet the locals is invited to contact the Municipality (tel. (04)929800), which will gladly arrange home visits.

The road clings close to the coast and within a few kilometres leads past the golden sands of **Akhziv**. A fee is charged at the entrance to this remote beach with full facilities, including showers and restaurant. On the mound overlooking it, on the seashore, are the wistful-looking ruins of an Arab village, deserted since the War of Independence.

Kibbutz **Gesher Haziv** (Bridge of Splendour), with its comfortable Guest House, is set on the hill opposite Akhziv. One of the largest turkey breeders in the country, this settlement takes its name from a sabotage mission at the bridge over the Keziv River, just north of Akhziv. Fourteen Hagana men died when this bridge was blown up in June 1946 as part of a country-wide campaign to disrupt British communications.

The road passes **Lehman Village**, named in honour of a former Governor of New York, Herbert H. Lehman. Soon after, it forks left for the chalk-white limestone cliffs and the border post with Lebanon at Rosh Haniqra. In the area there is a diving school, a camping site (Akhziv), and a youth hostel.

This is the southernmost point of a range of hills along the Mediterranean coast, known as the Ladder of Tyre (which is in Lebanon).

ROSH HANIQRA (Map: J3)

However inured you may have become to panoramic views of Israel, you will be left breathless by the breadth of scenery that lies below the cliffs. On a clear day you can see as far as Haifa. The coastline from Rosh Haniqra is both rocky and sandy. Here and there the rocks finger the surf while the Mediterranean Sea picks at the jagged coast, forming scores of inlets, salty pools and languorous lagoons.

A unique thrill awaits you when you take the cablecar down to sea level. There is a maze of sweet-smelling white limestone caves and passages looking down on the emerald-green and blue pools of sea water. The constant roar of the sea, the hissing surf and the heaving motion of the pellucid pools lend an air of fantasy to the grottos.

The cablecar operates throughout the year and is open daily from 8.30 a.m. – 5 p.m. A fee is charged.

Drive back down the hill, past the banana plantations of Kibbutz **Rosh Haniqra** and turn left (into Road No. 899). The flatness of the fields changes dramatically as you take the steep road up the mountainous border with Lebanon towards Kibbutz Hanita. Suddenly you are enveloped in a sea of pines that stretch for the next 30 km. These hills were once scabby with rocks, like the denuded Lebanese hills adjoining this route later on. The land reclamation schemes undertaken by Keren Kayemet LeIsrael have transformed this isolated region beyond recognition.

Kibbutz **Hanita,** founded in 1938, is one of several settlements that arose overnight with stockades and towers to plug the infiltration gaps used by hostile Arabs. The stockades and towers may still be seen. The kibbutz is set on the ridge of the mountain. A special feature is the kibbutz **Museum**, built on the ruins of a Byzantine church, which houses a fine collection of archaeological finds and flora and fauna connected with the area.

Leaving Hanita on Road 899, pass by the other farming settlements of **Ya'ara, Eilon** and **Goren**, noticing the many caves in the few slices of sheer rock bordering the road.

At the crossroads, 28 km. from Hanita, turn right towards Nahariyya, passing Kibbutz **Sasa** almost immediately (on Road No. 89).

The luxuriant vegetation continues, as do the widescreen overlooks across valleys and hills.

The road cuts through the ancient Druze village of **Hurfeish**, the epitome of all that is serene and virtuous about the Galilean villages. Some 2,000 people live here and each of the houses has some decorative stone work, with vines and fruit trees growing in the small plots.

To your left, high above the village, on the heights of Mt. Zebul, 814 m. above sea level, is the tomb of **Nebi Sabalan**, one of the prophets holy to the Druze community. Each year, in September, the Druze assemble on the mountain to pay homage.

Some 6 km. later there is a turn-off left to Zefat (Road No. 864). Detour towards Zefat for another 5 km. before arriving at the quaint village of Peqi'in.

PEQI'IN (Map: L4)

Peqi'in evokes feelings of awe in the hearts of secular as well as religious Jews because it is the only place in the Holy Land that has had continuous Jewish settlement from the days of the Second Temple, and because the noted scholar, Rabbi Shimon Bar-Yochai, lived here for many years.

Today there are only a few Jews, members of the Zinati family, living among the Druze and Moslem villagers.

In 1972 a band of students from Jerusalem set up a yeshiva in Peqi'in, with the aim of re-establishing the

Jewish community and restoring the old synagogue.

The **synagogue** is believed to date from the 2nd century CE. Although it was restored in 1873, stone carvings of the Holy Ark, a menora, shofar, lulav and etrog dating from the first synagogue are embedded in the walls. Parts of an ancient Scroll of the Law kept in the Ark are said to be 1,200 years old.

The stone houses have overhanging balconies fashioned with wrought iron and vines creeping along pole supports on the flat-topped roofs. Narrow streets lead to the synagogue and, further on, to the enclosed **spring.** This is where the 1st century CE rabbinical sage, Rabbi Shimon Bar-Yochai, and his son, Eleazar, are said to have got their water supply when hiding from the Romans for 13 years in a cave above the village.

Rabbi Shimon Bar-Yochai is believed to have written the **Zohar** (The Splendour), the treasured book of the Kabbalists, while living in the **cave**. To reach it, return to the entrance to the village and take the road forking left up the hill. Once you are past the village you arrive at some steps near a stone, with Hebrew writing noting that this is a holy site. The cave is on the left, near the top of the steps.

Rabbi Bar-Yochai's memory is so revered by the pious that on the festival of Lag Ba'Omer tens of thousands of pilgrims converge on his tomb in Meron.

Return to Road No. 89 and drive in the direction of Nahariyya, very shortly arriving at **Ma'alot**. This settlement is linked to the Arab village of **Tarshiha**, a little further along the road, and was used as the headquarters of Arab gangs until it was captured by Israelis in 1948. Schoolchildren were taken hostage and killed here by Palestinian terrorists in 1974.

Take the right fork on reaching Tarshiha and drive a few kilometres until you reach **Mi'ilya**. The Arabs living in this village are all of the Greek Orthodox faith and a number of their houses are built within and on the ruins of the Crusader castle, **Castellum Regis** (The King's Castle). Note how the two corner towers on the north side of the ruins stand at their original height. Castellum Regis was captured by Sultan Beibars in 1265.

Return towards Tarshiha, driving up the right hand fork (Road No. 8833) just after passing the police station. Pass En Yaaqov and brace yourself for another spectacular view. Ahead is the Mediterranean Sea and the Zebulun Valley that you drove through earlier. To the left is the Carmel mountain range and closer, on your left, is the silhouette of **Castle Judin**.

The road passes Ga'aton and soon branches left to Kibbutz **Yehiam** and the remains of the Crusader citadel.

Castle Judin, now known as **Metzudat Yehiam**, was built by the Order of Templars in the 12th century. Later it passed into the hands of the Teutonic Knights; it was destroyed in 1265 by Sultan Beibars, in preparation for his attack on Montfort Castle, a few kilometres northwest of Mi'ilya. Unlike many of the other Crusader forts that fell to the Moslems, this one was reoccupied and partially rebuilt in the 18th century by Sheikh Tahar al-Amr. This National Parks site is open daily, April – Sept. 8 a.m. – 5 p.m., Oct. – March 8 a.m. – 4 p.m. It closes one hour earlier on Fridays and holidays. Entrance fee.

Return to the main road (No. 89) and soon arrive at the point where it crosses Road No. 70. Kibbutz **Kabri** is on your immediate right. It was founded in 1949 by farmers who had been compelled to abandon their settlement at Bet HaArava, north of the Dead Sea, during the War of Independence. There is the **Nativ Hashayara** memorial here (one kilometre to the southeast) to 46 members of the Haganah convoy who were killed in an ambush while on their way to relieve Kibbutz Yehiam in 1948.

You have two choices for the remainder of the route back to Haifa. You may continue straight for 5 km., turning left (Road No. 4) at Nahariyya for the coastal drive through Akko. Or, and we recommend this route, you may turn left (Road No. 70) at this point for some more of that refreshing Galilean landscape.

Assuming you have turned left, pass the Netiv Hashayara memorial and a picnic area also on your left. Pass Sheikh Daud and Sheikh Danoun, then **Amqa**, a village abandoned by the Arabs in 1948 which still has ancient columns in some of the houses.

Bet HaEmeq, a kibbutz established by Hungarian and Slovakian survivors of the Holocaust, is close by.

The road winds through one of the largest olive groves in the Galilee. The groves continue through the large Arab villages, **Kafr Yassif**, and farther on **Kafr Jadeida**, culminating in a stunning view of the Zebulun Valley with its steam-roller-flat fields.

As you dip down a hill, the Carmel looms beyond the kilometres of sunflower fields.

The road meets up with Road No. 85 going left to Zefat

and right to Akko. Drive 8 km. to Akko and from there swing south to Haifa along the same highway (No. 4) you travelled at the start of this route.

ACCOMMODATION ON ROUTE No. 14

(See also general "Accommodation" section.)

HOTELS

AKKO
Argaman Motel Tel. (04) 916691. Sea Shore.
Nes Ammim Guesthouse Tel. (04) 922566.

NAHARIYYA
Carlton Tel. (04) 922211. 23 Ga'aton Blvd.
Astar Tel. (04) 923431. 27 Ga'aton Blvd.
Eden Tel. (04) 923246. Hameyasdim St.
Frank Tel. (04) 920278. 4 Haaliya St.
Kalman Tel. (04) 920355. 27 Jabotinsky St.
Panorama Tel. (04) 920555. 6 Hamaapilim St.
Rosenblatt Tel. (04) 820069. 59 Weizman St.
Erna Tel. (04) 920170. 29 Jabotinsky St.

KIBBUTZ GUEST HOUSES

Gesher Haziv Tel. (04) 825715. Western Galilee.
Nir Etzion Tel. (04) 842541. Carmel Beach Mobile Post.
Beit Hava Tel. (04) 922391. Shavei Zion.
Beit Oren Tel. (04) 222111. Mt. Carmel.

Amirim Tel. (06)989571. Vegetarian and naturalist accommodation. Western Galilee.

YOUTH HOSTELS

Shlomi. North of Nahariyya. Tel. (04) 808975.
Yehuda Hatzair. Kibbutz Ramat Yohanan, Tel. (04) 442976.
Akko. Old City near Khan el-Umdan, Tel. (04) 911982.

ROUTE No. 15 (Map: Northern Sheet G6 to M4)

The Bet HaKerem Valley and Galilee

Haifa – Akko (24 km.) – Meron (68 km.) – Zefat (Safed) (75 km.) (Road Nos. 4, 85, 89, 866.)

(Distances in brackets refer to start of route.)

The principal feature of this route is the Bet HaKerem Valley that separates the hills of the Lower Galilee from the mountains of the Upper Galilee, many of which top 1,000 m. above sea level. These are just the right kind of scenic wonders to put you in an elevated frame of mind for the ancient synagogues that await you at the end of the journey.

Follow Route No. 14 as far as Akko (on Road No. 4) and then notice the signpost directing you right (east) to Zefat (Road No. 85). The fields of sunflowers and other crops are a welcome relief from the industrial plants choking the road to Akko.

Wooded hills keep track of the road on the left but peter out into stony, forbidding heights around the villages of **Madj el-Kurum, Bina,** and **Deir el-Asad.** However, these villages retain their charm with vineyards and olive groves.

This is the heart of the **Bet HaKerem Valley** where the town of **Karmiel** received its first residents in 1964. Half the population of 20,000 are immigrants, with many hailing from North America. Karmiel's standardly designed flats contrast glaringly with the pastoral surroundings.

The road climbs sharply some 7 km. after Karmiel and passes by the pleasant sight of red-tiled bungalows, gently tucked among orchards at **Shazor.** Pass by **Rama** and then drive through a gigantic olive grove where time seems to have wrapped itself around the gnarled tree trunks. At the next fork, turn left onto Road No. 866. Kibbutz **Parod** is on the right, and immediately after it, adjacent to the roadside cafe, is the natural spring named after Israel's second president, Yitzhak Ben-Zvi.

A grim-looking fort, built by the British during the

1936 flare-up between Arabs and Jews, overlooks Moshav **Shefer.** Round the corner and pull over at the **Mitzpe Hayamim** (Seaview) observation point. From here the Sea of Galilee can be seen clearly, far below. The area between the Mediterranean Sea and the Sea of Galilee (which are both visible from here) is backed by the Carmel and the Lower Galilean hills.

It is now only a few kilometres of winding, mountainous road to **Meron.** On entering, turn left to the tomb of **Rabbi Shimon Bar-Yochai** and the nearby traditional burial places of Rabbi Hillel and other sages. Two ancient synagogues are also located nearby. For a full description of Meron's attractions and the route to Zefat (7 km. eastwards on Road No. 89) see Route No. 20.

ROUTE No. 16 (Map: Northern Sheet G6 to K7 and N6)

Across the Lower Galilee

Haifa – Bet She'arim (15 km.) – Nazareth (34 km.) – Kafr Cana (41 km.) – Tiberias (64 km.) (Road Nos. 75, 722, 754, 77.)

(Distances in brackets refer to start of route.)

A morning is sufficient for this trip but you should make sure that you arrive in Nazareth in time to see the main Christian shrines that are normally closed between noon and 2 p.m.

Drive north towards Derekh Ha'atzmaut and keep going east on Road No. 75, avoiding the left turn-off to Akko. The **Nesher Cement Works** that belch plumes of polluting smoke below the northeastern face of Mt. Carmel are some 3 km. later. Kibbutz **Yagur,** where the British authorities detained many people after the Haganah's central arms cache was discovered here, is 3 km. past Nesher. Here you turn right for Qiryat Tiv'on.

The road courses past the charming resort of **Qiryat Tiv'on,** set between the flat plains of the **Jezreel** and **Zebulun Valleys.** The houses, hotels and pensions are set amid cool forests of oak pine and many young travellers make their Galilean base in Tiv'on's Youth Hostel. The Bedouin housing project of **Basmat Tab'un** (about 4 km. to the northeast) is an interesting place to drive through.

The turn-off to Bet She'arim (Road No. 722) is on the eastern outskirts of the settlement and is clearly signposted. Turn right off the main road, right again and follow the road-signs down the cypress-lined road to the National Parks site.

BET SHE'ARIM (Map: J7)

There was a thriving Jewish community on these limestone hills from the 2nd-4th centuries CE. Jews fled here after the destruction of the Second Temple and the quashing of the Bar Kochba rebellion.

Bet She'arim became the fulcrum of Jewish national and spiritual life. The Sanhedrin, the Jewish Supreme Council, had its seat here. Here, too, lived Rabbi Yehuda Hanassi, who studied and taught while codifying Judaism's oral laws (the Mishna). When he died in 220 CE he was buried in the catacombs carved inside the limestone necropolis.

But the glory of Bet She'arim was snuffed out in 352 CE when the Byzantines destroyed the town and the grandiose synagogue in an attempt to cow the rebellious Jews.

Few excavations in Israel can equal the impact of the vast city of the dead, as the catacombs of Bet She'arim are called. Now incorporated in a national park, they make up immense labyrinthine vaulted chambers and contain scores of stone sarcophagi, most of which weigh five tons. Grave robbers have long since vandalized many of them. The inscriptions in Hebrew, Greek and Aramaic, and reliefs carved on some 200 sarcophagi, testify to the spiritual intensity and artistic fervour of the community.

A single chamber hacked into the side of the hill has been converted into a small museum. Open daily. Entrance fee.

Return to Road No. 75 and continue towards **Nazareth**, passing the turn-off right to **Afula**. The road climbs abruptly and soon passes by **Migdal HaEmek** perched in enviably quiet, rural surroundings. For those who are prepared to make a small detour to the valley below, there is a Museum of Pioneer Agricultural Settlements in **Kibbutz Yifat**.

Just outside Migdal HaEmek you should pull over to your right for the **Balfour Forest** and the observation point for a magnificent view of the Carmel range, the Jezreel Valley and the mountains of Gilboa and Ephraim. Also here is a **tree-planting centre**. Anyone who stops here between 8 a.m. and 2.30 p.m. weekdays (Friday 8 a.m. – 12.30 p.m.) may buy a sapling for a few shekels and plant it on the slopes nearby.

The remaining 4 km. to Nazareth are packed with scenic views. The Christian village of **Yafia,** fortified by the Jews during their revolt against the Romans in 66 CE, is close to the road, on your left.

On entering Nazareth, turn left down Paul VI Road. If there is space in the parking lot opposite the Government Tourist Office in Rehov Casa Nova, you are fortunate, as all the main sites are situated within easy walking distance from here.

NAZARETH (Map: K7)

The sacred Galilean town where Jesus spent much of his youth nestles between rolling hills, and nearly all its streets are sloped. Its spiked churches are overshadowed by the charcoal-grey roof of the monumental **Basilica of the Annunciation,** built over the ruins of churches dating from the 4th century. It is the largest church in the Middle East.

Everywhere there are signs of a burning faith. Churches rise over two places believed to be where the Archangel Gabriel informed Mary of the imminent birth of Jesus. Others shelter the **home of the carpenter,** Joseph, the **well** from which Mary drew water, and the mount from where Jesus escaped his angry congregation . . . "truly, I say to you, no prophet is acceptable in his own country" (Luke 4:24).

At the 200-year-old **Maronite** church in the Latin quarter, mass is said in Arabic and Aramaic.

Nazareth is far more of a city than Bethlehem but it has the same chasteness.

You can walk through most of the tourist sites in a couple of hours or less, depending on your sensibilities. But a worthwhile tour of the Basilica of the Annunciation takes at least an hour as it is as much a work of art as a house of prayer. As everything is relatively close to the Basilica we advise you to leave your car in the free parking lot on Rehov Casa Nova and walk from there.

However, you will need your car to see **Nazrat Illit** (Upper Nazareth), unless you take Bus No. 1 or 3 to get there. This new town is on the hills northeast of the old town and is a sterling example of city planners taking aesthetic considerations into account. From a modest beginning with 1,000 settlers in 1957, Nazrat Illit now has a population of 34,000.

Located 34 km. east of Haifa and 30 km. west of Tiberias, Nazareth overlooks the Jezreel Valley.

Climate: pleasantly cool in summer because it is set in the hills above the valley, and winter is less severe than in Upper Galilee.

There are about 58,000 people living in the old city, about half of whom are Moslem and half Christians.

Tourist Information Office: Rehov Casa Nova, opposite parking lot, tel. (06)573003,570555.

History

Nazareth was settled from the Middle Bronze Age onwards and silos, cisterns and oil presses show that it has been an agricultural village for several millennia.

Jesus was raised in Nazareth and the Christian religion had its beginnings here. The modern Hebrew word for Christians, "Notzrim," derives from the name of the town. There are numerous references in the New Testament to Nazareth, particularly to Jesus being chased out of the town after claiming to be the Messiah (Luke 4:21).

The Romans devastated Nazareth during the Jewish Revolt. After the collapse of Bar Kochba's rebellion, the city became a Jewish town made up of many refugees from Judaea.

The Byzantines expelled the Jews who had earlier sided with the invading Persians. Nazareth's Christian shrines were definitively located and the first churches were built during Constantine's reign.

The Moslems destroyed the city but the churches were rebuilt by the Crusaders. Nazareth was completely devastated by Sultan Beibars in 1263 and lay desolate for some 400 years. Thereafter the Franciscans returned under the tolerant rule of the Druze ruler, Fakhr al-Din.

Napoleon's troops held it briefly in 1799, when it was reclaimed by the Turks.

Nazareth Elit

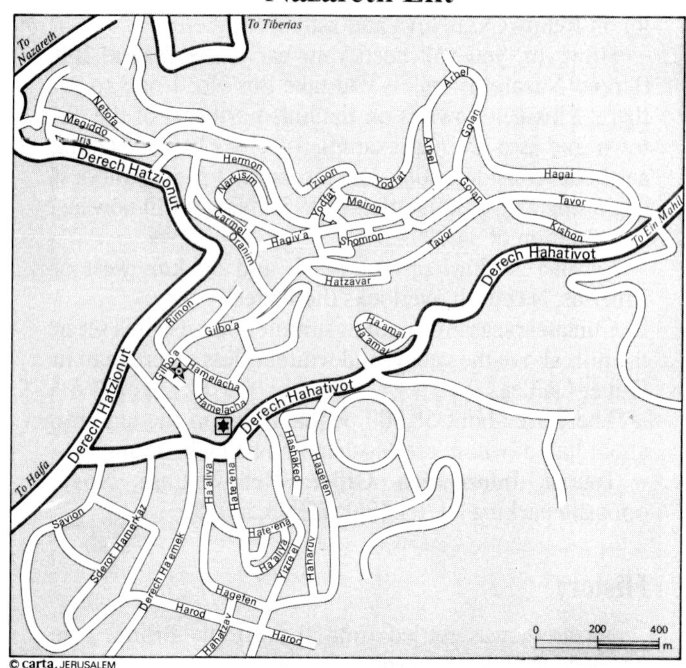

Nazareth

Before the outbreak of World War I the Germans established their military headquarters for Palestine in Nazareth. It surrendered to the British in 1918.

The town fell to Israeli troops two months after Independence and was the town with the largest concentration of Arabs in the pre-1967 borders.

Upper Nazareth received its first settlers in 1957, a factor that brought car assembly plants and textile, food and furniture factories to its environs.

Places of Interest

Basilica of the Annunciation: Rehov Casa Nova. Largest church in Middle East. Built over grotto where Archangel Gabriel appeared to Mary to announce the birth of Jesus (Luke 1:26–35).

The Basilica, planned by Professor Giovanni Muzio of Milan, and built in 1960–69, is over the lower church or crypt and the remains of pre-Byzantine, Byzantine and Crusader churches. Glorifies Mary and the mystery of the incarnation. The block of the two churches forms a parallelepipedon (with six faces).

The 6-m.-high presbytery is built over the main apse of the Crusaders. Within it are 35 choir stalls made of plain mahogany. Many of the wall paintings, mosaics, stained-glass windows and sculptures are gifts from countries around the world. In the courtyard behind the Upper Church there is a museum of the finds from excavations around the churches. Open 9 – 11.45 a.m., 2 – 5.30 p.m. Entry forbidden to persons wearing shorts. Taking photographs inside is forbidden.

Basilica of Jesus the Youth: Rehov Salesian. Built in 1906 by Frenchwoman, Madame Foache. Together with technical high school, it is supervised by Salesian Order of St. John Bosco.

Chapel of Our Lady of the Fright: on Mt. of Dread, in south of city, above Paul VI Road. Franciscan convent over site where Mary saw Jesus escape his pursuers by leaping from a precipice.

Church of the Annunciation (Greek Orthodox): northern end of Rehov Masqobia. Also known as St. Gabriel's Church. Built almost 300 years ago over well where Mary is said to have drawn water. Greek Orthodox believe Gabriel appeared to Mary near this site. Interior richly furnished with icons and wood-carved pulpits. Descend some steps to see source of spring feeding the well. Open: daily 8 a.m. – 6 p.m.

Frank Sinatra Club and Social Centre: Rehov Namsawi, east of Greek Orthodox Church of the Annunciation. Named after the entertainer who financed it. Social club for all faiths, library and lecture halls. Tel. (06)570016, 570018.

Market Place: at left, upper end of Rehov Casa Nova. Typical Oriental bazaar where nearly everything under the sun may be bought. Closed Sundays and Wednesday afternoons.

Maronite Church: Latin quarter.

Mensa Christi: on side-street near the market. Franciscan chapel around large block of soft limestone, traditionally accepted as a table used by Jesus and his disciples after the Resurrection. Church built in 1861.

Old Mosque: near market place. Also known as the White Mosque. More modern As-Salam mosque on Mosque Road, completed in 1965, has platform resembling Taj Mahal in India. Special wing for women.

Old Synagogue: in market place. Some maintain that Jesus prayed here. Known today as "Greek Catholic Church of the Old Synagogue". Last used in 1887. Has some Crusader walls. Open: Mon., Tues., Thurs., Fri. 9 a.m. – 12.30 p.m., 2.30–6 p.m. Wed. & Sat. 9 a.m. – 12.30 p.m. Closed Sundays. If locked ask market traders nearby for caretaker.

St. Joseph's Church: next to the Basilica of the Annunciation. Built over 13th century Crusader site, covering grotto of Joseph's home and workshop. Also known as the Church of the Nutrition and Joseph's Workshop. Open: 9–11.45 a.m., 2–5.30 p.m.

The roads (Nos. 754 and 77) from Nazareth to Tiberias are once more filled with the spell of the Galilean landscape. Seven kilometres from Nazareth, Road No. 754 winds round the predominantly Christian-Arab village of Cana. Park your car at the roadside and ask any one of the helpful villagers how to get to the nearby **Franciscan Church of the First Miracle of Christ.**

KAFR CANA (Map: L7)

Kafr Cana occupies a special place in the hearts of Christians as it was here, according to the Gospel of John (2:1–11), that Jesus performed his first miracle while attending a wedding feast, when he transformed water into wine.

The Franciscans believe that the church they built in 1881 stands over the site where the wedding feast was held because the crypt, which you may enter, is built around a dried-up well and a large rock with a scooped-out hollow obviously intended for washing.

The church stands over the ruins of a 6th century Byzantine building that was either a church or a synagogue.

A replica of the wine jars in use in Jesus' time rests above the slab of rock in the crypt.

The Franciscans supervise the **Chapel of St. Bartholomew** at the northern end of the village. St. Bartholomew was the Nathanael of the Gospel of St. John and was a native of Cana.

Other churches in this compact little village include two supervised by **Greek Catholics** and the **Greek Orthodox.**

The countryside along Road No. 77 rolls past a number of Arab villages until, 8 km. later, the road leads up to the Golani Crossroads (Tzomet Golani). Tiberias is straight ahead, 15 km. away, while Afula is to the right and Zefat to the left.

The **Golani Memorial and Museum,** in honour of one of Israel's most famous brigades, is located next to the junction. The remaining part of the journey is covered in Route No. 11, from Tel Aviv to Tiberias.

ACCOMMODATION ON ROUTE No. 16

(See general "Accommodation" section.)

HOTELS

NAZARETH

Grand New Tel. (06)573325. St. Joseph St.

Hagalil Tel. (06)571311. Paulus 6th St.

Nazareth Tel. (06)577777.

Nof Hacarmel Tel. (06)547847. P.O. Box. 332, Migdal Ha'emek.

Nof Ha'emek. Migdal Ha'emek. Tel. (06)547847/8.

YOUTH HOSTEL

Ramat Yohanan. 15 km. northeast of Haifa. Tel. (04) 442976.

CHRISTIAN HOSPICES

NAZARETH

St. Charles Borromaeus Tel. (06)554435. Roman Catholic (German). 316 St., House 12. Clergymen only.

Greek Catholic Theological Seminary Tel. (06)570540 P.O.B. 99.

Religieuses de Nazareth Tel. (06)554304 P.O.B. 274. Roman Catholic (French). Rehov Casa Nova.

Casa Nova Hospice Tel. (06)571367. Roman Catholic. P.O.B. 198.

Foyer des Pelerins Franciscains de Marie Tel. (06)554071 Roman Catholic (French). P.O.B. 41.

Christian Encounter Centre. Tel. (06)576410. P.O.B. 1548. Greek Catholic.

Tiberias

(Map: Northern Sheet N6)

Tiberias is without peer in Israel as a water sports playground, especially in spring, autumn and winter. It is situated on the shores of the Sea of Galilee, Israel's only fresh-water lake.

The newer part of the city, with modern hotels and palm-lined streets, roosts some 450 m. above the older part, where black basalt ruins of Moslem and Christian conquerors have a dignity all their own near the water's edge.

Recently, the older part was renovated and today boasts three hotels, commercial centres and a two-kilometre long promenade.

People are early risers because there is so much to enjoy in the cool of the first light. As the sun rises across the waters over the distant Golan Heights, fishermen cast their nets from bobbing boats, and truck drivers set off with their frozen catch for the markets further inland.

Before long the smooth-pebbled waterfront is alive with the roar of speed boats, water-skiers and the more restful kayaks and rowing boats. You may wish to soak up the sun on rafts anchored further out or hire fishing and skin-diving equipment at one of the many beaches with full facilities.

The acme of pleasure, however, is to lunch on St. Peter's fish, served up on platters at open-air restaurants on the waterfront. This is the same species that doubled as a money box when, according to the Gospel of St. Matthew, St. Peter paid his taxes with a shekel found in the mouth of a fish.

There is a more serious side to Tiberias. It is one of the four cities holy to Judaism (the others are Jerusalem, Hebron and Zefat), and it is the last resting place of many a famous rabbi. The cooler hours of the afternoon are the best for a walk to the old cemetery to see the **tombs of Maimonides** and **Rabbi Yohanan Ben Zakkai.** A bus takes you further uphill to the **shrine of Rabbi Akiva.** Then to **Hamat,** only 20 minutes south along the lakeside by foot, to see what is left of the earliest synagogues near the therapeutic wonders of the Hot Springs. Adjacent to the springs, up the hill, is the tomb of **Rabbi Meir Ba'al Haness.**

For sites around and about the Sea of Galilee take Route No. 17 for a circular tour of the lake. Read the tail-end of Route No. 11 for sites lying above Tiberias; Route No. 20 leads you north for many interesting hours of sightseeing.

Location: the shorefront and city are 210 m. below sea level, while the newer, western suburbs rise on the mountainside to a height of 249 m. above sea level.

Climate: hot and dry in the summer but a haven in winter when mild temperatures prevail.

Population: 36,000.

History

The area around modern Tiberias contained the fortified cities of Hammath, Rakkath and Chinnereth during the time of Joshua (Joshua 19:35).

Herod Antipas, son of Herod the Great, built a city on these ruins in 18 CE and named it in honour of the emperor Tiberius. It was the capital of the Galilee but devout Jews stayed away as ancient graves were discovered while foundations were being laid.

Tiberias surrendered to Vespasian in 67 CE but after the war many Jews fled here from Jerusalem. In the 2nd century CE the presiding Jewish **nassi** and his Sanhedrin resided here. It became a great seat of learning.The Mishnah and the Jerusalem Talmud were written in Tiberias between 200–400 CE and the vowel and punctuation system of Hebrew script was conceived here in the 8th century.

The influence of the rabbis was so strong that Roman statues were destroyed in the public baths. However, a

Tiberias

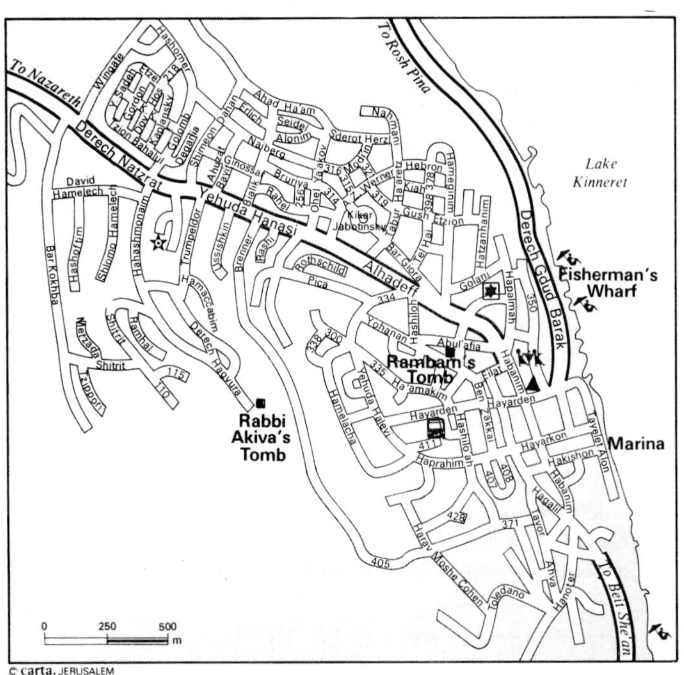

revolt against Roman influence was quashed in 351 CE.

Christians acknowledged the scholarly status of Tiberias. Jerome, an early church father, employed a man from Tiberias to help him translate the Bible from Hebrew into Latin. In the 5th century the Christian community even had a bishop, but Jews remained on after the Arab conquest when Tiberias was the capital of the Galilee and a textile and tapestry centre.

After defeating the Crusaders at the nearby Horns of Hittin, Saladin captured Tiberias in 1187.

Little of note took place until the 16th century, when a pair of former Spanish Marrano Jews, Don Joseph Nassi and Donna Gracia, persuaded Sultan Suleiman the Magnificent to let them rebuild the walls and bring in Jewish settlers. However, the town declined after a century.

A hundred years later, Sheikh Daher el-Omar rebuilt Tiberias and it again became a seat of learning. Hassidim settled in 1777 and the Egyptian Ibrahim Pasha constructed walls in 1833.

The great earthquake of 1837 levelled part of Tiberias.

During the 1936–39 disturbances many people lost their lives in the Arab-inspired riots.

After the War of Independence many newcomers brought renewed vitality to the town and Tiberias has continued to hold its position as the most important town in the eastern Galilee. Its climate and water sports assure it of continued popularity in the future.

WORSHIP

SYNAGOGUES
Etz Haim, Lakeshore.
Hanania, Ahva Quarter, southern Tiberias.
Sinior, Rehov Hashalom.

CHURCHES
Protestant:
Church of Scotland, Rehov Hayarden.
Greek Orthodox, Rehov Hayam.
Roman Catholic:
St. Peter's Terra Sancta, Rehov Hayam.

ACCOMMODATION

(See general "Accommodation" section.)

HOTELS

Jordan River Tel. (06)721111. Habanim St.
Galei Kinnereth Tel. (06)792331. 1, Kaplan Ave.
Moriah Tiberias Plaza Tel. (06)792233. P.O.Box 375.
Ariston Tel. (06)790244. 19 Herzl Blvd.
Ganei Hamat Tel. (06)792890. Near Hot Springs.
Golan Tel. (06)791901. 14 Achad Ha'am St.
Washington Tel. (06)791861. 13 Zeidel St.
Astoria Tel. (06)722351. 13 Ohel Ya'acov St.
Galilee (06)791166. Elhadef St.
Hartman Tel. (06)791555. 3 Achad Ha'am St.
Quiet Beach Tel. (06)790125. Gedud Barak St.
Tzameret Inn Tel. (06)794951. P.O.B. 3030.
Daphna Tel. (06)792261. P.O.Box 502.
Menora Gardens Tel. (06)792770.
Caesar Tiberias Tel. (06)723333.
Gai Beach Tel. (06)790790.
Ron Beach Tel. (06)791350. Gedud Barak St.

Holiday Tel. (06)721091. Gedud Barak St.
Dekel Palm Beach Tel. (06)790068. Migdal Beach.

YOUTH HOSTELS

Tiberias Youth Hostel (06)721775. Corner Alhadeff-Yarden, town centre.
Poria Taiber Youth Hostel Tel. (06)750050. 4 km. south of Tiberias.
Karei Deshe Tel. (06)720601. (Between Tiberias and Zefat).

CHRISTIAN HOSPICES

Church of Scotland Centre. P.O.B. 104. Tel. (06)790144
Terra Sancta. Franciscan. Tel. (06)720516. Old Town, on the shore of the Sea of Galilee.
Peniel-by-Galilee. YMCA (Protestant). Tel. (06)720685. P.O.B. 192

USEFUL ADDRESSES

Tourist Information Office: 23 Habanim St., Midrachov, tel. (06)720992, 722089. Open: Sun. – Thurs., 8.30 a.m. – 5 p.m., Fri. 8.30 a.m. – 2 p.m.

Post Office: Kikar HaAtzmaut, tel. (06)790066. Qiryat Shmuel branch, tel. (06)720894. Cables – tel. (06)730022.

Police: Derekh Nazrat, Kiryat Shmuel, tel. (06)792444. Emergency, tel. 100.

First Aid (Magen David Adom): HaKishon St. tel. (06)790111. Emergency, tel. 101.

Fire Brigade: tel. 102, (06)796222.

Places of Interest

Hamat: near Hamei Tiberias Hot Springs. Ruins of ancient synagogues and early settlements. Beautiful mosaic floor of Zodiac signs. Open: Sun. – Thurs. 8 a.m. – 4 p.m., Fri. 8 am. – 2 p.m. Entrance fee. Bus Nos. 2, 5. (See Route No. 17.)

Hamei Tiberias (Hot Springs): therapeutic waters; treatments in modern installation. Remnants of ancient baths. (See also "Health Resorts" and Route No. 17.)

The ancient boat : Less than 10 minutes by car from Tiberias, a boat of the type mentioned in the New Testament is displayed. The boat, discovered in the Sea of Galilee in 1985, is about 2,000 years old. It is being carefully restored, a process that archaeologists believe will take seven years. The display, located near the home of the late Yigal Allon in Ginossar, is open to the public Sun–Thurs.: 8 a.m.–5 p.m.; Fri. 8 a.m.–1 p.m., Sat. 9 a.m.–5 p.m. The admission fee includes a 15-minute film on how the boat was discovered. Tel. (06) 722905.

Tomb of Maimonides (Rambam): Rehov Hatanaim, left of Rehov Alhadeff as you walk away from the lake. Twelfth century Spanish-Jewish philosopher and talmudic scholar. Visited Tiberias shortly before his death in 1206. Cemetery open Sun. – Thurs. 8 a.m. – 5 p.m., Fri. 6 a.m. – 2 p.m.

Tomb of Rabbi Akiva: on hill in a western quarter of the town. Conspicuous shrine of 2nd century CE sage who supported Bar Kochba's rebellion. Skinned alive by Romans. Bus No. 4.

Tomb of Rabbi Meir Ba'al Haness: near Hamei Tiberias Hot Springs. White cupolas on building. Second century "miracle-maker." Bus Nos. 2, 5. (See Route No. 17.)

Tombs of the sages: same cemetery as tomb of Maimonides. Include tombs of Rabbi Yohanan Ben Zakkai, founder of 1st century CE rabbinical academy at Yavne, Rabbis Ami and Assi, of 3rd century, and 17th century Kabbalist, Rabbi Isaiah Horowitz.

War of Independence Memorial: prominent feature in front of Rassco Shopping Centre in the centre of town.

Tours from Tiberias

ROUTE No. 17 (Map: Northern Sheet M6 to N7 and N5)

Circling the Sea of Galilee (Anti-clockwise)

Tiberias – Hamei Tiberias (2 km.) – Deganya (10 km.) – En Gev (23 km.) – Kursi (Gergessa) (28 km.) – Capernaum (Kfar Nahum) (57 km.) – Tiberias (73 km.) (Road Nos. 90, 92, 98, 87.)

(Distances in brackets refer to start of route.)

The Sea of Galilee is surrounded by beaches, water-sport parks, fishing areas, picnic and camping grounds, guest houses and other tourist facilities.

Take the southern main road (No. 90) out of Tiberias, and drive along the many beaches and picnic sites on the western shore of the lake. **Hamat** is 2 km. from downtown Tiberias and is within the city's municipal area.

HAMEI TIBERIAS – HAMAT (Maps 3, 7, N6)

The origin of the springs reaches back millions of years when volcanic activity shaped the Jordan Valley. The 60°C centigrade temperature is fairly constant and the springs rise from a pool some 1,800 m. below ground.

The Romans built magnificent baths at Hamat when the city had a large Jewish population after the destruction of the Second Temple.

The city flourished under the Arabs in mediaeval times when more sumptuous baths were constructed for Arab emirs vacationing from abroad.

The bath house, tiled with marble slabs, was built in 1833 during the rule of the Egyptian, Ibrahim Pasha. Further development took place in 1932 when the springs were encased and the flow increased tenfold. The most recent thermal centre was erected in 1978. At present 17 of the underground springs are encased, giving an output of 2,400 cubic metres a day.

Visitors come from all over the world for treatment at Hamei Tiberias. Aside from the curative nature of the water, the area is an all-year resort as, lying 212 m. below sea level, it is warm throughout the winter. (See "Health Resorts.")

The fortified city of **Hammath** was apportioned to the tribe of Naphtali after the Israelite conquest of Canaan (Joshua 19:35).

Adjacent to the baths are the ruins of the early settlement of Hamat (1st-8th centuries CE); they include some of the largest and most beautifully conceived mosaics from ancient synagogues in Israel.

The site is maintained by the National Parks Authority and is open from 8 a.m. – 5 p.m. (4 p.m. in winter). Entrance fee.

Higher up the hill is the white-domed **Tomb of Rabbi Meir Ba'al Haness.** Many people ascribe special efficacy to prayers uttered at his tomb a few days before Lag Ba'Omer and on the festival of Shavuot. Pilgrims come from far and wide in cars, buses and trucks on these dates, when the rattling of tambourines and the ululating cries of women are the norm.

Continue on the route which follows the curves of the beach. Another road leads off right up the hill to Poriyya Hospital and a Youth Hostel before the right turn-off to Afula, which passes by Moshava **Kinneret** and Kibbutz **Kinneret,** the second oldest kibbutz in the country. Here you'll find the palm-tree grove known as **Rachel's Wood,** in memory of Rachel, a poetess who lived in these parts. Nearby, on the lake-shore, is **Tel Bet Yerah,** with remnants of an ancient Canaanite city of moon-worshippers. There are also remains from the Roman period. Kibbutz Kinneret and the Government Tourist Corporation have established a baptismal site ("**Yardenit,**" with kiosk and other facilities) for Christian visitors. It is located at the spot where the Jordan flows out of the Sea of Galilee, 8 km. south of Tiberias. Admission free.

DEGANYA (Map: N7)

The next stop is at the first entrance to Kibbutz **Deganya Aleph,** the mother of all kibbutzim, founded in 1909. Turn in right, after crossing the Jordan bridge.

It is a short walk through the kibbutz to the **A.D. Gordon Agricultural and Nature Study Institute,** named after the Second Aliya philosopher who lived and died here. The library has 55,000 volumes. Also a museum of the natural history of Israel and the archaeology of the Jordan Valley. Open: Sun. – Thurs. 9 a.m. – 4 p.m., Fri. 8.30 a.m. – 12 noon. Sat. 9.30 a.m. – 12 noon. Entrance fee.

Back on the main road, turn right very shortly afterwards into the second entrance to the kibbutz. Almost immediately, to your right, opposite the banana plantations, you will see the Syrian tank that was stopped by a "Molotov cocktail" in 1948. When the Syrians saw what had happened to this tank, the only one to break through the perimeter of the kibbutz during the three-day battle, they turned tail and abandoned their attempt to reach the Galilee and the Jezreel Valley.

The road to En Gev (No. 92) is lined with date palms before you reach Zemakh, with the turn-off, right, to Bet Shean. An impressive monument to the defenders of the area during the War of Independence stands at **Zemakh,** on the southern rim of the Sea of Galilee, to your left.

Nearby is the new cultural centre **Bet Gabriel**. Opened in May 1993, it includes a theatre, a small auditorium and a restaurant.

From Zemakh, there is a road southeastwards (No. 98) to **Hamat Gader** (El Hama in Arabic), which has been renowned for its mineral pools since ancient times. (Drive carefully!) The site was opened officially to the Israeli public in mid-1977. It offers bathing in a 42° centigrade mineral spring, in an open pool; an archaeological site (with findings from the Early Bronze Period and the 5th century CE); lookout on to the Yarmuk River and Jordan; picnic and barbecue facilities; crocodile park; refreshment centre, toilets, showers and first-aid station. (See "Health Resorts".)

Back on Road No. 92 along the eastern shore of the lake, heading north, you'll find Ma'agan Camping Site immediately on your left, with full facilities, a beach and lawns. Ahead of you is the meeting point of the Golan Heights and the Gilead Range, between which flows the Yarmuk River.

There are popular camping sites at Kibbutz Ma'agan and Kibbutz Ha'on (which also has an ostrich farm) and just before En Gev.

Turn left and follow the tarred road within the kibbutz down to the jetty, fishing boats, restaurants, Esco Music Centre and fee-paying beach area.

EN GEV (Map: 06)

Founded in 1937, **En Gev** was the first settlement on the eastern shore of the Sea of Galilee.

As you exit from En Gev, notice the steep, saddle-shaped, 350 m.-high mountain facing the gate. It is known as **Susita,** a Hebrew translation of the Greek name for it – Hippos (horse). Many ruins at its base, and especially on the summit, date from Greek and Roman times. However, the 7th century Moslem invaders destroyed much here and an earthquake did the rest. Until 1967 there was a border post at the top. It will take you about 45 minutes to climb to the summit up the spiralling footpath.

Water-sports facilities are offered at nearby Hof Golan, Luna Gal.

Five kilometres north of En Gev is Kursi, a national park at the site of the miracle of the Gadarene swine. Main attraction is a partially reconstructed Byzantine church and chapel.

KURSI (GERGESSA) (Map: O6)

On your right, the remains of the biggest Byzantine convent found in Israel. The place was identified by the early Christians as the site where the "Miracle of the Swine" occurred. Jesus exorcized the devils in a man and transferred them into a herd of swine (Luke 8:26., Mat. 8:28). The church dates from the 5th cent. CE, and was destroyed by the Persians in 614 CE. Car park. Entrance fee. Open 8 a.m. – 5 p.m.

The road above En Gev passes the settlements of **Neot**

Golan, Givat Yoav, Bnei Yehuda and **Ramot.** Some Syrian armoured units advanced close to these settlements on the opening day of the Yom Kippur War.

Ten km. later you come to Road No. 87. Nearby you can enjoy paddling a kayak down the Jordan River. Turn right at the Bethsaida (Bet Zayda) junction and continue north for half a kilometre. On your left is a sign directing you to the **Jordan River Park.** The park itself is well worth a visit, with excavations currently underway at the site of ancient Bethsaida, mentioned in the New Testament. Entrance to the park is NIS 10, but if you just want to go kayaking you don't have to pay. Just drive through the park to **Abukayak**, where you can rent kayaks (NIS 40 for a couple) or inner tubes (NIS 14 each), and paddle along a three-km.-long stretch of the Jordan (it takes about an hour). Open April–October, all week, 8.30 a.m.–4.30 p.m. Tel. (06) 921078, 961187.

Return to Road No. 87, turning right at Bethsaida junction. Cross the Jordan River on the northern shore of the Sea of Galilee and soon arrive at Moshav **Almagor** (turn right along Road No. 8277). Before the Six Day War it was the only Israeli settlement overlooking Syrian territory from a high vantage point, now the **Jordan River Park.**

Three km. west of Almagor are the remains of a 3rd century CE synagogue at **Korazin.** It was here that Jesus cursed the citizens for not repenting after he had been among them.

A couple of kilometres further on you'll find the guest farm, restaurant and stables of **Vered HaGalil**, at the junction of the main road (No. 90) down to Tiberias. The farm offers rides around the Galilee, ranging from half a day to 2 days or more.

Turn left towards the Sea of Galilee and very soon branch off left to the Italian Hospice of the Beatitudes. This reposeful church is set on top of the graceful **Mt. of Beatitudes,** where Jesus preached his immortal Sermon on the Mount (Mat. 5). From here there is a magnificent view of the Sea of Galilee.

Return again to the main road (No. 90) and follow the signposts left to Tabgha and Capernaum and Road No. 87 eastwards.

TABGHA (Map: N5)

It is revered by Christians as the site where Jesus performed the miracle of feeding some 5,000 people by multiplying five loaves of bread and two small fish (Mark 6:30–46). The **Church of the Multiplication of Loaves and Fishes** stands over the site of a former Byzantine church, of which some delicately styled mosaics remain.

Tabgha takes its present name from the Greek "Heptapegon," meaning seven springs.

A few metres further east, down by the shore, you will see a large rock (**Mensa Christi**) inside a church, and steps cut into more rock rising above the water level. The Franciscan monks hold that Jesus stood here while conferring the primacy of the church upon Peter (John 21).

It is only a short distance ahead to Capernaum.

CAPERNAUM (KFAR NAHUM)(Map: N5)

Both Jews and Christians hold this site dear. It was where Jesus lived for some time and where he admonished the residents in strong language. After his crucifixion and the destruction of the Temple in Jerusalem, many Jews fled here and soon developed a prosperous trading and fishing community.

The ruins of the splendid late 2nd or early 3rd century **synagogue** include the basalt-paved west street, a Corinthian capital adorned with symbols of a menora and a shofar, architectural fragments containing the Magen David (David's Shield), floral ornaments and the benches of the elders. The lateral nave has four reconstructed columns. The second from the right carries a Greek inscription honouring the Jewish donors.

The land was purchased in 1894 by Franciscan fathers who rebuilt a monastery next to the synagogue. The church is on the site of a 4th century structure marking St. Peter's house. (Nearby is a Greek Orthodox Church.) Open: seven days a week: 8.30 a.m. – 4.30 p.m. Entrance fee.

Retrace the route to the main road and turn left on Road No. 90. The area is saturated with vineyards, olive groves, tall palms and orchards. Pass by Kibbutz **Ginosar** and its marvellous Guest House. The brand-new **Yigal Allon Museum of the Galilee** is located here, as is the 2,000-year-old boat recently found in the Sea of Galilee. Both are well worth a visit. Entrance fee: NIS 8. Open Sun. –Thurs. 8 a.m.–5 p.m., Fri. 8 a.m.–1 p.m., Sat. 9 a.m.–5 p.m. Tel. (06) 721495, 06 722905. Pass Tree View beach,

Tamar beach and camping site, Migdal camping site and Villa Melchett beach and camping site. All this is in the biblically-referred-to Land of Gennesaret (Mark 6:53).

At a point only 4 km. north of Tiberias you arrive at the fishing village of **Migdal** (on the right). It is said to be the birthplace of Mary Magdalene. Towards the end of the Second Temple it was a flourishing Galilean city. Josephus Flavius fortified it before switching loyalty.

Round the curves of the shore-front road and enter Tiberias.

ACCOMMODATION ON ROUTE No. 17

(See also general "Accommodation" section.)

GUEST FARM

Vered Hagalil Tel. (06)935785. Guest farm, horse-riding, restaurant, swimming pool.

KIBBUTZ GUEST HOUSES

Lavi Tel. (06)799450. Kibbutz Lavi.
Nof Ginosar Tel. (06)792161. Kibbutz Ginosar.
En Gev Tel. (06)758027. Sea of Galilee.
Haon Tel. (06)757555. M.P. Jordan Valley.
Kinar Tel. (06)763670. N.E. Sea of Galilee.
Ma'agan Camping village. Sea of Galilee. Tel. (06)753753.
Ramot Resort Hotel Tel. (06) 732636. East of Sea of Galilee.

YOUTH HOSTEL

Karei Deshe (Tabgha). Tel. (06)720601

CAMPING

(On the shore of the lake)
Ma'agan. Kibbutz Ma'agan Tel. (06)753753.
Ha'on. Kibbutz Ha'on Tel. (06)757555.
En Gev. Kibbutz En Gev Tel. (06)758027.

ROUTE No. 18 (Map: Northern Sheet N6 to P1 and N4)

Northern Golan and Galilee Enclave

Tiberias – Pool of Ram (78 km.) – Banias (93 km.) – Tel Hai (132 km.) – Metulla (140 km.) – Hazor (177 km.) (Road Nos. 90, 91, 98, 99.)

(Distances in brackets refer to start of route. Be careful near uncleared minefields.)

On the map the **Golan Heights** look like a bulge in the northeastern corner of Israel.

The Golan's known history is very long. It was one of the first territories held by the tribe of Menashe, which conquered it from King Og (Deut. 3:11); it is known in the Old Testament as Bashan. Jews lived in the Golan even in the late Roman and Christian eras, when more central places like Jerusalem were forbidden to them. The ruins of 26 synagogues have been found on the Golan.

During the Ottoman Period (1517–1917 CE) the Golan came under Syrian administration, as part of the Turkish Empire.

This volcanic high plateau then passed into British and French hands before reverting to Syrian control. It was sparsely populated by Bedouin and Druze. In 1948, the Syrians turned it into a military area and almost completely emptied it of civilians. As it towers over the Hula Valley, it was used for the constant harassment of the Jewish villages and towns in the valley below. The Syrian bunkers can be seen to the present day, and the remains of their army camps are strewn all over the area.

In the Six Day War (1967) the Golan was taken by the Israeli Defence Forces in retaliation for Syrian attacks and in order to prevent an attempt to divert the River Banias (one of Israel's main water sources).

The empty spaces are now being cultivated and the Golan is no longer one big army camp. **But there are still uncleared mine fields. Do not ignore warning signs and take care around fenced areas.**

In the 1973 Yom Kippur War the Syrians almost succeeded in retaking the Golan, as Israeli forces there were totally unprepared. In the central area the Syrians almost reached the Bridge of **Bnot Yaaqov.**

After the war a U.N. force was stationed along the eastern border of the Golan, with its main base in what used to be the Syrian H.Q. in the town of **Quneitra,** now in a demilitarized zone.

In 1982 the Golan was declared a part of Israel. The Druze residents in their five villages in the northeastern part of the plateau comprise the only original ethnic group that has remained in the area. Some of them accepted Israeli citizenship, others preferred to remain "Syrians abroad" (see the chapter dealing with Communities in Israel).

The Golan area is where you'll find Israel's highest mountain: the **Hermon** (2,224 metres high). The Banias (Hermon) River flows through it. The Yarmuk River separates the Golan from the Kingdom of Jordan.

Set aside at least five hours for this trip, which takes in the **Golan Heights** with dramatic vistas of much of northeastern Israel, National Parks sites, picnic spots and cascading waterfalls.

Drive north of Tiberias along the snaking road (No. 90) that provides a marvellous opportunity to look down on the entire Sea of Galilee. Don't stop at any of the points before Rosh Pinna as these are covered in Route No. 17 and there is a lot to see.

ROSH PINNA (Map: N4)

This small moshava, set on the slopes of Mt. Canaan, has preserved its rural atmosphere since it was founded in 1882.

Its name derives from the Hebrew for "cornerstone", as it was the first Jewish settlement in recent times in the Galilee. Restored early pioneer houses and the synagogue can be visited, and the town is a pleasant spot for a leisurely stroll. For details of the restoration work, phone (06)936603.

The first Jew to be hanged by the British Mandatory authorities, Shlomo Ben-Yosef, is buried here. A memorial stone stands near the highway (No. 89) to Zefat. (See Route No. 19.)

After skirting Rosh Pinna, the road to the left goes to Hazor and Metula. Two kilometres further on, take the right fork (Road No. 91) and pass the cowsheds of **Mahanayim.** South of the kibbutz is the regional airfield. The **Hula Valley** opens up on your left and soon you reach **Mishmar Hayarden,** built anew after the previous settlement, located further east, was completely destroyed by the Syrians in 1948.

A road branches off left to **Gadot,** the settlement that suffered greatly from Syrian shelling until the Golan Heights were captured in 1967. Continue along Road No. 91. One kilometre later the road descends and crosses the **Jordan River** over the **Bnot Yaaqov (Daughters of Jacob) Bridge.** The ruins of **Chastelet** (Mezad Ateret), the Crusader castle built in 1178 and destroyed the following year by Saladin, are close by to your right. Observe, too, the remains of an undated Khan (inn) that used to serve travellers.

The bridge is associated with many other famous battles in history. This is where the British finally put an end to Turkish hegemony in the area during World War I. The British also broke through at this place to advance on Vichy-controlled Syria in World War II. The bridge witnessed fierce battles as the Israelis stormed the Golan Heights in 1967 and repulsed the Syrians in 1973.

The road climbs and you begin to appreciate the strategic value of the Golan Heights when you peer down on the telescoped and vulnerable Hula Valley far below.

Continue on round a corner and swing left to Mitzpe **Gadot** (Lookout over Gadot). Observe the Syrian bunkers. The large black basalt stone memorial contains the names of the Israeli soldiers who died in action while seizing this site.

The road passes turn-offs to a number of new agricultural settlements. It also runs very close to a good example of swirling tuff – the fragmentary material ejected by exploding volcanoes millennia ago. (Road No. 9088, to your right, takes you to the new town of Katzrin. See end of Route No. 19.)

Ten kilometres after the bridge, you cross the fenced-off T.A.P. oil pipeline that starts at Bahrein in the Persian Gulf and crosses Saudi Arabia, Jordan, Syria and Israel before reaching the Lebanon. Stretching over 1,750 km., it is one of the longest oil pipelines in the world.

There are more roads branching off to farming settlements, but you are advised to keep to the main road as the area is dotted with minefields, which are, of course, marked off with yellow and red warning signs.

Eventually, Road No. 91 passes the fields of **Ortal** and **En Zivan.** Travellers who were in this area, on the perimeter of Quneitra, in the months immediately following the 1967 war, will readily appreciate the giant strides made in farming on previously neglected but fertile land.

The road forks, and taking the left hand road (No. 98) observe the Syrian town of Quneitra straight ahead. The road passes settled areas, including Kibbutz **El Rom,** 72 km. from Tiberias, and a number of Druze villages. In spring, the area is a mass of perfumed greenery.

Drive on until you reach **Mas'ada,** a Druze village 14 km. northwest of Quneitra and very close to the **Pool of Ram** (Birket Ram). Banias is 11 km. to the left (Road No. 99) but you should continue left over the bridge to Majdal Shams (on Road No. 98).

A few kilometres up the hill, the road turns right to the large Druze settlement at **Majdal Shams** (Tower of the Sun) perched at the foot of lofty **Mt. Hermon,** 2,224 m. above sea level. Majdal Shams was strafed by Syrian aircraft during the Yom Kippur War in 1973, and fierce fighting took place on Mt. Hermon.

Covered by snow in winter, Mt. Hermon has been developed as a skiing centre by the nearby settlement of **Neve Ativ**, where accommodation is available all year round.

If you are here in winter you should continue on through Majdal Shams to the parking lot and immediately transfer to an Egged bus heading for the ski slopes, where there are full skiing facilities, including several chair-lifts. When you drive back via Mas'ada towards Banias, stop at the **Pool of Ram.** (You can also drive via **Neve Ativ** and the **Castle of Nimrod** on Road No. 989.)

Fed by springs and melting snow from the Hermon, this elliptical pool is set in the crater of a long-dormant volcano. The walls of the crater above the level of the blue water are lush and scented in the summer months by fruit trees. In the winter, snow covers the high banks to a depth of 60 centimetres. Archaeological excavations here have uncovered some of the earliest tools found in Israel, made by the ancestors of modern man in the Lower Palaeolithic period, over 70,000 years ago.

The pool is 900 m. long and 600 m. wide; it is by no means only a scenic delight – the Druze villagers living nearby fish daily for the carp and hafaf that were first placed here in 1958. It is also a swimmer's paradise in the summer – conjuring up visions of Switzerland with its motionless, clean and fresh beauty.

On Road No. 99 to **Banias** (Banyas) you begin to wind round hills and gorges, each of which seems to outdo the previous one in its allure. But on the way down the northern Golan Heights you are constantly reminded of its military associations when you pass interesting monuments, such as the one at **Ein Fit** inscribed with a date – 10 June 1967 – and commemorating Israeli casualties. Nearby is **Mitzpe Golani,** another memorial and observation point.

The Hula Valley spreads out below and the road passes very close to innumerable Syrian bunkers. Soon, however, the road passes a picnic site set in olive groves and then crosses a narrow bridge before the self-service restaurant ahead and the parking lot at Banias, to your right.

BANIAS (Map: O1)

The first impression is one of rushing water. This is the Banias Spring or Hermon River that rises from under a cave and is one of the three sources of the Jordan River.

Walk over the small bridges spanning the stream and approach the large **cave** cut into the face of the high mountain. On your right you can see four decorated niches carved into the rock face of the hill. One of them has a Greek inscription on it. These are the only remains of the **Greek temple** that once stood here, named Panias in honour of **Pan,** the Greek god of woods and nature.

An earthquake destroyed this temple and the one built later at the same site by Herod's son, Philippus. The second temple and city were named Caesarion in honour of Augustus Caesar but were later known as Caesarea Philippi.

Banias was for a long time a strategic site as it lay astride the road from Akko and Tyre to Damascus. The Egyptians were defeated by the Seljuks here in 198 BCE.

Banias was a prosperous city in the early Arab era and was called the granary of Damascus. Its thick woods were a favourite hunting ground.

The Crusaders fortified their settlement, some of the ruins of which may be seen today. However, there are far more impressive and mighty ruins of the castle of **Subeibe** (Qala'at Namrud, or **Castle of Nimrod**), standing on a mountain-top 3 km. east of Banias (and approached along

Road No. 989). There was protracted fighting between the Crusaders, Ayyubids and Mamelukes for control of this vital pass. The area round the castle is now a national park, and is open to the public. Entrance fee.

Back on the road down the Golan, take the left turning marked by an orange sign for "Banias" to the parking lot for the **Banias waterfall.** Walk about 100 m. to the steps leading down to the gorge. The smell of the damp, leafy vegetation follows you for the next 100 m. to the pool below the twin waterfalls. See how the small stream above, at Banias, has now become a swift flowing river of cool mountain water.

There is more to see so don't stay too long. Further down, in the water, there is a Syrian tank that rolled off the bank during the 1967 war.

The road coils lazily downhill, brushing past another memorial to Israeli soldiers next to a Syrian tank.

Take the right turn to **Tel Dan,** stopping, if you wish, at **Ussishkin House** – a nature and history museum of the flora, fauna geology and archaeology of the Hula Valley and surrounding areas, with audio-visual show. Open: Sun. – Thurs. 9 a.m. – 5 p.m. (in winter till 3.30 p.m.), Fri. 9 a.m. – 3.30 p.m., Sat. 10 a.m. – 5 p.m. Tel. (06)941704, 951703. Entrance fee.

Continue along this turn-off to the **Dan Nature Reserve.** This is a wooded paradise around the **Dan River.** The green path signifies a half-hour walk through the dense vegetation, while the yellow one alerts you to an hour's meandering. The reserve has a restaurant (which offers trout from Kibbutz Dan) and picnic facilities. Entrance fee.

Back on the main road (No. 99) you soon pass Kibbutz **Dafna** and **Kfar Szold,** the latter named after Henrietta Szold, the first president of Hadassah. The Tal camping ground is also to the left.

You will also see a signpost to the National Parks site of **Hurshat Tal** (Forest of Dew). The Dan River flows through the park, as green as an English meadow, while an artificial lake, in which you may swim, has been carved between many of the ancient oaks, some dating back 2,000 years. Legend has it that when 10 messengers of Mohammed halted here for an overnight stay, they found it a desolate stretch. They stuck sticks in the ground to tether their horses and when they woke up in the morning, they found that the sticks had sprouted into giant oaks.

There is a restaurant and there are picnic facilities. Open daily in spring and summer. Closed October to March. Entrance fee.

The last part of the descent passes Kibbutz **Hagoshrim Guest House,** Kibbutz **Ma'ayan Barukh,** at which you can see the **Hula Valley Museum of Prehistory**, with a rich collection of prehistoric tools and implements from the area and an ethnographic collection. Open: daily 9 a.m.–noon. Tel. (06)954611. Entrance fee. After crossing the bridge and the branch road to the textile plant, you are at a T-junction; turn right, on Road No. 90 to Qiryat Shemona, left, and Tel Hai and Metulla, right. Cross over and enter Tel Hai.

TEL HAI (Map: N1)

Annual pilgrimages by youth groups and veteran members of the HaShomer (The Watchman) association take place here in commemoration of the inspiring Jewish defence of this hill in 1920. Eight defenders of this early Upper Galilean settlement, including Joseph Trumpeldor, the one-armed founder of the **Hehalutz** Zionist pioneering movement in Russia, fell to armed Arab gangs. The eight included two women and the nearby development town of **Qiryat Shemona** (shemona=eight) is named in their honour.

The **Tel Hai Courtyard Museum** has been restored to its original shape after being partially destroyed by the Arabs. The grounds of this walled enclosure include agricultural equipment used by the pioneers in Tel Hai. There is an audiovisual presentation. The rooms where the defenders were shot have photographic exhibits showing life here in those early days. Open Sun. – Thurs. 8 a.m. – 4 p.m.; Fri. 8 a.m. – 1p.m.; Sat 8.30 a.m. – 2 p.m. Entrance free. A youth hostel is situated within the grounds. Tel. (06) 951333.

To get to the cemetery where the defenders are buried, walk or drive a short way up the hill, turn right and then sharp right again. A sculptured lion by Avraham Melnikeff squats on blocks of stone and is a memorial to the Tel Hai eight. Inscribed on this striking monument are the last words of Trumpeldor: "It is good to die for one's country."

Kibbutz **Kfar Giladi** and its Guest House are adjacent to the cemetery. Founded in 1916, Kfar Giladi has the

Haganah Museum – Bet Hashomer, recording the history of settlement and defence in the region. Open: daily 9 a.m. – 12 noon, 4–6 p.m. (summer) and 3–5 p.m. (winter). Fri. and eve of holidays 9 a.m. – 12 noon. Entrance fee. Tel. (06)946373.

The road up the **Naphtali Mountain range** soon branches off to link up with Route No. 19 at Metzudat Yesha, 15 km. away on Road No. 886. However, you should drive down back to Road No. 90 which leads left to Metula. Four km. later, after veering left, turn right to the parking lot before the **Iyon River Nature Reserve.** This can also be reached from the northern edge of Metulla. If you walk a few hundred metres from here, you reach the uniquely shaped **Tannur Waterfall,** so named because it resembles an Arabic adobe baking oven. The Hebrew word for oven is Tannur. The waterfall is dry in the summer months but presents a remarkable spectacle during the rainy winter months between December and March. And there is water from melting snow until May. The site is open seven days a week 8 a.m. – 5 p.m. Entrance fee.

Metulla is about one kilometre further north, squeezed into the northernmost tip of Israel in ethereal, lovely surroundings. The farmers of Lebanon can be seen working in their fields bordering the town.

Some 1,500 people live in Metulla, founded in 1896 on lands bought by Baron Rothschild from Druze villagers. There are no factories. It is solely a farming area and it is a good retreat for city dwellers and tourists yearning for a few days of cool mountain air. There are a number of hotels and good pensions set in this unruffled resort settlement, 525 m. above sea level. (See Accommodation at end of the route.)

The **Canada Centre**, a state-of-the-art sports, cultural and recreational centre, has recently been built here. It is open every day from 10.00 a.m.–10.00 p.m. and includes indoor and outdoor swimming pools, two squash courts, a firing range, an Olympic-size basketball court, a tennis court, a football field, the biggest ice-skating ring in Israel, and aerobics room and a fitness room. There's also a health club, a beauty parlour, a sports shop and an Italian restaurant and cafeteria. Tel. (06) 950370, 950371.

From Metulla, you can walk or drive up to "**the Good** Fence", the border crossing to Lebanon. Originally the site of a clinic whose good works crossed barbed-wire fences, the post now sees a lot of two-way commercial and agricultural trade, as well as a daily influx of Lebanese workers. On a clear day, you can see wide vistas of Lebanon from here.

Backtrack to **Qiryat Shemona,** a development town of approximately 16,000 people, many of them new immigrants, who had to live with numerous rocket attacks from Palestinians in Lebanon before the 1982 Lebanon war. Pass the bus station on the road leading south, then the ancient tel of the biblical city **Abel Beth Maacha**, then observe the fish ponds, fields and orchards that you will pass by all the way through the Hula Valley until you reach Tel Hazor, 20 km. south.

The **Hula Valley** is one of the greatest land reclamation schemes undertaken in Israel. In the early fifties it was a forsaken swamp, whose malaria-infested marshes had only a rich variety of flora and fauna.

The work involved in making it into the semi-Eden it is today involved deepening and straightening the Jordan River so that water could be led into it from the valley. Years of back-breaking work culminated in 1957 with the successful drainage of the marshes.

Drive on past the road leading up to Metzudat Yesha, as this is covered in Route No. 19.

Visit the **Hula Nature Reserve**, the last remnant of the original swamps, and the first of Israel's 120 nature reserves, established in 1956. There is an audio-visual presentation shown every 15 minutes, in Hebrew and English, as well as a guided tour lasting one hour. The reserve has several observation points for watching the amazing variety of wildlife, especially birds. There are also water buffalo, swamp cats, mongoose, and coypu, and several rare plant species. Autumn, winter and spring are the best seasons for a visit. Open: daily, 8 a.m.–4 p.m. Entrance fee. Tel. (06)937069.

A little to the south of the Hula Reserve is the **Dubrovin Farm** reconstructed just as it was in pioneer days. It shows the lives of farmers in the region in the early 1920s, including the Dubrovin family home, garden and smithy. There is a restaurant at the site. Open: Sun.–Thurs. 9 a.m.–4 p.m., Fri. 9 a.m.–2 p.m., Sat. and holidays 9 a.m.–4 p.m. Tel. (069)37371.

Eight km. later, from the Hula Reserve, turn left for the **Hazor Museum** and the Guest House of Kibbutz **Ayelet Hashahar,** probably one of the best known in the country.

It would be a mistake not to visit the Hazor Museum

if you have time to see the ruins of the ancient tel on the other side of the main road. Even a cursory glance at the masses of pottery vessels, gold jewellery, javelin heads and basalt statues from Canaanite temples 37 centuries old will be sufficient to heighten your interest in seeing the places where they were found. Open daily 8 a.m. – 5 p.m. (4 p.m. in winter). Entrance fee: adults NIS 6, children NIS 3. Tel. (06) 934855. The ticket to the ruins includes cost of entry to the museum.

HAZOR (Map: N4)

Hazor and Massada are the most exciting chapters in modern Israeli archaeological excavations. The finds of Professor Yigael Yadin and his team at Hazor between 1955–59 conclusively date Joshua's conquest of the Promised Land to the 13th century BCE. Biblical accounts of Joshua's slaying of the King of Hazor and the burning of this, the largest metropolis of Canaan, can be found in Joshua 11:10–13. Judges 4:2 narrates how the Canaanite King Jabin ruled here and I Kings 9:15 reveals that King Solomon converted it into a royal, fortified city.

All this was confirmed by the Yadin expedition. The archaeologists exposed much of the bottle-shaped mound, 600 m. long and 200m. wide, and the rectangular plateau lying to the north of it measuring 1,000 m. by 700 m. As they dug away the layers of earth, they found **Canaanite temples** from the 17th-13th centuries BCE, earlier buildings from the 27th century BCE, the Solomonic **casement wall,** stone pillars of Israelite **store-houses,** and everything that is housed in the museum.

The most spectacular find of all, since restored by the National Parks Authority, was the 38 m. deep **shaft and tunnel** that the Israelite King Ahab built in the 9th century BCE. When you walk down the 123 steps of the spiral staircase leading to the tunnel, you are awestruck by the technological prowess of Ahab's builders, whom we encountered along Route No. 11 at Megiddo and on Route No. 8 at Sebastia.

Hazor is the largest tel in the country, and because it dominated the Hula Valley it was built upon by each successive conqueror. The excavators peeled away the ruins of no fewer than 21 towns, one above the other.

Open: daily April – September 8 a.m. – 5 p.m. October

– March 8 a.m. – 4 p.m. Entrance fee. Tel. (06)937290.

Head back to Tiberias, 35 km. south (Road No. 90).

ACCOMMODATION ON ROUTE No. 18

(See also general "Accommodation" section.)

HOTELS

North Kiryat Shmona Tel. (06)944703.
Arazim Metula. Tel. (06)944144.
Hamavri Metula. Tel. (06)943237, 940150.

KIBBUTZ GUEST HOUSES

Ayelet HaShahar Tel. (06)932611. Upper Galilee.
HaGoshrim Tel. (06)956231. Upper Galilee.
Kfar Blum Tel. (06)943666. Upper Galilee.
Kfar Giladi Tel. (06)941414. Upper Galilee.
Yaffa Pension Metula. Tel. (06)940607.
Menora Hotel Metula. Tel. (06)942361.
Sheleg HaLevanon Metula. (06)944015.

YOUTH HOSTELS

Tel Hai. Near Kfar Giladi — Tel. (06)940043
Nature Friends. Rosh Pinna — Tel. (06)937086
Karei Deshe. (Tabgha) — Tel. (06)720601

BED AND BREAKFAST

Some kibbutzim offer bed and breakfast accommodation in members' homes, sometimes including visits to see kibbutz artists at work. Among these kibbutzim are **Kfar Hanassi, Gadot, Manara, Ayelet Hashachar, Ya'ara and Sasa.**

ROUTE No. 19 (Map: Northern Sheet N6 to O7 and P4)

The Southern and Central Golan

Tiberias – Hamat Gader (El Hamma) (19 km.) – Kfar Haruv (32 km.) – Gamla (60 km.) – Katzrin (74 km.) (Road Nos. 90, 98, 808, 9088.)

(Distances in brackets refer to start of route. Be careful around uncleared minefields.)

This half-day route touches the southern border between the Golan Heights and the Kingdom of Jordan, takes you up the heights on a scenic road, and covers sites from prehistory to the Roman period. It also follows the southern route of the Israeli army in 1967, and the Israeli counter-attack in the 1973 Yom Kippur war.

Take the southern road (No. 90) out of Tiberias (Route No. 17) and go southeastwards to **Hamat Gader** (El Hamma). As you proceed along this road, you will see the Yarmuk River on your right; it marks the border with Jordan. Hamat Gader was a health centre in Roman times; the site includes a 42°C pool and the ruins of an elaborate Roman bath and theatre. Refreshments, shower facilities, etc., are available. There is a large crocodile farm, open to visitors. Entrance fee. (See "Health Resorts.")

From Hamat Gader, going back the way you came, you very soon reach a narrow, winding road going uphill to your right. This is not for novice or nervous drivers. As an alternative, go back to the junction, where you turn right towards En Gev, passing Haon, and then right at Kursi to reach Ramat Magshimim by a wide, modern road. If you do decide on the first route, continue on it for about 13 kms. along the plateau and you will come to Kibbutz **Kfar Haruv**. A secondary road that goes around the kibbutz on your left takes you to an observation point and an old Syrian stronghold. The Sea of Galilee lies below you, and the greenery of kibbutz En Gev.

Rejoining the main road (No. 98) you drive straight on towards **Ramat Magshimim,** where you take the left turn on Road No. 808 to ancient **Gamla.**

Don't take the first fork left at Tzomet Daliyot, but the

one slightly further on, which takes you to Gamla. (If you take the first road, you will soon find a sign pointing right to Gamla along an unpaved road.)

Gamla was the last fort taken by the Romans when putting down the revolt of the Jews in Galilee and the Golan that ended with the destruction of the Temple in Jerusalem.

Josephus Flavius describes the siege that took a month and occupied three Roman legions (60,000 troops) led by Titus (later a Caesar). The last Jewish defenders with their women and children jumped into the abyss, preferring death to slavery. As you stand by the car park looking at the conical hill, it is easy to see the advantages of the fort's position. A footpath leads down the valley and up to the archaeological site where the remains of a fortified wall and a big public building, probably a synagogue, are to be found. Archaeological work is still going on here.

There are a number of possible walks from the car park. They all start with a path that leads north through the biggest Copper Age burial ground in the Golan, strewn with almost 200 enormous dolomite stones (**dolmens**) in table-like constructions that served as tombs for the men who lived here some 6,000 years ago.

One path leads to the rocks through which Wadi Gamla winds its way. It affords a lovely view of this wild gorge; in winter, there's a waterfall. South of the parking lot is an observation point and a memorial to the settlers of the Golan Heights.

Leaving Gamla the way you came, you turn left on Road No. 808, continuing north until you reach a crossing; turn left (west) onto Road No. 87 until you get to another crossing. Here you turn right on Road No. 9088 towards **Katzrin.** Turn right to Katzrin Industrial Centre; 200m further on, to the left, is the Golan Heights Winery, which produces some of Israel's finest wines (Golan, Gamla, Yarden, etc.). There is a visitors' centre with guided tours of the winery, including wine-tasting, for a small fee.

Before you reach the town you will find a sign pointing to your right that says: **"Katzrin Synagogue."** A short ride on a secondary road brings you to the archaeological site of one of the many ancient synagogues found on the Golan. This was one of the first places settled by the 12 tribes of Israel around 1300 BCE. The synagogue probably dates from the 4th century CE.

When you drive to nearby Katzrin, try to look in at the **Golan Archaeological Museum,** which will give you a general idea of archaeological excavations and finds in the area. Highlights include the heroic story of the Jewish city of Gamla and Jewish, Christian, and pagan settlement during the Byzantine period.

At nearby Park Qatzrin, the open-air museum and synagogue in the ancient village recreates Jewish daily life during the Talmudic period. The park also includes an outdoor exhibit of modern basalt sculpture and its natural environment. Open Sun. – Thurs. 8 a.m. – 4 p.m. Fridays 8 a.m. – 1 p.m. Saturdays and holidays 10 a.m. – 4 p.m. Entrance fee. Tel. (06)961350.

Katzrin, a town founded in 1967, serves as the urban centre of the Golan. It is a good example of a modern, planned Israeli town. Several restaurants and shops are centred in a service area. The town has some industry and provides services to the agricultural settlements of the Golan.

Back on the main road, turn right and return to Tzomet Katzrin. The right fork brings you, 14 km. later, to Arik's Bridge over the Jordan River. Drive around the Sea of Galilee to Tiberias.

ROUTE No. 20 (Map: Northern Sheet N6 to M4 and N2,3)

Eastern Upper Galilee

Tiberias – Rosh Pinna (26 km.) – Zefat (34 km.) – Meron (41 km.) – Bar'am (52 km.) – Metzudat Yesha (77 km.) – Tiberias (121 km.) (Road Nos. 89, 90, 899.)

(Distances in brackets refer to start of route.)

Drive out of Tiberias on Road No. 90, which swerves north along the Sea of Galilee. Follow Route No. 17 in reverse until you reach the Vered HaGalil farm guest house 21 km. away. Keep to the main road until you reach **Rosh Pinna** 5 km. later (see Route No. 18).

Turn left up the main Rosh Pinna Street and climb the mountain road (No. 89). You will be able to pull over at an observation point near the Shlomo Ben-Yosef Memorial, for a view of the plain between the Sea of Galilee and the Hula Valley, backed by the Bashan and Golan mountains.

The road continues to weavc and twist, rising all the time through invigorating mountain scenery. After 8 km. the road goes straight on for Akko. You should branch off left to Zefat.

ZEFAT (SAFAD) (Map: M4)

A divine presence seems to hover over the mountainous peaks of Zefat, one of the four cities holy to Judaism.

Its old city, balancing precariously on the west, overlooks the humped Galilee as far down as the waters of the Sea of Galilee. It is a world unto itself. Something of its golden age in the 16th and 17th centuries, when erudite rabbis and Kabbalists lived and studied here, seems to linger on. Yet Zefat is unassuming, and its cobbled streets and winding alleys are squeezed between whitewashed walls of low and curiously angled houses.

There are overhanging balconies where you will see wrinkled and devout inhabitants. Yiddish and Hebrew filter through the iron grille-work and out of the painted shutters. This is ironic in a way since it was Ladino speakers who gave the town a great name in the 16th century.

Zefat's synagogues are as small as the one-roomed Pennsylvanian Amish schools. Their exquisite precision of design makes for intimacy, warmth and piety.

The cool mountain air and winter snow apparently stimulate the sensibilities of a great number of creative artists, for they have chosen to make Zefat their home.

Their quarter also exudes an overpowering charm. In fact, the Artists' Quarter, which is part of the old city, is far more of an aesthetic adventure than tramping through Jaffa because nothing has been touched up to flutter the tourist. Everything is preserved in its original state.

Zefat may be seen in less than a day, but such is the magic of its spiritual touch that you will find yourself wanting to return again and again to its dizzying confines.

You can take a two-hour walking tour that will bring you to at least three ancient synagogues, explaining their history and giving you a taste of Kabbala, Jewish mysticism. The tour starts out across the street from the Tourist Information Office at 21 Jerusalem St.

The schedule is as follows: Summer – Sunday–Thursday: 10.00 a.m., 2 p.m.; Friday: 10.00 a.m. Winter – Sunday–Thursday: 10 a.m., 2 p.m.; Friday: 10 a.m. For more information, call (06)974597.

Location: Zefat hangs high in the Upper Galilean mountains, peering down on the Sea of Galilee, southeast, looking across to Mt. Meron in the west, and lying about 15 km. south of the Lebanese border.

Climate: cool, mountain air and invigorating summers. Snow often falls during the winter when it is usually chilly and even icy. Zefat is 900 m. above sea level.

Population: most of Zefat's 20,000 or so residents are people who settled in the new area after the War of Independence. In the old city, however, there are many religious families with age-old ties to the city.

Tourist Information Office: 22, Rehov Yerushalayim, tel. (06) 930633. Open: Sun. – Thurs. 8.30 a.m. – 12.30 p.m., 4 – 6 p.m. Fri. 9 a.m. – 12 noon.

Zefat

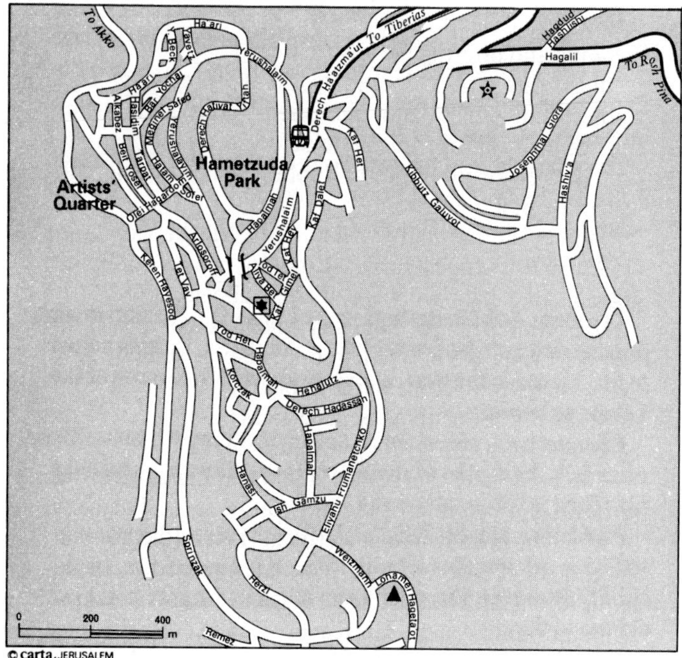

History

The Talmud refers to the city as Tzefiya, and in the last years of the Second Temple it was fortified by Josephus Flavius before he became a turncoat.

The Crusaders turned it into an administrative centre, building one of the largest Frankish castles in the Middle East. It was besieged by Saladin in 1188.

When Sultan Beibars finally took it in 1266, he decapitated the men and sold the women and children into slavery.

As the Crusader cities along the coast fell to the Mamelukes, many Jews moved to Zefat. The town prospered and was the capital of a province and a lively commercial centre. Zefat took in many Jews following their expulsion from Spain in 1492. During the 16th century it positively shone with learning.

The rabbis and the sages were all attracted by the proximity of the tomb of Rabbi **Shimon Bar-Yochai** at Meron. He was the author of the "Zohar" (or Book of Splendour), which was the basic book of the Kabbalists. It is a mystical commentary on the Five Books of Moses and proceeds from the premise that every letter, word and line in the scriptures is significant, containing a higher mystical meaning and offering the key to life.

Illustrious rabbis flocked to Zefat's precincts. They studied and taught and published books and poems, spurred on by the opening in Zefat in 1563 of the country's first Hebrew printing press; Rabbi **Moshe Galante** published the first book there.

Among the luminaries was Rabbi **Moshe Cordovero** (1522–1570), whose "Pardes Rimonim" (Grove of Pomegranates) is a standard work on the Kabbala.

His brother-in-law, **Solomon Alkabetz,** composed the hymn, "Lecha Dodi," which to this day is sung by Jews everywhere to welcome in the Sabbath.

Many of the poems of **Israel Najara** (1555–1628) have become part of Sephardi synagogue ritual.

The greatest teacher of all, Rabbi **Isaac Luria,** was a hermit in Egypt before arriving in Zefat in 1569. The name by which he is known to posterity is **Ha'Ari** (the lion). By the time he died, only three years later, he had become a living legend and bequeathed a system of Kabbala known as the Lurianic system. His teachings were embodied in a book, "Etz Hayim" (Tree of Life), published by his disciple **Haim Vital** (1543–1620).

Joseph Caro's magnum opus, the "Shulkhan Arukh," was completed in 1536.

A breakdown in law and order along the Galilean highways, together with a plague in 1742 and an earthquake in 1759, account for Zefat's decline. However, the Jewish population increased somewhat with the arrival of some Russian Hassidim in 1776.

Napoleon's troops were garrisoned in Zefat to secure the highway to Damascus.

The Crusader castle was completely destroyed in the earthquake that shook the town in 1837, and many of the loosened stones were used in building other houses in the city.

During the War of Independence, Zefat's religious community helped fortify the Jewish quarter on the Sabbath, with Rabbi Avraham Zida Heller donning his Sabbath clothes before joining in the defence. The Arabs originally held the Citadel and Mt. Canaan but fled after the Jews stormed the Citadel during a night-time operation.

Zefat has since flourished as a vacation centre and Jewish pilgrimage site.

Legends

Many legends and tales are woven around the lives of the great Renaissance rabbis and authors of Zefat.

One of them earned Rabbi Yossi Banai the affectionate title of "HaLavan" (the white one). The story goes that a tyrannical Arab governor of Zefat ordered the Jews to bring him a certain number of white chickens, or face expulsion. The people prayed at the grave of the rabbi and, miraculously, all the chickens in the town turned white.

Another legend relates how the poet, Israel Najara, left his native Zefat to sing in the inns of Damascus. He pined so much for the Galilean mountain air that he decided to return. On the way he was accosted by robbers who decided to kill him, but they granted his sole request to be allowed a final prayer. He picked up his flute and played the haunting melody of a prayer. It so captivated the robbers' camels that they rose and began to dance. The robbers panicked and fled while the dancing camels followed Najara to Zefat.

Synagogues

The ancient synagogues of Zefat are west of Kikar HaMeginim, reached by descending the slopes from Rehov Yerushalayim into the old city.

Abohav: named after the 15th century Kabbalist, Rabbi Isaac Abohav. Ancient Torah Scroll used only on Rosh Hashanah, Yom Kippur and Shavuot. Wall facing Jerusalem was only one not damaged by the 1837 earthquake.

Alshekh: beautiful domed ceiling in 16th century synagogue. Named after Rabbi Moses Alshekh (1508–1600), author of commentary on the Torah.

Banai: believed to be Rabbi Yossi Banai's house. One of the most attractive, with adjoining courtyard. The 16th century rabbi is buried within. Ancient Torah Scroll carried in joyous procession to Meron on Lag Ba'omer. Stone floor, wooden ceiling and benches around three sides. Women's gallery. Yeshiva within small adjoining room. If locked, ask for caretaker.

Caro: off Rehov Beit Josef, just after Rehov Alkabetz. In honour of Rabbi Joseph Caro (1488–1575), who codified daily religious practices in "Shulkhan Arukh." He is said to have worked and prayed here. Admirable simplicity and intimacy of interior. Small domed room beneath synagogue believed to be where angel appeared as wandering preacher, inspiring him to write "A preacher of righteousness."

Ha'Ari (Ashkenazi): Rehov Najara. Traditionally the site where Rabbi Isaac Luria went to welcome the Sabbath. Built after his death and damaged in 1837 earthquake. Fifteen years later rebuilt on 16th century foundations. Superlative art work on Holy Ark, with intricate carvings and reliefs dating from 19th century. Make it a point to talk to the caretaker of the synagogue (and perhaps give him some money). He knows a lot about the town's history, both ancient and modern.

Ha'Ari (Sephardi): at base of old city, close to ancient cemetery. Most famous of all Zefat's synagogues. Exquisite decorations and architecture. Great craftsmanship in central bimah, neatly enclosed by low, arched ceiling and benches round sides. Finely-carved wooden doors. With surrounding wall, served as Haganah stronghold during War of Independence. Caretaker expects donation before opening doors.

Other Sites

Artists' Quarter: Kiryat HaOmanim. Turn right at traffic light on southern tip of Rehov Yerushalayim. Cluster of quaint, stone houses with studios built around former mosque, now serving as site of general exhibition of Zefat artists. Open: Sun. – Thurs. 9 a.m. – 7 p.m. in summer (winter 9 a.m. – 5 p.m.) Fri. 9 a.m. – 2 p.m. Sat. 10 a.m. – 1 p.m.

Caves: there are a number of caves in and around Zefat. Most famous is Cave of Shem V'Ever, close to bridge above Rehov Yerushalayim and close to Rehov Palmach. Musty interior. Presided over by old man who lights candles and recites prayers, after which he expects donation. Said to be place where Shem and Ever, son and great-great grandson of Noah, studied.

Cemetery: at base of slopes on extreme west of city. Adjacent to Ha'Ari road by car. Modern cemetery has graves of underground fighters executed in Akko by British in 1947, and of men who fell in War of Independence.

Ancient cemetery further south has tombs of learned rabbis of 16th century including Ha'Ari, Cordovero, Alkabetz and Alshekh. Karaites of Damascus are said to have built domed tomb traditionally regarded as site of grave of prophet Hosea.

Citadel Hill: Givat HaMetzuda. Park above centre of city with magnificent view over Zefat as far as Sea of Galilee. Handed over by British to Arabs in April 1948. Captured by Jews four days before Independence. Memorial to soldiers of 1948 on crown of hill, above ruins of Crusader fortifications. Restaurant. Band during summer.

Davidka monument: Rehov Yerushalayim above old

city. Primitive mortar developed by Israeli forces in 1948.

Old Turkish Government House: Rehov Aliya Bet.

Museums

Hameiri House: A historic house in the Old City dating from 1517, which now houses a museum, a research institute for the history of Zefat, and an educational centre. Hundreds of items show the life of Jewish community of Zefat through the years. Open: Sun.–Fri. 9 a.m.–2 p.m. Entrance fee. Tel. (06) 971307, 921932. P. O. B. 1028.

The Israel Bible Museum: the Bible in Art: on northern rim of Citadel Hill. Open: March – Sept. Sun. – Thurs. 10 a.m. – 6 p.m., Sat. 10 a.m. – 2 p.m.; Oct. and Nov. Sat. – Thurs. 10 a.m. – 2 p.m.; Dec. and Feb. Sun. – Thurs. 10 a.m. – 2 p.m. Sat. closed. Closed Fridays. Closed January. Admission free.

Museum of the Art of Printing: within Artists' Quarter. First Hebrew press in Holy Land, founded in Zefat in 16th century. Display of 500 years of printing. Open: Sun. – Thurs. 10 a.m. – 12 noon, 4–6 p.m. Fri. 10 a.m. – 12 noon Sat. 10 a.m. – 12 noon. Admission free. Tel. (06) 920947.

Ethiopian Folkart Centre: Eshtam House, Old City. Documentation and information centre. Original handicrafts. Exhibition and sale. Open: Sun. – Thurs. 10 a.m. – 4 p.m. Fri. 10 a.m. – 1 p.m. Admission free.

A Walk In Zefat

Start the walk from the **Town Hall** near the entrance to town, diagonally opposite Gan Rothschild, on the main street, **Rehov Yerushalayim.** At the first corner to the left, just past the Town Hall, the road leads to the **Israel Bible Museum**, where the permanent exhibit of works by international artist Phillip Ratner is housed. The museum is in the former home of the Turkish governor in Zefat.

From the Museum the road leads further uphill to the ruins of a 13th century **Crusader fortress.** Today, at **Hametzuda**, a park has been developed on the site where there is also a **memorial** to those who fell in the 1948 War of Independence. There are breathtaking views in every direction.

Descend from the park alongside the Israel Bible Museum and return to Rehov Yerushalayim. A short distance along Zefat's main street, you come to two narrow lanes to your right: **HaMeginim** and **Bar Yokhai,** both of which lead into the old city and its synagogue quarter. Most synagogues have a deacon (shames) on the premises who will be happy to show you the house of worship and tell you something of its history.

Return to Rehov Yerushalayim and continue to a flight of stairs, just before the bridge, which leads down to the **Artists' Quarter.** Also in the Artists' Quarter is the **Museum of the Art of Printing.** Zefat was the first town in the land where books were printed.

Leave the Artists' Quarter and climb the stairs leading to the bridge. Alongside them, next to the bridge on **Rehov Hapalmakh,** is the **Cave of Shem and Ever.** A white-domed building marks the site of the cave.

After the bridge to your left is Rehov Aliya Bet with the **"Saraya"** – Old Turkish Government House. Return to Rehov Yerushalayim. (An organized daily walking tour leaves from 18 Rehov Yerushalayim at 9.30 a.m. It lasts two hours and takes you to the old city and synagogues. Tel. (06)972763.

Up the road that leads to Amuka is **Bat Ya'ar**, a farm that organizes trips on horseback around the area, jeep trips and adventurous outdoor activities such as rappeling down cliffs. The farm has a restaurant.

Continue driving west on Road No. 89 for 7 km. of hilly, wooded countryside until you arrive at a picnic site at the entrance to Meron. Then turn left after the Delek gas station for a look at the principal sites.

MERON (Map: M4)

This small village is the focal point of one of the most colourful annual pilgrimages in the calendar of Jewish holidays.

On **Lag Ba'Omer,** the 33rd day after the counting of the Omer, from the eve of Passover, tens of thousands of young and old trek up the slopes of 1,200-m.-high **Mt. Meron** to the **Tombs** of **Rabbi Shimon Bar Yochai** and his son, **Eleazar**.

The Kabbalists hold that Rabbi Bar Yochai vowed to

the Almighty that the Torah would never be forgotten. It is in fulfilment of this vow that the ancient Scrolls of the Law are taken in joyous procession from Zefat's old synagogues to the rabbi's tomb.

If you happen to be here during Lag Ba'Omer, usually in May, you will find large tent cities where the pilgrims slaughter many sheep and cattle during the few days they camp here.

There is a **Yeshiva** within the compound of the tombs of the rabbi and his son. The court where the tombs are located was built by Rabbi **Abraham ben Mordechai Galante** in the second half of the 16th century.

Walk further up the mountain, up some steps a few hundred metres further off, and you'll come to one of the oldest Galilean synagogues, built in the 3rd century CE. Its east wall is carved out of the sheer rock scarp.

Many Jewish sages are buried in Meron. Among them is one of the most revered of all – **Rabbi Hillel,** of the 1st century CE, whose liberal teachings are the inspiration behind many of the rabbinical decisions in our time. His cave-tomb is reached by a path leading down to the valley from the left of the Yeshiva.

Rabbi Shammai, a contemporary of Hillel, is believed to be buried close by, in the massive double sarcophagus set on the hill facing Hillel's tomb.

At the top of this hill lies the excavated synagogue of Khirbet Shema, in use throughout the 3rd–5th centuries CE. An unusual feature is the fixed shrine for Torah Scrolls; most of the synagogues of this period, such as that at Capernaum, had mobile Arks.

Return now to the gas station and turn left after it in the direction of Sasa. (You're still on Road No. 89.) Pass Moshav **Sifsufa** and turn left before **Jish (Gush Halav),** on the slopes of a hill on your right. Jish is the Arabic name of the village occupied by Maronites (Catholics) who originate in the Lebanon. The sect is named after St. Maron, a 6th century holy man.

Jewish historians will recall that John of Giscala (Gush Halav), one of the leaders of the revolt against the Romans in the 1st century CE, came from here.

Drive on, with Mt. Meron on the left. A signpost points left to Rosh Haniqra at the northwestern edge of Israel; Bar'am and Metzudat Yesha are to the right along Road No. 899. The ruins of the village of Bar'am, destroyed shortly after the War of Independence, and uninhabited today because of a government decree, stand wistfully on a rise in the landscape. There is a parking lot to the right off the main road, next to the National Parks site.

Set high up in the mountains, almost on the border with Lebanon, **Bar'am** has the best preserved of the early Galilean synagogues. It dates from the end of the 2nd century or the early 3rd century CE.

The most impressive part of this synagogue, the main facade, stands to this day. Three stone portals seem to defy time and the elements. The centre portal is crowned by a semi-circular arch, decorated with a bas-relief of vine leaves and clusters of grapes. Part of the ornamental lintel has a sculptured garland set between two lions. Open: Sun.–Thurs. 8 a.m.–4 p.m., Fri. 8 a.m.–3 p.m. Entrance fee. Tel. (06)940400. Nearby is Kibbutz Bar'am.

The 25 km. drive from here to **Metzudat Yesha** takes you through scenery that is every bit as captivating as that in Jerusalem. But the predominant colours here are olive green and rock grey. The road clings to the Lebanese border, on the other side of which farmers grow Turkish tobacco and other crops.

The Israeli side is dotted with frontier settlements. A number of memorials stand on the side of the road. They provide silent evidence of the fact that terrorists from across the border brought murder to an area that was free of incidents until the end of the 1967 war. Notice how the orchards of Kibbutz Malkiya end within centimetres of the security fence.

Continue along the weaving road until, just before Metzudat Yesha, Road No. 886 leads off left to Tel Hai, 20 km. away (see Route No. 18).

METZUDAT YESHA (Map: N2)

Bitter fighting raged around this British police post during the War of Independence, because it commands the heights above the Hula Valley and is at an important intersection for the roads leading above the Naphtali mountains to Metula, as well as the roads filtering down to the Upper Galilean settlements.

From the observation post you can see far across the Hula Valley and across to the Golan Heights.

The memorial behind the observation post lists the names of the Israelis who fell in action during the battles of 1948 in this area. Here, too, are buried some of the twenty-eight fighters who attempted to destroy the fortress.

Continue down the hill to the Hula Valley and turn right for the return trip to Tiberias on Road No. 90. The route now links up with Route No. 18. If you did not have time to see Hazor along that route, you have another opportunity now.

ACCOMMODATION ON ROUTE No. 20

(See also general "Accommodation" section.)

HOTELS

BETWEEN ROSH PINNA AND ZEFAT
Seaview Hotel Tel. (06)937014, 937013. Vegetarian and fish restaurant, health farm.

ZEFAT

Rimon Inn Tel.(06)920665. Artists' Colony.
Zefat Tel.(06)930914. Mt. Cana'an.
Central Tel.(06)972666. 37, Jerusalem St.
David Tel.(06) 971662. Mt. Cana'an.
Ron Tel.(06)972590. Hativat Yiftah St.

Berlinson House (Tel Aviv) Tel.(06)972555.
Pisga Tel.(06)730105. Mt. Cana'an.
Ruckenstein Tel.(06)920060. Mt. Cana'an.
Hadar Tel.(06)930068.
Nof HaGalil Tel.(06)931595. Mt. Cana'an.

YOUTH HOSTELS

(See also Route No. 18.)
Bet Benyamin. Zefat Tel. (06) 937086.

ROUTE No. 21 (Map: Northern Sheet N6 to M9)

The Valley of Bet Shean

Tiberias – Kokhav Hayarden (29 km.) – Bet Shean (45 km.) – Sakhne (48 km.) – Ma'ayan Harod (64 km.) (Road Nos. 71, 90, 669, 717.)

(Distances in brackets refer to start of route.)

This very short route is packed with adventure and brings you close to the Jordan River, to the Bet Shean, Harod and Jezreel Valleys, and to many frontier settlements. At the end of the trip you have the choice of returning to Tiberias or proceeding to Haifa or to Jerusalem (through Samaria) and on to Tel Aviv.

Drive south along the **Sea of Galilee** on Road No. 90 towards Hamei Tiberias, following the beginning of Route No. 17 as far as **Zemakh.** There you should take the right turn towards Bet Shean.

The first kibbutz you pass is **Sha'ar Hagolan,** which has a fine prehistory museum, then **Afiqim,** with its furniture factory, and, as you bear right, **Ashdot Ya'aqov,** one of the largest kibbutzim (which has been divided into two for political reasons).

If you turn off to the right to Menahemya, you can visit Israel's only Medical Museum, **Bet Harofeh**, which has exhibits and an audiovisual presentation on the history of medicine. One wing of the museum is devoted to the history of Menahemya, the first modern Jewish settlement in the Bet Shean Valley. Open: Sun.–Thurs. 9 a.m.–2 p.m. Entrance fee: adult NIS 3, children NIS 2.50. Tel. (06)751554.

Lying in the Jordan Valley, these settlements are like closed ovens in the long summer months. In the early days, before air-conditioning became a familiar sight on these kibbutzim, primitive cooling systems, with water dripping down grass-covered window-screens, brought some relief.

Round the corner and cross the bridge over the Jordan. You are now in the **Bet Shean Valley,** bounded on your left by the **Gilead Mountains** in Jordan, whose beautv inspired the poet to write in the Song of Songs (6:5), "Your hair is like a flock of goats moving down the slopes of Gilead."

All is quiet, with the snaking Jordan River forming the border between Jordan and Israel. However, the scene was far from tranquil for the two years succeeding the 1967 war. This was the only border that rumbled with artillery, mortars and tanks. Border patrols were fired on by bazooka-carrying groups hiding in the thick reeds guarding the river. In winter, infiltrators drifted across the swollen river on tractor tubes, bringing with them their store of weapons and explosives.

Today the area is as silent as the waters of the Jordan. But if you stop at any of the kibbutzim or moshavim – **Gesher, Hamadiya, Ma'oz Haim, Kfar Rupin** – ask to see the concrete-lined subterranean shelters. They were "home" for many people during many a long night.

If you look beyond the fields you will see the slashed, defaced earth of part of the **Afro-Syrian Rift** that ends in Africa.

Turn right when the signpost directs you to Kokhav Hayarden, and continue up the tarred mountain road (No. 717) for 6 km. until you reach the parking area.

KOKHAV HAYARDEN (Map: M8)

In Hebrew the name means "Star of the Jordan." The Crusaders, who raised the giant castle on the 500 m. high mountain, named it Belvoir. It is almost a castle in the air. From here a spectacular panorama unfolds. Down below, the Sea of Galilee is clearly visible, with the Jordan River leaking out at its southern extremity. To the south – biblical **Mt. Gilboa** and the Jezreel Valley. The hills of Galilee are in the north-west.

The Knights of the Order of the Hospitallers bought this site in the 12th century from the Velos family, members of the Galilean Dukedom. Then, when they had built the seemingly impregnable castle, they successfully withstood attacks by the Saracens. Finally, it was captured by Saladin. When the National Parks Authority restored the site, they found that many of the stones used in building it had been brought up from a 3rd century CE synagogue at the Jewish townlet of Kokhav, 700 m. lower down and southeast of the fortress.

Open: seven days a week. Apr. – Sept. 8 a.m. – 5 p.m. Oct. – Mar. 8 a.m. – 4 p.m. Entrance fee.

The road through the Bet Shean Valley (No. 90) passes the settlements of Neve Ur, Yardena, Bet Yosef and Hamadiya in quick succession. There is a turn-off right to Afula; the road you're on crosses a bridge and continues straight on to Bet Shean.

If you want to get even closer to the Jordan River and meet some of the friendliest kibbutzniks in the country, why not take the left fork (Road No. 71) to Kibbutz **Ma'oz Haim.** Pass factories employing Bet Shean residents and fork left again. Ma'oz Haim is one kilometre further on, just past Kibbutz **Neve Etan**.

The name "Ma'oz Haim" means "Haim's Stronghold," and it commemorates Haim Sturman, a HaShomer veteran who was killed by an Arab-planted mine which exploded when he was on a land-purchasing mission in the area. You will learn more about him in the museum named after him at Kibbutz En Harod later on along this route.

Ma'oz Haim, founded in 1937, was in the forefront of the shelling after the Six Day War. Its prize dairy herd was decimated during one bombardment.

At the end of the cotton fields, on the banks of the Jordan River, you can see the **Sheikh Hussein Bridge** which was destroyed in 1948. Some believe that it was at this point of the river that the Midianites fled from Gideon's army (Judges 7:24).

It may well have been over the fields of present day Ma'oz Haim that King Saul's body was carried for cremation and burial on the Gilead (I Samuel 31:8-13).

To get to Bet Shean take the left fork on the road back, pass a war memorial and factories, and you are within the precincts of the city.

BET SHEAN (Map: M9)

A Talmudic sage is credited with the remark that "if paradise is in the land of Israel then its gate must be Bet Shean."

The present town is the home of some 15,000 people. It lies close to the prominent tel of Bet Shean where archaeologists have uncovered the remains of 18 cities. The tel was settled more than 7,000 years ago and the town's name is believed to derive from a Canaanite god.

Bet Shean is closely associated with nearby Mt. Gilboa where, according to the Bible (I Samuel 31:9), King Saul was slain. The main thoroughfare running through the modern town is dedicated to King Saul's memory and named after him.

Your first port of call should be the **Municipal Museum,** to your right, a few hundred metres after you pass the memorial on your way in. The collection gives you an immediate insight into the antiquity of the town and the valley as most of the exhibits are Canaanite, Israelite and Roman. Open: Sun. – Thurs. 8 a.m. – 3.30 p.m. Fri. 8 a.m. – 12.30 p.m. Entrance fee.

At the museum, you could ask the director to show you around the 6th century Byzantine Monastery of Lady Marie, located at the northern edge of the town. The monastery ruins and the exquisite mosaic floors are worth a visit.

As you drive along the main road through the town, several signposts direct you to the spectacular **Roman theatre**. This lies to the south of the mound where over 20 successive settlements have been excavated, dating back to the 5th millennium BCE. Ongoing excavations near the theatre are revealing the remains of the **Roman-Byzantine city** of **Scythopolis**, destroyed by an earthquake in 749 CE. Many structures are currently being restored, so the most impressive feature is the Roman theatre, which could seat about 7,000 people. It was built around 200 CE and has eight vaulted entrances (vomitoria) around its circumference, and two main entrances along the axis of the stage. There were three tiers of seats, the first of which is completely preserved. The huge stone stage, now reconstructed with a wooden floor, was backed by a colonnaded structure, richly decorated with marble, statues and reliefs; it is now being restored. Performances of all kinds are held here, including an annual festival with musicians and dancers from around the world.

You can also see the Byzantine bathouse, an elaborate building with nine halls, paved in marble mosaic. Or you can stroll down Palladius' Street, a long colonnaded street paved with basalt slabs laid in a herringbone pattern and flanked by a raised pavement and colonnaded porticoes, on to which opened a row of marble-fronted shops. Mosaics with geometric and floral patterns were found here, including a beautiful 6th century medallion showing the head of the city's guardian goddess. The city also possessed a semi-circular Roman temple, dedicated to Dionysos, the god of wine and the city's patron deity. Two other Roman colonnaded streets and a row of Byzantine shops have been found, as well as the basilica – the hall that served as the city's main public building.

You can also visit a potter's workshop from the Early Arab period, complete with ten brick kilns and drying rooms, and a street and residential quarter from the Byzantine period. On the southern edge of the ancient city is the Roman amphitheatre, where chariot races and gladiatorial contests took place; it is still being excavated. Open: Apr. – Sept. Sun. – Thurs. 8 a.m. – 5 p.m. Oct. – March 8 a.m. – 4 p.m. Fri. closes one hour earlier. Sat. 8 a.m. – 5 p.m. Entrance fee.

Continue along Rehov Shaul Hamelekh, following the signpost left to Gan Hashlosha (Sakhne) on Road No. 669.

Mt. Gilboa looms over the kibbutz fields and you soon pass the detour to Kibbutz Tirat Zvi, 12 km. southeast and built on the banks of the Jordan River. The National Parks site of **Gan Hashlosha (Sakhne)** is further along the main road.

This restful park with unsullied grounds and natural swimming pools (all year temperature 28° C) below waterfalls beckons if you're in the mood for a quick dip and languid sunbathing. A **Museum of Regional and Mediterranean Archaeology** is located in the park. It has exhibits on discoveries in the Beth Shean Valley. Open: Sun.–Thurs. 8 a.m.–2 p.m., Sat. 10.30 a.m.–1 p.m. Entrance fee. Tel. (06) 583045.

The ravishing beauty of the site is enhanced by hundreds of trees, boulders and thick green lawns, making it an ideal picnic spot. Open daily. Entrance fee. The restaurant is open 8 a.m. – 4 p.m.

Near the exit there is a turning left to the farming settlement of **Ma'ale Gilboa**. A coiling tarred road leads up for 9 km. to the summit of Mt. Gilboa. If you have time on your hands it is worth the detour as the view from the heights overlooking the Harod and Jezreel Valleys is quite astonishing.

While driving up **Mt. Gilboa** you also get a chance to see many wild flowers among pine, carob and eucalyptus trees. Notable among the flowers is the delicate Mt. Gilboa Iris that grows nowhere else on earth. It grows here in spring in spite of David's curse, on learning of the death of Saul and Jonathan on these slopes: "Ye mountains of

Gilboa let there be no dew or rain upon you, nor upsurging of the deep!" (2 Samuel 1:21).

Continuing along the route below, the road passes Kibbutz **Bet Alpha** and next to it Kibbutz **Hefzibah,** into which you should turn for a look at the famous synagogue mosaic.

The pioneer farmers on this kibbutz were digging an irrigation ditch in 1928 when they accidentally exposed what is still the best preserved mosaic floor of an ancient synagogue in Israel. What they stumbled on has become known as the 6th century CE synagogue of Bet Alpha. The National Parks Authority has helped maintain it by covering it with an enormous building.

A large central panel holds the 12 signs of the Zodiac in exquisite colours. Their names are written in Hebrew and Aramaic. A lower panel illustrates Abraham's intended sacrifice of Isaac. Above a ram tied to a tree are the words, "Behold the Ram." The hand emerging from heaven is captioned "Lay not" (thine hand upon the boy). The names Abraham and Isaac are inscribed above their heads.

The kibbutzniks sell table mats, book markers, ashtrays and other objects carrying colourful representations of the mosaics. These may be bought at the site or at the nearby cafe within the kibbutz. The site is open Sun. – Thurs. Apr. – Sept. 8 a.m. – 5 p.m. Oct. – March 8 a.m. – 4 p.m. Fri 8 a.m. – 4 p.m. Sat. 8 a.m. – 5 p.m. Entrance fee.

Follow Road No. 669 past more cultivated fields and turn left towards Afula on reaching the forbidding Shatta Prison, which is on Road No. 71.

The first turning right after the turn-off right to **Tel Yosef** brings you to the artistically inclined Kibbutz **En Harod,** near where the Mamelukes defeated the Mongols in 1260. There are two museums worth seeing. The first is **Mishkan Le'omanut,** En Harod's Museum of Art. The rich variety includes Jewish folk art, modern Israeli painting, sculptures and graphic art. Open: Sun.–Thurs. 9 a.m.–4.30 p.m., Fri. 9 a.m.–1 p.m., Sat. 10 a.m.–4.30 p.m. Entrance fee. Tel. (06) 531670.

Drive on for a few seconds until you reach **Bet Sturman,** a museum-institute for research on the eastern Jezreel Valley. The photographic display shows pioneer life on the settlements. Open: Sun. – Thurs. 8 a.m. – 3 p.m. Sat. 10 a.m. – 2 p.m. Entrance fee. Tel. (06) 531605, 533284.

After returning to the main road turn right, pass **Geva,**

and almost immediately take the left turn towards **Moshav Gidona**. There is a camping site near the moshav houses, with a shop and a kiosk. To the right of this is the National Parks site of **Ma'ayan Harod.**

MA'AYAN HAROD (Map: L9)

This charming picnic and swimming area is set below the heavily wooded northern face of Mt. Gilboa, at the bottom of which a stream emanates from the base of a cave. It is believed to be the same spring where the divinely-inspired Judge, Gideon, chose his troops for the attack on the Midianite (Bedouin) throngs who had invaded the area. According to Judges 7:6, Gideon watched 10,000 men drink at this spring and chose only the 300 who drank standing up. He then launched a surprisingly novel night-time raid on the enemy, completely routing them.

The vaulted tomb above the spring contains the remains of Yehoshua Hankin, who purchased 600,000 dunams of land – including this tract – for Jewish settlement, so earning for himself the epitaph "The Redeemer of the Valley".

Note that the artificial lake used as a swimming pool at Ma'ayan Harod is closed on Thursdays, when the water is changed. Open: Sun. – Thurs. Apr. – Sept. 8 a.m. – 5 p.m. Oct. – March 8 a.m. – 4 p.m. Fri. closes one hour earlier. Sat. 8 a.m. – 5 p.m. (summer), 8 a.m. – 4 p.m. (winter). Entrance fee.

Next to the National Park is a camping site with full facilities. Tel. (06)581660.

You now have several alternative destinations ahead of you. If you wish to travel to **Tel Aviv,** return to Road No. 71, and turn left onto Road No. 675. After 12 km. turn left onto Road No. 65. Drive along this road until you get to Highway No. 2.

To get to **Afula**, you should turn left from Ma'ayan Harod onto Road No. 71 for 10 km.

To return to **Tiberias** you may either backtrack over the entire route or drive on to Afula and join up with the second half of Route No. 11, leading you up and around Mt. Tabor on Road No. 65.

To get to **Haifa** from Afula, take Road No. 60 north, No. 73 west, and then No. 75.

The Negev

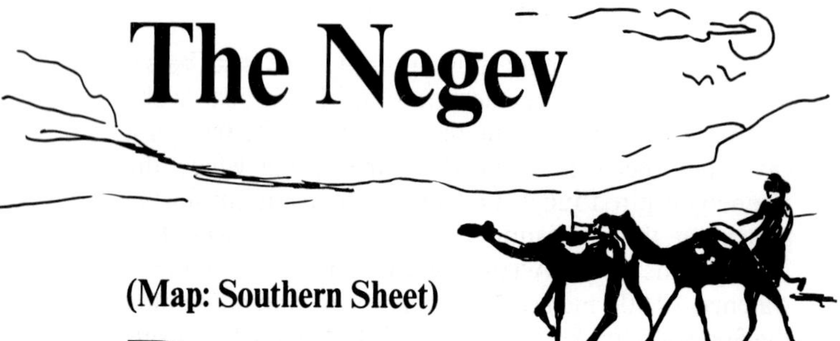

(Map: Southern Sheet)

Deceptively quiet and barren, the Negev packs more surprises than meet the eye, between the Bedouin market in Beer Sheva and the coral reefs of Elat.

There are scattered oases, great stretches of hard limestone dolomite rock and red Nubian sandstone, flat vistas of saline earth and craters that tell the story of geological shifts and erosion from time immemorial.

All our Negev routes radiate out of **Beer Sheva**, a third of the way between Tel Aviv and Elat. Follow one of these routes south and you'll see how the wind and rain and erosion have given the desert a swirling choreography all of its own. Mountains swoop and hills ribbed with layers of rock change colour by the minute with the rise and fall of the sun.

During the winter months you may even witness the phenomenal torrential floods. They follow rainfall of only a few centimetres which cannot be absorbed by the cracked ground. When the floods have spent themselves, the Negev breaks out in exquisite colour with myriad wild flowers, reed grasses and tamarisks.

Our routes to Elat direct you through development towns such as **Dimona** and **Mitzpe Ramon**. They are indicative of the huge deposits of manganese, sulphur, fluorite, mica, phosphates, bitumen, clay and gypsum secreted below the desert.

Further south, on Route No. 23, are the copper deposits, extracted from the legendary **King Solomon's Mines**. The green rock waste – Elat stone – is used for earrings, brooches, rings and ashtrays and sold all over the country, but particularly in Elat.

Also along this route, between the Dead Sea and Elat, is the **Arava**, an elongated expanse of yellow, ochre and pink. Forming part of the Afro-Syrian Rift Valley below the Mountains of Moab, it will undoubtedly be the highlight of your trip through the desert. In Hebrew it means desert plain. But in every language it spells miracle for here the young kibbutzniks and moshavniks are turning the dust bowl green with their off-season fruit, vegetable and flower gardens. They're accomplishing this in spite of sizzling 40-degree centigrade temperatures, and land and wells heavy with salt.

Much of their water is piped from the north. But along Routes 23 and 24 you'll arrive at the ruined cities of **Shivta, Avdat** and **Kurnub** (Mamshit) where the Nabateans learned more than 2,000 years ago how to catch and store vital rainwater and so survive in the bleak wilderness.

Beer Sheva is also the starting point for outings to **Arad**, the mountain-fortress of **Massada**, and the **Dead Sea** where, at the lowest point on earth, you will see a moonscape of mounds bleached detergent-white by the sticky salt, and where you can have the thrill of a lifetime reading a newspaper while floating on the glazed sea.

A word of caution before you start off: travellers are advised to take along spare packs of food and cans of water in case they have a breakdown. There is regular traffic along Route No. 23 as well as gas stations and roadside cafes. But Route No. 24, from Mitzpe Ramon south, has fewer of these facilities and traffic is lighter.

As a result of Israel's evacuation of Sinai, new military facilities and many new roads are being built in the Negev; not all of them are indicated on the maps.

Beer Sheva

(Map: Southern Sheet F23)

A watering hole for Abraham's sheep has become, nearly 4,000 years later, an oasis of civilization in the surrounding desert. It stands as the gateway to the Negev, straddling the roads leading south and those cutting across–country from the Dead Sea to the coast.

This has made it **the Capital of the Negev** and the obvious choice for industrial plants processing minerals from the desert. It is also perfectly positioned for tourists making stopovers on their way to and from Elat and the Dead Sea. The Egyptian border is 70 km. west of the city.

Everything in Beer Sheva seems geared to modernization. The Ben–Gurion University campus stands as proof of progress in the wilderness. All around are flats for new immigrants, with finishing touches of stucco and paint distinguishing them from the drab apartments of the fifties and sixties.

Beer Sheva nevertheless remains rooted in the past and tied to the lore of the wilderness. The weekly Thursday morning Bedouin market is the highlight of a visit. It heralds the appearance of robed and veiled nomads, cutting across the skyline in a file of goats and camels laden with bales full of wool, embroidered materials and trinkets. Remember to get there shortly after sunrise, because within a few hours they and their camels disappear over the hills from where they came.

A number of art galleries may be found on Rehov Smilansky in the old city. Coffee and cakes are served in the courtyards of the old Arab houses.

Location: on a plain 107 km. southeast of Tel Aviv, 286 km. north of Elat, 62 km. west of Massada (or Dead Sea) and 60 km. east of Ashqelon (or the Mediterranean Sea).

Climate: hot and dry, typical of the desert. The nights are cool and sometimes even cold during summer. The low humidity is ideal for persons suffering from asthma.

Population: about 134,000.

Tourist Information Office: Rehov Ben-Zevi 61, opposite the Central Bus Station, tel (057) 236001.

History

Beer Sheva's history reaches back to the Chalcolithic age (4000 BCE), 1,500 years before Abraham, when it was inhabited by a highly gifted agricultural people who first lived in subterranean dwellings. Excavations have revealed their jewellery, pottery, basket–work and ornaments – all fashioned by skilled craftsmen.

Above all, Beer Sheva is the town most closely associated with the Patriarchs. Isaac and Jacob lived here and Abraham gave it its name – The Well of the Oath – for it was here that he made his covenant with Abimelech: "And Abraham took sheep and oxen, and gave them unto Abimelech; and both of them made a covenant . . .

"Wherefore he called that place Beersheba; because there they sware both of them." (Gen. 21: 27 and 31.)

After the Exodus of the Israelites from Egypt, Beer Sheva was allotted to the Tribe of Simeon, and it was then the most southerly point of permanent habitation in the country, hence the biblical expression "From Dan to Beersheba." Further south was the domain of nomad shepherds.

When the Jews returned from their Babylonian captivity in the sixth century BCE, Beer Sheva was one of the towns they resettled: "And the rulers of the people dwelt at Jerusalem: the rest of the people also cast lots, to bring one of ten to dwell in Jerusalem the holy city, and nine parts to dwell in other cities . . .

"And they dwelt from Beersheba unto the valley of Hinnom" (Nehemiah 11: 1, and 30).

The earliest settlement of the present site, for the remains of ancient Beer Sheva lie 5 kilometres to the northeast, took place during the late Roman and Byzantine periods. Parts of a mosaic floor of a Byzantine church discovered here are on exhibit in the Negev Museum. The earlier settlement (Tel Sheva) has been excavated, and some of the objects found there are on display at the site.

Until the beginning of this century, Beer Sheva was just a collection of wells where Bedouin watered their flocks. In 1900, the Turkish authorities built a small town to serve as an administrative centre for the Negev's Bedouin tribes. During World War I, the Germans connected it by rail with the Sinai peninsula, and in 1917 the town fell to the British General Allenby in his northward advance. By 1948, its inhabitants numbered some 3,000.

During the War of Independence, Beer Sheva was held by the Egyptians who strongly fortified it; but they were overcome by Israeli forces in "Operation Ten Plagues" on 21 October 1948. Since then, Beer Sheva has grown into a town of 134,000 inhabitants who originate from every quarter of the globe. Many Soviet Jews have settled here. In the first years of the State of Israel it was very much a "Wild West" frontier town and it retains something of this flavour to this day.

Places of Interest

Abraham's Well: corner of Derekh Hebron and Rehov Keren Kayemet. Legend attributes this stone–enclosed well to that dug by the Patriarch Abraham.

Bedouin Market: held on Thursdays from 7 a.m. – 4 p.m. Visitors can take their pick from a large selection of Bedouin handicrafts such as beaten copperware, jewellery, embroidered camel bags and hand–woven rugs. The market takes place on Rehov Hebron, opposite the wholesalers' market.

Bedouin Village: Tel Sheva, 5 km. northeast of city adjacent to Tel Beer Sheva. Government housing for Bedouin who have left nomadic way of life. Residents wear contemporary clothing. Many engaged in earthworks and building trades. But adjacent to modern housing are tents and goat herds of nomadic Bedouin.

Ben–Gurion University of the Negev: Rehov Ben–Gurion. New campus with ultra modern buildings. Tours may be arranged by contacting the University's Public Relations Department, tel. (057) 461280, in advance. These tours are perhaps the most impressive of their kind.

Industrial Area: northeast of city, off Hebron Road.

Includes plants for bromine compounds, chemical works, Israel Aircraft Industries.

Music Conservatory: Derekh Hameshachrerim, near Municipality.

Negev Museum: Derekh Ha'atzmaut. In the hall of a former mosque. Exhibits include contemporary art and excavated objects from many surrounding sites; well worth a visit for insight into history of settlement of the region. Open: Sun. – Thurs. 10 a.m. – 6.30 p.m. Fri., Sat. 10 a.m. – 1 p.m. Entrance fee, except for Saturday.

Institutes for Applied Research (affiliated to Ben–Gurion University): 1, Derekh HaShalom, close to the Municipality. Research is conducted here into irrigation with brackish water; introduction and development of salt- and drought-resistant crops; algal biotechnology for production of valuable biochemicals; membrane and ion-exchange technologies; utilization of raw materials found in the Negev and the Dead Sea; industrial catalysis and biocatalysis; microencapsulation of biologically active materials; utilization of non-conventional energy sources. Prior appointments needed for visits in mornings only. Tel. (057) 461901.

Soroka Hospital: Rehov HaHaroshet, opposite University. Among the best in the country.

Tel Beer Sheva: 5 km. northeast of Beer Sheva on Hebron road. Biblical site excavated by Institute of Archaeology, Tel Aviv University; open 9 a.m.–4 p.m. Entrance fee..

Memorial to the Negev Palmach Brigade: situated to the northeast of the city, Hebron Road. A good road leads to the memorial which is open to the public throughout the year. Admission free.

Israeli Military Cemetery: Rehov Hatzerim.

British Military Cemetery (1914–18): Rehov Ha'atzmaut, next to the Youth Hostel.

WORSHIP

SYNAGOGUES

Or Haim (Sephardi). Rehov Ha'avot, Old Town.
Rabbi Klein (Ashkenazi). Rehov Ha'avot, Old Town.
Struma (Ashkenazi). Shikun Aleph, near Kupat Holim.
Conservative. Sderot Yerushalayim 72, tel. (057)421424.

CHURCHES

Roman Catholic. 51 Rehov Hashalom.

Protestant. American Mission, Rehov Ha'avot, Old Town.

For further information call at The Bible House, Rehov Rambam, tel. (057) 277022.

ACCOMMODATION

(See general "Accommodation" section for additional information.)

HOTELS

Desert Inn Tel. (057) 424922.
Zohar Tel. (057) 277335. 3 Shazar Blvd.
HaNegev Tel. (057) 277026. 26 Ha'atzmaut St.
Arava Tel. (057) 278792. 37 Histadrut St.
Aviv Tel. (057) 278059. 48 Mordei Hagetaot St.

YOUTH HOSTEL

Beer Sheva. 79 Ha'atzmaut St. Tel. (057) 277444.

USEFUL INFORMATION

Magen David Adom: tel.101; corner Sokolov and Weizmann St.
Police: tel. 100.
Fire Brigade: tel. 102.
Government Tourist Information Office: Rhov Ben-Zevi 6A, Tel.(057) 236001.

ROUTE No. 22 (Map: Southern Sheet F23 to L22)

Beer Sheva – Arad (45 km.) – En Boqeq (74 km.) – Massada (90 km.) (Road Nos. 31, 60, 90)

(Distances in brackets refer to start of route.)

Follow Derekh Hebron (Road No. 60) northeast out of Beer Sheva, passing through the industrial sites and crossing the railway line before roads branch off left to the **Negev Brigade Memorial**, right to **Tel Sheva**, and the next right to the affluent suburb of **Omer**, 9 km. northeast of Beer Sheva.

Turn right (onto Road No. 31) for Arad 13 km. after leaving Beer Sheva. The desert is absolutely bleak, with some of the pebbled hills looking as smooth as ski slopes from a distance.

Twenty–one kilometres later there is a turn–off left to **Tel Arad**, 4 km. away. Excavations show the remains of a Canaanite city in existence about 1,000 years before Abraham wandered through this area. There is an Israelite citadel from Solomon's time with a synagogue inside resembling the biblical description of Solomon's Temple. Entrance fee.

Continue 11 km. to Arad.

ARAD (Map: K23)

You won't be the first to rub your eyes in disbelief on entering Arad. When the first families moved into tents and asbestos huts here in 1962, there wasn't a single tree or road. There were only the crinkled desert surfaces and the stretched goatskin tents of the Bedouin.

Today Arad boasts flowering, tree–lined boulevards, deluxe hotels with swimming pools, supermarkets, and spacious villas whose market value has soared over the years. There are more than 15,000 residents.

Three factors have made it the most dynamic development town in Israel. First and foremost it was settled by young Israelis, who were later joined by thousands of new immigrants yearning for the challenge of building a new town out of nothing. The development of the Dead Sea Chemical Works and the discovery of gas at nearby Rosh Zohar called for a new town to house the workers. Finally, the dry, pollen–free air, with sunny days, proved a boon to people suffering from asthma. The town authorities are determined to protect the environment and a team of experts has the power of veto over every kind of vegetation planted in Arad. (See "Health Resorts.")

As a result tourism is booming. The hotels are built on the eastern border, close to the edge of the plateau, and overlooking the Dead Sea some 1,000 m. below. (See "Accommodation" section at the end of the route.) There are about a dozen eating places – restaurants, snack bars, felafel stands, pizza and ice cream parlours – at the Commercial Centre. Light meals are served at the Paz petrol station, at the entrance to Arad.

Government Tourist Information Office:

New Visitors' Centre, tel. (057)954409. Open: daily 9 a.m. – 12 noon, 4 – 7 p.m.

There are two roads from Arad to Massada. The one leading northeast along Rehov Moab winds down hilly terrain for 22 km. However, the ascent is on foot, up the Roman ramp, and since there is no through road to the Dead Sea, you must return all the way back to Arad. Take the other road, eastwards, down to the Dead Sea if you want to take the cablecar up Massada or continue to En Gedi and points north.

The first route is normally used by visitors wanting to climb Massada the easy way. It takes about 15 minutes over the western Roman ramp to the summit, as opposed to the 60–minute walk up the eastern face on the Snake Path.

At the end of this road, at the base of Massada, you can see the mound where the remains of the defenders of Massada were buried with full military honours in 1969. Close by are some of the Roman siege camps and dykes. However, they are out of bounds to visitors because they have not yet been thoroughly excavated.

The second, busiest route from Arad to Massada spirals down southeast on Road No. 31. Six kilometres from Arad a road branches off right to Elat. After a further 12 km. you arrive at sea level; the Dead Sea lies 403 m. below this point.

Drive on for 3 km. and stop at the observation post. Look down the normally dry river bed of **Nahal Zohar**. See the brick walls clinging to the same coloured mound resembling congealed jelly. That's **Metzad Zohar** (Glorious Stronghold), built by the Romans and Byzantines to guard the way to Edom. If you want to walk down the 800 m. long path, tread carefully. It will be easier if you have rubber–soled shoes.

Continue on for a few hundred metres where another observation spot overlooks much of the Dead Sea area, with the salt–encrusted earth flashing and sparkling in the sunlight. Descend to Road No. 90, which runs parallel to the Dead Sea. There is a gas station and restaurant at the **Neve Zohar** junction, where you will also find a museum and a youth hostel.

THE DEAD SEA (Map: L, M18–24)

The Dead Sea is very much alive. Health spas and hot springs dot its western bank, and luxury hotels have sprung up in the last few years to meet the tourist boom.

People from all over the world come for therapeutic treatment to this place (see "Health Resorts"), because the water contains unique health-promoting salts.

A swim in the Dead Sea is tantamount to a full cosmetic treatment. But bathers should beware not to go for a dip if they have any cuts, and not to splash around, as a mere drop of this salt water in any wound or in the eyes stings sharply. Freshwater showers are necessary after a swim to wash off the sticky salt.

The Dead Sea is 55 km. long and varies between 18 km. and 3 km. in width. It has a maximum depth of 430 m.; it is fed by the Jordan River and a number of rivers and springs that bring flood waters after the infrequent rains of the Judaean Desert.

The Dead Sea dates back some 100 million years, but geologists reckon that the shallow southern tip was formed a mere few thousand years ago, which coincides with the cataclysmic Sodom and Gomorrah story in the Bible.

The road leading right from the junction leads to **Sedom**, 9 km. away. Here are situated huge plants (of the Dead Sea Works) to extract minerals from the frothy water.

On your right is the Mountain of Sedom, gouged with many caves. The chalk–white **Flour Cave** is midway between Sedom and the junction on the upper plateau of Mishor Amiaz; it takes its name from the fine white dust carpeting its interior.

Nothing remains of biblical Sodom and Gomorrah, but a wind–carved sculpture on the mountains is pointed out as **Lot's wife**, who was turned to a pillar of salt after looking back on the ruined cities (Genesis 19:26).

(If you continue along the road south of Sedom for 14 km. to another junction you will link up with Route No. 23 to Elat.)

Turn left at the junction for the resort area of **Neve Zohar**. There is a gas station, camping site, and restaurant. The **Hamei Zohar** hot springs have modern installations. The **Bet Hayotzer Museum** here displays a variety of exhibits connected with the Dead Sea region.

Pass the Moriah Hotel and arrive at **En Boqeq**, with the

Tongue jutting out across the Dead Sea just to the north. Lying at the Delta of Nahal Boqeq, this resort has hotels and restaurant and beach facilities. (See "Health Resorts.") Close by are the ruins of **Metzad Boqeq**, a Roman fortress.

Drive on parallel to the Dead Sea until you come to the Massada turn–off 15 km. later.

MASSADA (Map: L22)

Towering 430 m. above the Dead Sea, Massada (Hebrew for fortress) is a boat–shaped, craggy mountain. Upon it one of the greatest epics in the history of mankind was played out.

When the Jewish rebellion erupted in 66 CE, a group of Zealots headed for Massada. They knew that Herod had built, about 100 years earlier, an impregnable fortress on its summit which he intended to use as a sanctuary in the event of Cleopatra or local dissidents trying to usurp his throne.

The Zealots seized it from the Roman garrison and settled into the sumptuous palaces, hanging villas and rooms within the casemate wall surrounding its heights. It seemed they could not be dislodged. Herod had built well. There were giant cisterns hacked within the rock to receive the flood waters following the rains. There were barracks, defence towers and arsenals.

With the fall of Jerusalem four years later in 70 CE they were joined by survivors fleeing the capital and some Essenes from Qumran. Their numbers swelled to 960 men, women and children. During the next two years they remained the only pocket of resistance in Palestine, continuing to harass the Romans by using the royal citadel as their base.

In 72 CE the Roman Governor, Flavius Silva, arrived at the foot of Massada, with the Tenth Legion, auxiliaries and 10,000 Jewish slaves. He built a dyke around the base of the mountain and eight siege camps to prevent escape. On the western side, he later built a ramp of beaten earth, stones and logs. While he did this, the Jews hurled down boulders and rounded rocks and fired arrows from their bows. In time the Romans positioned a siege tower on the ramp and then a battering ram. The year was 73 CE. The siege was approaching its denouement.

The Romans set fire to the wall, but wind drove the

flames into the face of the attackers. The defenders took heart, but then the wind changed and the wall burned.

All this has come down to us through the Jewish historian Josephus Flavius, who recorded the events after he became a turncoat and joined the Romans. His account of what happened next makes compelling reading, and the oration of the leader of the defenders, Eleazar Ben Ya'ir, ranks with Henry V's electrifying summation before Agincourt, and Churchill's galvanizing war–time speeches.

"Let our wives die before they are abused," he implored, "and our children before they have tasted of slavery; and after we have slain them, let us bestow that glorious benefit upon one another mutually, and preserve ourselves in freedom, as an excellent funeral monument for us."

He then exhorted them to destroy their money and burn the fortress but to spare their provisions "for they will be a testimonial when we are dead that we were not subdued for want of necessaries, but... preferred death before slavery."

Josephus' account of the drama notes that after this speech there were some who balked at the idea of killing their families. Ben Ya'ir again appealed to them. He reminded them that Jerusalem had fallen and that the great Temple had been burned. "Now, who is there that revolves these things in his mind, and yet is able to bear the sight of the sun?" he asked. "Let us die before we become slaves under our enemies, and let us go out of the world, together with our children and our wives, in a state of freedom. Let us therefore make haste and instead of affording them so much pleasure, as they hope for in getting us under their power, let us leave them an example which shall at once cause their astonishment at our death and their admiration of our hardiness therein."

Josephus writes that before Ben Ya'ir had finished they "all cut him off short and made haste to do the work..." They "gave the longest parting kisses" to their wives and children and then slew them. Then they cast lots to choose 10 men to despatch the remainder. Again they cast lots to select one to kill the survivors. With this done, the lone Jew "ran his sword entirely through himself."

Details of the mass suicide and the oration were provided later by two women and five children who hid in the underground caves and lived to tell the tale.

Massada was excavated by Professor Yigael Yadin for 12 months from 1963 to 1965. The Israeli army and thousands of volunteers from 28 countries came to help sift the rubble and restore what was found. While discovering much evidence of those fateful hours, they also determined that the Romans maintained a garrison on Massada for several decades after its capture. The last inhabitants were a handful of reclusive 5th century monks.

Today Massada has become a symbol for men who cherish freedom. The defiant cry of recruits to the Israel Defence Forces Armoured Unit swearing the oath of allegiance in an annual ceremony on its summit: "Massada shall never fall again!"

Our guided walk on Massada leads you to the principal sites with notes on what was found.

Most people walking up the **Snake Path**, named after the winding ascent on the eastern face, start an hour before dawn to get to the summit in time for the sunrise over the Mountains of Moab. Later in the day the blistering sun makes climbing a wearying sweat. Entrance fee. There are water points on the cliff.

The **cablecar** whisks you up in no time at all. The last cablecar leaves the summit at 4 p.m. during the week but at 2 p.m. on Friday. A fee is charged.

Massada is open all the year round (except Yom Kippur) from 7.30 a.m. – 3.30 p.m.

A sound and light show is presented in April – October. It is narrated in Hebrew on Tuesday and Thursday and in English on Wednsday. In July, the show starts at 9 p.m., in August at 8 p.m., in September and October at 7 p.m.

The Massada Museum: at the eastern base near the hotel, hostel and restaurant, includes a model of the fortress and some of the finds from the summit. It also contains photographic illustrations of the siege and the manner in which water was channelled to the cisterns. The Museum is open from 8 a.m. – 4 p.m. Admission free.

From here it is possible to join Route No. 1 to En Gedi and Jerusalem (in reverse).

A Walk On Massada

This walk will take at least an hour, even if you browse only cursorily at each of the numbered locations on our map. But remember that the numbers on our map, which

Massada

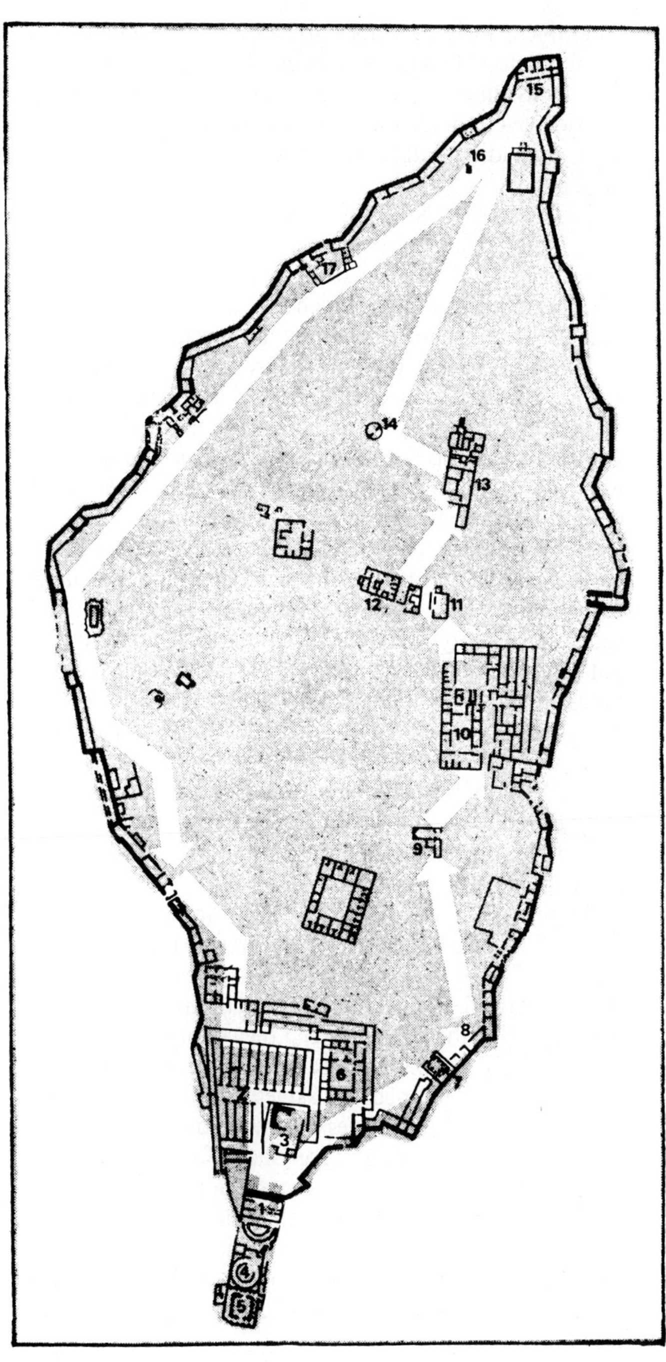

go anti–clockwise, do not correspond with some of the numbers atop Massada, so you should disregard the latter. We also assume that you have entered the gate on the **eastern side**, overlooking the Dead Sea. Recently, shaded rest areas, including bathroom and drinking facilities, have been added.

Walk across to No. 1 on the northern tip of the mountain. This is the upper terrace and living quarters of Herod's private hanging **palace–villa**. The dwelling rooms are paved with mosaics which are among the oldest in Israel. Note the semi–circular porch at the northern edge.

Now walk back to the **store–houses** at No. 2. Built from dolomite stone quarried on Massada, they were destroyed by the Zealots and by earthquakes. Remains of wine, oil and flour jars, together with coins, were found here. As with other restored buildings on Massada, everything below the painted black line is original.

Between the store–houses and the steps leading down to the middle terrace of the palace–villa is the large **bath–house,** No. 3. There is a hot room, cold room, tepid room and disrobing room. The round clay bricks in the hot room supported the upper floor. Impressions of clay pipes for hot air circulation can be seen on the wall plaster. The small bathing pool covering frescoes in the disrobing room was added by the Zealots.

Walk west towards the steps and descend to the **middle terrace**, No. 4, about 20 m. down. This was built for Herod's leisure hours. The circular building probably had rows of pillars supporting a roof.

More steps continue down to the lower terrace, No. 5, about 15 m. below. Again, this was erected for leisure and pleasure. The Herodian artists tried to give the impression that the plastered walls were panelled in stone and marble when painting the walls between the columns and Corinthian capitals. The bath–house on the east, to which access is forbidden, contained the skeletons of a young man, woman and child. The scales of armour, arrows, inscribed potsherds and parts of a prayer shawl found next to the man can be seen in the museum at the foot of Massada. The sandals and plaited hair of the woman are on display at the Shrine of the Book in Jerusalem. They are believed to have been among the last defenders of Massada. Coins inscribed with "The Freedom of Zion," and food, were also found on this terrace.

Return to the summit and walk to the **administration**

building, No. 6, adjoining the western end of the store-houses. There is a **mikve** (ritual bath) in its northeastern corner.

Now walk along the **casemate wall** on the west. Built around the entire summit, it was a popular Herodian structure with double walls partitioned into rooms for stores or dwellings. Many of the Zealots lived in them.

The **Synagogue** is No. 7 on the walk, overlooking Silva's camp. It is the oldest synagogue in Israel. Two parchment scrolls buried within it contained fragments from the books of Deuteronomy and Ezekiel. Also found were coins from the revolt, pottery inscribed with Hebrew names, Herodian jars, burned furniture, glass and a wash basin.

A short distance away, at No. 8, is another **casemate room** where the first of 14 biblical, sectarian and apocryphal scrolls was discovered on Massada. Written on parchment, it was from the Book of Psalms. Here, too, were found parts of Leviticus and a scroll believed to have been written by the Essenes of Qumran. Seventeen silver shekels, struck during the five years of the revolt and inscribed "Jerusalem the Holy," were also extracted from the rubble.

Cross over to the 5th century **Byzantine chapel** at No. 9. The mosaic floor is decorated with rings around pomegranates, figs, oranges and grapes.

Walk southwest to the **Western Palace** at No. 10. It is divided into an administrative building, dwelling quarters, a service wing and storerooms. The only coloured Herodian mosaic floor on Massada is in the entrance hall to the throne room. There are also humble, Zealot additions, including a cooking stove. A small bath–house is in the service chambers. From the edge you can see the ramp and the western entrance.

Continue over to the **swimming pool** at No. 11. Steps lead down to the base where coins of the revolt were discovered. Nos. 12 and 13, east and south of the swimming pool, are Herodian **villas** in which the Zealots added walls and partitions.

Walk east to the niched circular structure at No. 14. It is dubbed the **Columbarium** because it resembles a dovecote. However, experiments have shown that the holes are too small to house pigeons. No one knows with any certainty what its purpose was but one theory is that the niches held the ashes of non–Jews cremated on Massada.

Proceed to No. 15, a **lookout tower** on the southern wall high above Roman siege camps. A few metres below the casemate wall, but out of bounds to visitors, are a number of **caves** in which the excavators found the skeletons of 25 men, women, children and an embryo. These, and the skeletons found in thc palace–villa, are believed to be the remains of the Jewish defenders. They were buried with full military honours near the Roman ramp on the western base of the mountain.

Turn east, towards one of the many **cisterns** at No. 16. Steps lead down to the enormous reservoir, cut into the rock. Floodwaters were channelled through a hole in the roof.

Walk northeast towards the wall and stop at the **mikve** at No. 17. It proves decisively the ardent religious nature of the defenders of Massada. There are three pools. The smallest is for washing hands and feet before immersion. Diagonally opposite it is a pool to collect rainwater. A pipe connects this with the actual mikve.

Continue along the eastern **casemate wall**, observing the cramped quarters in which many of the Zealots lived for so long. Most of these quarters contained their household utensils, but the majority of the rooms are fenced off and may not be entered because of the danger of collapse.

The wall leads up to the Snake Path gate by which you entered Massada.

ACCOMMODATION ON ROUTE No. 22

(See also general "Accommodation" section.)

HOTELS

ARAD
Margoa Tel. (057) 957014. Mo'av St.
Masada Tel. (057) 957140. P.O.B. 62.
Nof Arad Tel. (057) 957056. Mo'av St.
Arad Tel. (057) 957040. 6 Hapalmach St.

DEAD SEA, EN BOQEQ, NEVE–ZOHAR
Moriah–Dead Sea (Spa Hotel) Tel. (057) 584221. Mobile Post, Dead Sea 84960.
Ein Boqeq Tel. (057) 584331. Mobile Post–Dead Sea 86930.

Galei Zohar Tel. (057) 584311. Mobile Post–Dead Sea 87930.
Lot Tel. (057) 584321. Mobile Post, Dead Sea 86930.
Moriah Gardens Tel. (057) 584351. Mobile Post–Dead Sea 84960.
Tsell Harim Tel. (057) 584121. Mobile Post, Dead Sea 86930.
Hod Hamidbar, Tel. (057) 584644. Mobile Post, Dead Sea 86930

YOUTH HOSTELS

Arad. Tel. (057) 957150.
Massada. Tel. (057) 584349.

ROUTE No. 23 (Map: Southern Sheet F23 to K26 and G42)

The Arava

Beer Sheva – Mamshit (Kurnub) (40 km.) – Solomon's Pillars (226 km.) – Elat (261 km.) (Road Nos. 25, 90.)

(Distances in brackets refer to start of route.)

Warning: the banks on the sides of the asphalt road are of soft earth.

This is the most favoured road to the coral reefs of Elat because it is quicker than Route No. 24 through Mitzpe Ramon, because there are far more signs of human life, and because there are many roadside refreshment stands.

Take Road No. 25 leading out of Beer Sheva to Dimona and pass the signpost at the outskirts of the city directing you to Mamshit (Kurnub) National Park. The road passes through a monotonous sequence of brown hills over which groups of Bedouin have occasionally pitched their goat-skin tents and tethered their camels.

After 37 km. pass by the southern entrance of **Dimona**, a development town founded in 1955 to provide those who worked at the Dead Sea with a more salubrious place to live in. Dimona has grown and has a population of about 29,300; many of them work in the textile mills and the nearby atomic reactor.

A few kilometres further on you will see a signpost pointing right to Kurnub. A short approach road brings you to the foot of a hill sprawling with the restored buildings of this ancient settlement.

MAMSHIT (KURNUB) (Map: H26)

The traders and skilled water–conservationists known as the Nabataeans built this city in the 1st century CE. It was later taken over by the Romans (who called it Memphis) and expanded vigorously under the Byzantines before being deserted after the Moslem conquest of 636 CE.

Much of the strong city wall built by the Romans still stands. The impressive remains of the 6th–7th century Byzantine churches have large, colourful mosaics over parts of the floors.

As you wander around the ruins of Nabataean constructions that were added to, and used, by successive occupiers, make sure to walk down towards the part near the entrance booth. Here you will find one Nabataean room that was plastered and painted over by the Romans. The frescoes – which are unique for their period and place – include a representation of Eros and Psyche sitting on a couch, and identified by their Greek names.

A few metres left of this room was the scene of a sensational find during the excavations from 1965–67. A bronze jar hidden in a stairwell contained more than 10,000 silver Roman coins from the 1st and 2nd centuries CE. They are now in the Israel Museum in Jerusalem.

Other sites to see at Kurnub (Arabic for what is known in modern Hebrew as Mamshit) include reservoirs, baths, a Nabataean palace and Nabataean and Roman graves one kilometre north of the town. Open daily. Entrance fee.

Return to the main road and turn right, soon passing the turn–off left to Arad and Massada. The road rises and then, while descending, you are treated to a cineramic vision of the Arava, the Mountains of Moab and a part of the Dead Sea Works to your left.

Turning right at the junction, you now begin to drive along Road No. 90 through the 180–km.–long Arava Valley. Here and there are kibbutzim and moshavim where men and women are braving the scorching sun and defying the saline soil to bring the land back to life. Twenty–four kilometres later, you come to **En Hazeva**, a settlement with a gas station and refreshment facilities, as well as a serpentarium.

At **En Yahav**, some 18 km. further south, there is also a restaurant and a gas station.

Thirty–three kilometres further you will come to **Moshav Paran**. It takes its name from the biblical Wilderness of Paran and the Paran Brook close by.

Forty km. further you come to the Qtura junction. (From here there is a new road to Elat. Ten km. to your right you arrive at Shizafon junction. You then take the new road to your left (south) through Biqat Uvda and Biqat Sayyarin to Ein–Netafim and Elat.)

Five km. after the Qtura junction, the road (No. 90) leads close by a hill, on the left, on top of which is **Kibbutz Grofit**. The settlement's orchards stand out like rays of hope in the Arava. (See end of Route No. 24.)

Five kilometres later, you're at the turn–off to **Yotvata**, a kibbutz which has a milk bar. Elatites rely heavily on Yotvata for their milk supplies. Near the main road here are the recently excavated remains of a Roman fort. (See Route 24.) Nearby: **Hai Bar,** a nature reserve; a **tourist centre** that provides information about the flora, fauna, archaeological sites and history of the area; and the Ye'elim camping site.

Continue for another 13 km. before following the signpost right to **Timna Park** and **King Solomon's Pillars**, reached at the end of a 7 km. tarred road.

These 50 m.–high pillars of Nubian sandstone brood over the Negev like strange sentinels. Polished by wind and sand, they are tinted with subtle shades of pink, cream, yellow and white. They are splendid reminders that nature can surprise even the most blasé of travellers.

Just around the right hand corner you can see the stone outlines of a former Egyptian–Kenite temple, dating from the 13th century BCE, at the time of the exodus of the Hebrews from Egypt. Entrance fee.

Back on the main road there is a turn–off right, a few kilometres later, to the **Timna Copper Mines**, close to where King Solomon is believed to have mined 3,000 years ago.

You are now 25 km. north of Elat and should read the tail–end of Route No. 24 for a description of the remaining part of your journey.

ROUTE No. 24 (Map: Southern Sheet F23 to F30 and G42)

Central Negev

Beer Sheva – Shivta (54 km.) – Sede Boqer (89 km.) – En Avdat (93 km.) – Mitzpe Ramon (139 km.) – Elat (286 km.) (Road Nos. 40, 90, 211.)

(Distances in brackets refer to start of route.)

While this route is longer and more wearying than Route No. 23 through Dimona and the Arava to Elat, it passes through more majestic landscape in the heart of the Negev and is specked with colossal ruins of ancient civilizations. There is a new road, not covered in this route, that goes from Shivta westwards to Nitzana and then southwards along the Egyptian border to Eilat (road No. 10).

A few words of caution: the banks on the sides of the asphalt road are of soft earth. Travellers should take water flasks in the car for their own drinking needs and for the radiator in the unfortunate event of a breakdown. The petrol tank should be filled and the water flasks topped again at Mitzpe Ramon as there are no facilities between this point and the end of the Wilderness of Paran, 100 km. away.

Drive straight down Rehov Keren Kayemet, past Abraham's Well, ignoring the turn–off left to Derekh Hebron (No. 60).

Follow Road No. 40 south. The earth is packed hard in this bleak landscape but there are many signs of soil erosion. An afforestation scheme stands out in this home of many roaming Bedouin. Drive carefully as there are several blind corners and hills.

Thirty kilometres later pass by kibbutz **Mashabei Sadeh** and stop to look at the memorial soon after, at the crossroad to Revivim and Nitzana. The **Bir Asluj Memorial**, set amidst the trees of a picnic site, commemorates the Israelis who died liberating this area from Egyptians in December 1948.

Take Road No. 211 to **Nitzana**. Pass the tarred road left to Sede Boqer 16 km. further south.

The signpost to Shivta is 20 km. east of the Sinai border

and 50 km. from Beer Sheva. A tarred road (left) leads to the National Parks site 4 km. away.

SHIVTA (Map: D27)

Shivta's colossal ruins reach back to the 1st or 2nd century BCE when the great Nabataean traders built it. It is the largest restored settlement of the six Nabataean settlements in the Negev. The Nabataeans chose this site because goods traded with the Far East and Arabia were transported from Elat through here and on to Gaza and Rafah.

While they were energetic tradesmen, the Nabataeans were even more famous as water conservationists. They set the pattern for others intent on settling in this desiccated region. Their method was to catch rainwater, and to harness the flood–waters that flow suddenly in the Negev.

They built reservoirs cut out of rock and lined with a covering of small stones and a kind of cement that prevented seepage. They also constructed dams, and built terraces; roofs were flat and cisterns were used. The water they collected was used to irrigate their farms; the produce from Shivta also maintained their strategically sited camp at Nitzana, 20 kilometres southwest.

With the Roman conquest, Shivta was used as a supply centre for the northern Negev. It flourished again under Byzantine occupation from the 4th–6th centuries when it was used to protect the Negev populations and pilgrims on their way to Mt. Sinai.

However, following the Moslem conquest, it declined and was deserted after the 14th century. It was excavated by a joint Anglo–American expedition in 1935.

The ruins include reservoirs, wine presses, Byzantine churches and residences. Be sure to see the extraordinarily well–preserved Byzantine dwelling house. It has three curved stone arches on the ceiling and a stone table and chairs in a corner. Open daily. Entrance fee.

Having visited Shivta, turn right into Road No. 211 and 16 km. later take Road No. 40 for Sede Boqer and Elat.

The road passes over arid hills until you descend and see the lush orchards of Kibbutz Sede Boqer and the stark range of mountains behind them. Turn right at the crossroad and carry on to the kibbutz which is opposite you.

SEDE BOQER (Map: E27)

Founded in 1952, it became a dateline for journalists filing stories around the world when David Ben–Gurion, then Prime Minister, made this his second home in 1953. His hut, which includes his library, is open Sun. – Thurs. 8.30 a.m. – 3.30 p.m., Fri., Sat. & holidays 9 a.m. – 2 p.m. Meals are served at an inn and a pub, and fruit from the kibbutz is on sale. For details of guided tours, phone (057)960320, (057) 558444.

While walking through the residential area notice how the houses are enclosed by walls on their east. These act as breakers against the stinging sand storms that come in from this direction.

About 250 people live here, including rotating groups of visiting youngsters who come from abroad to further their knowledge of Judaism and the Hebrew language.

Leave the kibbutz and turn left. Within minutes you arrive at the turn–off to **Midreshet Ben-Gurion (College of the Negev)**. The buildings on your right make up an environmental education high school and a school of field studies on the rim of the Zin Canyon. The buildings on your left make up the Jacob Blaustein Institute for Desert Research and the residential quarters. Ben–Gurion and his wife, Paula, are buried nearby. The college shows an audio-visual presentation about the life of David and Paula Ben-Gurion. Sun.–Thurs.: 8.30, 9.30 and 10.30 a.m., and 2.30 p.m.; Fri. 8.30, 9.30 and 10.30 a.m.; Sat. and holidays 9.30, 10.30, 11.30 a.m. and 2 p.m. Tel. (057)565717.

Drive 3 km. down the gravel path until you reach the parking area of the National Parks site of En Avdat.

EN AVDAT (Map: E28)

In English it translates into "Spring of Avdat" but it is far more than that. The pools lie between giant cracks in the earth and walking to them from the parking lot puts man back into his proper perspective.

There is not a sound to be heard here, except the noises of the fleet–footed gazelles and ibex that you may see near the entrance.

Walk along the pebbled, dry river bed between massive walls of the canyon. Nature has carved huge caverns in the walls and they are made even more attractive by the lavender–coloured caparis flowers that cling to the rock surfaces.

To get to the top of the first pool (En Mor) walk several hundred metres and then cross to the right, following the beaten path, up 60 stone steps. Walk a little further and you arrive at the top of the waterfall for a vision of stark and grand scenery that will leave you momentarily stunned.

However, more awaits you further on. Follow the path alongside four–metre–high bamboo growing in profusion. Round the curved walls and you are soon at the second pool.

En Avdat is fed by a spring and the floodwaters that rage through the blistering Negev after a few minutes of rainfall. The soil is too dry to absorb the waters and they very soon churn up everything lying in their raging path. When the floods have spent themselves, a residue of water remains and that is why vegetation and animal and plant life flourish in this sector.

Note: Swimming and hunting are prohibited at En Avdat. Entrance fee for the park.

When you return to the main road, No. 40, turn left to Elat, drive on for about 8 km. and then turn left at the **En Avdat** signpost. The National Parks Authority has installed iron balconies and a staircase at the observation post and you can get a look at this pool from about 100 m. up.

While you're here you may like to see how sounds carry by shouting a few words. You will be amazed at the reverberations of the echo.

Back on the main road (No. 40) you can see part of the ruins of ancient Avdat clinging to the hill ahead. There is a kosher restaurant and gas station at the entrance to this next National Parks site.

AVDAT (Map: E28)

If you were astonished by the high quality of the buildings at Shivta you will be awed beyond expectation by the sight that greets you at Avdat (Avedat). For here you see limestone caves with sculptures, burial niches in the white limestone, and, on the summit of this commanding height, the proud remains of a very large settlement.

Avdat was built by the Nabataeans in the 2nd century

BCE and takes its name from Obodas (Abdat) II, King of the Nabataeans.

Avdat also dominated the trade routes but during the early period of Roman rule it declined when trade was diverted to the road linking Elat with Damascus. It recovered its importance when the Romans again fortified the area and when the Byzantines settled.

There are some fine churches, complete with inscriptions on some of the drums of the columns. Interspersed throughout the ruins are the cisterns and conduits that enabled people to live here. The solid remains of a huge Roman tower can be seen next to the southern gate of the Byzantine citadel, and visitors should not miss the steam room of the bath house that shows how hot–air vents were utilised below the floor.

The lower parking area is close to limestone caves with discernible sculptured animals' heads in the corners and crosses on the ceiling. These were Nabataean caves that were later used by the Byzantines.

Other sites include a magnificent three–storey Roman house near the upper parking lot and, beyond the main body of buildings, the former Nabataean kiln and workshop with thousands of sherds of pottery there for the picking. Open daily. Entrance fee.

About 22 km. remain (on Road No. 40) between here and Mitzpe Ramon and the drive is uneventful.

A few kilometres before Mitzpe Ramon, there is another road to your right, No. 171, which leads to road No. 10. You can take this road and drive to Elat along the Egyptian border.

MITZPE RAMON (Map: F30)

You are now about 900 m. above sea level and on the rim of the **Ramon Crater**, a unique geological phenomenon comprising ancient rock strata and well–preserved fossils (Triassic and Jurassic).

Fossilized life dating back almost 200 million years shows that this area was the domain of long–extinct marine reptiles.

Gradually the grey and lava black mounds in the depths of the canyon were exploited for their ceramic clay, gypsum and glass–sand ingredients.

Mitzpe Ramon began in 1954 as a camp for men building the highway south to Elat. If you drive past the houses, up the hill, and turn left to the **Nabataean Inn**, you get a truly superb view of the canyon from the observation post. Next to the inn, you'll find a gas station and a park of modern sculptures. There is a youth hostel in Mitzpe Ramon, tel. (057) 588443, and a field school for groups and hikers in the area, tel. (057) 588616, operated by the Society for the Protection of Nature in Israel. The Nature Reserves Authority has a Visitors' Centre here, with an exhibit on the area, which organizes tours and hikes (tel. (057) 588691).

Nearby is the only alpaca farm in the Middle East, which may be visited (entrance fee; tel. (057) 588047).

This is also the inhospitable territory through which Moses led the Israelites, for it forms part of the **Wilderness of Zin** (Numbers 20).

Statistics alone are impressive – the Ramon Crater is 8 km. wide, 37.5 km. long and 300 m. deep. To the west of this look–out point is **Mt. Ramon**, rising 1,035 m. above sea level, making it the highest point in the Negev desert. A modern observatory has been built here.

Remain in low gear as you descend into the crater for the road winds sharply over its 300 m. descent. The jagged walls of the crater have a hushed force about them while the dappled colours of burnt sienna, beige and black down below make it look as if some artist has been at work.

Roman roads are still recognisable and are used by the mining companies in transporting minerals out of the crater. The roads connected towns on the trade routes, and Nabataean potsherds have been found in profusion.

The road courses up and down over hills until it suddenly leaves you suspended above a big bowl of earth known as The Plain (Hameshar). It is dotted with broken tamarisks.

You think you have reached the lowest part of this terrain but again the road looks down on another flat and stony basin. You cross **Nahal Paran**, which, after the winter floods, has to be detoured as the water lingers across the road until it evaporates or finally sinks in. If it is impassable when you reach it, make sure that your detour is over stony ground because tyres get bogged down quickly in the softer earth over which water has already evaporated.

The scenery throughout is bold and expansive, with the sun playing tricks with the colours of the mountains, and the prickly acacia bushes holding out in a wilderness of erosion.

Ninety–five kilometres after Mitzpe Ramon, the road climbs. When you reach a point where the road begins to descend, you are confronted with your first view of the Arava, its pink sands splashed over the sides of the Edom mountains before you in Jordan.

Within a few minutes you are at a crossroad, Qetura, with Elat 52 km. to your right on Road No. 90 and Sedom and the Dead Sea to your left, some 140 km. away. (From Shizzafon or the **Tzomet** (junction), which you passed 15 km. earlier, there is a new road, No. 112, to Elat through Biq'at Uvda and Biq'at Sayarim, along the Egyptian border.)

The **Arava** is part of the great Afro–Syrian Rift Valley that runs all the way down to Kenya, and at first glance it seems almost as forbidding as the route you have just crossed. But after a few kilometres you pass Kibbutz **Grofit**, whose green orchards break the barren monotony.

There is a cafe at the entrance to Kibbutz **Yotvata**, a few kilometres further on. The large dairy herd here supplies Elat with much of its milk requirements. (See Route No. 23.)

The **Hai Bar National Biblical Wild–Life Reserve** is located here. Entry is via the Tourist Centre opposite the kibbutz. It serves as a breeding centre for a unique collection of animals in danger of extinction, most of which lived in the area in biblical times. Drive along the 8 km. round road and see the white oryx, addox, ostrich, wild ass, etc., which roam the reserve freely. Recommended visiting hours 7.30 – 11.30 a.m. Also open in the afternoon. Entrance fee.

About 12 km. from Yotvata, a tarred road leads to **Timna Park** and **Solomon's Pillars**, and a little further south another road branches right to the **Timna Copper Mines**. The recently opened Timna Valley Preserve covers an area of about 60 sq. km. and includes many varieties of desert flora and fauna. The ancient mines from the Chalcolithic – Early Bronze Age are the earliest shaft and gallery mines discovered to date and may be examined by visitors. An entrance fee is charged. It is advisable to leave Solomon's Pillars for the return journey, or for the tail–end of Route 23, because by now you should be hot and tired enough to flop into the cool waters of the Red Sea at Elat.

The Jordanian port city of Aqaba is the first sight to

greet you as you near Elat. Then the hotels on the north beach, and the downtown parts of Elat, appear on the horizon.

Pass Kibbutz **Elot** on the outskirts of Elat. Drive straight through, past the airport, and you are in the centre of a tropical paradise.

Elat

(Map: Southern Sheet G42)

Introduction

Elat's rich underwater life and its location at the junction of two deserts make it a unique seaside resort with a year-round tourist season.

Wedged between the magnificent, rugged mountains of Jordan, Saudi Arabia and the Sinai, the emerald-green and aquamarine waters of the Gulf of Elat (Aqaba) contain some of the most wonderful coral flora and fauna in the world.

You don flippers and snorkel and wade into the clear waters, gliding between spectacularly coloured schools of fish, some bloated to the size of a football.

The Red Sea is a top attraction for undersea divers from Europe, since it is the closest tropical sea for them. And Elat is a highly developed diving centre, with an underwater observatory that opens up the coral reefs to non-divers as well as divers. Experienced deep-sea fishermen can make use of the high-speed boats purchased by a local hotel to catch marlin, barracuda, sharks and other big fish.

Elat is a border town. Like most such places it attracts refugees from culture, the international backpack brigade, tourists in search of the exotic, and rip-off artists. It is also the home of a growing number of hard-working, honest Israelis who, for one reason or another, opted for a challenging life in this scorched developing region rather than a more comfortable existence in the north.

Prices of goods and services in Elat have been reduced by an average of at least 17 per cent as a result of the transformation of the town into a **Free Trade Zone** on November 1, 1985.

Tourists benefit, under this new scheme, from reduced prices in stores, restaurants, places of entertainment and tourist attractions, as well as hiring of sea-sport and diving equipment and taxi services.

These reductions are mainly due to the abolition of VAT – currently 17 per cent in other parts of the country – on all goods and services in Elat. Additional reductions have also been made.

At the same time, duty-free stores in Elat are being expanded to offer tourists a wide variety of both local and foreign goods exempt from all taxes and duties against payment in foreign currency.

Under this new scheme, tourists arriving directly at Elat have been exempt, as from November 1985, from paying airport tax; and airline companies, including charter operators, have been exempt from all airport taxes (air control tax, landing and take-off fees, porterage and passenger services), thus enabling them to reduce the price of each tourist's fare.

Drivers should of course make it a point to fill up their tanks in Elat – not only at the beginning of a journey but also at the end if possible.

A short drive south of Elat, along the tarred highway, you'll find **Coral Beach,** with every facility and boats, water skis and wind-surfing and skin-diving equipment for hire. Here, too, you board glass-bottomed launches for cruises over the coral reef, and look at the wonderful underwater life from the observatory.

At sunset along the Gulf, the sea, the barren hills and mountains and sky merge into misty, soft shades. The giant rock-forms turn peach, rust red, apricot and plum above the creamy beige sands. The harsh glare of the desert disappears with the sun and the blanket of night like a squid's cloud darkens the underwater world and its fantastic living forms.

For those who want to be entertained at night, Elat has piano bars and discotheques (in the better hotels and the new tourist centre near the airport), a cinema that changes its programme every two days or so, restaurants that serve huge platters of Red Sea fish, and moody coffee houses. Young tourists tend to gather at the new tourist centre, where the spell of the sea, with the lights of Aqaba across the bay, ships anchored motionlessly near the port and bonfires on the beach are a great attraction. Elat goes to bed late, and some bars and discotheques remain open until the early hours.

Getting There: if you're not driving, there are buses and taxis (sheruts) from Jerusalem and Tel Aviv, four to five hours away. Arkia Airlines offer regular flights to Elat from these two cities, and the trip takes less than an hour. There are charter flights to Elat from Britain, France, Germany and the Scandinavian countries.

Climate: temperatures rise to 40°C and higher in summer, and rarely fall below 18°C in winter. The humidity, however, is low; the dryness of the air is good for rheumatism and makes the heat easier to bear. But the combination of low humidity and high temperatures makes people dehydrate very rapidly. Visitors are advised to drink at least four litres of liquids – preferably uncarbonated – a day, especially in the summer months.

Population: Some 30,000 residents, with a large, fluctuating number of visitors.

History

Elat is first mentioned as one of the points along the route taken by Moses and the Hebrews (Deuteronomy 2:8). Specific mention is made of it during King Solomon's reign when he "built a fleet of ships at Ezion-Geber, which is near Eloth on the shore of the Red Sea in the land of Edom" (1 Kings 9:26). This may have been 12 km. south of the modern town where there is a natural, current-free harbour between the island and the mainland.

The Judaean kings also used Elat as a port but under the Ptolemies it was renamed Berenice. The Nabateans called it Aila while the Moslems named it Aqaba, the name retained for the modern Jordanian port city 5 km. east of Elat.

Jews are thought to have lived here until the Crusaders captured it in 1116. It was of great strategic importance, being on the principal land route linking Egypt and Syria, where Moslem pilgrims and traders crossed on their way to Medina and Mecca.

The Crusaders built a fortress on Coral Island, 12 km. south of Elat. In those days the granite rock, 300 m. off the mainland, was known as Jazirat Fara'un (Pharaoh's Island) or al-Qureiye, which they corrupted to Ile de Graye. Before Saladin captured the island in 1170, the Crusaders sailed from it to attack Arab ships in the Red Sea. Later the Mamelukes and the Turks fortified the island but it gradually became deserted.

Elat was a mere British police outpost known as Umm Rash-rash when the Israeli Army raised the flag in March 1949. But development was painfully slow until the blockade of the Straits of Tiran was lifted in the Sinai Campaign of 1956.

Thereafter, Elat became the country's lifeline to Africa and the Far East. The town's existence was again threatened when Egypt closed the Straits at the mouth of the Gulf of Elat in 1967. Shipping was safeguarded with the capture in the Six Day War of the islands in the Straits, together with Sharm el-Sheikh on the mainland.

However, Elat's ports were idle again in 1973 when Egyptian war vessels blockaded the Bab el-Mandab Straits (Gate of Tears), at the southern entrance to the Red Sea, during the Yom Kippur War.

Elat now has a modern port, and oil pipelines run from here to Haifa and Ashqelon. After the overthrow of the Shah of Iran early in 1979, and the subsequent opening of the Suez Canal to Israeli shipping, activity at Elat's oil port was considerably reduced.

Places of Interest In And Near Elat

Coral Beach: south of port. Coral deposits and multi-coloured fish in underwater nature reserve. Skin-diving equipment for hire. A glass-bottomed boat leaves daily for a 3 – 3/4 hr. cruise to Coral Island. A night cruise, viewing underwater sea-life with arc lamps, leaves Coral Beach every Fri. and Sat. night at 10 p.m. Buses run every 30 minutes seven days a week. Open: 8 a.m.–5 p.m. Entrance fee. Tel. (07)373988.

Dolphin Reef: Here, about 2 km. south of Elat, you can meet dolphins and sea-lions in their ocean home. The site provides a private beach, snorkelling equipment, a dolphin and sea-lion observatory, and an educational centre which screens films on underwater life, and provides equipment for underwater photography, as well as guided "diving with the dolphins". Bus. No. 15 from the city centre. Tel. (07) 371846.

Elat Express Minitrain: a miniature train gives tours around the lagoon. Boarding near Galei Elat and Lagoona Hotels on the promenade. Operates every hour on the hour from 4 – 11 p.m. Fee: adults NIS 6.50, children NIS 4.50. Tel. (07)331937, 332068.

En Netafim: West of Eilat, near the Egyptian border. Drops of water falling through narrow outlets in steep granite walls of ravine on edge of Sinai desert. Accessible by track through majestic scenery, one km. from the main road.

Har Tzefakhot: small mountain west of Coral Beach, near Underwater Observatory. Reached through a wadi by foot. Wonderful view of the bay, Mountains of Edom, Jordanian port of Aqaba and Elat and vicinity. Best seen in afternoon light.

Israel Palace Museum: Near Caesar Hotel. Handmade dolls in dioramas portraying history of Jewish people. Open: summer – Sun.–Thurs. 9 a.m.–1 p.m., 5.30 p.m.–9.30 p.m., Fri. 9 a.m.–1 p.m. Winter – Sun.–Thurs. 9 a.m.–noon, 4–8 p.m., Fri. 9 a.m.–1 p.m. Entrance fee: adults NIS 9, children NIS 5. Tel. (07)376161.

Malkit: 457, Schunat Ha'Dekel. Specializes in the cutting and polishing of Elat stone, a unique combination of chrysocol, malachite, turquoise and azurit. The first workshop/factory in Elat to polish these stones and create jewellery with gold, silver and other metals. Malkit was established by Zvi and Frieda Weiss and is today a family concern. It is one of the few handiwork shops where the old tradition of Oriental filigree is perpetuated. Visitors to the workshop usually avail themselves of the chance to have jewellery designed to their specifications. Free transport is arranged to the factory. Exhibition open daily. Hours: Sun. – Thurs. 8 a.m. – 7 p.m., Fri., Sat. and Holidays 8 a.m. – 1 p.m., 4 p.m. – 7 p.m. Tel. (07)373372, 375650.

Minigolf – The Promised Land: A tour round Israel in miniature. Includes minigolf, cafeteria, bar, restaurant. Israeli folk-dancing daily at 9 p.m. Next to Shulamit Gardens Hotel. Open: 8.30 a.m. – midnight.

Municipal Library: Opposite Municipality. Established by United Jewish Appeal. Hebrew, French and English books and periodicals. Children's and adults' sections. Open: Sun., Mon., Tue., Thurs. 11 a.m.–6.45 p.m. Wed. closed. Fri. 9 a.m.–11.45 a.m.

Ostrich Farm: The farm has 30 ostriches and other animals. Ostrich riding demonstration daily at 6.00 p.m. Cafeteria, pub, souvenirs. In Nahal Shlomo. 5 km south of Elat. Open: Sun.–Wed. 9 a.m.–9 p.m., Thurs. – Sat. 9 a.m. – midnight. Entrance fee till 8 p.m. Tel. (07)373213.

Solomon's Pillars: within the Timna Valley Preserve 25 km. north of Elat. Fifty-metre-high redstone pillars. At base are ruins of Egyptian temple dating to time of Hebrew Exodus (Routes 23 and 24).

Texas Ranch: Coral Beach, opposite pier for glass-bottomed boats, a 30-dunam (7.5 acre) Wild West town constructed as a movie set and now a tourist site with a saloon bar, a shop, a courthouse, etc. Horse-riding facilities, camel rides. Open: 9 a.m.–7 p.m. Entrance fee (Bus 15).

Underwater Observatory and Aquarium or "Coral World": Coral Beach, tel. (07)376666. Located 7 km. from the town centre. The project comprises three one-storey buildings with distinctive, rounded roofs, on the beach, and an observatory which has been placed in position 100 metres out to sea, in a part of the coral reef known as the Japanese Gardens. A pier connects the observatory to the coast. Of the three buildings, two are the Maritime Museum and the Aquarium, and the third is a cafeteria. Three open seashore pools contain sea turtles and sharks and a circular tank, 20 metres in diameter, encloses a coral reef. Since the water in the gulf is generally crystal clear, it is possible to watch exotic tropical fish darting in and out of the corals or swimming by in shoals. The underwater observatory is one of seven in the world. It opens up an incredible world that was previously accessible only to divers, and everyone who visits Elat should make a point of going to the observatory and spending at least an hour taking in the brilliant rainbow-coloured fish and the other forms of sea life. A section of the Museum is devoted to fluorescent corals and luminescent fish. A submarine provides underwater tours along the coral reef. Open Sun. – Thurs. 8:30 a.m. – 5 p.m. Fri. 8.30 a.m. – 3 p.m. Entrance fee. Bus to town every 20 minutes. (No. 15).

Wadi Art Gallery: A permanent exhibition of paintings, sculpture, lighographs and ceramics by Israeli artists. Located in Elat's oldest house, the picturesque Beit Williams, Wadi Shlomo, near Texas Ranch, Coral Beach, tel. (07)372727.

Wadi Taba: 8 km. south of Elat. Border post manned by Egyptian Camel Patrol before 1967; today it is the border again. Unique double-stemmed palms. There is an Egged bus every 30 minutes.

Note: To cross the border, inquire at Egyptian Consulate, Elat. tel. (07)376882.

The Gulf Of Elat

About half a century ago, the British scientist Crossland described the Red Sea and the Gulf of Elat (Aqaba) as "the most desolate sea." Since then, it has become one of the world's most intensively studied seas, and a major tourist attraction.

The Red Sea is a geologically young one. It was created relatively late with the formation of the Great Syrian-East African Rift. This great trench in the crust of the earth runs from Northern Syria through the Jordan, Dead Sea, and Arava valleys, along the Gulf of Elat and the Red Sea to East Africa.

The Red Sea is actually an appendix of the Indian Ocean, which rushed in to fill the deep abyss created by the Rift in this area. Geologists view it as an initial phase in the creation of a new "embryonic" ocean.

The Gulf of Elat marks the northernmost extent of the tropical coral reefs. The profusion of underwater life is due to several factors.

Although the southern tip of the Red Sea opens out into a warm ocean, there is a gradual lowering of temperature from south to north. The winter temperatures in the Gulf of Elat, which range from 21°–25°C, are ideal for tropical marine life.

Another factor is the salinity of the Red Sea, which is appreciably higher than that in the open ocean. Evaporation in this area, with its arid shores and high radiation, is far more intensive than in mid-ocean.

The temperature conditions combined with the shallow threshold separating the Red Sea from the Indian Ocean, have led to the evolution of many plant and animal species which may be considered endemic to the Red Sea.

The Red Sea corals are arranged as fringing reefs along the coast line. Corals are tiny animals living in dense colonies, depositing limestone skeletons on the site. These skeletons accumulate, forming the reef in the course of thousands of years.

Such stony corals have a symbiotic relationship with microscopic algae living inside the coral tissue, and are therefore restricted to the shallow parts of the sea where the sunlight vital to algae penetrates. This factor determines the location of the reefs.

In most tropical seas, the reefs are further away from the beach and much less diversified. The transparent water in the Gulf of Elat, and the proximity of the reef to the shore, make this complex, fascinating world easily accessible to the observer without necessitating elaborate equipment.

A man-made contribution to the unique qualities of the region is the Suez Canal, which serves as a water bridge between the Red Sea and the Mediterranean. The dynamics of plant and animal migration through the canal have intrigued scientists for decades.

One of the more sensational recent finds of oceanographic research in the region is the strange phenomenon of the "Red Sea hot brines." These are stagnant water masses at a depth of 2,000 metres below the surface of the sea, which reach temperatures of 56°C due to volcanic activity.

The relatively concentrated and heavy brine contains minerals such as copper, iron and tin. Technological development may make the extraction of these minerals economically feasible in the future for the benefit of Saudi Arabia and the Sudan in whose waters these brines are located.

The development of bathing beaches and port installations affected the corals in the region. In 1966, a tiny area was proclaimed a nature reserve. This reserve stretches south along the shore for 2.5 kilometres, from the Elat

"Coral Beach" to the international border at Taba.

The beaches are great favourites of scuba divers. The Nature Reserves Authority patrol the coast.

The situation in the near future, in the wake of the Israel-Egypt peace treaty, seems far from promising as far as nature conservation is concerned. The small nature reserve at Elat remains Israel's only diving and underwater nature site.

Hotel and tourism projects are already threatening this minimal area. We may shortly be faced with a situation where beachfront hotels have no beach to speak of.

The Red Sea and Gulf of Elat are virtually landlocked seas, their waters remaining in a closed area with very little movement to and from the Indian Ocean. Polluted water therefore has little chance of exchange and purification as in the large open ocean. Pollution, once begun, may easily become chronic in the Red Sea.

Coral Reefs

The warmth of the Gulf of Elat, and its clarity – allowing solar penetration to great depths – provide optimal conditions for the growth of corals.

A coral reef, of the **fringing reef** type, developed some 20 m. off the shoreline and caused the formation of the **shallow lagoons.** The sandy bottom of the lagoon is inhabited by numerous burrowing creatures, such as **sand dollars, sea cucumbers, snails, sea urchins** and **star fish.**

Stony corals are the major contributors to the reef formations and serve as a base for other sessile organisms. Most of the corals consist of colonies of very small animals (polyps), all of which are inter-connected and grow in size through the budding of new polyps. The corals may be divided into **stony corals** and **soft corals.** The **stony corals,** which produce calcium carbonate skeletons, are the reef-building species. Some of these are solitary **(fungia)**; some form flat or rounded skeletal masses **(brain coral),** while others form branching growth forms. **Soft corals,** on the other hand, look like fragile trees and bushes waving slightly in the water. Among the most colourful of these are the **gorgonarian,** or fan corals. The **fire coral** (not a true coral) is noted for its high concentration of poisonous cells which, on contact, inflict a burning rash.

The stony corals provide shelter and substratum for many organisms, especially the numerous coral-reef fish and invertebrates. **Giant clams, sea anemones** and **sea urchins** are common in the cracks and crevices of the reef flats.

The reef's wall is a meeting place between live coral and the open sea. The fish that inhabit the reef survive by unique adaptations to their environment.

The **damselfish** appears among the corals' branches; the colourful **butterfly fish** swim in couples through cracks in the reef; schools of **goldfish** take refuge between the corals in time of danger. Some fish live in defined areas among the reef, such as the **clown anemonefish,** seeking shelter among the tentacles of the sea anemone, and the **cleanerfish,** which invites big fish into its "cleaning station" where it cleans even their teeth. Fish moving in groups along the reef are the **surgeonfish** which, at the base of its tail, conceals a sharp, folded spine, and the **parrotfish** with its beak-like mouth adapted to scraping coral rocks. The beautifully coloured **lionfish** which, with its array of venomous spines, discourages attack, the **moray eel,** which has its den in the coral caves, and the **groupers,** are the predators of the coral reefs.

The open-sea fish are streamlined for rapid swimming. Typically, their backs are bluish in colour, their bellies silver-gray. The **tuna, jackfish,** and young **barracuda** swim in schools; the **trumpetfish** has long, tooth-lined jaws and a very narrow body. Various types of sharks are also found in these waters: the **black-tipped** and **white-tipped sharks.**

Manta rays, bat rays, sizable **sea turtles,** and octopus are also to be found posing for the photographer.

Tour Yam, located on Coral Beach (Tel. (07) 372802), offer glass-bottomed boats and cruise vessels for individuals or groups. Also regular tours to the coral reefs. Recommended by the Tourism Ministry. You can also explore the undersea world on the **Jules Verne Explorer**, a high-tech observatory ship with underwater window-walls and a large terrace on deck (with restaurant). The two-hour tour operates day and night, with a special tour to Coral Island twice a week. Tel. (07)334668, 377702.

Suggestions For Visitors To The Gulf Of Elat

- Carry with you and consume more drinking water than you crave; dehydration is the biggest health hazard of the desert.

- Avoid overexposure to direct sunlight; wear protective clothing and a head covering; apply sun screen.

- The swimmer is advised to wear protective foot covering (e.g., sneakers), and to use a diving mask when entering the water. There are stinging corals and poisonous fish, as well as sea urchins that can cause painful injuries. Try to avoid bodily contact with all corals.

- Sharks may be stimulated to attack by shiny objects, erratic movements, and fresh blood in the water. If you spot sharks near the reef, do not fish, swim, or snorkel; if sharks approach while you are in the water, remain calm and slowly seek the protection of reef or beach.

- Boating requires licensing and equipment according to law. Don't boat near swimmers; don't approach the reef by boat, as you may endanger divers. In any case, please inquire in which areas boating is permitted. Care should be taken near the Egyptian coast of Sinai.

- Eat fresh fish, but be sure it's fresh. The heat of the desert promotes rapid spoilage. Don't eat unfamiliar species – some may be poisonous.

Sources Of Additional Information

Nature Reserves Authority

Jerusalem: 78 Yermiyahu St. Tel. (02) 536271.

Elat: Coral Beach, P.O. Box 667. Tel. (07) 373988.

Israel Diving Federation

Tel Aviv Port; tel. (03) 457432. P.O. Box 6110, Tel Aviv.

Elat office (07) 373145, 373146, 373147. Located at Caravan Hotel.

Information also available at all hotels and diving centres, and the Elat Field School.

A Note For Divers

The Red Sea is one of the best spots in the world for scuba diving.

The Dead Sea on the road to En Gedi. (Below) Massada.

What To Bring

- Your diving card stating experience and qualifications. Israelis are safety-conscious (though you wouldn't believe it from the way they drive) and their standards are high. By law, you cannot hire scuba gear or get air for your cylinders if you don't have a diving card.

- Small personal diving equipment – regulator, depth gauge, buoyancy-compensator vest, compass, etc. Weight belts and cylinders, as well as other equipment, may be rented.

For Your Safety

- Exercise after your journey in order to loosen up; also do a little skin-diving to test your stamina before your first day of scuba.

- Do not dive alone. Diving without a partner is forbidden.

- Marker buoys must be placed at all diving sites.

- The clarity of the water is deceptive – plan your dive accordingly. Use your depth gauge as well as common sense. Observe safety regulations. Achieve maximum depth at the beginning of each dive, and ascend slowly.

- The smallest visible air bubble ascends at about 18 m. (60 ft.) per minute. Let all your bubbles climb faster than yourself and you won't exceed the safe rate of ascent.

- The flora and fauna are breathtaking and distracting – check your watch more frequently than usual and make sure you have enough air for decompression stops. If transport is not immediately available at the site, dives requiring decompression stops are not recommended. Unless you rate the equivalent of a "Three Star" CMAS diver (" Second Class" in England, "Advanced" in America, and formerly "Second Echelon" in France), dives requiring decompression stops are not recommended.

- Tables have no safety margin whatsoever: make an unlisted and unrequired decompression stop at 3 m. (10 ft.) for three minutes on all dives of 12 m. (40 ft.) or more.

- A small nitrogen residual will make a big difference on a deep dive. A large nitrogen residual will make little difference on a shallow dive.

- Notify a responsible person of your itinerary, intended destination and estimated time of return. Authorities should be notified if you fail to return on time. Diving centres have logs where you file your dive plans.

- Within 12 hours of any dive do not climb to an altitude of more than 700 m. (2,300 ft.) above sea level whether by plane, train, car or foot. Take the last day off before your flight home to enjoy the snorkeling and the sun on the beach.

Diving Centres

To qualify for a diving licence, one has to take a course (varying in length from five days to two weeks) at a recognized centre, during which one learns how to breathe through a mouthpiece attached to compressed air tanks; how to control the speed of one's descent and ascent; what depths and air pressures are safe and for how long; how to work out the amount of air you have left, and how to help someone in distress.

The **Aquasport International Red Sea Diving Centre** is situated on Coral Beach, 5 km. south of the town of Elat. Tel. (07) 372288. Regular 5-day scuba courses are given in the internationally staffed diving school; 250 scuba units are available to certified divers. Also courses in night diving, deep diving, research diving and underwater photography. Wind-surfing courses and equipment for hire on beach in front of the centre. (Wind-surfing is becoming increasingly popular; you carry the board under one arm and the mast, sail and bar under the other; at sea, you have all the pleasure of sailing on a surfboard. The techniques can supposedly be mastered in 10 lessons.) Within walking distance of the centre, there are reefs of outstanding interest.

Solomon's Pillars.

Timna Park.

The Hai Bar Wildlife Reserve at Yotvata, about 40 km. north of Elat.

Bus No. 15 serves Elat/Coral Beach every 30 minutes, 7 days a week.

Other centres

Manta – diving and water sports school at the Caravan Hotel, tel. (07) 373145.

Lucky Divers, Khan Centre, tel. (07) 334706.

Red Sea Sports Club, Caravan Sun Club, Elat, tel. (07) 373145, 376569, 379685.

Exploring The Desert With The Experts

Perhaps the best bargain for instructive and enjoyable – though not pampered – tours are the hikes and vacation camps run by the Society for the Protection of Nature in Israel (SPNI).

Experienced guides who love their work and can cope with any emergency explain the natural and human history of particular areas and reveal hidden places of beauty and interest. Children are welcome on many trips, except those limited to "good hikers", that is individuals with the experience and stamina required for long treks over difficult country.

Nights are usually spent in sleeping bags under the stars or at field study centres. Toilet facilities in the desert are of course non-existent. ("When in the desert do as the Bedouin do.") Evening "entertainment" for those who want it includes campfires and lectures on the terrain or the wildlife.

The Elat SPNI Field School sells an excellent map of the region, showing possible hiking routes. Visitors are warned, however, against going into the desert without an experienced guide. It is extremely dangerous to do so at all times of the year – in summer, the heat can be disastrous; in the rainy season, flash floods are a menace.

The Field School offers free information to members and non-members alike. Tel. (07) 372021.

Other SPNI offices in Israel:

Tel Aviv: 4, Hashfela St. (near the Central Bus Station), tel. (03) 3350635.

Jerusalem: 13, Heleni Hamalka St., tel. (02) 252357, 244605.

Haifa: 8, Herzliya St., tel. (04) 511448.

Birdlife

Elat is the best place within the Mediterranean Basin and one of the best places in the world for observing bird migration. Birds that migrate between Eastern Europe and Africa in spring and autumn use warm air currents along the Syrian African Rift Valley. Some of the migrants rest on their way, in the area of the Salt Ponds and in the nearby agricultural fields of Kibbutz Elot. In spring 1986 more than one million (!) raptors, from 30 different species, were counted over Elat. Elat is also an excellent spot to observe Passerines, Water Fowl and Sea Birds: more than 400 different species have been recorded. For birdwatchers and nature lovers there is a signposted path for observing the birds, a Ringing Station for Raptors and Passerines, and in addition a huge park is being prepared for visitors.

Visitors to Elat who are interested in birds should get in touch with the Birdwatching Centre (P.O.B. 774, tel. (07) 376908), which provides guided tours and information on an autumn migration survey and a bird-ringing station. At Neot Hakikar Office, Etzion Hotel, Hatmarim Blvd. Open: Sun.–Thurs. 8 a.m. – 1 p.m., 4 – 7.30 p.m.

ACCOMMODATION

(See also general "Accommodation" section.)

HOTELS

King Solomon's Palace Tel. (07) 334111. North Beach.
Moriah Eilat Tel. (07) 361111. North Beach.
Neptune Tel. (07) 334333. North Beach.
The New Caesar Tel. (07) 333111. North Beach.
Galei Eilat Annex to Neptune. North Shore. Tel. (07) 334222.
Lagoona Tel. (07) 333666. North Beach.
Riviera Tel. (07) 333944. Apartment Hotel.
Red Rock Tel. (07) 373171. North Beach.
Shulamit Gardens Tel. (07) 333999. North Beach.
Sport Tel. (07) 333333. North Beach.
Americana Eilat Tel. (07) 333777. P.O. Box 27.
Coral-Sea Tel. (07) 333555. Coral Beach.
Edomit Tel. (07) 379511.
St. Tropez Beach Tel. (07) 376111. North Beach.

Elat

Elat: The Marina

Adi Tel. (07) 376151. Tzofit St.
Dalia Tel. (07) 334004. North Beach.
Etzion Tel. (07) 3741315. Hatmarim St.
Melony Club Aparthotel Tel. (07) 331181. 6 Los Angeles.
Club In Coral Bcach. Tel. (07) 334555.
Red Sea Tel. (07) 372171. Hatmarim Blvd.
Princess Taba Beach. Tel. (07)365555.
Orchidea Taba Beach. Tel. (07)360360.

KIBBUTZ HOTELS

Y'elim Tel. (07) 374362. Mobile Post Eilat.

YOUTH HOSTEL

Elat. Tel. (07)370088.

USEFUL ADDRESSES

Government Tourist Information Office: Khan Centre, Ofira Park, P. O. B. 86, tel. (07)334353. Open: Sun. – Thurs., 8 a.m. – 6 p.m. Fri. 8 a.m. – 1 p.m.

Magen David Adom (First Aid): Sderot Hatamarim, tel. (07) 372333 or emergency, 101.

Police: tel. (07)372444, 372222. Emergency, tel. 100.

Fire brigade: tel 102.

Post Office: Sderot Hatmarim. Open. Sun., Mon., Tues., and Thurs., 8 a.m. – 12.30 p.m. and 4 – 6.30 p.m., Wed. 8 a.m. – 2 p.m., Fri. till 1 p.m.

We want to hear from you on ways to improve this guide!

Write us at:

BAZAK
P.O.B. 4471
Jerusalem 91043

index

★★★ A must ★★ Special interest ★ Interesting

A Archaeology
C Christians
J Jews
M Moslems
V View

Elat: negotiating the price of a camel ride near the Underwater Observatory.

The Marina.

The Red Sea. View of Aqaba.

Camping on the beach.

Diving in the Red Sea

Red Sea

Notes

Notes

Examining sea life at close range at the Underwater Observatory.